G000256093

WINGS
OF FAME™

Aerospace Publishing Ltd
AIRtime Publishing Inc.

VISIT THE WORLD'S No. 1 AVIATION WEBSITE

air-recon.com

News • Comment • Competition • Aircraft encyclopedia • Air Force information • Full details of World Air Power Journal, Wings of Fame *and other products*

www.air-recon.com

Published quarterly by
Aerospace Publishing Ltd
179 Dalling Road
London W6 0ES, UK

Copyright © Aerospace Publishing Ltd 2000

ISSN 1361-2034
Aerospace ISBN 1 86184 061 6
(softback)
1 86184 046 2
(hardback)
AIRtime ISBN   1-880588-23-4

Published under licence in USA and Canada by AIRtime Publishing Inc., 10 Bay Street, Westport, CT 06880, USA

Editorial Offices:
WINGS OF FAME™
Aerospace Publishing Ltd
3A Brackenbury Road
London W6 0BE, UK
E-mail: info@aerospacepbl.co.uk

Publisher: Stan Morse
Managing Editor: David Donald
E-mail: dave@aerospacepbl.co.uk

Editor: John Heathcott
E-mail: john@aerospacepbl.co.uk

Contributing Editors:
Paul E. Eden
Dave Willis
Jim Winchester

Picture Manager: Nick Stroud
E-mail: nick@aerospacepbl.co.uk

US Correspondent:
Robert F. Dorr
Russia/CIS Correspondent:
Yefim Gordon
Canada Correspondent:
Jeff Rankin-Lowe

Artists: Mike Badrocke
Tony Bryan
Chris Davey
Keith Fretwell
Dean Morris
John Weal
Iain Wyllie

Origination by
Chroma Graphics, Singapore
Printed by
Officine Grafiche DeAgostini,
Novara, Italy

All rights reserved. No part of this publication may be reproduced, stored in a retrieval system or transmitted, in any form or by any means, electronic, mechanical, photocopying, recording or otherwise, without the permission of the publishers and copyright holders.

For their assistance in the preparation of this volume of *Wings of Fame*, the authors and publishers gratefully acknowledge the assistance of the following:

For material and illustrations the author of the Bristol Type 188 article must thank Duncan Greenman, Heritage Technical Archivist, and David Charlton, Photographer, both British Aerospace Airbus, Bristol, and the staff of the Public Record Office.

Thanks also to Dave Walton at DERA for his assistance in obtaining Bristol Type 188 photographs

For assistance with the Tradewind article, the author would like to thank Alex 'A. J.' Lutz at the San Diego Aerospace Museum and Richard C. Knott

Ian Thirsk and Philip Birtles for their invaluable assistance in sourcing Mosquito photographs

The editor of WINGS OF FAME™ welcomes photographs for possible publication, but cannot accept any responsibility for loss or damage to unsolicited material.

Wings of Fame™ is a registered trademark in the United States of America of AIRtime Publishing Inc.

Wings of Fame™ is published quarterly and is available by subscription and from many fine book and hobby stores.

SUBSCRIPTION AND BACK NUMBERS:

UK and World (except USA and Canada) write to:
Aerospace Publishing Ltd
FREEPOST
PO Box 2822
London
W6 0BR
UK
(No stamp required if posted in the UK)

USA and Canada, write to:
AIRtime Publishing Inc.
Subscription Dept
10 Bay Street
Westport
CT 06880, USA
(203) 838-7979
Toll-free order number in USA:
1 800 359-3003

Prevailing subscription rates are as follows:
Softbound edition for 1 year: $59.95
Softbound edition for 2 years: $112.00
Softbound back numbers (subject to availability) are $16.00 each, plus shipping and handling. All rates are for delivery within mainland USA, Alaska and Hawaii. Canadian and overseas prices available upon request. American Express, Discover Card, MasterCard and Visa accepted. When ordering please include card number, expiration date and signature.

U.S. Publisher:
Mel Williams
Subscriptions Director:
Linda DeAngelis
Charter Member Services Manager: Janie Munroe
Retail Sales Director: Jill Brooks
Shipping Manager: E. Rex Anku

WINGS
OF FAME

CONTENTS

Volume 18

Convair R3Y Tradewind

Seen through the prism of half a century's hindsight, the Tradewind looks like a dinosaur – a huge creature whose time came and went – but it would be a mistake to dismiss the Tradewind: Convair's big, shoulder-winged, four-engined 'boat contributed more to aviation than is generally acknowledged **4**

Robert F. Dorr

F-105 in Southeast Asia

Asked to perform what amounted to a strategic bombing role in Vietnam, the Thunderchief fighter-bomber spent 10 years in the region, eventually taking on a Wild Weasel role. Though 'Thud' losses were high, the type's importance in the Vietnam conflict cannot be understated **16**

Larry Davis

de Havilland Mosquito: Part 1

The de Havilland Mosquito was originally proposed in 1938 as a fast, unarmed bomber and was rejected out of hand by an RAF hooked on the idea that a bomber needed to be heavily armed and certainly not constructed largely of wood. In this first part of a two-part look at the Mosquito, the genesis of the aircraft and its photo-reconnaissance and bomber variants is examined in detail **38**

Martin Bowman

Bristol Type 188

Today, many historians and enthusiasts turn their backs on the stainless steel Type 188, but it remains an aircraft of great interest, and still looks incredible. It was in some ways a remarkable achievement, not least since it actually survived the swathing cuts brought about by the 1957 Defence White Paper **92**

Tony Buttler AMRAeS

Avro Canada CF-100 Variants

The only Canadian-designed and -built jet fighter to achieve operational status, the 'Clunk' had its beginnings in January 1945, when the RCAF issued a set of specifications for what would be its major post-war fighter aircraft. Here the variants and operators of the CF-100 are described **102**

Jeff Rankin-Lowe

Air war over Malta, 1940-43

When recounting the history of Malta during World War II, it is the fortunes of the fighting forces which operated from the island, and the suffering of its civilian population that are most often recorded. It is less frequently emphasised that Malta was a vital base for offensive operations against the Axis, and a real threat to the enemy dictators' ambitions in North Africa and the Middle East. Here the three turbulent years in the history of the island – 1940-43 – are described **132**

Francis K. Mason

Luftwaffe Markings: Part 3

The third and final in this series of articles looks at revisions of, and additions to, the two basic systems of markings already described and the ways in which certain branches of the Luftwaffe introduced their own marking schemes for tactical formation and recognition purposes **146**

John Weal

Index **158**

Convair R3Y Tradewind

'The Flying LST'

It would be tempting to dismiss the Convair R3Y Tradewind as an idea that came too late. By the mid-1950s, many were saying that land-based aircraft could readily achieve the one mission hitherto reserved for flying-boats, that of hauling heavy cargoes across vast distances. Seen through the prism of half a century's hindsight, the Tradewind looks like a dinosaur – a huge creature whose time came and went – but it would be a mistake to dismiss the Tradewind: Convair's big, shoulder-winged, four-engined 'boat contributed more to aviation than is generally acknowledged.

The big Convairs were the world's first production turboprop seaplanes, and appeared when flying-boats still had more than another decade of service ahead in the US Navy. They were nearly twice as fast as the older water-based transports and could climb as quickly as World War II fighters. More than 142 ft (43.28 m) long and tipping the scales at some 175,000 lb (79380 kg) when ready to fly, the Tradewinds were impressive in every sense. Indeed, given the world-wide shortage of refuelling aircraft today – the US Navy no longer operates any dedicated air-refuelling tanker – the Tradewinds would be as useful at the turn of the century as they were in its middle.

The Tradewind was powered by turboprop engines but, unfortunately, the engine in question was the Allison T40, possibly the worst gas turbine engine every to be employed operationally in American service. At the time, turboprop power was the answer to all future conditions, especially for heavy-lifting jobs where speed and time were less critical than payload. It was not yet evident, or even viewed

as likely, that pure jet power (turbofan power, as it turned out) would push outsized aircraft like the C-5 Galaxy and Antonov An-124 Ruslan through the sky. The turboprop offered both performance and economy; the pure jet engines of the time had neither. The T40, though, was the wrong turboprop engine, not merely unreliable but, in fact, temperamental and even dangerous.

Turboprop development

It should be noted that competing turboprop engines – the Westinghouse T30 and Pratt & Whitney T34 – had their own problems, primarily in that the science of metallurgy was not keeping up with the ability of gas turbine powerplants to create heat. Virtually every turboprop and turbojet engine developed by industry in the late 1940s was inadequate for the airframes of the time, and there were numerous examples of delays and difficulties with production warplanes because powerplant technology lagged far behind the rest of aeronautical progress.

The last R3Y-1 (main picture) ordered was completed as the first R3Y-2. Obvious differences between the latter and the XP5Y-1 (right) include the redesigned bridge containing all the crew members above the cargo hold, the new bow and weather radar at its tip, an enlarged fin fillet and the horizontal tailplane. The turret positions on the flanks of the XP5Y-1's forward and rear fuselage were unique to that model, though they were never equipped with their intended armament.

Nevertheless, the R3Y Tradewind became a feature of US naval aviation in the 1950s. To tell the R3Y story, it is necessary, first, to cover the P5Y patrol aircraft which came first. The original P5Y designation, as set forth in preliminary specifications issued by the Consolidated Aircraft Corporation on 23 November 1942, was a twin-engined version of the US Army's four-engined B-24D Liberator bomber. The aircraft was intended to compete with the Vega P2V, a design based on the PV Ventura patrol bomber. The Navy essentially vetoed the idea of a twin-engined Liberator in late 1942, so this XP5Y-1 was not built, although Consolidated

R3Y-1 Tradewind BuNo. 128445 makes its initial take-off run on its first flight on 25 February 1954 after having taxied down the slipway under its own power. The first flight of this aircraft, the second Tradewind to take to the air, was terminated early after a minor malfunction in one of the Allison T40-A-10s – a sign of things to come.

continued work on a twin-engined, patrol version of the B-32 Dominator, which, in the end, was never built either.

The P5Y designation was re-established in a Navy document dated 3 August 1946. This time, the aircraft in question was a four-engined flying-boat intended for sustained operations from water bases. The giant seaplane's genesis went back at least three years earlier. Consolidated had become Consolidated Vultee in March 1943 (when founder Reuben Fleet sold his interest in the former company), and it was soon known by the shortened version of its name, Convair. That year, the US Navy had expressed an interest in a new long-range, multi-role flying-boat. Convair's design team went to work on a four-turboprop design and a contract was awarded on 27 May 1946. By then, of course, the war was over and Convair was looking for peacetime work at its San Diego, California facility. Hopes were high

when a contract was awarded for constuction of two XP5Y-1 (Model 117) prototypes, which were eventually assigned Bureau Numbers 121455/121456.

Radio-controlled model

Convair engineers built an impressive, radio-controlled flying model of the XP5Y-1 to evaluate the unusually long, slender hull with its atypically high length-to-beam ratio of 10:1 (compared, for example, to 5:1 for the PBY Catalina). Exhaustive hydrodynamic studies were carried out and, as a result, the aircraft which followed was always an easy one to handle when manoeuvring on water.

The new aircraft was a high-winged flying-boat with a conventional, two-step hull. A cantilever wing with a 145-ft (44.19-m) span was mounted almost halfway back on the hull, giving the aircraft an appearance of speed. The tail assembly was characterised by a noticeable

amount of dihedral in the horizontal plane, and had a high single vertical fin which gave the XP5Y-1 a height of 51 ft 5 in (15.68 m). Convair intended that the craft would be powered by four Westinghouse XT30 (Model 25D) turboprop engines driving Hamilton Standard super hydromatic, four-bladed propellers having a diameter of 15 ft 1 in (4.59 m). Westinghouse was having serious problems at the time with the development of several gas turbine engines. The XT30 was delayed and so the XP5Y-1's manufacturer turned to another engine that was even more experimental. The change in powerplant was formalised in February 1947, at which time it was apparent that engine delays were going to become significant. At one time, a plan existed to fit the second prototype with R4360 reciprocating engines, but this was never accomplished.

As eventually fitted, the XP5Y-1 was powered by four Allison T40-A-4 turboprop engines,

Above: Ellis 'Sam' Shannon joined Consolidated Vultee from Martin in 1943 as a test pilot. His test-flight career included the B-24, B-32, XB-46, XP-81, L-13, B-36, XF-92, XF2Y and the Convair twin propliners, as well as the XP5Y.

Top left: The first XP5Y-1 sits outside the Convair factory awaiting its T40 turboprops engines. The aircraft would have to wait 15 months before taking to the air.

Left: Seen prior to its first flight, the first XP5Y-1 its seen tethered to a floating dock specially constructed for engine testing.

each driving two three-bladed Aeroproducts 15-ft (4.57-m) diameter contra-rotating propellers through a common gear box. As with other T40 variants, the engine consisted of two gas turbine units laid side-by-side so that, in a sense, this could have been considered an eight-engined aircraft. In the case of the 'dash 4', a long, three-piece extension shaft gave the engine nacelles a misleadingly slender appearance. This powerplant, and the production 'dash 10' variant found on the subsequent R3Y, ultimately became one of the most trouble-prone powerplants in the Navy's history. It looked like an aerodynamic miracle, and the long extension shafts connecting the powerplant to the propellers gave the installation a clean and straightfoward appearance, but the arrangement led to a clamour of propeller noise inside the fuselage.

There were bigger problems, though, and eventually the turboprop engines would create undue vibration in certain speed regimes. Initially, engine development problems caused the first flight of the XP5Y-1 to occur nearly three years later than originally planned. The aircraft was rolled out in December 1948 and

began a long period of sitting outdoors, minus engines. When the second XP5Y-1 was completed in June 1949, it, too, sat on a beaching cradle on the concrete at Lindbergh Field, without engines.

Range of duties

It was intended from the beginning that this aerial behemoth would perform a varied range of duties. With long range and a diverse weapons load, the aircraft was undoubtedly inspired by the recently-concluded war with Japan, fought over vast distances by far-reaching naval fleets. The principal function of the XP5Y-1 was meant to be ASW (anti-submarine warfare), for which it was expected to carry a formidable load of bombs, mines, rockets and torpedoes. It would be configured with advanced radar, ECM (electronic countermeasures), and MAD (magnetic anomaly detection) equipment. In one of several ASW mission profiles envisioned for the aircraft, it would carry 57,428 lb (26048 kg) of fuel plus four Mk 41-1 torpedoes at a gross weight of 165,000 lb (74844 kg), cruising at 161 kt (297 km/h) to a radius of 1,065 nm (1972 km).

The timing seemed flawless. There were, as yet, no submarine-launched ballistic missiles threatening North America, but Western intelligence credited the Soviet Union with 450 submarines, a grossly-inflated estimate that was more than enough to snatch away the US Navy's command of the sea. An expert who worked on ASW in 1950 recalls that, "you were bound to get ahead in the Pentagon if you kept ringing the alarm bell about the Soviet submarine threat." An article in *Collier's* magazine in 1950 portrayed Russian U-boats as dominating the world's shipping lanes and, as this expert recalls, "scared the hell out of everybody."

The XP5Y-1 was also viewed as the ideal aerial platform for long-range mine-laying missions. With 20,000 lb (9072 kg) of mines (like all ordnance planned for the flying-boat, carried internally), the XP5Y-1 could cruise at 230 kt (424 km/h) to a combat radius of 1,115 nm (2065 km). Some observers in the Navy questioned whether an aircraft of this size engaged in laying mines in a heavily defended harbour might be too vulnerable. In addition to the mine-laying mission, the Navy expected to use the XP5Y-1 for nocturnal attacks on

The XP5Y-1 runs down San Diego Bay, displaying the upper surfaces of its wings to advantage. The rear of the engine nacelles remained in natural metal.

'Riding the step' the XP5Y-1 builds up speed as it prepares to lift off. Convair spent much time and money investigating the P5Y's hydrodynamics, with the result that the type was exceptionally easy to handle on the water.

shipping, as it had done with the Catalina.

No defensive armament was installed in the XP5Y-1, but the aircraft was intended to have five 0.50-in (12.7-mm) machine-gun positions, of which two were located on each side of the hull fore and aft, and one accommodated a 20-mm cannon in the tail. The side-mounted guns were in sleek barbettes and were to be operated by gunners via remote control.

First flight at last

During test flights, the XP5Y-1's maximum speed exceeded 350 mph (563 km/h), so the flying-boat moved swiftly even while demonstrating its enormous bulk and weight of 165,000 lb (74484 kg) or more. The first flight took place on 18 April 1950 at San Diego, with company pilot E. S. 'Sam' Shannon in the left seat, co-pilot Donald P. Germeraad in the right, and Bob McGeary facing sideways at the flight engineer's console. Germeraad, who had

The anonymous all-over blue scheme of the first prototype XP5Y-1 had gained white photographic calibration stripes by the end of June 1950. Here it passes NAS North Island.

already piloted several types of flying-boats, would eventually be even more important to the programme than Shannon, whose only sea experience thus far was at the controls of an L-13B liaison aircraft with pontoons. To commemorate this maiden air voyage, the Consolidated Vultee Aircraft Corporation issued a special postal envelope. However, the company had precious little to cheer about: the big flying-boat was in the air just 29 minutes and the episode proved only that it could, indeed, fly.

In San Diego, which is very much a Navy town, many at Convair considered the P5Y to be a great, majestic ship of the skies, able to operate from waters around the world to carry out diverse missions for the Fleet. In the boardroom, where Convair was losing more than it was making on an obscure liaison plane called the L-13, the whine of the P5Y's turboprops must have sounded like money in the bank. In reality, there was to be no black ink at the bottom of this ledger, even though the XP5Y-1 moved ahead in August 1950 to establish a turboprop endurance record of eight hours and six minutes.

That month, the triumph of the P5Y also became the end of the road. The Navy decided not to proceed with the big 'boat as a maritime reconnaissance platform, but Navy experts did

agree to proceed with a version of the Convair aircraft as a passenger and cargo carrier.

The XP5Y-1 flew for more than three years as a test aircraft, completing 42 flights. All this time, the second XP5Y-1 sat, awaiting engines. In time, the Navy's plan to fly the second aircraft was put on hold, and available engines were used to support the first ship. The second XP5Y-1 was eventually scrapped in 1957 without ever taking to the air. By then, all hopes for this aircraft as a maritime patrol craft had been dashed.

When the end came, it was abrupt. The XP5Y-1 programme had its final curtain with the crash of the prototype off San Diego on 15 July 1953, during flutter tests. Engineer Bud Davies, who was on board that day, believes the outcome would have been very different but for the "cool proficiency [and] bravery" of pilot Germeraad. "On the fateful dive," recalls Davies, "the pulse input produced a short severe shudder in the aircraft structure and we were aware that we had suffered damage. First flight engineer Bob McGeary was sent aft to investigate for damage. Two small windows in the aft end of the hull permitted inspection of the horizontal stabiliser's moveable surfaces. Bob choked up and said, 'The elevator torque tube is sheared in two inside the hull!' This left us with virtually no longitudinal control, except

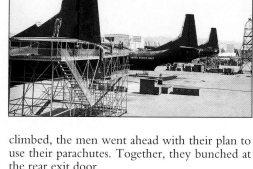

Above: The Tradewind's 'Achilles' heel' was undoubtedly its Allison T40 turboprop engine. Initial ground tests of the installed engines were conducted without gearbox cowlings or spinners.

Top and top right: Convair's flightline and final assembly area contained BuNos 128446 (nearest the camera), 128445, (R3Y-2) 128450, 128449 and 128447 at the time of these photographs.

Below: With Convair workers and test crew peering out of doors and riding on the beaching cradle, R3Y-1 BuNo. 128446 taxis into the San Diego Bay from the Convair seaplane ramp.

climbed, the men went ahead with their plan to use their parachutes. Together, they bunched at the rear exit door.

"Lloyd Bennett, who was in front of me, fell down in the aisle. I reached down and, grasping his collar and the bottom of his parachute back-pack, lifted him clear off the floor – despite the mild *g*-loading of the pull-out. By the time I reached the door, the aircraft was climbing rapidly and I did not hesitate in going out. I cleared the props and the hull, although some of the others scraped paint off the hull.

"Clear of the ship, I opened my 'chute. I was by far the highest 'chute and I counted seven others. One was missing! It had to be the captain because that's the kind of guy he is." The eight other crewmen believed Germeraad had gone in with the XP5Y-1 when the aircraft performed four spectacular hammerhead stalls, each a little lower, and on the fourth plunged vertically straight into the water near San Diego's Point Loma, never having shed any major parts. The others did not know that the XP5Y-1 had been spiralling toward upscale private homes along the shoreline and had crashed harmlessly at sea, rather than killing people on land, because of Germeraad's emergency flying skills. In fact, the pilot had bailed out at the last instant and Germeraad was alive and well, rescued like the others by the Coast Guard. "Turbo Plane Lost", headlined the *San Diego Union* the next day.

Its nose at a 90° angle when it hit the sea, the XP5Y-1 was gone forever.

Transport version

The loss of the XP5Y-1 was high drama, especially with its vision of the giant craft going into the waves at 90 like a dagger. By this time,

with engine power.

"Germeraad flew the aircraft down the coast to near the Mexican border where we turned northward again. The plan was to bail out five of the nine-man crew and four of us would attempt to bring the aircraft in. But first the captain said, 'We'll try a simulated landing at 10,000 ft [6096 m].'" The attempt confirmed that a bailout was necessary and it was decided that all nine would jump, abandoning the XP5Y-1. With difficulty, while the aircraft

an unstoppable momentum had begun, and Convair was making relentless progress toward completion of a transport based on the patrol craft. The US Navy was firmly committed to the flying-boat as an important ingredient in its aerial arsenal, and apparently never hesitated to move ahead with the longer, sleeker, more powerful R3Y-1.

The Navy had issued a contract for six R3Y-1s, or Convair Model 3s (BuNos 128445/128450), on 16 August 1950, three years before the crash of the XP5Y-1 patrol ship. More than two years before the crash, on 10 February 1951, the Navy increased its purchase by five airframes (BuNos 131720/131724). Although the patrol and transport aircraft were superficially almost alike in appearance, there were important changes: with a fuselage length of 139 ft 8.3 in (42.60 m), the R3Y-1 was fully 12 ft 2.7 in (3.71 m) longer than the patrol aircraft and, when fully loaded, was about 22,000 lb (9979 kg) heavier. The R3Y-1 also had configuration differences in engine and empennage shape.

Design changes

The R3Y-1 differed from the XP5Y-1 in having a strengthened wing, a revised vertical tail, and a flat horizontal stabiliser (with no dihedral). Convair also redesigned the fin, giving it a more squared-off appearance and, as a result, a distinctive dorsal fillet with a break leading into the vertical tail. There was a new nacelle shape for its Allison T40-A-10 turboprop engines, each rated at 5,850 shp (4364 kW). Rather than being bisected by the airfoil, the engines were raised above the wing level. Where the XT40-A-4 employed by the XP5Y-1 had been a lengthy design with reduction gearbox and concentric propeller shafts, the -10 engine of the R3Y-1 had a far shorter shaft.

The R3Y-1 had a conventional, two-step flying-boat hull, but without internal bulkheads above the cargo deck, meaning that the interior of the fuselage was a vast open space that could be used in a variety of ways. In this roomy interior, the Navy could seat 80 troops in rearward-facing seats, carry 72 litter patients and eight medical attendants, or haul up to 48,000 lb (21772 kg) of cargo, all in air-conditioned, pressurised comfort. Then as now, not enough thought had been given to the advantages of 'roll-on, roll-off' capability, so the R3Y-1 lacked the capability to load vehicles or to easily load and unload anything. A rectangular 12-ft (3.65-m) cargo door at the aft port fuselage was inadequate for any sort of serious cargo.

In the early 1950s flying-boats were very much a part of the Naval Air Transport Service's operations. Martin JRM Mars 'boats were plying Pacific routes, hauling troops and supplies en route to the Korean War. The Navy had only recently retired its last PB2Y-1R Coronado four-engined transport 'boat, and had a vast fleet of PBM-3R and -5R Mariner twin-engined 'boats that performed transport duty. Soon to be on the drawing board was a huge Navy flying-boat powered by jet engines, the Martin P6M Seamaster. Land-based aircraft could not match flying-boats for hauling capacity (the Air Force had but a single XC-99, and could carry only limited cargoes on anything but its outsized C-124 Globemaster). Even with questionable engines, an inadequate method of loading, and

all of the growing pangs that came with any new design, the Convair R3Y-1 Tradewind seemed like a logical and sensible idea.

It was equally logical, then, that the Navy would envision not only a sea bridge of R3Y transports circumnavigating the world's oceans but, in addition, a series of bases at sea where the transports could refuel. The Navy was at work on floating water bases for the R3Y-1 long before it addressed two other innovations that seem obvious in retrospect – roll-on

Top: BuNo. 128446 moves away from the Convair floating dock in San Diego Bay, under the gaze of company employees (with one on the cradle) and at least two photographers.

Above: BuNo. 128448 could be identified by its discoloured nose radome. Each R3Y also carried an individual nose-number which reflected the airframe construction sequence.

Below: Passing over San Diego Bay prior to its record-breaking delivery flight to NAS Patuxent River, Md. in late February 1955, BuNo. 128448 passes close to a US Navy tender and submarine.

Inside the Tradewind

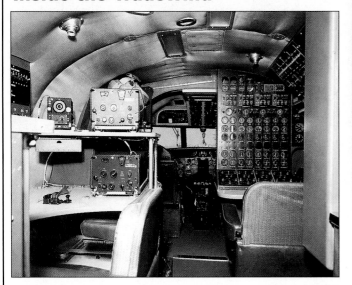

A flight engineer monitors his dials aboard an R3Y-1. In front of him were four columns, each two dials-wide, providing data for each of the coupled T40s, while the panel directly to his right was the fuel management board. Next to his right hand are the throttle levers. In the R3Y-1 the engineer's position was at a lower level in the fuselage. With the redesign of the R3Y-2's cockpit this was moved to a spot directly behind the cockpit.

Below: The R3Y-1 could seat a total of 90 passengers (but is seen here rigged for 80) on rearward facing seats arranged five abreast with a central aisle. The door at the end of the cabin leads to the washroom.

Below right: Vital for long-distance flights was the washroom (or 'heads', to use the naval term), located at the rear of the main cabin. Two were provided in an R3Y-1.

Looking forward in the cockpit of the R3Y-2 (above) are the engineer's position to the right and the radio operator's desk on the left. Behind the radio operator's position was a small galley (below).

Below right: Experience in Korea had shown the need for aero-medical transport on a large scale, and the R3Y-1 Tradewind was able to carry 72 litters and 8 attendants.

Below left: The empty Tradewind main cabin shows the attachment points for the seats and the litters.

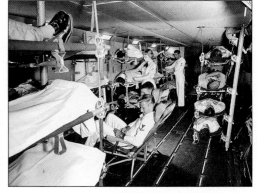

capability in the transport role, and a new and unforeseen duty as an air-refuelling tanker.

The name Tradewind was selected for the R3Y-1 and it was christened by swimming star and actress Esther Williams in a ceremony on 17 December 1953, the 50th anniversary of the Wright Brothers' first powered flight. Swimmer/actress Williams was a favourite with the Navy leadership, having starred in Hollywood's forgettable *Skirts Ahoy!* the previous year, in part to promote naval service during the Korean War – but when she penned an autobiography decades later, she did not deem the christening important enough to mention.

After two months of final preparations, Germeraad took the big blue R3Y-1 aloft from San Diego Bay for its first flight, on 25 February 1954. A planned three-hour initial flight was cut to two hours when problems developed with the number two engine and Germeraad had to feather it. There were no significant

problems with the big aircraft, as far as anyone could tell, and in a post-flight interview Germeraad praised the Tradewind's handling qualities, even though he knew the aircraft was seriously underpowered. While flight work on this aircraft proceeded, Germeraad – whose Tradewind experience had begun in the right seat – became the manufacturer's chief engineering test pilot.

The Navy's Bureau of Aeronautics gave the go-ahead for development work and initial production, and for Phase One and Phase Two testing of the R3Y-1 Tradewind. The first phase, which dealt with the structural integrity of the aircraft, was carried out under the manufacturer's watchful eye in San Diego. Phase Two service-test trials were completed a continent away at the Naval Air Test Center, Patuxent River, Maryland.

On 18 February 1955, Germeraad took the R3Y-1 to San Francisco bay where he

demonstrated its capabilities to observers from Naval Air Stations Alameda and Oakland. A tourist observing from the San Francisco-Oakland ferry described the flying-boat as "a big blue wall plunging through the water". Four days later, a Convair press release spoke of a projected cross-country speed dash to be made by the fifth R3Y-1 (BuNo. 128449); in fact, a different R3Y-1 made a transcontinental flight on 24 February 1955. This apparently was the fourth aircraft (BuNo. 128448) which appeared at Patuxent for Phase Two and for Board of Inspection and Survey trials. All these years later, it is unclear whether any record was set on that flight.

R3Y-2 bow-loader

Effort to develop an improved version dubbed the R3Y-2 was moving in fits and starts. The Navy was groping for a strategic role – carrier aviation was being cut from the three-

pronged striking force that eventually became the strategic triad (bombers, land-based missiles, and SLBNs or submarine-launched ballistic missiles) – and the SLBN had not yet proven itself. The Navy believed the future was nuclear, and wanted a part of it, so it was developing a concept for floating pontoon docks under the Mobile Base Concept (MBC) to allow the jet-powered Martin P6M-1/-2 Seamaster to become part of the United States' atomic striking force. Not only was the Seamaster perceived as a long-range bomber, but the Navy was also looking at a nuclear-powered version of it. The bases that would be placed at sea in littoral waters near allied nations would threaten the Soviet Union with their P6M-1s, while being protected by F2Y-1 Sea Dart floating-boat fighters and serviced by surface vessels and R3Y Tradewinds. This plan to have flying-boats available for action anywhere in the world demanded improvements to the Tradewind design – the aircraft which, in the end, became the only member of the MBC trio to achieve operational status.

The principal improvement in the 'dash 2' Tradewind was the addition of a clamshell nose door to enable cargoes to be rolled on and off from the front of the aircraft. Side-opening nose doors were a feature of the Air Force's C-124 Globemaster but the Tradewind's door opened by folding straight up, a design echoed by the C-5 Galaxy that still lay more than a decade ahead. The configuration – like that of the LST (Landing Ship Tank) assault ships developed for amphibious island campaigns in World War II – was called the Bowloader concept and would enable the R3Y-2 to tie up to an MBC floating dock to off-load and on-load its cargo. The Navy ordered five R3Y-2s (BuNos 131720/131724) in February 1953 after arrangements for six R3Y-1s had already been completed.

The R3Y-2 had a raised bridge which placed the entire flight crew above the passenger/cargo level. This change was easily accomplished, since the aircraft had been designed from the outset without bulkheads; the change increased the overall internal capacity of the fuselage, raising the personnel load from 80 to 103 and the alternate capacity for litters from 72 to 92. A blunter shape to the nose was punctuated by a thimble-shaped radome, housing weather radar, which could be reached through an access door inside the nose. To roll cargo on and off beneath the opened nose door, the R3Y-2 introduced a pair of folding loading ramps on which a vehicle could be driven. The R3Y-2 dispensed with a mooring hatch on the port side of the nose, unique to the R3Y-1 model, that was used to drop anchor.

First R3Y-2 flight

The first R3Y-2 flew on 22 October 1954. Germeraad was pilot, and others onboard were co-pilot Jack Elliott, flight engineers B. P. Gray and R. M. Bloom, and flight test engineers Jim Mason and E. H. Davies. The press billed the aircraft as 'The Flying LST' and reported the duration of the first flight as one hour and 23 minutes. Germeraad's log book makes it one hour and 52 minutes. The aircraft flew again on 4 November 1954 and thereafter sorties became more frequent, Germeraad flying approximately every other day throughout November.

Perhaps too many sailors and Marines had succumbed to the glories of the 1949 film *Sands of Iwo Jima* with John Wayne, or to the real-life Inchon landing in Korea in 1950. In any event, there was an infatuation with Marines storming the beach in the early 1950s, and naval officers and aeronautical experts spoke routinely of the Tradewind replacing the landing boat. It was, of course, the small, light Higgins boat – not the LST – that had made amphibious warfare successful in World War II, and the Tradewind lacked the low profile or nimble quickness of that vessel. To make matters worse, the clamshell cargo door would blind both pilots at the very time the Marines hit the beach. Even so, fanciful art appeared in literature of the 1950s showing the Bowloader re-enacting the Pacific Island campaign. More quietly, the Navy sought to proceed with the MBC concept.

Tests in San Diego Bay showed that the R3Y-2 Bowloader could, indeed, bring guns, trucks, troops and cargo to the beachhead. While the Tradewind approached the shore, the bow opened upward and the twin folding ramps extended forward and down to enable troops or equipment to off-load quickly. The pilots were to keep two engines turning, one

Caribbean Sea Tradewind *R3Y-2 (BuNo. 131723)* is seen at NAS Alameda resting on the motorised beaching cradle designed by Convair for use with the Tradewind.

Below: Each R3Y had a port-side main cargo door. Opening upwards, the aperture was 120 in (3.05 m) wide by 88 in (2.24 m) high, and sported a portable cargo loading platform and hoist to ease loading, especially in the water.

Bottom: The bow-loading R3Y-2 was fitted with a hinged nose (with a cut-out to allow the pilot to see ahead) incorporating ramps for the direct loading and unloading of troops and equipment.

The R3Y-2 was envisaged as a 'flying LST'. It would approach the beach (left) with the inner engines shut down to reduce spray while Marines were landed by helicopter behind the beach to secure the area. The R3Y-2's nose would then open (below) and the Marines and their equipment would be disgorged. Using its contra-rotating propeller's ability to be reversed, the Tradewind would then back away once it had unloaded. These amphibious landing trials seen here took place near San Diego using Marine Corps personnel from Camp Pendleton. The Tradewind's crew experienced some difficulty maintaining station during unloading, and reversing away from the beach proved difficult.

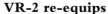

on each wing, to hold the Tradewind steady while unloading took place. The Tradewind would subsequently back away from the beach on all four engines with propellers reversed. The crew would then make a fast getaway, for the Tradewind could reach take-off velocity less than a minute after turning into the wind and going to military power.

It looked impressive in San Diego and it was tried elsewhere. On 21 April 1957, the *South Atlantic Tradewind* (BuNo. 128450), piloted by Lieutenant Commander E. G. Calles, landed near MCAS Kaneohe Bay, Hawaii for a 10-day familiarisation period with the 1st Marine Brigade. Troops loaded and unloaded on the beaches on the leeward side of Oahu, while Marine HRS-2 helicopters whirred overhead. The Tradewind crew found it difficult to hold the flying-boat steady during loading and unloading operations and sometimes had difficulty backing away from the beach when the procedure was completed. The reversing procedure was applicable to everyday use and did make the Tradewind somewhat more flexible in a docking situation than earlier, piston-engined flying-boats.

This arrangement would have proven problematic, to say the least, on a 'hot' beach. There were, after all, no plans to equip the

Tradewind with guns, nor any other way to protect it from shoreline defences. The tactic might have worked in a benign environment, such as the one Marines encountered later when they landed at Beirut in 1958.

In the end, there were to be no floating bases and no amphibious assaults on enemy-held beaches. Still, the R3Y Tradewind became far more than an aeronautical curiosity. The Naval Air Transport Service (NATS) was operating both land-based transports and flying-boats (JRM Mars) in the Pacific. On 31 March 1956, the fifth and last R3Y-2 (BuNo. 131724) became the first ship to be delivered for operational duties when it arrived at NAS Alameda to join squadron VR-2 commanded

by Captain W. A. Sullivan. The plan was to begin replacing the Mars on flights between the San Francisco Bay area and Hawaii as soon as aircraft and crews were ready.

VR-2 re-equips

South Pacific Tradewind was the name assigned to this first VR-2 Tradewind, an R3Y-2 model, which participated in a ceremonial flyby together with VR-2's much-travelled *Philippine Mars*, alias JRM-1 BuNo. 76820. Soon afterward, the squadron received R3Y-2 131723 which became the *Caribbean Sea Tradewind*. The Navy formed VR-2 to operate both models of the Tradewind, the earlier R3Y-1s now being called 'cruiser bow' variants to distinguish them from R3Y-2 bowloaders. An R3Y-1 (BuNo. 128449) became the *China Sea Tradewind* shortly after its delivery on 17 May 1956.

The next aircraft to become operational was R3Y-1 BuNo. 128449, which became the *Coral Sea Tradewind*. On 10 May 1957, this aircraft suffered an engine failure followed by an emergency landing in San Francisco Bay, and had to be written off.

VR-2's inventory was filled out by R3Y-2s BuNos 128450 and 131722, which became the *South Atlantic Tradewind* and the *Arabian Sea Tradewind*. After these came R3Y-1 BuNo. 128446, the *Indian Ocean Tradewind*. On 18 October 1956, this R3Y-1 made a Honolulu to San Francisco flight in six hours and 45 minutes; this quick crossing of approximately 2,400 miles (3862 km) of ocean failed to match the record of six hours and 11 minutes attained the previous year by a land-based United Air Lines Douglas DC-7, but it clipped more than three hours from the previous 10-hour 21-minute mark set in 1948 by the JRM-2 *Caroline Mars*. The aircraft was piloted by Lieutenant Commander C. E. Felock, with 15 others aboard including company pilot Germeraad. At the time, a news story on the

The US Navy wanted the R3Y to be operated as part of its proposed Mobile Base Concept, flying in supplies to the base and providing assault transport in the 'flying LST' role. Here Marines simulate a landing in San Diego Bay.

Two R3Y-2s are flanked by R3Y-1s of VR-2 during one of the unit's training flights over the southern California coast. VR-2's primary role was undertaking replenishment flights between the US mainland and Hawaii.

event culminated with a sentence that indicated the brief future for the R3Y: "The three R3Y-1s and four R3Y-2s delivered to the squadron to replace the Mars seaplanes have not yet been assigned a mission [emphasis added] and are being used for training."

The need to supplant and eventually replace the Mars was evident to all. VR-2 was operating five JRMs in a situation that amounted to a logistical and maintenance nightmare, since these aircraft represented three models with three engine types – the JRM-1 powered by Wright R-3350-8s, the JRM-2 with particularly maintenance-intensive Pratt & Whitney R-4360s, and the JRM-3 with Wright R-3350-24s. One Mars had already been lost at sea in a horrendous fire and another had been phased out. Maintaining the aircraft that remained, and despatching them on a daily flight in each direction between California and Hawaii, was proving uneconomical.

The Mars series undoubtedly had racked up a list of achievements, including carrying 225,000 passengers over 13 million miles (20.9 million km). The Mars 'boats were capable of only about 200 mph (321 km/h) in the air, compared with an economic cruise of 300 mph (480 km/h) for the Tradewind. While the Mars lumbered slowly to gain altitude, the Tradewind climbed as fast as a World War II fighter. It seemed sensible, therefore, to proceed with plans to equip VR-2 with 11 Tradewinds, comprising five R3Y-1 cruise loaders and six R3Y-2 Bowloaders.

Motorised beaching cradle

The Tradewind soon reached operational status. VR-2 received not only the aircraft but also a motorised beaching cradle, designed by Convair and manufactured by the Union Steel Company. The cradle was a steerable unit normally operated by three men. Weighing a remarkable 25,000 lb (11340 m), the cradle was 49 ft (14.93 m) in length, 25 ft (7.62 m) wide, and 16 ft (4.87 ft) high, with a draft of 6 ft (1.82 m). Vinyl covered all parts of the cradle which made contact with the underside of the Tradewind, so as not to scratch the aircraft. The

intent was for the R3Y to contact the cradle in the water and then pull up the ramp under its own power, beaching itself.

The final flight by a Mars with VR-2 took place in August 1956, and VR-2 shifted entirely to the Tradewind. (Ironically, the Mars flying-boat would still be in operation decades later, fighting fires in Canadian forests, while the newer, faster, seemingly better-performing Tradewind would be gone in less than two years.) VR-2 began filling out its operational roster with crews trained under two crews who previously underwent instruction at Convair. The Tradewind had now been in development for nearly a decade and seemed, finally, on the brink of success.

However, the troublesome T40 engine had not reformed, and Navy crews reported power deficiency at altitude and poor balance between the dual balance sections. The contra-rotating propellers overheated, oscillated and went out of synchronisation. The gear boxes were trouble-prone. The Tradewind also offered other problems, including malfunctions of the

Fleet Logistic Support Squadron Two (VR-2)

Left: VR-2 Philippine Mars (JRM-3 BuNo. 76820) taxis while the South Pacific Tradewind (R3Y-2 BuNo. 131724) overflies the giant during Tradewind delivery ceremonies on the last day of March 1956.

Below: As well as gaining individual names, the Tradewinds received VR-2's 'RA' tail-code. Indian Ocean Tradewind (R3Y-1 BuNo. 128446) taxies in to Keehi Lagoon on Oahu in October 1956.

Fleet Logistic Support Squadron Two (VR-2) of the Fleet Logistics Air Wing provided the air transport link between Alameda and Honolulu. It initiated the first USN trans-Pacific flights on 15 May 1942 using Douglas R4Ds. From February 1946 it employed the lumbering JRM Mars, built especially for the route, having previously used the XPB2M-1R Mars prototype between January 1944 and March 1945. The Mars were supplemented from 31 March 1956 by the first of five R3Y-1s and six R3Y-2s, the final JRM being retired by VR-2 in August 1956, prior to delivery of the last Tradewind. When the Tradewinds were stricken on 16 April 1958, VR-2 was disbanded.

One accident too many...

Bow cruiser R3Y-1 BuNo. 128446 was the second R3Y Tradewind built, and gained the most flying hours of any of its breed – 716 in all. It joined VR-2 at NAS Alameda as the unit's seventh Tradewind, being christened *Indian Ocean Tradewind,* and breaking the Honolulu-Alameda speed record on 18 October 1956 with a time of six hours 45 minutes. '446's career – and that of the Tradewind in US Navy service – came to a grinding halt with an accident on 24 January 1958.

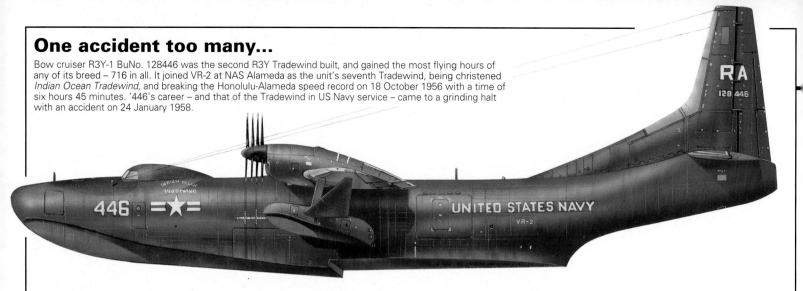

Above: A victim of the frequent engine problems, VR-2's R3Y-1 BuNo. 128448 sits on a mud-bank awaiting salvage. On 10 May 1957, during a routine training flight, the no. 3 engine went out of control and all attempts to rein it in failed. After a steep dive an emergency landing was executed in San Francisco Bay at 200 knots (230 mph/370 km/h), the craft being uncontrollable below 180 knots (207 mph/333 km/h). The resulting landing punctured the hull and ended the flying days of the Coral Sea Tradewind, *the aircraft being salvaged and stripped for parts.*

Below: After covering 385 miles (620 km) following the disintegration of a gearbox and loss of the propellers from its no. 2 engine, R3Y-1 BuNo.128446 thrust itself onto a rock sea-wall in San Francisco Bay, tearing a large hole in its bow. The hole made by the no. 2 propeller is visible in the fuselage. As a HUP-2 Retriever rescue helicopter approaches, spray is kicked up from the out-of-control no. 1 engine. Attempts to shut down this engine from the cockpit were to no avail and one of the 17 crew on the aircraft, an engine mechanic, crawled inside the vibrating wing and shut down the engine manually. Though the accident brought an immediate and final grounding for the Tradewind fleet, 128446 had nonetheless broken the Honolulu – San Francisco speed record once again!

automatic pilot and rudder flutter at high speeds, but it was the inability to get the T40 working right that sealed the Tradewind's doom. Even as regular flights traversed the eastern Pacific in 1956 and 1957, the handwriting was on the wall.

Far from rectifying the Tradewind's powerplant problems, the Navy was busy carving out a new role for the big aircraft. The Navy has always wanted its own fleet of long-ranged, land-based tankers – it still does – and the Tradewind seemed perfectly suited. The flying-boat would be equipped with four reeled hoses enclosed within streamlined aluminium honeycomb and fibreglass pods, two under each wing, operated from two consoles located in the hull. The Tradewind would carry sufficient fuel to enable a flight of four fighters to make a long-distance water crossing. The Navy modified two R3Y-2 Tradewinds to the tanker configuration in 1956 and began trials using F2H-3 Banshee fighters of squadron VF-23 and F9F-8 Cougars of VF-123 as receivers.

In due course, four Tradewinds (one R3Y-1 and three R3Y-2s) were brought to tanker standard, with unchanged designations. The four external hose units and structural modifications increased the weight of the aircraft by 6,600 lb (2994 kg). Fuel for receiver aircraft came from the Tradewind's outer wing

F2H-3 Banshee BuNo. 126417 of VF-23 is seen being filmed by one of the Tradewind's crew while connected to the port outer hose. R3Y-2 BuNo. 131722 retains its production line number '9' and has yet to gain its VR-2 codes and Arabian Sea Tradewind *name.*

A rather weather-beaten Caribbean Tradewind (BuNo. 131723) was photographed off Catalina Island during in-flight refuelling trials with F9F-8P Cougars, on 17 December 1957. Note that the aircraft is fitted with just two refuelling pods on this occasion.

tanks and could be cross-fed to either side. In operations with F2H-3 Banshees and F9F-8 Cougars, it was decided that the inner two refuelling pods, which hung from slanted pylons immediately adjacent to the outer engines, were unsafe. They worked properly but subjected the receiver aircraft to turbulence from the Tradewind's contra-rotating propellers. In actual operations, the Navy decided to use only the outer two refuelling pods, which were flush with the underside of the wing at the tip.

The last straw

Just as a crash had terminated the XP5Y-1 – albeit, only after a variety of difficulties made themselves abundantly evident to the Navy brass – a crash ended the R3Y Tradewind programme. When it happened, it was only the latest in a continuing story of technical troubles. The ill-starred *Indian Ocean Tradewind* (BuNo. 128446) continued its tradition of record-breaking flights with a sortie that set a new mark, but also caused the Navy to scuttle the Tradewind programme when the flight ended in catastrophe. On 24 January 1958, BuNo. 128446 was flying from Hawaii to California when the gearbox for the number two engine blew apart only a couple of hundred miles from arrival at Alameda. A propeller tore off the engine mount and ripped a hole into the side of the fuselage at the leading edge of the wing. The pilot declared an emergency, descended abruptly, and picked up an escort of a Coast Guard P4Y-1G Privateer and an Air Force SA-16 Albatross as he brought the aircraft down

for a trembling, shuddering landing with the weather closing in on all sides.

Indian Ocean Tradewind ran amok on the bay, the pilot having control of the starboard engines only. With some difficulty, he put the aircraft down on the water but the R3Y-1 was still out of control and ploughed into a seawall, ripping out the forward hull. It was an ironic stroke that the flight had set another record, this time of five hours and 52 minutes. The disaster made BuNo. 128446 a complete write-off and resulted in an immediate grounding of all R3Y-1 and R3Y-2 Tradewinds. The cantankerous T40 engine had finally inflicted more damage than the Tradewind programme could absorb.

Based on the mortal mishap to *Indian Ocean Tradewind*, which in turn prompted a Navy Bureau of Aeronautics recommendation to the Chief of Naval Operations dated 7 March 1958, the Navy shut down the Tradewind programme completely. Its termination became official on

16 April 1958. VR-2 was disestablished and its members scattered. The R3Ys were struck from inventory in March 1959 and, while they awaited the scrapper's torch at Alameda, the Navy ordered their vertical fins to be cut off to make them less noticeable. Soon afterward, every one of the 11 flying-boats in the R3Y series, like the two P5Ys before them, was cut up for scrap. The on-site dismantling and destruction of these great flying-boats was completed in the spring of 1960. Today, the largest surviving remnant is a T40 engine displayed at the San Diego Aerospace Museum, a few miles from where the big 'boats were manufactured.

Convair worked briefly on its parasol-wing, three-engined, long-range patrol aircraft – the XP6Y-1 – but by 1960 the Navy was no longer interested. The company soon ended its activity in the flying-boat business and its employees with expertise in the field moved on to other things.

Robert F. Dorr

Seen during the first live fuel transfer on 10 October 1956, R3Y-2 BuNo. 131722 refuels four F9F-8 Cougars of VF-123 simultaneously off the southern Californian coast.

Specification

R3Y-1 (*R3Y-2)

Type: heavy transport flying-boat (*tanker and assault transport flying-boat)
Powerplant: four 5,850-eshp (4364-kW) Allison T40-A-10 turboprop engines
Weights: normal take-off weight 165,000 lb (74844 kg); maximum take-off weight 175,000 lb (79380 kg)
Dimensions: span 145 ft 9 in (44.42 m); length 139 ft 8 in (42.57 m); (*141 ft 1⁷⁄₁₀ in [43.00 m]); height 44 ft 10 in (13.67 m), wing area 2,100 sq ft (195 m²)
Performance: maximum speed 360 mph (579 km/h); cruising speed 300 mph (483 km/h); maximum range 4,000 miles (6437 km)

Thunderchiefs arrived in Southeast Asia finished in an aluminised lacquer. The first aircraft reached their Thai bases in 1964 and were immediately thrown into combat. This F-105D is hauling the heaviest load carried by Thunderchiefs in-theatre – 16 750-lb M117 low-drag, general purpose (LDGP) bombs. The load deprived the aircraft of the ability to carry external fuel tanks, making it even more reliant on in-flight refuelling for the long journey to North Vietnam.

1st Lt Chuck de Vlaming of the 354th TFS was photographed in his F-105D, The Grim Reaper, on its way to a target during 1968. Fighting became so intense and F-105 losses reached such levels, that it was soon statistically unlikely that an F-105 pilot would complete a tour of 100 combat missions.

'Thud', *n.* nickname applied affectionately to a species of fighter-bombers found in considerable numbers over North Vietnam, noted for extraordinary ability to carry out 75 per cent of USAF missions despite heaviest concentrations of flak, missiles, etc. in history; excels in SAM suppression role; official name of this unusual species: Republic F-105 Thunderchief.

When the USA went to war in Southeast Asia during the first half of the 1960s, the USAF made a strange decision: it would use tactical fighters as strategic weapons, and B-52 strategic bombers as tactical weapons. The weapon system chosen for the strategic bombing campaign was the Republic F-105 Thunderchief fighter-bomber. The F-105 had been developed in the mid-1950s as a nuclear strike fighter for the Tactical Air Command, making its first flight in October 1955. By the time the Vietnam War began, the F-105 had changed considerably. The F-105D, considered the ultimate in Thunderchief design, had the R-14A radar and ASG-19 Thunderstick nav/attack system. Huge for an aircraft in the 'F-for-Fighter' category, the F-105D was 64 ft 4 in (19.61 m) long with a wingspan of 34 ft 11 in (10.64 m) and a height of 19 ft 8 in (5.99 m). Weighing over 52,500 lb (23814 kg), the F-105D was powered by a single Pratt & Whitney J75-P-19W turbojet engine rated at 24,500 lb st (108.98 kN) with afterburning.

The F-105D had a maximum speed of 1,390 mph (2237 km/h) or Mach 2.1, a rate of climb in excess of 34,000 ft (10363 m) per minute, a service ceiling of more than 52,000 ft (15850 m) and an unrefuelled ferry range of 2,070 miles (3331 km). Of course, with inflight-refuelling the range was indefinite but limited to the endurance of the pilot. However, the unrefuelled range was somewhat shorter, and shortened still further when the aircraft was combat loaded with bombs, missiles, drop tanks and ECM pods, and the use of the afterburner, which was virtually a standard procedure over North Vietnam, further curtailed range. Designed originally as a trainer, the two-seat F-105F Thunderchief had similar specifications.

In the Vietnam War the F-105D was modified to carry a maximum amount of non-nuclear ordnance on five hardpoints, one on the centreline and two under each half of the wing. The normal ordnance load was a single MER (multiple ejector rack) on the centreline with up to six 750-lb bombs, but there were times when heavier ordnance was required, such as 3,000-lb M118 bombs, and these were usually carried under the wing. Moreover, each Thunderchief entering North Vietnamese airspace was required to carry items like ECM pods and AIM-9 Sidewinder short-range AAMs for defensive purposes. Thus a fully loaded 'Thud' could not even approach the stated

'Thuds' and Weasels

The F-105 Thunderchief in SEA, 1964-1974

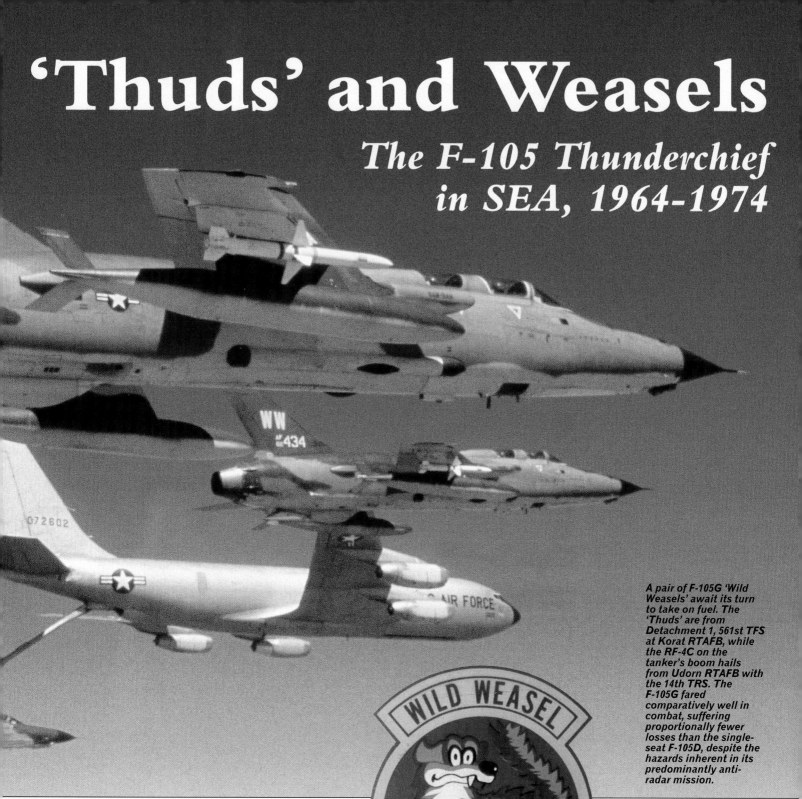

A pair of F-105G 'Wild Weasels' await its turn to take on fuel. The 'Thuds' are from Detachment 1, 561st TFS at Korat RTAFB, while the RF-4C on the tanker's boom hails from Udorn RTAFB with the 14th TRS. The F-105G fared comparatively well in combat, suffering proportionally fewer losses than the single-seat F-105D, despite the hazards inherent in its predominantly anti-radar mission.

maximum speed, while in 'clean' condition, it could leave almost every other fighter aircraft in the dust, especially 'down in the weeds' where the 'Thud' generally operated during the Vietnam War.

The first F-105 aircraft to enter the conflict were those assigned to the 36th TFS (Tactical Fighter Squadron), which deployed from Yokota Air Base in Japan to Korat in Thailand on 9 August 1964. Four hours after landing at Korat, the 36th TFS had eight aircraft armed on ready alert. Their mission was ResCAP (Rescue Combat Air Patrol). Specifically, they were tasked to fly ResCAP for pilots downed in Laos. At least that was their 'official' mission, but in reality the F-105s were at Korat to supply air support for CIA operations in Laos. Several other units deployed to South East Asia (SEA) in response to the Gulf of Tonkin Crisis of August 1964, including the 80th, 357th, 67th, and 44th TFSs, and many of these squadrons would figure prominently in F-105 operations well into 1970. All the squadrons that deployed to SEA were on a TDY (temporary duty) status, assigned initially to the 2nd Air Division (2nd AD) and to provisional wings, until activation of the two permanent wings at Korat (388th TFW) and Takhli (355th TFW) RTAFBs.

On 14 August 1964, Lt Dave Graben's 36th TFS F-105D (62-4371) became the first casualty of the Thunderchief war in SEA. Graben's 'Thud' was hit by 37-mm anti-aircraft fire during a ResCAP for a the pilot of a CIA-operated North American T-28 downed in the Laotian

Left: The origins of the 'YGBSM' patch can be traced back to the first Wild Weasel F-100s. When the new mission was explained to the first pilot/EWO crews at Eglin AFB in late 1965, one of the crew members allegedly exclaimed, "You gotta be shittin' me!", hence "YGBSM". The five-initial abbreviation for that immortal phrase was thus adopted as the unofficial motto of Weasels crews, whether they were flying F-100s, F-105s or F-4s.

Above: 'Straight' F-105Fs were an increasingly rare sight in combat, especially as aircraft were consumed by the EF-105F/F-105G conversion process. This 36th TFS F-105F was photographed returning from a rocket strike against targets in the Plain de Jarres area of Laos in January 1965. Note the empty rocket pod on the starboard outer wing pylon.

Armourers reinstall the ammunition drum of a 335th TFS F-105D on the ramp at Takhli in 1968. The F-105 carried a single 20-mm M61A1 rotary cannon. The weapon fired from a trough in the lower left forward fuselage.

jungle. Hit in the engine and stabiliser, Graben took the wounded and burning 'Thud' to 39,000 ft (11885 m), which 'starved' out the fire, then brought the machine safely back to Korat. It was the beginning of the legend of how tough the F-105 was. However, Graben's 'Thud' was declared a total loss and was therefore the first of 334 F-105s lost to hostile fire in the Vietnam War.

Six months after opening Korat to F-105 operations, the 36th TFS deployed to another Thai air base, namely

Takhli, about 100 miles (160 km) to the north-west. The 36th TFS's place at Korat was taken by the 35th TFS and other squadrons from both the continental USA and the PACAF (Pacific Air Forces) command. From these two air bases in Thailand, the 'Thuds' operated on a daily basis, flying deep into North Vietnam for the next six years. With combat operations increasing every day at Korat and Takhli, the 13th Air Force activated two permanent wings, the 6234th TFW at Korat and the 6235th at Takhli.

Barrel Roll

On 10 December 1964, Operation Barrel Roll was initiated as the first open US air support of Royal Laotian troops involved in combat with the North Vietnamese and the Pathet Lao communist forces attempting to overthrow the legitimate government. The first Barrel Roll mission, on 15 December 1964, saw F-105Ds of the 80th TFS make up a strike force with a trio of McDonnell RF-101C Voodoo reconnaissance aircraft that were acting as both pathfinder and bomb damage assessment aircraft. MiGCAP was flown by eight North American F-100D Super Sabre fighters. This was the first co-ordinated strike by F-105s, and their introduction to something new to air warfare – rules of engagement.

The target was the bridge complex on Route 8 near the village of Nape. Two bridges spanned the river: one was of the sunken log type and the other was made of steel and concrete. The F-105s were armed with CBU-24 cluster

Republic F-105D Thunderchief 563rd TFS, 6235th Combat Support Group Takhli RTAFB, 1965

Revised instrumentation
In the F-105D, Republic replaced the traditional circular instrument dials of the F-105B with vertical and horizontal tape-type instruments. These were arranged in a 'T'-shape on the instrument panel and were theoretically easier to read than dials.

62-4398
'398 was an F-105D-30-RE of the penultimate single-seat production block. Production of the F-105D ended in 1963/1964, so when this aircraft was lost to enemy action on 3 July 1965, it became just one more 'Thud' that the USAF was unable to replace.

Combined airbrake and nozzle
The F-105's cleverly designed exhaust nozzle performed dual functions. With afterburner selected, all four of the exhaust nozzle's petals automatically opened to an angle of 9°, increasing nozzle area. When used as an airbrake, all four petals could be fully opened in flight. With the undercarriage extended, only the horizontal petals could be fully opened, thus shortening the aircraft's landing run.

Underwing warloads
Early on in the conflict, the AGM-12 Bullpup AGM had been available to the Thunderchief squadrons. It was quickly realised that there was no place for such an indifferent weapon in combat however, and 'iron bombs' became the weapons of choice. The 750-lb M117, illustrated here on the centreline MER and the 500-lb Mk 82 (on the outer wing pylons) were the most common bomb types employed.

bombs and rocket pods, which were hardly weapons of choice to knock out a hard target like a bridge. Based at Takhli, the pilots from the 80th TFS first had to fly to Da Nang because the 'rule' (based on the 1962 Geneva Accords) stated that to hit targets in Laos, the aircraft had to be 'based' in South Vietnam. At Da Nang, the Thunderchiefs were armed and refuelled, and then took off back toward northern Laos. The pilots then learned the real 'rules': first, the Thunderchiefs had to fly well into northern Laos before being able to turn south toward the target, which was some 100 miles (160 km) away; second, the pilot was not allowed to attack the bridge unless there was a truck or some type of military vehicle on it (there always was such a vehicle even if the bridge was empty!); and third, the pilot was not permitted to fire on anything more than 300 yards (275 m) from the road unless, of course, he was being fired upon from that area. Those were the 'rules of engagement' at that time, and they were constantly expanded over the next six years. It is worth remembering that at this time the official

line was that the USAF 'had no units operating in Thailand', a fact that was admitted only in 1966. Barrel Roll continued into 1965.

On 7 February 1965, following a Viet Cong attack against a US base camp inside South Vietnam, President Lyndon B. Johnson ordered Operation Flaming Dart as the first attacks against targets inside the borders of North Vietnam. On that same day, US Navy aircraft attacked the Dong Hoi army complex, one of the main training bases for the Viet Cong, and on the following day USAF F-105 and F-100 aircraft, along with South Vietnamese air force (VNAF) Douglas A-1 Skyraiders led by VNAF Air Vice Marshal Nguyen Cao Ky, struck Dong Hoi again, and also hit the communications centre at Vinh Linh.

The Viet Cong answered that attack by blowing up the US barracks at Qui Nhon, killing 23 US personnel. President Johnson ordered Flaming Dart II, the first integrated attacks by USAF, US Navy and VNAF aircraft on targets in the panhandle region of North Vietnam, i.e. Route Pack 1, just north of the DMZ (De-Militarised Zone) separating North and South Vietnam. The Flaming Dart operations also brought more F-105s, including the aircraft of the 12th, 354th and 561st TFSs, into the conflict.

Early in 1965, PACAF divided North Vietnam into

These 'shark-mouthed' F-105Ds were from the 23rd TFW. Both aircraft are armed with rocket pods and M117 bombs on centreline MERs. The green stripes around the aft fuselage of the rear aircraft were applied for a Stateside exercise named Desert Strike. Such was the speed of F-105 deployments that the opportunity to remove them did not arise.

Good Vibrations *is armed with a mix of conventionally fused 500-lb Mk 82 LDGPs and Mk 82s fitted with extended fuses. Known as 'Daisy Cutters', the latter were especially effective against soft targets such as personnel and trucks.*

J75 turbojet
The addition of water injection to the Pratt & Whitney J75 turbojet produced the J75-P-19W, which powered the F-105D and F, and produced 26,500 lb st (117.85 kN) at sea level.

Drop tanks
Two 450-US gal (1703-litre) underwing tanks were typically carried in combat, although carriage of a third, 650-US gal (2460-litre) tank on the fuselage centreline was also possible. The drop tanks were used in sequence to refill the internal tanks as fuel was consumed.

The Vulcan cannon of 61-0132 was responsible for the destruction of a MiG-17 on 23 August 1967, in the hands of 1Lt David B. Waldrop III. The pilot and F-105D hailed from the 34th TFS of the 388th TFW at Korat. Note the aircraft's empty bomb rack and wing pylons, and the deflection of the horizontal nozzle petals.

Right: On 10 March 1967, Captain Max C. Brestel downed two MiG-17 'Fresco' fighters on the same sortie, while flying F-105D 62-4284. Both kills were scored with the gun, and the same weapon was used to accomplish a third kill, again a MiG-17, on 27 October 1967. On the latter occasion, '284 was being flown by Capt. Gene I. Basel, but remained with the 354th TFS, 355th TFW throughout.

seven areas for tactical purposes. These were called RPs, standing for Route Packages or Route Packs. As the number of the RPs went up, so too did the intensity of the North Vietnamese defences. RP-1 was immediately above the DMZ. RP-6 was the last major area, taking up the entire north-east portion of North Vietnam, including both the main port city of Haiphong and the capital city of Hanoi. Within RP-6 were all the main rail lines that brought supplies and equipment from Red China. RP-6 was divided into two areas, namely RP-6A and RP-6B. RP-6A was the target-rich area in and around the city of Hanoi. Nowhere were the defences deadlier. It would later be documented as the 'most heavily defended area in the history of air warfare'. When a strike went 'downtown', i.e. within the Hanoi city limits, the 'pucker factor' went up

five notches because Hanoi was the home of SAMs.

Operation Rolling Thunder began on 2 March 1965. In answer to continuing, and ever increasing attacks by the VC against both South Vietnamese and US installations in South Vietnam, President Johnson ordered a new series of air attacks against targets in North Vietnam that were not in retaliation for an attack by the Viet Cong against US or South Vietnamese personnel. The idea was to strike selected targets inside North Vietnam in an attempt to slow the communist aggression in the south. Just as the noise of thunder would increase and decrease, so would the American air attacks increase and abate in response to North Vietnamese or VC attacks south of the 17th Parallel.

Rolling Thunder begins

Postponed twice, first by a failed coup in Saigon and second by bad weather, the initial Rolling Thunder attacks took place on 2 March 1965 against the Xom Biang ammunition depot, just 10 miles (16 km) across the DMZ. Over 100 USAF fighters struck Xom Biang, destroying the target. At the same time, VNAF A-1s hit the North Vietnamese naval base at Quang Khe, about 65 miles (105 km) to the north. But the North Vietnamese air defences were starting to get better – much better. Five aircraft were lost, comprising three of the 67th TFS's F-105Ds (61-4214, 62-4325 and 62-4260) and two F-100Ds. Three of the pilots were recovered by USAF Kaman HH-43 'Pedro' helicopters out of Da Nang, but one F-100 pilot was captured, and Captain R. V. Baird, a pilot of the 67th TFS, was killed.

Initially, the targets were selected on a daily basis by the

By November 1966, Korat had all the trappings of a major US air base, as indicated by the sign and revetment. Built from heavy-gauge metal and filled with soil, the revetments helped keep aircraft free of unwanted attention from rocket-firing enemy sappers and minimise shrapnel damage.

F-105Ds unload M117s over a North Vietnam target on a Rolling Thunder strike. All four have QRC-160 ECM pods.

A handful of F-105Ds were modified under the Thunderstick II programme to give them a true blind-bombing capability. The system, which included a LORAN receiver for highly accurate navigation, was installed in a bulged spine (above) with other new avionic equipment. Assessed briefly in combat prior to 1968, the system proved too complex to be adequately maintained in the field. F-105Ds were therefore forced to rely on pathfinder aircraft, such as the Douglas EB-66 (left), for guidance during radar bombing sorties.

JCS (Joint Chiefs of Staff) and politicians in Washington. As the Rolling Thunder attacks elicited little response from the North Vietnamese, the scope of the operation was slowly expanded. The JCS drew up a list of selected targets in the area of North Vietnam between the 17th and 19th Parallels. The target list was approved all the way up the chain of command to President Johnson, who reserved the final decision as to whether or not a specific target would be struck. The target list included POL (petroleum, oil and lubricant) depots, storage facilities, bridges, military facilities and barracks, ammunition depots, road and rail networks, etc. It is significant to note what were excluded from the target list: airports (civilian and military), harbour complexes, anti-aircraft sites and major cities. And the 'rules of engagement' were strictly enforced.

Fresh aircraft and crews

As the Rolling Thunder campaign continued through 1965, PACAF began rotating F-105 squadrons through Korat and Takhli, bringing fresh aircraft and crews into the conflict, and as a result squadrons from the 4th, 8th, 18th, and 23rd TFWs deployed to the war zone. During the first 11 months of 1965, neither Korat nor Takhli was 'home plate' for one of the recognisable wings in the USAF. Both bases were initially organised under the control of 2nd AD, then as 'provisional wings' made up of the TDY squadrons rotating in and out of the war. Korat was home to the 6234th TFW (Provisional), activated on 5 April 1965. The 6234th TFW initially comprised elements of the 35th TFS, TDY from Yokota AB, the 44th TFS from Kadena AB, and elements of the 354th and 421st Squadrons from McConnell Air Force Base, Kansas. In early 1965, the 12th and 67th TFS deployed from Kadena on Okinawa to Korat, taking the place of two of the previous squadrons, again on a TDY basis. They arrived in time to add 25 F-105D aircraft to the first Rolling Thunder mission. The

469th TFS, attached to the 18th TFW at the time, sent five F-105D aircraft to Korat.

On 3 March 1965, under Operation One Buck 10, the 354th TFS rotated back to Kadena, taking the place of the 469th TFS, which returned to McConnell AFB, a move that was not to last. On the same day that the 469th TFS returned to McConnell, 13 March, the 354th TFS returned six of its F-105Ds to Korat, becoming officially operational with all aircraft by 19 March. Interestingly, the 469th TFS, even while in SEA, still had a nuclear strike mission, standing ZULU alert on Formosa, which was finally dropped on 18 March when the unit returned to McConnell AFB.

Takhli was home for the 6235th TFW (Provisional), activated on 8 July 1965, and elements of the TDY squadrons already in place at Takhli. On 8 November 1965, the 355th TFW was transferred from McConnell AFB to Takhli. At the beginning of 1964, the 355th TFW had four squadrons attached: the 354th, 357th, 421st, and 469th TFSs. Before the Gulf of Tonkin Crisis erupted, the 355th had deployed aircraft and personnel to California for participation in Operation Desert Strike. Between 1

This 1965 shot of 'Thuds' on the ramp at Takhli, demonstrates the level of US bombing operations from Thai bases. It also serves to demonstrate the fact that US tactical aircraft were transitioning from 'natural metal' to camouflage finishes at about this time.

In SEA, the largest weapon, in terms of weight, employed by the F-105 was the 3,000-lb M118. The considerably greater size of the weapon when compared to the M117 or Mk 82 is readily apparent.

North Vietnamese air defence systems, which were constantly being improved, increased and replenished by the USSR. But the North Vietnamese were also preparing for an extended war. Their Soviet backers brought in some very sophisticated air defence hardware to use against the 'Yankee Air Pirates'. Most of the AAA (anti-aircraft artillery) was radar-directed, varying in calibre from 37-mm to 85-mm, and notably accurate. The North Vietnamese also received supplies of Soviet SAMs (surface-to-air missiles), initially in the form of the SA-2 'Guideline' using the 'Fan Song' radar guidance unit. The SA-2 could be very deadly, especially if the strike force was caught by surprise. Flying above a cloud deck was an invitation to disaster. If the strike force did not know about a SAM launch until the missile broke through the cloud deck, it was too late. At least one aircraft would probably be lost.

'Painted' by 'Fan Song'

In 1965, the only way the pilots of strike packages could know they were under attack by a SAM was to see the launch. If they were lucky, one of the ECM aircraft assigned to the mission, such as a Douglas EB-66 or Lockheed EC-121, would pick up the SAM guidance radar signals and warn the pilots of the strike package that their aircraft were 'being painted' by a 'Fan Song' guidance radar. The pilots would then start to look very hard for anything unusual. If a pilot saw the launch, he could go into a 'split S' manoeuvre, breaking down and into the SA-2's climbing flight path. With a little jinking, he could usually force the SA-2 out of its manoeuvring envelope, and the missile would not be able to follow the F-105's flight. With a cloud deck however, the pilot had two choices: either fly above it and take his chances on the SAMs catching him unaware, or fly below it and be subjected to the heavy and very accurate AAA fire. Such was the dilemma of the Rolling Thunder strike force commanders.

Good Golly Miss Molly of the 469th TFS was photographed while leading a second F-105D on a strike over North Vietnam in the summer of 1968. By mid-1966, with losses reaching unacceptable levels, the carriage of at least one QRC-160 ECM pod by each strike package became mandatory. In 1966 alone, 103 'Thuds' were lost to AAA, with losses to the same cause falling to 69 in 1967 and 28 in 1968.

January 1965 and 30 June 1965, all squadrons within the original 355th TFW were deployed, at one time or another, to areas of the Far East to take part in the increased air operations against North Vietnam. Following activation at Takhli, the 355th had three squadrons attached: the 333rd TFS transferred permanently (PCS) from the 4th TFW to the 355th, the 354th TFS that had originally been assigned to the 355th, and the 334th TFS that had originally been allocated on a TDY basis to the 4th TFW. On 14 March 1966, the 388th TFW was activated at Korat, initially comprising the 421st and 469th TFSs, and later the 13th and 34th TFSs. The stage was now set for the next three years of war involving the F-105 and its crews.

President Johnson halted the bombing twice in 1965, for six days in mid-May and again from Christmas Eve 1965 to the end of January 1966, while attempting to get the North Vietnamese to the peace table. Neither halt accomplished anything other than to give a respite to the beleaguered

Although F-105Ds often carried AGM-45s, the aircraft were unable to locate targets for the missile's sensors. It was therefore standard practice for F-100F Super Sabre or EF-105F Wild Weasels to fly in 'hunter-killer' teams with Shrike-armed 'Ds'. The former detected the targets, while the latter 'killed' them.

*Both of these aircraft have their bomb doors sealed shut with metal straps, the bomb bay being redundant over Vietnam, having been designed for nuclear weapons. After the 1968 bombing halts, F-105Gs were frequently employed on straight bombing missions, hence **Honey's** load of Mk 82s. The Weasel aircraft belongs to the 333rd **TFS**, while **Rosa E**, the F-105D, is a 44th **TFS** machine.*

The USAF knew about the construction of the SA-2 installations as early as April 1965, when an RF-101 Voodoo photographed five such emplacements under construction near Hanoi. But the 'rules' did not allow any of these sites to be attacked since they were not yet operational. Even later, after these same SAM sites had become operational, attacks were not permitted on any site unless this had first launched a missile! On 24 July 1965, a flight of McDonnell F-4C Phantom IIs of the 47th TFS came under attack by three SAMs just west of Hanoi: the SA-2 missiles knocked one of the F-4s out of the sky, and damaged two of the remaining three aircraft. Three days later, F-105s attacked that particular SAM site, destroying it. But it was much too late for the downed F-4C crew, as the pilot was posted KIA (killed in action) and the navigator was taken prisoner.

Countering the SAM threat

Something had to be done to counter this new and very deadly defence. The USAF's answer was two-fold: first was the development and employment of an airborne jamming system, compact enough to be carried by a fighter aircraft; and second was the development of some type of suppression system or aircraft. Until such aircraft became available, the F-105s would have to defend themselves in other ways. On 31 October 1965, the first of a very dangerous type of mission was flown. This was the Iron Hand mission, a deliberate attack against the North Vietnamese SAM sites using US Navy Douglas A-4E Skyhawk aircraft as bait. The Skyhawks were equipped with sensors to pick up the missile system's radar signals and a flight of F-105s waited to spring the trap. At least that was the plan. On this day, an A-4E from VA-164, piloted by Lieutenant Commander Richard Powers, launched from USS *Oriskany* and staged into Korat for the mission. Powers led eight F-105Ds against a pair of SAM sites in North Vietnam. Although four SA-2 missiles were launched against the Iron Hand flights, there were no hits and the 'Thuds' knocked out both sites. Tragically, anti-aircraft fire struck Powers' Skyhawk and he was forced to eject. He did not survive his captivity.

The airborne jamming systems were already available in specialised aircraft such as the RB-66 jet bomber. Moreover, small individual jamming pods had also been under development for some time, but these were not in production and available to combat units during the first 12 months of the air war. The USAF had begun development of the ECM pod in the late 1950s, but it was not until early 1961 that General Electric was contracted to develop a pod small enough to be carried by a fighter. This was the General Electric QRC-160 (QRC standing for Quick Reaction Capability) series of ECM (electronic countermeasures) pods. The QRC-160-1, standardised as the ALQ-71, was about 8 ft (2.44 m) in length, and was tuned to the frequencies of Soviet anti-aircraft radars, including the 'Fan Song' guidance radar used by the SA-2 SAM. The QRC-160-2, standardised as the ALQ-72, was

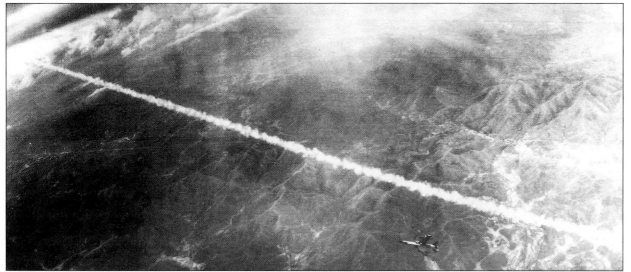

This incredible image was captured by the strike camera of a second F-105D. The contrail was left by an SA-2 missile, which narrowly missed the hard-manoeuvring F-105D at the foot of the photograph. Given adequate warning of the SAM's launch, an alert 'Thud' driver could often out-manoeuvre an incoming missile.

Thorsness and Dethlefsen: Medal of Honor recipients

Of 12 USAF Medal of Honor winners, two were F-105 Wild Weasel pilots.

Lietenant-Colonel Leo K. Thorsness

On 19 April 1967, the then Lieutenant-Colonel Thorsness (right), was on a SAM suppression mission over North Vietnam. He and his EWO Captain Harold E. Johnson, had already destroyed one radar with ARMs and a second with bombs, when their wingman was downed by AAA. As the unlucky crew took to the silk, Thorsness circled their position so that he could accurately relay it to the rescue forces. However, his attention was soon diverted by a MiG-17, which he duly dispatched with 20-mm cannon fire. Finding himself low on fuel, Thorsness then went off in search of a tanker. However, before he found fuel, he was informed that the two rescue helicopters sent to pick up the downed airmen were being harassed by four MiGs. Without refuelling therefore, Thorsness returned to the area, damaging one of the MiG-17s and forcing all four away. Now, desperately low on fuel, he learned of another aircraft in an even more critical fuel state. It seemed that the second aircraft would be lost and a new rescue situation would develop if this second aircraft did not refuel immediately. Thorsness therefore elected not to hook up with a nearby tanker, leaving this for the other stricken machine and himself landing at a forward operating base. Thorsness and Johnson's 357th TFS, 355 TFW EF-105F is pictured below.

Captain Merlyn H. Dethlefsen

Merlyn H. Dethlefsen (right, with the rank of Major, receiving his medal from President Johnson and with wife Jorja and children Julie and Jeffrey looking on), with EWO Captain Mike Gilroy, was part of a flight of EF-105Fs sent against a strong establishment of anti-aircraft defences on 10 March 1967. The defences protected an industrial complex which was to be attacked in the wake of the Wild Weasels. As the anti-radar attack was initiated, the leader's aircraft was immediately taken out of action, while Dethlefsen's was severely damaged. Realising that the safety of the main attack force and the success of its mission now rested in his hands, Dethlefsen continued to attack the defences at close range with repeated bomb and strafing attacks. Despite the overwhelming AAA, SAM and fighter defences fielded by the enemy, Dethlefsen succeeded in silencing the enemy search radars, allowing the main attack force to pass unmolested and to attack the target with impunity. The bombers suffered no losses. Detlefsen and Gilroy's 357th TFS, 355 TFW aircraft is seen in the air-to-air view to the right.

While few in-theatre jets could match the F-105 for outright speed 'on the deck', the aircraft was by no means a dogfighter. This 'Thud', with a MiG-17 glued to its tail, was photographed with the gun camera of second Thunderchief.

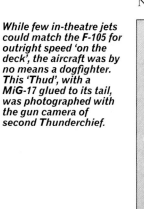

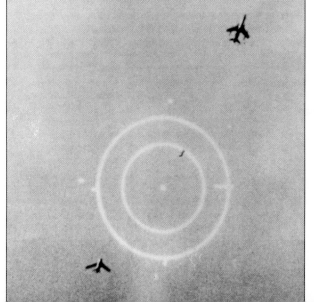

similar in size but its purpose was to jam the fire-control radars of Soviet fighter aircraft. Both pods were deployed to the war in SEA beginning in 1966, with the first pods going to the F-105 squadrons that were penetrating North Vietnamese airspace on a daily basis.

The situation with regard to F-105 losses to AAA and SAMs became so critical in 1966 that the 7th Air Force issued orders that no F-105 aircraft were permitted to enter North Vietnamese airspace without at least one of the ECM pods under their wings. On many occasions, in fact, two pods were carried. In tight formations of up to 16 aircraft the ECM pods were very effective, but any machine that strayed away from the flight found that its individual ECM pod could offer only limited protection.

The other system developed specifically to counter the air defence threats encountered over North Vietnam, was the defence-suppression type of aircraft, commonly called the 'Wild Weasel'. This could not only locate an enemy defensive radar site, be it AAA, SAM, or GCI (ground-controlled interception), but carried the specialised weapons, such as anti-radar missiles and cluster bombs, to attack and destroy these sites.

Project Wild Weasel

It was in the summer of 1965 that the US Air Force had begun a crash programme to produce a system to counter the increasing SAM threat over North Vietnam. On 18 August 1965, the USAF panel made its recommendations for what became known as Project Wild Weasel. Applied Technology Inc. was the supplier of the electronic monitoring equipment, and North American Aviation supplied the required two-seat F-100F Super Sabre. The F-100F was chosen because operation of the electronic systems called for a pilot to fly the aircraft and an EWO (electronic warfare officer) to monitor the equipment, and the type was also readily available. Into the modified F-100F went the Vector IV RHAW (radar homing and

Republic F-105G Thunderchief

333rd TFS, 355th TFW Takhli RTAFB, 1969

Under Project Wild Weasel III the equipment originally fitted to 'Weasel' F-100Fs was installed in 86 F-105F airframes to create the 'EF-105F'. An official designation change to F-105G came in 1967, and was soon accompanied by a significant increase in capability. *Cooter* (63-8320) was an early-standard F-105G (lacking the fuselage-mounted AN/ALQ-105 jammer, but fitted with wingtip ALR-31 antennas) flown by Major Wallace and Captain Hoynacki of the 333rd TFS. It sports two kill markings for air-to-air victories claimed, though only a 'half kill' was officially credited. The 'owl and moon' motif on the forward fuselage is a 'zap' provided by the 497th TFS. This aircraft survived the war and was presented to the USAF Museum for display.

Undernose fairing

From 1965, in-theatre tactical aircraft were modified by the installation of the AN/APR-25 RHAW system. On F-105s, the forward antenna of this system was located in a wedge-shaped housing beneath the nose. The antenna was also used by the AN/APR-26 launch warning receiver. To the rear, an aft facing strike camera occupied a second fairing.

AGM-45 Shrike

Shrike was the original US anti-radar missile. It could detect and home only on to frequencies programmed on the ground and therefore required good Sigint data for successful operation. Nevertheless, the weapon remained the most important ARM in the US inventory until the advent of AGM-88 HARM, continuous development having overcome its shortcomings, allowing it to outserve the Standard ARM.

Inflight refuelling

A rare breed indeed, the F-105 was blessed with both types of US fuel receiving equipment. A standard receptacle was housed in the upper nose, offset slightly to port, while a probe could be extended from the upper forward fuselage, again to port, but just below the windscreen.

AGM-78 Standard ARM

In order to create a more powerful ARM, the body and motor of the USN's Standard AGM was initially mated to the electronics of the AGM-45-A3. This restricted the AGM-78A to attacking only radars of a pre-set frequency, although later variants of the weapon had more flexible receivers, which could monitor a wide range of frequencies.

Wingtip receivers

Small antennas located at the wingtips of F-105G aircraft, served the AN/ALR-31 RHAW receiver. AN/ALR-31 provided for automatic direction-finding and homing on a threat emitter. The antennas also serve as the principle identification feature of the early F-105G, when compared to the EF-105F.

When the 561st TFS first deployed to Thailand, not all of its F-105Gs had the internal ALQ-105 system installed. However, the AGM-78 missile, which was not widely available to the EF-105F, identifies Red Ball as the later Wild Weasel variant.

An EF-105F unleashes a load of 500-lb bombs. Fs and Gs flying straight bombing missions often flew with the rear cockpit vacant.

Specially modified for pin-point single-aircraft strikes on difficult targets, the 'Ryan's Raiders' aircraft were all modified EF-105Fs. Whar's Dem MiGs? of the 44th TFS, demonstrates the special camouflage applied to 'Raiders' aircraft. This comprised a wrap-around scheme of FS.30219 Tan and FS.34159 SAC grey-green.

led a flight of F-105Ds on the USAF's first suppression mission of the war. All such defence-suppression missions, regardless of service, were undertaken with the operational code Iron Hand. Captains Al Lamb (pilot) and Jock Donovan (EWO) scored the first SAM site 'kill' on 21 December 1965.

'EF-105F' takes the stage

Although the F-100F programme was successful, the USAF knew it would never meet the entire spectrum of needs associated with the SEA air war. The F-100F simply did not have the performance needed to stay with F-105 strike packages. As a result F-105 strike aircraft had to slow to the speed of the Wild Weasel F-100F, making the entire strike force even more vulnerable to interception by AAA, SAMs and MiG fighters. Thus the F-105F was the next logical step in the development of the Wild Weasel concept, and the APR-25/26 RHAW system and IR-133 scan receiver were installed into a modified F-105F. On 15 January 1966 the first Wild Weasel III F-105F (unofficially designated 'EF-105F') made its first flight. On 28 May 1966, the first five such aircraft arrived at Korat AB. Initially, the EF-105Fs were integrated into the F-100F Wild Weasel Detachment at Korat but later, after the F-100Fs had been withdrawn from combat, the EF-105F machines were assigned as a flight within the 13th TFS. The EF-105F scored its first 'kill' (a GCI site in RP-1) on 7 June 1966.

As with the F-100F, the first batch of EF-105F machines escorted strike flights from both the 355th and 388th TFWs. As more EF-105Fs were delivered, however, each wing developed its own set of rules regarding the Wild Weasels. In the 388th TFW, the EF-105Fs were all assigned to the 13th TFS, making it the only squadron in the USAF dedicated to the defence-suppression mission. In the 355th TFW, the EF-105F aircraft were formed into elements and flights within all three squadrons. The tactics were basically the same for both wings. The EF-105F flights would go in ahead of the strike flights and 'troll for SAMs', i.e. deliberately make a target of themselves for the SAMs. If a North Vietnamese radar 'illuminated' them, the Weasels had various weapons aboard to take out both the radar and the SAM site itself. The AGM-45 Shrike anti-radar missile was available beginning in the spring of 1966, and the CBU-24 cluster munition was the standard weapon for use against the SAM launchers. At times, the EF-105Fs flew with Shrike-armed F-105D Thunderchiefs to create 'hunter-killer' teams: the EF-105F would find the SAM site and the F-105D would kill it! On every mission, at least one of the invaluable Wild Weasel aircraft was always 'First In and Last Out!'

There were other special projects involving the F-105F. One was Project Northscope, while another was Project Combat Martin. During January 1967, General John Ryan, commanding the Strategic Air Command, saw a need for an all-weather nocturnal capability over North Vietnam. By March of that year, training had begun at Yokota AB in Japan. The initial programme involved a dual pilot concept for a modified F-105F. All the aircraft modified for Northscope were EF-105F machines, which each received the R-14A radar modified to allow an expanded radar scope picture with a faster sector sweep. This gave the rear pilot a better target definition, allowing for much greater accuracy during night attacks. The rear cockpit was also fitted with a weapons release capability.

warning) system that was standardised as the APR-25. The APR-25 monitored the S, C and X bands for radar signals. The next system installed was the IR-133 panoramic scan receiver, which analysed the various threat signals as to type, i.e. AAA, SAM or GCI. Lastly, and the most important as far as pilots were concerned, was the WR-300 LWR (launch warning receiver). It had been discovered that the 'Fan Song' radar increased in power (intensity) just before and during the missile launch. The WR-300, standardised as the APR-26, detected these power increases and indicated an impending SAM attack with a small red indicator that simply, but very clearly stated LAUNCH! The APR-25/26 RHAW combination was added to all SEA aircraft beginning in 1966.

Following a six-week training course at Eglin AFB, the first four F-100F Wild Weasel aircraft deployed to Korat AB in Thailand on 21 November 1965, landing on Thanksgiving Day 1965. The new SAM suppression aircraft were assigned to the 6234th TFW at Korat as Detachment Wild Weasel, and were tasked with leading and escorting strike flights from both Takhli and Korat. On 1 December 1965, Major Garry Willard, Commander of the Wild Weasel Detachment, with Captain Walt Lifsey as his EWO,

The first four Northscope crews, known as 'Ryan's Raiders', arrived at Korat on 24 April 1967. All 'Raider' aircraft and crews were assigned to the 13th TFS, which coincidentally had the Wild Weasel role within the 388th TFW. The crews flew their first night mission on 26 April, striking the Ron Ferry complex. By 22 May, there were 12 Northscope crews at Korat, but PACAF had already changed its thinking about the 'Raider' concept, and accordingly changed the crew composition from two pilots to a standard Wild Weasel crew of a pilot and an EWO. In this way, PACAF increased the number of crews available without increasing the personnel required as the Wild Weasel crews were already in place. There was one hitch, however, as most of the Wild Weasel EWOs had little or no navigator training and even less bombardier training. Most had been trained as EWOs on RB-66 and Boeing B-52 aircraft, and now had to undertake a crash course on navigation and bombing with the R-14A radar.

Between 26 April and 4 October 1967, the 'Raiders' flew 415 sorties to RP-1, RP-5 and RP-6A. All missions were 'one plane, one target' sorties. Beginning in July, the 'Raider' aircraft were used as pathfinders on daylight missions. Three 'Raider' aircraft were shot down before the programme was shut down late in 1967. When the 13th TFS was transferred to the 432nd TFW on 20 October 1967, the mission was taken over by the 44th TFS.

Combat Martin and Linebacker

USAF engineers reasoned that if they could develop a system to monitor and jam North Vietnam's air defence radars, they could also create a system to inhibit the MiG fighter threat. The result of this effort was the Combat Martin F-105. Late in 1967, at least 12 EF-105Fs were modified by installation of the Hallicrafters QRC-128 airborne jamming system designed to jam the communications link between the North Vietnamese

While 'Thuds' did tangle with MiGs, the majority of 'mud-movers' would rather avoid any contact with enemy fighters. One method of defeating the enemy's aerial defences was tried with the Combat Martin aircraft. These machines attempted to jam voice communications between the MiGs and their GCI controllers.

In mid-1966, F-105 pilots joked that by the time a 'Thud jockey' reached his 66th mission, he would have been shot down twice and rescued once. The harsh reality was that the crews were caught up in a grim war, flying strategic missions in a tactical aircraft and being controlled by politicians thousands of miles away. The conflict in Vietnam accounted for the majority of the F-105 fleet and for the lives of an equally appaling number of crews.

The large blade aerial and a rear cockpit without an ejection seat indicate that this is a Combat Martin aircraft. The 561st's Captain Kennedy flew this machine, with 'Colonel Computer' as his backseater.

Below: Forced to land at Nakhon Phanom RTAFB in September 1968, this 354th TFS EF-105F found itself sharing the ramp with an aircraft that might well have provided rescue support had the 'Thud' crew ejected – a 1st SOS A-1E. Note that the Thunderchief wears the reverse pattern camouflage that was applied to one in five F-105s in SEA.

Take-off for a heavily-laden F-105 in Thailand's hot and humid conditions represented an almost unequal struggle between engine thrust and gravity. Ideally, a long runway was needed. However, relatively short runways were the norm, often forcing aircraft like Damn You Charley Brown to take off with near empty tanks and rendezvous almost immediately with a KC-135 tanker.

the most satisfying of the war – and also the most heavily defended! The Thai Nguyen steel works, the Paul Doumer bridge complex, the north-east railway into China, etc, were all hit during that two-year period. In 1966 alone, the F-105 squadrons lost a total of 111 aircraft, and another 97 aircraft went down in 1967. Statistically, it was virtually impossible for a pilot to complete his 100-mission tour!

When they were not over North Vietnam, the 'Thuds' were tasked with attempting to stop the flow of supplies coming down the Ho Chi Minh Trail, or supporting troops fighting the Khmer Rouge in northern Laos. During the communists' 1968 Tet offensive, F-105s flew hundreds of sorties helping the beleaguered Marines at Khe Sanh, and this was one of the few times that the 'Thuds' out of Korat and Takhli were used for the close air support of troops in contact in South Vietnam.

On 31 March 1968 President Johnson, in an attempt to coax North Vietnam to the peace table, announced the first of his bombing halts, restricting all attacks to below the 19th Parallel. On 31 October 1968 he halted all bombing of North Vietnam. The F-105 war was winding down. In November 1968 the 388th TFW at Korat began conversion to the new F-4E Phantom II, transferring all its remaining F-105 assets to Takhli and the 355th TFW, which soldiered on and flew the last Thunderchief strike missions of the war. Although not officially tasked with strikes into North Vietnam, the crews of the 355th TFW were allowed to undertake PRSs (protective reaction strikes) against north Vietnamese air defences that were harassing the sorties of RF-4C reconnaissance aircraft. The RF-4C flights always had both Wild Weasel and MiGCAP support. A PRS could be called in on any target that threatened the reconnaissance package.

The 355th TFW concentrated the bulk of its missions against targets along the Trail, hitting the choke points at Tchepone and the Mu Gia Pass, attempting to strangle the flow of supplies into South Vietnam. On 10 December 1970, the 355th TFW stood down at Takhli having flown its final F-105D strike mission on 9 October. The remaining F-105Ds were transferred to the 18th TFW at Kadena, or returned to bases in the USA. The last 12 Wild Weasels, mostly of the upgraded F-105G variant, were transferred to Korat, where they were integrated with the aircraft of Detachment One of the 12th TFS, which was the sole remaining SAM-suppression unit in SEA. Det One was redesignated as the 6010th Wild Weasel Squadron, then redesignated as the 17th WWS a year later, just in time for the predicted North Vietnamese Easter offensive and the Linebacker campaigns that followed. When the North Vietnamese launched their all-out offensive on 30 March 1972, President Richard M. Nixon countered by ordering Operation Freedom Train, which removed all the former bombing restrictions on targets in North Vietnam.

When Linebacker was initiated on 10 May 1972, the only remaining F-105s in SEA were the 16 machines of the 17th WWS at Korat. As the Linebacker sorties mounted, the small Wild Weasel force rapidly became overwhelmed. It was not uncommon for the crews to fly four or five missions daily, against a vastly improved North Vietnamese air defence system. PACAF became concerned about the toll that all these missions was taking on the small number of Wild Weasel crews and aircraft remaining in the theatre. PACAF took the initial step of rotating more air crews to the 17th WWS, and then ordered the establishment of 'hunter-killer' teams of F-105G and F-4E aircraft. This effectively doubled the size of the Wild Weasel force. The missions kept coming however, day and night, and the 'hunter-killer' teams were also rapidly taxed to their limits.

The Weasels: reinforced then withdrawn

The USAF then ordered Operation Constant Guard, a reinforcement of all forces operating in SEA. Constant Guard sent additional Wild Weasel forces to Korat in the

ground controllers and the MiG interceptors. The QRC-128, being a very large and complex system, was installed in the rear cockpit of the EF-105F in place of the rear ejection seat, and the pilots referred to their new back-seater as 'Colonel Computer'. Besides the obvious empty rear cockpit, the Combat Martin aircraft were easily distinguished by the large blade antenna on top of the fuse-lage. Combat Martin aircraft were assigned to both F-105 wings until the 388th TFW transitioned to the F-4E. Following deactivation of the 355th TFW in December 1970, all remaining Combat Martin aircraft, in both SEA and the USA, were demodified and brought up to F-105G Wild Weasel standard.

With the exception of the Linebacker campaigns of 1972, the years of 1966 and 1967 contained the greatest amount of combat for the F-105 crews. The targets were

The Phantom largely ousted the F-105D from SEA. This mixed gaggle of F-4Es and F-105Gs, represents another variation on the 'hunter-killer' team, with the 'Thuds' taking out enemy radars so that the F-4s could finish off the target with 'slick' bombs and CBUs.

form of the 12 F-105Gs of Detachment One of the 561st TFS from McConnell AFB. Arriving in mid-April 1972, these 12 aircraft would supplant the 17th WWS. Throughout the remainder of Linebacker, the 'hunter-killer' teams combining the F-105Gs of the 17th and 561st TFSs and the F-4Es of the 388th TFW ferreted out North Vietnamese air defences, escorting F-4 aircraft equipped with laser-guided bombs and also conventionally armed B-52 bombers. When Linebacker II began on 18 December 1972, the greatest bombing raids of the war were always preceded by the F-105G. Once again, the Wild Weasels were 'First in and Last out!' The final Wild Weasel mission landed at Korat on 29 December 1972.

The USA's involvement in the war with North Vietnam ended on 27 January 1973 with the signing of the Paris Peace Accords. The F-105 war continued for almost two more years, however. Wild Weasels continued to escort RF-4C reconnaissance flights that were monitoring the terms of the truce, as well as B-52 Arc Light strikes in Laos and Cambodia, as the North Vietnamese had moved heavier air defences, including SAMs, into both countries. On 15 August 1973, all US operations in SEA were halted by the cut-off of funding by the US Congress. Within a month, Det One of the 561st TFS had been transferred back to the USA and assigned to the 35th TFW at George AFB, California. The last F-105G left Korat on 29 October 1974, when the 17th WWS was also transferred to George AFB to become the 562nd TFS.

The combat era of the F-105 Thunderchief had ended. The war in SEA had cost a total of 385 F-105s in the form

of 296 F-105D and 38 F-105F/G machines to enemy action, including 22 to North Vietnamese MiG fighters, 32 to SAMs, and 280 to anti-aircraft fire. An additional 51 aircraft had been lost to operational problems such as inflight engine fires, collisions with other aircraft, etc. F-105 air crews shot down 27½ North Vietnamese MiG fighters, 24½ of them with the 20-mm M61A1 Vulcan cannon, two with AIM-9 Sidewinder missiles, and one using a combination of both. The number of pilots killed in action will probably never be known as a result of the number of aircraft shot down over Laos, for which no accounting has ever been made, and the number of crew members who simply disappeared during their capture by the North Vietnamese.

Larry Davis

As an EF-105F, 63-8320 (seen here in F-105G configuration) was responsible for a MiG-17 kill on 19 December 1967. The crew, Major William M. Dalton and his EWO Major James L. Graham, shared credit for the shoot-down, recording ½ a kill each. Two other kills were claimed in this aircraft – one with cannon fire and the other when the pilot ejected an MER in front of an on-coming MiG!

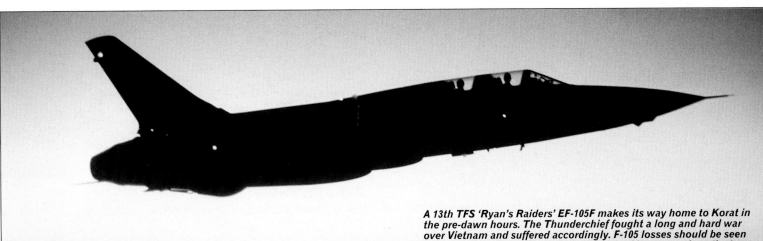

A 13th TFS 'Ryan's Raiders' EF-105F makes its way home to Korat in the pre-dawn hours. The Thunderchief fought a long and hard war over Vietnam and suffered accordingly. F-105 losses should be seen in the context of the 'Thud's' combat record however, since the type flew the majority of strikes by tactical aircraft over the North, and was also largely responsible for the hazardous anti-SAM mission.

F-105 Deployments

This section covers all deployments to SEA by F-105 Thunderchief squadrons or detachments during the war in that troubled part of the world. The bases from which the F-105 operated are listed alphabetically, and the squadron deployments are listed chronologically. In the USAF there are two basic deployments – TDY for Temporary Duty, and PCS for a permanent change of station. Two bases, the Royal Thai Air Force bases at Korat and Takhli, were the main bases for the majority of F-105 operations in the Vietnam War, and for all missions flown into North Vietnam.

The deployment of F-105 Thunderchief squadrons in the years between 1964 and 1966 is extremely hard to chronicle as a result of the fact that most of the units deployed back and forth between bases in the Far East, i.e. Yokota AB and Kadena AB in Japan, and the bases in SEA. Squadrons from Kadena and Yokota were some of the first units deployed, and their places at Kadena and Yokota were filled by other TDY squadrons from Tactical Air Command units in the USA. By mid-1966, the total number of TDY squadrons operational in SEA was

18. The TDY dates often overlap and one TDY did not necessarily end at exactly the same time that another began. As one TDY unit left, another was usually already in place. After a certain amount of time, usually 30/90-day intervals, the TDY squadrons would switch bases. An example of this was the 80th TFS at Yokota: originally assigned to the 8th TFW, late in 1964 the squadron deployed to Osan AB, South Korea for ZULU (nuclear strike) alert on a 30-day TDY, then from February 1965 went to Takhli for 30 days, and finally back to Yokota before the cycle was repeated. This went on until August 1965 in the form of 30-day deployments back and forth.

When the 80th TFS was at Takhli, either the 35th or 36th TFS was at Yokota and the other was at Osan for ZULU duty. When more than one unit was deployed to Korat or Takhli (after January 1965), one of the TDY squadrons from the USA would stand ZULU alert at Osan, or fill in at Yokota. This system was required because the USAF was committed to SEATO (South-East Asia Treaty Organisation) and PACAF taskings at the same time. There is even, in at least one instance, a case where a squadron was deployed to Takhli for a single specific mission, then rotated back to Japan on the following day. Moreover, all this does not include the effect of TDY detachments that went to Da Nang Air Base in South Vietnam (RVN, or Republic of Vietnam). By June 1966, the 13th Air Force had two permanent F-105 wings operating in SEA, and only the 334th TFS was still on TDY status.

Korat Royal Thai Air Force Base, Thailand

Located 5 miles (8 km) south of the city of Nakhon Ratchasima, the third largest city in Thailand, on the Mae Nom Mon river, Korat is 157 miles (253 km) north-east of Bangkok, the capital of Thailand, about 100 miles (160 km) east of Takhli AB, and some 485 miles (780 km) from Hanoi, the capital of North Vietnam. Korat had a single 9,850-ft (3002-m) runway, with 1,000-ft (305-m) overruns, and is only some 600 ft (183 m) above sea level. The first US personnel arrived at Korat in April 1962 to train Royal Thai Air Force personnel and to fly clandestine reconnaissance missions in 'Thai Air Force' Lockheed RT-33 Shooting Star tactical reconnaissance aircraft. Korat initially came under the control of 2nd Air Division and all TDY units came under its operational control. At times, Korat was the home for over 6,500 airmen and 34 individual units, including a RTAF squadron and a Bristol Type 170 Freighter transport detachment of the RNZAF.

6234th TFW (Provisional)

TDY 5 April 1965 to 8 July 1965
PCS 8 July 1965 to 8 April 1966
On 5 April 1965 the 6234th Tactical Fighter Wing (Provisional) was established at Korat, and assumed control of all the units then on base. The status of the 6234th TFW was changed from temporary to permanent at Korat on 8 July 1965, remaining in control of all TDY units operating from Korat until activation of the 388th TFW on 8 April 1966.

388th TFW

PCS 8 April 1966 to 23 December 1975
On 8 April 1966 the 6234th TFW (Provisional) was inactivated as primary tenant of Korat and replaced by the 388th TFW, which had been based at McConnell AFB, Kansas from 1 October 1962 to 8 February 1964 with F-105D/F aircraft. The 388th TFW was replaced by the 23rd TFW in February 1964, and on 14 March 1966 was assigned to Pacific Air Forces before being assigned to the 13th Air Force on the day the wing was activated at Korat. The 388th TFW was attached to 7th Air Force and 13th Air Force until 23 December 1975, when it moved to Hill AFB, Utah.

The 388th TFW was one of two F-105 Thunderchief wings in Southeast Asia. The wing's normal strength was 72 F-105s in the form of 54 F-105D single-seat strike/attack aircraft and 18 EF-105F two-seat Wild Weasel machines. The squadrons initially assigned to the 388th TFW were the 421st, 469th and 13th TFSs, the last replaced later by the 44th TFS. Beginning in May 1969, in anticipation of transition to the new McDonnell Douglas F-4E Phantom II, the 388th TFW transferred the first 18 of its F-105s to the 355th TFW at Takhli.

Through the glorious history of the F-105 era, pilots of the 388th TFW scored many 'firsts' and other successes. F-105 pilots in the 388th TFW scored a total of eight victories over North Vietnamese MiGs. The first air-to-air victory was scored by Major Fred Tracy of the 421st TFS on 29 June 1966. Only three pilots are known to have flown at least 200 missions to North

Above: This 44th TFS F-105D exhibits two interesting markings features. The white letter 'B' on the fin is an early 44th marking, while the USAF legend and serial have been applied in tan (FS 30219), rather than the usual white.

Right: This Combat Martin aircraft was with the 44th TFS in 1968. At least 13 EF-105Fs were so modified.

Vietnam in the F-105, and all of them were assigned to squadrons in the 388th TFW: these pilots include Major Larry Waller, who flew 100 missions with the 355th TFW and then flew a second series of 100 missions when assigned to the 388th TFW. The second pilot to record 200 missions was the legendary 1st Lieutenant Karl Richter, who was shot down on his 198th 'official' mission, although a check of squadron records revealed that Richter had actually flown over 230 missions, at least 32 of which were never logged on his record. The only other 200 mission pilot was Captain Peter Foley of the 469th TFS.

The 388th TFW was awarded the Presidential Unit Citation for operations between 10 March and 1 May 1967. In addition, the Wing was awarded four Air Force Outstanding Unit Awards with Combat 'V' Device while flying the F-105 in SEA. The Republic of Vietnam Gallantry Cross with Palm was awarded the 388th TFW for its service throughout the SEA war.

36th TFS 'Flying Fiends'

TDY 9 August 1964 to February 1965
The 36th TFS was the first F-105 squadron to deploy to the war in SEA, taking 18 F-105Ds from Yokota AB, Japan to Korat AB, Thailand on 9 August 1964, landing at 1020 hours local time. Four hours later the aircraft were armed and flying their first

mission, a ResCAP over a downed pilot in Laos. At Korat, the 36th TFS was under the control of the 2nd AD. The TDY at Korat for members of the 36th TFS lasted 89 days, and the squadron then returned to Yokota. In February 1965 the 36th TFS again deployed to the SEA war, this time to Takhli RTAFB. During its TDY at Korat, the 36th TFS lost one aircraft to North Vietnamese

Capt Robert Amos, standing beneath '357th', celebrates his 100th mission. After the usual soaking by fire hose, the 100-mission pilot was given a champagne toast and paraded before the 100-mission celebration board.

anti-aircraft crews. On their silver aircraft, the unit markings consisted of a PACAF badge on the vertical tail, a red arrow device on the sides of the intakes, and red ailerons; some of the aircraft had the 36th TFS badge on the nose.

67th TFS 'Fighting Cocks'

TDY August 1964 to May 1965
The 67th TFS deployed from Kadena AB, Okinawa to Korat AB, Thailand in August 1964, where it came under operational control of the 2nd Air Division. The 67th TFS deployed from Korat AB to Da Nang AB for operations in South Vietnam beginning on 25 December 1964 with Detachment Two, 18th TFW, under the control of 2nd AD. Det Two's deployment ended in January 1965 and the aircraft then returned to Korat AB for continued operations against North Vietnam. During the period of TDY at Korat and Da Nang, the 67th TFS lost at least nine aircraft, including three aircraft shot down on the first Rolling Thunder mission of the war. There are an additional six aircraft losses for the 18th TFW, which could be from the 12th, 44th or 67th Squadrons. The 67th TFS returned to Yokota AB in May 1965. Aircraft markings on the silver aircraft during this period were a PACAF badge on the vertical tail and a narrow red band just behind the radome; some of the aircraft had a 67th TFS badge on the nose.

44th TFS 'Vampire Bats'

TDY August 1964 to May 1965
PCS 25 April 1967 to 15 October 1969
The 44th TFS deployed from Kadena AB, Okinawa to Korat AB, Thailand in August 1964, where it came under the operational control of the 2nd Air Division. Aircraft of the 44th TFS deployed from Korat AB to Da Nang AB for operations in South Vietnam on 25 December 1964 as part of Detachment Two, 18th TFW, returning to Korat AB on 13 January 1965. At Da Nang, the 44th TFS was still under the control of the 2nd Air Division. On 5 April 1965, the 44th TFS came under the control of the 6234th TFW (Provisional) at Korat. The assets of the 44th TFS were absorbed by the 13th TFS when that unit was activated at Korat. During the TDY period, the 44th TFS lost one F-105D, while scoring one MiG victory on 13 May 1967. During the TDY period, the silver F-105s had a PACAF badge on the vertical tail and a medium blue band painted behind the radome; some of the aircraft had the 44th TFS's 'Vampire Bat' emblem painted on the nose. Early camouflaged aircraft had a small letter 'B' on the vertical tail surface before standardised codes were applied in 1967. Aircraft of the 44th TFS at Korat wore the letters 'JE' on the tail, with yellow on the canopy rails and radar reflector. Aircraft participating in the Northscope operation

This brace of 12th TFS F-105Ds was photographed enroute between Da Nang and Korat early in 1965.

had a distinctive wrap-around camouflage with the 'JE' tail code.

On 25 April 1967, the 44th TFS was transferred PCS from the 18th TFW at Kadena AB, Okinawa to the 388th TFW at Korat AB, taking over all remaining F-105 assets of the 421st TFS. On 20 October 1967, the 44th TFS absorbed the remaining assets of the 13th TFS and assumed that unit's Wild Weasel role, including the Northscope mission and its specialised aircraft. The 44th TFS was transferred PCS from Korat AB to Takhli AB on 15 October 1969 during the transition of the 388th TFW from the F-105 to F-4E.

357th TFS 'Licking Dragons'

TDY August 1964 to 12 December 1964
The 357th TFS deployed from McConnell AFB, Kansas to Korat AB, Thailand in August 1964, where it came under the operational control of the 2nd Air Division. On 12 December 1964 the 357th TFS returned to McConnell AFB. During the TDY to Korat, the 357th TFS lost two F-105 warplanes to enemy action. However, there are six aircraft losses attributed to aircraft from the 355th TFW, some of which may have been aircraft with the 357th TFS. The 357th TFS re-deployed to Takhli on 12 June 1965 under the control of the 6235th TFW (Provisional). On silver aircraft, the unit markings at this time were four-inch black/yellow/black tail stripes with the TAC badge and lightning bolt in the centre of the vertical tail. On camouflaged aircraft the striping was reversed (yellow/black/yellow) and the TAC badge removed.

35th TFS 'Black Panthers'

TDY September 1964 to November 1964
The 35th TFS deployed from Yokota, AB, Japan to Korat AB, Thailand in September 1964, where it came under the control of

the 2nd AD. In November 1964, the squadron was under the control of the 6441st TFW, resuming ZULU nuclear alert status. Unit markings on silver aircraft included a PACAF badge on the vertical tail surface, a blue arrow device on the sides of the intakes, and blue ailerons.

469th TFS 'Fighting Bulls'

TDY 30 November 1964 to 13 March 1965
PCS November 1965 to 31 October 1972
On 30 November 1964, the 469th TFS deployed from McConnell AFB, Kansas where it had been assigned to the 355th TFW, to Kadena AB, Okinawa, assuming the mission status of squadrons already deployed to the war in SEA. The 469th TFS moved to Korat AB, Thailand in January 1965, where it came under the control of the 2nd AD. Interestingly, the 469th TFS still retained a nuclear mission until 18 March 1965, even though it was already committed to the combat in SEA. The 469th TFS returned to McConnell AFB on 13 March 1965. In November 1965, the 469th re-deployed PCS to Korat where it was now attached to the 6234th TFW (Provisional) for air operations in Laos and North Vietnam.

On 8 April 1966, the 469th TFS was placed under the control of the newly activated 388th TFW at Korat AB. In April 1968, the 469th TFS became the first squadron to record over 30,000 combat flight hours in SEA. The 469th TFS flew the F-105D until that type was replaced by the F-4E Phantom II on 7 November 1968. On that date, the 40th TFS arrived at Korat with 18 new F-4Es and crews. All remaining 469th F-105s were transferred to Takhli on that date. The 40th TFS was redesignated as the 469th TFS and remained at Korat until 31 October 1972. By the end of F-105 operations in SEA the 469th TFS had lost a total of 47 aircraft to enemy action, while recording two MiG victories.

During the TDY period, the silver F-105Ds

had unit markings consisting of four-inch green/white/green tail stripes on the top of the vertical fin, with the TAC badge and lightning bolt in the centre of the fin. Some early camouflaged aircraft had a four-inch green band at the top of the fin. Tail codes were applied beginning in 1967, and aircraft assigned to the 469th TFS wore the tail code letters 'JV' together with green canopy rails and radar reflectors.

12th TFS 'Foxy Few'

TDY 25 December 1964 to 15 March 1965, and 15 June 1965 to 25 August 1965
The 12th TFS deployed six F-105D warplanes from Kadena AB, Okinawa to Da Nang AB for operations in South Vietnam on 25 December 1964 as Detachment Two of the 18th TFW. The deployment ended on 1 February 1965 when the detachment transferred to Korat AB, Thailand with the remainder of the squadron. At Da Nang, the 12th TFS was under the control of 2nd AD. Detachment Two of the 12th TFS deployed from Da Nang AB, to Korat AB, Thailand on 1 February 1965, where the squadron was still under the control of 2nd AD. The squadron returned to Kadena on 15 March 1965. Three months later, on 15 June 1965, the 12th TFS re-deployed to Korat AB under the control of the 6234th TFW (Provisional), remaining there until 25 August 1965. The 12th TFS lost four aircraft during the two TDYs to Korat. On silver aircraft, the markings were a PACAF badge on the vertical tail surface and a yellow band around the rear of the radome.

354th TFS 'Bulldogs'

TDY 3 March 1965 to 12 June 1965
On 3 March 1965, during Operation One Buck 10, the 354th TFS deployed TDY from McConnell AFB, Kansas to Kadena AB, Okinawa, before taking its first six F-105Ds to Korat AB, Thailand on 13 March. At Korat, the squadron was under the control of 2nd AD until 5 April 1965 when it was transferred to the control of the newly activated 6234th TFW (Provisional). The personnel of the 354th TFS returned to McConnell AFB on 12 June 1965, and remained there until transferring PCS to Takhli AB with the rest of the 355th TFW on 27 November 1965.

During their TDY period at Korat, the pilots of the 354th TFS flew a total of 1,271 sorties, which included 637 Rolling Thunder, 102 Barrel Roll/Steel Tiger, 36 Yankee Team, 81 ResCAP, 57 MiGCAP, 28 Queen Bee, 11 Boxtop, 54 weather reconnaissance, 147 training and 126 other combat support missions. During the TDY period, the 354th TFS lost a total of three aircraft including two shot down by MiGs on 4 April 65, and another to AAA the same day. On silver aircraft, the unit markings consisted of four-inch stripes in

Pictured on a transit flight during a Kadena deployment, this F-105D belonged to the 421st TFS.

blue/white/blue on the top of the verical fin, with the TAC badge and lightning bolt in the centre of the vertical tail surface. On camouflaged aircraft the stripe colours were reversed and the TAC badge removed.

421st TFS 'Cavaliers'

TDY 15 September 1964 to 23 November 1964, and 7 April 1965 to 20 August 1965
PCS 8 April 1966 to 25 April 1967

On 15 September 1964, the 421st TFS deployed on a TDY basis from McConnell AFB, Kansas to Korat AB, Thailand, where the unit was under the control of 2nd AD. The 421st TFS returned to McConnell AFB on 23 November 1964. Under Operation Two Buck 3, the 421st TFS re-deployed to Kadena AB, Okinawa before moving to Korat on 7 April 1965, where the squadron was now under the control of the 6234th TFW (Provisional). The 421st TFS returned to McConnell AFB on 20 August 1965. During the TDY, the 421st TFS lost three F-105D warplanes to North Vietnamese TFW (Provisional). The 421st TFS returned to McConnell AFB on 20 August 1965. During the TDY, the 421st TFS lost three F-105D warplanes to North Vietnamese defences.

On 8 April 1966, the 421st TFS returned

An AIM-9B under the starboard wing was usually paired with an ECM pod to port. Mickey Titti Chi, a 34th TFS 'Thud', was lost to enemy action on 10 July 1967.

Right: Lt Col Ralph Kuster and Pucker Bird, *flew the 'Raiders" mission with the 13th TFS in 1967.*

to Korat as one of the three squadrons assigned PCS to Korat under the control of the newly activated 388th TFW. The 421st TFS returned to the USA on 25 April 1967, where it was assigned to the 15th TFW at McDill AFB, Florida. All the squadron's remaining F-105s were transferred to the 44th TFS on 24 April 1967. By the end of the 421st TFS's F-105 operations in SEA, the squadron had lost a total of 21 Thunderchiefs to enemy action, while scoring a single MiG victory on 21 September 1966.

Although aircraft of the 421st TFS were camouflaged in 1966, no tail codes were applied. Squadron markings included painting the bottom of the main gear doors red with white stars, and painting the canopy rail and radar reflector red with white letters.

Project Wild Weasel Det., 6234th TFW

21 November 1965 to 11 July 1966

On 21 November 1965, the Project Wild Weasel Detachment assigned to the 33rd TFW at Eglin AFB, Florida, deployed to Korat AB, Thailand with four F-100Fs modified for the defence-suppression mission, commonly referred to as Wild Weasel. Arriving at Korat on Thanksgiving Day, 25 November 1965, the detachment was under the control of the 6234th TFW

Wearing the post-summer 1972 'WW' tailcodes of Det One, 561st TFS, Tuffy was an F-105G.

(Provisional), flying its first mission on 1 December 1965.

On 28 May 1966, the first five F-105F Wild Weasel 3 aircraft deployed to Korat, and were assigned to the Wild Weasel Detachment of the 6234th TFW. On 11 July 1966, the F-100Fs were replaced by EF-105F machines, and the detachment was transferred PCS to the 13th TFS at Korat. The Wild Weasel Detachment's EF-105F shad no distinctive unit markings at this time.

13th TFS

PCS 15 May 1966 to 20 October 1967

On 15 May 1966, the 13th TFS was activated at Korat AB, Thailand under the control of the newly activated 388th TFW, taking over the F-105Ds originally assigned to the 44th TFS, which had rotated back to Kadena AB. On 11 July 1966, the 13th TFS absorbed the modified F-105Fs of the Wild Weasel Detachment 6234th TFW,

Below: Full afterburner helps a fully-laden 34th TFS aircraft leave Korat's runway in 1968.

the only squadron in SEA dedicated to the role of SAM suppression.

In April 1967, the 13th TFS carried out the Northscope night/all weather missions, commonly called 'Ryan's Raiders'. On 20 October 1967, the existing EF-105Fsof the 13th TFS were transferred to the 44th TFS, and the 13th TFS was transferred to the 432nd TFW at Udorn AB, Thailand. During its operations with the F-105 Thunderchief, the 13th TFS lost 13 aircraft to enemy action. During the time the 13th TFS was assigned to the 388th TFW, no tail codes were applied and aircraft had only the canopy rails and radar reflectors painted yellow as a unit marking. Aircraft participating in Northscope had a distinctive wrap-around camouflage.

34th TFS 'Fighting Rams'

PCS 15 May 1966 to 23 December 1975

On 15 May 1966, the 34th TFS was activated at Korat AB, Thailand under the control of the 388th TFW. The 34th TFS was equipped with the Republic F-105D, flying attack missions throughout SEA, before transitioning onto the F-4E in

Far right: This 17th WWS F-105G is notable for its weapons fit. Using two of the Navy-developed twin Shrike launchers, a total of four AGM-45s could be carried, along with the mandatory pair of underwing tanks.

Below: Afterburner helps a 6010th WWS F-105G haul an unusal load into the hot, humid air of Thailand. The aircraft carries an AGM-45 and 450-US gal (1703-litre) tank to port, a 600-US gal (2271-litre) tank on the centreline, and Shrike and AGM-78 missiles to starboard.

November 1968. The squadron remained at Korat until 23 December 1975, when it was transferred to Hill AFB, Utah. During the period from 15 May 1966 to November 1968, the 34th TFS lost a total of 28 F-105s to enemy action, while scoring 5½ MiG victories. Tail codes were applied during 1967 and aircraft of the 34th TFS carried the tail code letters 'JJ' together with black canopy rails and radar reflectors.

Detachment One, 12th TFS

TDY 24 September 1970 to 1 November 1970
Detachment One of the 12th TFS deployed 12 EF-105F/F-105G Wild Weasel aircraft from Kadena AB, Okinawa to Korat AB, Thailand on 24 September 1970 to augment the 12 EF-105F/F-105G aircraft transferred from Takhli. Detachment One, 12th TFS, under the control of the 388th TFW, became both the sole remaining EF-105F unit and the only operational Wild Weasel unit in SEA. On 1 November 1970 the designation was changed to the 6010th WWS. The F-105Gs of the 12th TFS carried the tail code 'ZA', and had yellow canopy sills and radar reflectors.

6010th WWS

PCS 1 November 1970 to 1 December 1971
The 6010th Wild Weasel Squadron replaced Det One, 12th TFS, as the sole Thunderchief-equipped unit in SEA.

Equipped with F-105G Wild Weasel aircraft, the 6010th WWS remained at Korat under the control of the 388th TFW until the designation was changed to the 17th WWS on 1 December 1971. The aircraft of the 6010th WWS carried the tail code 'ZB'.

17th WWS

PCS 1 December 1971 to 15 November 1974
The 17th WWS took over the assets of the 6010th WWS on 1 December 1971 as the sole F-105 squadron in SEA. Equipped with F-105G Wild Weasel aircraft, the 17th WWS was instrumental in the suppression of communist air defences during the Linebacker I and II campaigns flown during 1972-3, losing six F-105Gs to enemy action. The last 17th WWS F-105G (and final F-105 take-off in SEA) departed Korat for the USA on 29 October 1974. On 15 November 1974, the 17th WWS returned to the USA under Operation Coronet Exxon. All returning 17th WWS aircraft were turned over to crews of the 562nd TFS at George AFB, California. Wild Weasel F-105Gs of the 17th WWS carried the 'JB' tail code, with a blue band on the top of the vertical tail, blue canopy rails and radar reflector.

Detachment One, 561st TFS

TDY 7 April 1972 to 5 September 1973
On 7 April 1972, under Operation Constant Guard I, Detachment One of the 561st TFS

deployed from McConnell AFB, Kansas, to Korat AB, Thailand in response to the North Vietnamese Easter offensive. Under operational control of the 388th TFW at Korat, Det One, 561st TFS was integrated with the F-105Gs of the 17th TFS, participating in both the Linebacker I and II operations, and losing one aircraft to enemy action. On 5 September 1973, under Operation Coronet Bolo 1, Det One, 561st TFS was relieved from combat duty in SEA and transferred to George AFB, California, where the squadron was assigned to the 35th TFTW, whose primary mission was the training of crews for the defence-suppression role. When initially deployed to Korat, the F-105Gs of Det One retained their stateside tail code of 'MD' but later, during the Linebacker campaign, the tail code letters were changed to 'WW' to reflect the Wild Weasel mission.

Sent to Southeast Asia to reinforce the 17th Wild Weasel Sqn, Det One, 561st Tactical Fighter Sqn deployed to Korat as part of Operation Constant Guard 1.

Above: On 1 December 1971, the 6010th WWS changed its numberplate to 17th WWS. In the process it became the last F-105 unit in SEA.

Takhli Royal Thai Air Base, Thailand

The Royal Thai Air Base at Takhli is located 160 miles (257 km) north of Bangkok, and slightly more than 520 miles (837 km) from Hanoi, North Vietnam, almost the same distance as Korat RTAFB, which lies some 100 miles (161 km) to the east. Takhli had been a bomber base for the Imperial Japanese army air force during World War II, and had a single 9,800-ft (2987-m) concrete runway. USAF personnel began upgrading Takhli for jet aircraft operations in 1961, and F-100 aircraft from the 510th TFS, 405th FW, began operations from Takhli in June 1962 as part of the Sawbuck operation.
During the initial operations, Takhli was referred to as a FOB (forward operating base). The 355th TFW's official history notes that "at the FOB, there was no running water, they only had four-hole

latrines, and limited sleeping quarters until 20 April 1965, when more huts were built. There was no recreation facilities, no sports, and R&R was taken either in Bangkok or at Kadena." By July 1965, there were 45 'hooches' or sleeping quarters for the 1,200 personnel assigned to Takhli. Each hooch held 30 men, which meant they had to sleep in shifts. By December 1965, the population of Takhli had grown to over 2,600 men with 110 'hooches'.

6441st TFW (Provisional)

TDY May 1965 to 1 July 1965
The initial TDY squadrons were under the control of the 2nd AD until May 1965. At

that time the host tenant at Takhli became the 6441st TFW (Provisional), TDY from Yokota AB, Japan in May 1965. All TDY squadrons operating from Takhli came under the operational control of the 6441st TFW (Provisional). The 6441st TFW returned to Yokota when the 6235th TFW was established on 8 July 1965

6235th TFW

PCS 8 July 1965 to 8 November 1965
On 1 July 1965, the 6441st TFW (Provisional) was replaced at Takhli AB by the 6235th Combat Support Group, later the 6235th TFW. Squadrons assigned included the 80th TFS, 563rd TFS and the 9th Reconnaissance Task Force, the last with Douglas RB-66C aircraft. On 8 July 1965,

the 6235th TFW was activated at Takhli AB and assigned to the 13th Air Force. The 6235th TFW remained at Takhli until replaced by the PCS move of the 355th TFW from McConnell AFB, Kansas to Takhli on 8 November 1965. All TDY units operating from Takhli until that date were under the control of the 6235th TFW. By the end of July 1965, the TDY squadrons at Takhli had flown a total of 884 sorties, dropping over 2,000 tons of bombs and firing more than 2,800 2¾-in (70-mm) HVAR rockets and over 112,000 rounds of 20-mm ammunition. The month of July had been costly however, as five F-105Ds were shot down, three in the 563rd TFS, one in the 80th TFS, another not assigned to a squadron. Seven more F-105s went down in October 1965.

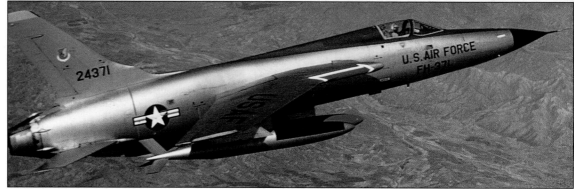

355th TFW 'Professionals'

PCS 8 November 1965 to 10 December 1970
The 355th TFW was activated at George AFB, California on 8 July 1962 with the 354th, 357th, 421st and 469th Squadrons. The 355th TFW moved to McConnell AFB, Kansas on 21 July 1964. On 2 October 1965, with all the squadrons already in SEA at various bases, the 355th TFW was alerted for a PCS transfer to Takhli, being activated on 8 November 1965. Three squadrons were attached - the 354th TFS from the original 355th Wing, the 333rd TFS transferred PCS from Seymour Johnson AFB, and the 334th TFS which remained TDY to Takhli until late 1966.

The 355th TFW flew continuously until December 1970. Late in 1968 the 355th TFW became the last unit in SEA flying the F-105D. When the 388th TFW converted to the F-4E, the 355th TFW absorbed all its remaining F-105 aircraft from Korat. The 355th TFW flew its last combat mission (also the final F-105D attack mission of the Vietnam War) on 9 October 1970: the

During its operations in South Vietnam, the 563rd TFS employed weapons such as the BLU-1/B firebombs under this F-105D, to attack troop concentrations.

Top: A mixed force of 333rd ('RK' tailcode) and 354th ('RM') F-105Ds replenishes its tanks. Refuelling often took place at lower than ideal altitudes, due to the 'Thud's' lack of ceiling at high combat weights.

mission was flown by four aircraft of the 333rd TFS. The 355th TFW was inactivated at Takhli on 10 December 1970 and all remaining F-105s, with the exception of 12 F-105G Wild Weasel machines, were returned to McConnell AFB and turned over to crews from the 23rd TFW. The 12 F-105Gs were flown to Korat AB and assigned to the newly created 6010th Wild Weasel Squadron.

The 355th TFW, known alternatively as 'The Bridge-Bustin' Professionals' and also as 'PACAF's Pride', had a very enviable record while flying the F-105. The pilots of the 355th TFW flew a total of 101,304 sorties for more than 263,650 hours of combat. The 355th TFW hit 12,675 targets, dropping 202,596 tons of bombs, and the wing's pilots accounted for 20½ North Vietnamese MiG fighters, the first being downed by 1st Lieutenant Fred Wilson, Jr, a pilot of the 333rd TFS, on 21 September

This 36th TFS F-105D had the dubious honour of being the first F-105 to be damaged by enemy action, struck by ground fire on 14 August 1964. The aircraft was pictured en route to Korat.

1966. Two pilots in the 355th TFW were awarded the Medal of Honor: Captain Merlyn Dethlefsen for the 10 March 1967 mission to Thai Nguyen, and Major Leo Thorsness for his mission on 19 April 1967. Both men were Wild Weasel pilots of the 355th TFW.

The 355th TFW was awarded the Presidential Unit Citation (Vietnam) for the campaign of 1 January to 10 October 1966; a second PUC(V) for the campaign of 11-12 August and 24-28 October 1967; and a third PUC(V) for the campaign of 12 April 1968 to 30 April 1969. The 355th TFW was awarded the Air Force Outstanding Unit Award with Combat 'V' Device for actions flown between 12 October 1966 and 11 April 1967; a second OUA with 'V' for 12 April 1967 to 11 April 1968; and a third OUA 'V' for 1 July 1969 to 24 November 1970. The 355th TFW was awarded the Republic of Vietnam Gallantry Cross with Palm for actions between 22 April 1966 and 10 December 1970.

36th TFS 'Flying Fiends'

TDY February 1965 to October 1965
The 36th TFS went TDY from Yokota AB to Takhli AB in February 1965 under the control of the 2nd AD until May 1965, when the 6441st TFW was activated at Takhli. The 36th TFS was the second squadron in the three-squadron rotational deployment between Yokota AB, Osan AB on ZULU alert, and Takhli AB, losing six aircraft and six pilots between 22 August 1965 and 22 October 1965. The 36th personnel rotated back to Yokota AB, assigned to the 6441st TFW, which had also just returned to Yokota from Takhli.

During the TDY tour, the 36th TFS flew a total of 1,175 sorties. It suffered the loss of seven aircraft during the TDYs to Korat and Takhli, including two F-105Ds on 5 October 1965 and another two on 15 October 1965. On silver aircraft, the markings consisted of a PACAF badge on the vertical tail surface, a red arrow device on the engine air intakes, and red ailerons.

80th TFS 'The Headhunters'

TDY February 1965 to 26 August 1965
The 80th TFS deployment consisted of a 30-day rotation between Yokota AB, Japan, to Osan AB, South Korea on ZULU alert, then to Takhli AB, beginning in February 1965 before being replaced by elements of the 36th TFS on 26 August 1965. At Takhli, the 80th TFS was under the control of the 2nd AD, then the 6441st TFW (Provisional) in May 1965, and the 6235th TFW in July 1965. The 80th TFS lost two aircraft during the TDY at Takhli. On silver aircraft the unit markings consisted of the PACAF badge on the vertical tail surface, a yellow arrow device on the sides of the intakes, and yellow ailerons.

561st TFS

TDY 6 February 1965 to 10 July 1965
The 561st TFS, one of three squadrons attached to the 23rd TFW at McConnell AFB, Kansas, deployed to Takhli AB, Thailand on 6 February 1965, under the control of the 2nd AD, the 6441st TFW (Provisional) in May 1965, and the 6235th TFW in July 1965. Detachments of the 561st TFS's F-105Ds deployed to Da Nang AB for operations in South Vietnam. The squadron returned to McConnell AFB in July 1965. On silver aircraft, the unit markings consisted of the Tactical Air Command badge on the vertical tail surface, and black and yellow checks painted on the rudder.

563rd TFS 'Ace Of Spades'

TDY 8 April 1965 to 15 August 1965
The 563rd TFS deployed from McConnell AFB, Kansas to Takhli AB, Thailand on 8 April 1965, operating under control of the 2nd AD, the 6441st TFW (Provisional) in May 1965 and the 6235th TFW in July. Detachments of aircraft from the 563rd TFS were deployed to Da Nang AB in the spring of 1965, for operations in South Vietnam, before returning to McConnell AFB on 15 August 1965. The 563rd TFS lost seven aircraft during its TDY to Takhli. On silver aircraft, the unit markings at this time consisted of the Tactical Air Command badge on the vertical tail surface, a white band and black 'Ace of Spades' device on

These 80th TFS aircraft were photographed on the move between standing nuclear alert at Osan and deploying to Takhli for Rolling Thunder missions in 1965.

Below: Four F-105Ds from the 334th TFS 'Eagles' provide an excellent example of the change over from 'natural metal' to camouflage. Note the squadron's distinctive tail marking, which consisted of a blue band with white spots. As can just be seen, this marking was retained even when the aircraft adopted camouflage.

the tail tip, and red/white stripes on the rudder, wing tips and stabiliser tips.

35th TFS 'Black Panthers'

TDY May 1965 to June 1965 and October 1965 to 9 November 1965

The 35th TFS was the third squadron on regular 30-day rotational deployment between Yokota AB, Osan AB ZULU alert, and Takhli AB. Beginning in May 1965, the 35th TFS was at Takhli, then re-deployed to Takhli in October 1965, returning to Yokota on 9 November 1965. However, over the next two years, aircraft and personnel from the 35th TFS augmented units in combat operations at both Korat and Takhli. The 35th TFS lost one aircraft during the TDY to Takhli. Unit markings on silver aircraft included a PACAF badge on the vertical tail surface, a blue arrow device on the air intakes, and blue ailerons.

562nd TFS

TDY 15 August 1965 to 8 December 1965

The 562nd TFS deployed from McConnell AFB, Kansas to Takhli AB on 15 August 1965, taking the place of the 563rd TFS, which had been at Takhli since 8 April 1965, operating under the control of the 6235th TFW. The 562nd TFS was involved in one of the first raids near Hanoi, the North Vietnamese capital, when it struck at the Lang Met bridge about 50 miles (80 km) from Hanoi. The 562nd TFS lost three aircraft during the TDY to Takhli. On silver aircraft, the unit markings consisted of the Tactical Air Command badge on the vertical tail surface and red/white shark's teeth on the nose.

335th TFS 'Chiefs'

TDY 3 July 1965 to 15 December 1965

On 3 July 1965, the 335th TFS deployed from Seymour Johnson AFB, North Carolina as part of Operation Two Buck 13 to Yokota

AB with the assignment of supporting other PACAF units already operating in SEA. On 8 November 1965, the 335th TFS deployed to Takhli for operations under the control of the newly activated 355th TFW. The 335th TFS returned to Seymour Johnson on 15 December 1965. The 335th TFS lost one

Right: Parked up at Andersen AFB, Guam, these 335th TFS aircraft would soon be sent to Yokota to cover for squadrons already in combat. In December 1965, they moved on to Takhli.

Below: The 562nd TFS also stopped over on Guam, on its deployment from McConnell AFB, Kansas to Takhli. The aircraft still wear their Desert Strike markings.

F-105D during the TDY. The 335th TFS was awarded the Vietnamese Air Defense Medal for its service. Unit markings at this time consisted of the Tactical Air Command badge on the vertical tail surface, and the top of the tail was painted green with a white 'V'.

334th TFS 'Eagles'

TDY 28 August 1965 to 10 October 1966
On 28 August 1965, as part of Operation Two Buck 13, the 334th TFS deployed from Seymour Johnson AFB, North Carolina to Takhli AB, Thailand, arriving on 1 September and coming under the command of the 6235th TFW (Provisional) until the 355th TFW was activated on 8 November 1965. Thirty days after its arrival at Takhli, the 334th TFS lost its commanding officer when Lieutenant Colonel M. J. Killian was shot down by a North Vietnamese surface-to-air missile. The 334th TFS returned to Seymour Johnson AFB in October 1966.

During its extensive TDY to Takhli, the 334th TFS lost seven aircraft. It was awarded the Air Force Outstanding Unit Award, Presidential Unit Citation, Vietnam Defense Campaign Medal, and the Vietnam Air Defense Medal. Unit markings at this time consisted of a Tactical Air Command badge on the vertical tail, and the top of the fin painted blue with white dots. Camouflaged aircraft carried only the blue band with white dots on the tail tip.

354th TFS 'Bulldogs'

PCS 27 November 1965 to 10 December 1970
The 354th TFS, one of the original 355th TFW squadrons at McConnell AFB, was the first PCS squadron assigned to the 355th TFW when it transferred to Takhli on

Top: Photographed taking on fuel during a February 1965 Flaming Dart mission, this 354th TFS F-105D is unusual in using the probe to take on fuel, rather than the more often employed receptacle. Featuring both receiving systems, the Thunderchief could at any time, refuel from boom- or drogue-equipped tankers.

Above: A seldom seen F-105D warload of two 2,000-lb Mk 84 and two 500-lb Mk 82 LDGP bombs, along with a centreline fuel tank and no ECM pod, suggests that this 354th TFS aircraft might well have been preparing to launch against a choke-point on the less-heavily defended Ho Chi Minh Trail.

Left: Captains Warren Kerzon (pilot) and Scottie McIntyre killed ten SAM sites in 333rd TFS EF-105F Root Pack Rat. Weasel crews usually began their training together and remained paired once deployed for combat.

A 44th TFS EF-105F, again with the Mk 84/82 bomb combination, prepares for a Barrel Roll strike supporting ground forces fighting the Khmer Rouge in northern Laos during 1969. In the background, awaiting a spell on the tanker, is a 357th TFS machine.

357th TFS 'Licking Dragons'

TDY 12 June 1965 to 29 January 1966
PCS 29 January 1966 to 10 December 1970

The 357th TFS had been TDY at Takhli from 12 June 1965 when it relieved the 354th TFS. It remained TDY with the 6235th TFW at Takhli until assigned to the newly activated 355th TFW on 29 January 1966, the third squadron permanently assigned. The 357th TFS remained with the 355th TFW until the wing was inactivated on 10 December 1970. Pilots with the 357th TFS scored a total of four MiG victories between 19 April 1967 and 19 December 1967. Forth aircraft were lost to enemy action.

Tail codes were applied beginning in 1967, aircraft of the 357th TFS having the letters 'RU', together with the canopy rails, radar reflector and intakes in yellow with black trim.

44th TFS 'Vampire Bats'

PCS 15 October 1969 to 10 December 1970

The 44th TFS was transferred from the 388th TFW at Korat to the 355th TFW at Takhli on 15 October 1969 following conversion of the 388th to the F-4E. Transfer of the 44th TFS to Takhli meant that the 355th TFW was the sole remaining Thunderchief-equipped wing in SEA, and the squadron was inactivated with the rest of the 355th TFW on 10 December 1970. The 44th TFS lost nine aircraft to enemy action during the war in SEA.

Tail codes were applied beginning in 1967, aircraft of the 44th TFS having the letters 'RE' together with their canopy rails, radar reflector and intakes in black with silver trim.

27 November 1965, operating continuously until inactivation of the 355th TFW on 10 December 1970. Pilots from the 354th TFS scored a total of eight MiG victories between 10 March 1967 and 27 October 1967. Total losses for the 354th TFS were 46 aircraft to enemy action before the unit was inactivated in December 1970.

Early camouflaged aircraft carried a medium blue band with white trim on the top of the vertical tail surface. Tail codes began to be applied in 1967, and aircraft of the 354th TFS carrying the letters 'RM', together with canopy sills, intakes and radar reflectors painted medium blue with white trim.

333rd TFS 'Lancers'

PCS 8 December 1965 to 10 December 1970

The 333rd TFS was the second squadron permanently assigned to the 355th TFW at Takhli. It was transferred PCS from the 4th

TFW at Seymour Johnson AFB, North Carolina on 4 December 1965. Initially, the 333rd TFS was to make the transfer to Korat AB, which was then changed to Takhli when the 355th was activated. With some aircraft arriving on 2 December 1965, the entire 333rd TFS was in place by 8 December. The 333rd TFS was the first squadron not originally assigned to the 355th Wing at McConnell to be permanently assigned, relieving the 335th TFS. 1st Lieutenant Fred Wilson, a 333rd pilot, scored the first air-to-air victory for the 355th TFW, when he shot down a MiG fighter on 21 September 1966. Pilots from the 333rd TFS shot down a total of 7½ North Vietnamese MiGs. Losses to enemy action totalled 37 F-105s.

The 333rd TFS remained with the 355th TFW until the wing was inactivated on 10 December 1970. Early camouflaged aircraft had a red tail stripe with white

borders. Tail codes were applied beginning in 1967, and aircraft of the 333rd TFS carried the letters 'RK', with canopy rails, radar reflectors and intake lips painted red with white trim. Aircraft of the 333rd TFS flew the final F-105D mission of the war on 9 October 1970.

Below: Takhli's Weasel force was arranged differently to that at Korat. Whereas the latter base deployed all its Weasels in one squadron, Takhli's were divided into flights, with one flight assigned to each squadron. This is a 357th TFS EF-105F.

Right: The AGM-12C Bullpup was a little favoured weapon. It offered the potential of rocket-assisted, pinpoint strikes, but lacked the punch to destroy the type of targets against which such a weapon might be employed. The carrier aircraft in this case is a 354th TFS F-105D.

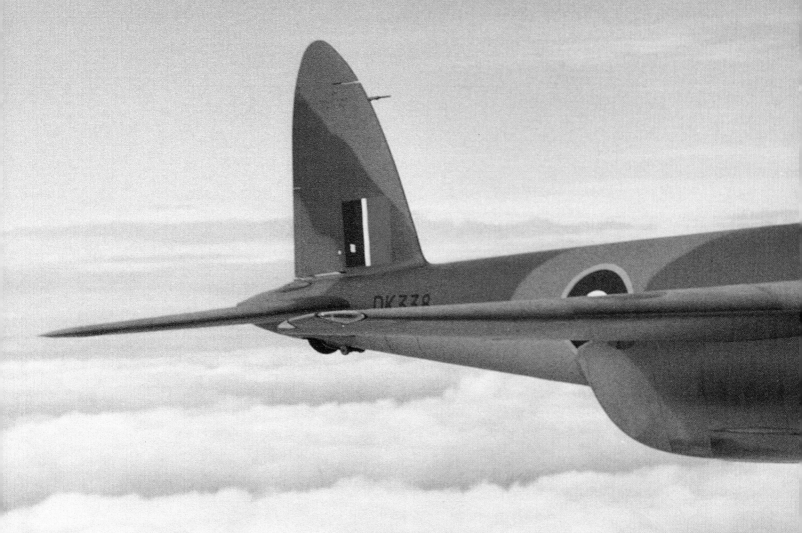

Posing for Charles E. Brown's camera, Mosquito B.Mk IV DK338 is seen in early 1942 prior to delivery to No. 105 Sqn, RAF, the first unit to operate the type in a bombing role. DK338 did not enjoy a long RAF career. On 1 May 1943 it departed Marham for a raid on Eindhoven. Tragically an engine failure caused the aircraft to crash near the airfield, killing its crew, F/Os O. W. Thompson DFC, RNZAF and W. J. Horne DFC.

de Havilland DH.98 MOSQUITO
(Bomber and PR variants)

One of the outstanding products of the British aircraft industry during World War II, the de Havilland Mosquito was originally proposed in 1938 as a fast, unarmed bomber but was rejected out of hand by an RAF hooked on the idea that a bomber needed to be heavily armed and certainly not constructed largely of wood. However, the outbreak of war and some concerted lobbying finally convinced RAF Bomber Command to order the Mosquito against a requirement for a light bomber. The type's versatility soon became apparent and it was as a photo-reconnaissance platform that the Mosquito first saw operational use. The 'Wooden Wonder' was the RAF's fastest bomber until the Canberra entered service in 1951 and was its the fastest aircraft of any type from September 1941 until 1944. In this first part of a two-part review of the Mosquito, the genesis of the aircraft and its photo-reconnaissance and bomber variants are examined in detail. Mosquito fighter and fighter-bomber variants and the Sea Mosquito will be described in a future issue of *Wings of Fame*.

E0234 sits in the open air for the first time after reassembly at Hatfield prior to its first flight. Camouflaged tarpaulins protect the yellow aircraft from the attentions of enemy reconnaissance aircraft. As the project was strictly speaking still a private venture, the Class-B serial was carried on the Mosquito's first two flights; it was, from then on, serialled W4050.

Right: It is 25 November 1940 and the DH.98 prototype has landed after Geoffrey de Havilland Jnr (with John Walker in the right-hand seat) have completed the first flight of the DH.98 prototype. Here Geoffrey de Havilland chats with colleagues after the successful flight.

In this view of the prototype, the short engine nacelles and one-piece flaps that characterised the early Mosquitoes are evident.

T he genesis and development of the Mosquito occurred in an era when Duralumin and other metals had long since replaced wood and wire, but that did not stop Geoffrey de Havilland's British aircraft manufacturing company from developing an amazing twin-engined aircraft of wooden construction that would strike 'Moskitopanic' into the hearts of its enemies in World War II.

The Mosquito's origins were in de Havilland's successful early use of simplified structures: the cabins of aircraft such as the DH.18, 29, 34 and 50 were literally spacious plywood boxes, with no internal bracing. By 1925 the first of the DH.60 Moth series appeared, later becoming one of the most successful light aircraft in aviation history.

In 1934, in great secrecy, de Havilland produced three diminutive, streamlined DH.88 Comet low-wing monoplane racers, each powered by two 230-hp (172-kW) DH Gipsy Six R (Racing) engines. Wooden construction and stressed-skin covering not only reduced all-up weight but also hastened production. All three Comets took part in the 1934 London-Melbourne Centenary Air Race, which was won by DH.88 *Grosvenor House*, crewed by Tom Campbell Black and C. W. A. Scott. In 1935 two more DH.88 Comet Racers were built. This type ultimately played a crucial role in the development of the Mosquito. In the late 1930s these same manufacturing techniques were successfully applied to the four-engined DH.91 Albatross commercial monoplane, whose manufacture was mainly of wood and stressed-skin construction; it was capable of cruising at 210 mph (338 km/h)) at 11,000 ft (3353 m). The Albatross flew for the first time on 20 May 1937 at Hatfield and a total of seven of these beautiful aircraft was built.

On 8 September 1936 de Havilland took an interest in Air Ministry Specification P.13/36, which called for a "twin-engined medium bomber for world-wide use." Further, it stated that the aircraft must have the highest possible cruising speed. Ideally, the new machine would be

a medium bomber, general reconnaissance and general-purpose aircraft in one basic design, "with possibly two 18-in torpedoes carried". It would be armed with two forward- and two rearward-firing Browning machine-guns (remotely-controlled guns was another consideration), have horizontal bomb stowage, in tiers if necessary, and would be suitable for outside maintenance at home or overseas. Notably, P.13/36 called for a top speed of not less than 275 mph (443 km/h) at 15,000 ft (4572 m) on two-thirds engine power and a range of 3,000 miles (4828 km) with a 4,000-lb (1814-kg) bomb load.

'Miniature Albatross' proposal

De Havilland had bad memories of submitting competing designs to the military in the 1920s, when all of his ideas had been considered too revolutionary. DH therefore proposed a modified miniature version of the Albatross airliner design to meet the specification. It could certainly carry a 6,000-lb (2721-kg) bomb load to Berlin and back at 11,000 ft (3353 m). Pacifists in Parliament were appalled and it appeared that de Havilland's doubts were well-founded, but he persevered with the Albatross proposal. In April 1938 studies were conducted for a twin Rolls-Royce Merlin-engined version of the airliner. There was nothing radical about this, but what would the Air Ministry make of a wooden design being submitted to carry bombs 3,000 miles (4828 km) in war? On 7 July Geoffrey de Havilland sent a letter detailing the specification to Air Marshal Sir Wilfred Freeman, an old friend of de Havilland's from World War I, now the Air Council's member for Research and Development. Sir Geoffrey was to recall later in his autobiography, *Sky Fever*, that "it only needed one

Prototypes

Contract B.69990/40, for 50 Mosquitoes, was placed to Specification B.1/40 on 1 March 1940. Amended to 21 aircraft in June 1941, these were completed (with Merlin 21 powerplants) as follows:

W4050	first prototype
W4051	photo-reconnaissance prototype
W4052	F.Mk II prototype
W4053	turret fighter and later trainer prototype
W4054/56	bomber Mk I prototypes
W4057	PR.Mk I, later B.Mk V bomber prototype (projected bomber variant strengthened to carry a 50-Imp gal (230-litre) drop tank or 500-lb bomb under each wing; failed to enter production)
W4058/59	PR.Mk I
W4060/61	PR.Mk I (long-range)
W4062/63	PR.Mk I (long-range and tropicalised)
W4064/70	PR.Mk I/bomber conversion (later known as B.Mk IV Series I)

The PR.Mk Is converted to B.Mk IV Series I standard also included W4071/72, though these appear to have fallen outside the original batch of 21 aircraft. The balance of the original order (27 aircraft) was completed as Mk II fighters and Mk III trainers.

Left: W4050 made four test flights from Hatfield on the afternoon of 10 January 1941, some six weeks into the intensive testing programme. Here the aircraft lands after one of these sorties.

Below: W4050 was re-engined with two-stage Merlin 61s in June 1942. Standing on the left in this view is John de Havilland, killed in a collision between two Mosquitoes in 1943.

meeting with this wise and far-sighted man to discuss our plans and get his full approval."

In the event, the Merlin-engined Albatross lost out to the Avro Manchester and the Handley Page HP.56, both to be powered by two Rolls-Royce Vulture engines (although plans for the Vulture-engined HP.56 were scrapped in 1937). The loss of this contract was a blessing in disguise, for de Havilland now opted for a very radical approach to the design of a twin-engined bomber. DH proposed deleting armament altogether to save about one-sixth the total weight of the aircraft; in turn, this would make production much easier and hasten service delivery. Losing the armament (although chief designer, Ronald E. Bishop, did make provision under the floor for four 20-mm cannon), meant that the crew could be reduced to a pilot and a navigator only.

The Munich Crisis of 1938 provided much needed impetus, and de Havilland proposed its unarmed, twin-engined wooden bomber with a crew of two. Speed would be the new bomber's only defence, so, predictably, the Air Ministry rejected the company's proposal. They wanted only heavily armed, conventionally built, all-metal bombers. War with Germany was declared on 3 September 1939 and de Havilland saw no reason to modify its proposal, but, likewise, the Air Ministry saw no reason to accept it.

Eventually, and mainly due to Sir Wilfred Freeman's support, de Havilland's unarmed bomber proposal finally won acceptance. On 29 December 1939 the project received official backing, and on 1 January 1940 a single prototype of the unarmed bomber – the fastest in the world – powered by two Rolls-Royce Merlin engines was ordered. On 1 March 1940 a contract was placed for 50

DH.98 Mosquito aircraft, although, following the Dunkirk debacle of May 1940, there was no surplus capacity available for aircraft like the Mosquito. To save the project altogether, de Havilland promised the Ministry of Aircraft Production that the 50 Mosquitoes would be delivered by December 1941.

W4050, the bomber/photo-reconnaissance prototype – referred to originally as E0234, the Company B-Class

With two-stage supercharging, Merlin 60/70 series powerplants transformed the Mosquito's performance at altitude. UK-built production aircraft were so-equipped from the Mk IX onwards. W4050 was to be the principal Mosquito trials airframe and was tested with all manner of modifications. Here DH Technical School apprentices start to dismantle W4050 for instructional use, some time in 1944. Amazingly, W4050 has survived and is displayed at the de Havilland Heritage Museum at London Colney.

W4051 was the last of the three Mosquito prototypes to fly, on 10 June 1941, having earlier donated its fuselage to enable the repair of W4050 after a mishap. '4051 was completed with a production standard fuselage, enabling its use operationally by No. 1 PRU at Benson to which it was delivered in July.

Mosquito production was initiated at de Havilland's Hatfield headquarters, at which bomber and PR aircraft production was to be concentrated. A shadow factory was established at nearby Leavesden, for fighter and fighter-bomber production, and further facilities were provided at the factories of Standard Motors (Coventry), Percival Aircraft (Luton) and Airspeed Aircraft (Southampton). Post-war, as Hatfield was busy with new projects, not least of which was the Comet airliner, the final Mosquitoes were built in the ex-Vickers factory at Hawarden between 1948 and 1950. Overseas production was carried out by de Havilland subsidiaries in Canada (from 1942) and Australia (in 1943), both factories developing their own variants that differed only in minor detail, apart from being powered by American-built Packard Merlins. Including overseas production, 7,619 Mosquitoes were completed in all, 6,710 of which were built during World War II. Of the latter, 3,054 were built at Hatfield. Canadian production accounted for 1,076 aircraft while the Australian production line completed 212 examples.

Prime Minister Winston Churchill, with Sir Geoffrey de Havilland to his right and company chairman Alan S. Butler to his left, inspects the Hatfield factory on 19 April 1943.

marking, and the first of three Mosquito prototypes – was built in strict secrecy at Salisbury Hall near Hatfield. A team of nine designers led by chief designer Ronald E. Bishop handled the DH.98 design which, although constructed of wood, was far from straightforward. Techniques and processes used on previous DH designs could not always be applied to the DH.98, which required higher load factors. W4050 was completed at Salisbury Hall, Hertfordshire and assembled at nearby Hatfield. On 25 November it made its first flight at Hatfield with Captain Geoffrey de Havilland, Jr, the chief test pilot, at the controls and John E. Walker, chief engine installation designer, in the right-hand seat. The aircraft flew like the pedigree machine it was, and once minor problems were eliminated during testing, the Mosquito proved to be a thoroughbred. Official trials at the A&AEE Boscombe Down in early 1941 confirmed that the aircraft met or exceeded de Havilland's speed and handling expectations. On 18-19 July, during further speed trials, W4050, fitted with Merlin 61 engines, reached 433 mph (697 km/h) at 28,500 ft (8687 m), and on 20 October

Right: Wings were built up on large jigs such as this. The upper surface of the wing is seen here, prior to the attachment of the outer skin.

Below: The Mosquito's fuselage was constructed in two halves using wooden, and later concrete, moulds. This starboard side of a bomber or PR fuselage has part of the cockpit floor and other equipment fitted.

Below right: Before the two fuselage shells were joined, they were mounted side-by-side for easy access to equipment and wiring.

W4050 achieved a speed of 437 mph (703 km/h) in level flight. Using two-stage Merlin 77s, W4050, which made its last flight around December 1943, produced a maximum speed of 439 mph (706 km/h) in level flight

W4051, the photo-reconnaissance prototype, was the second Mosquito completed at Salisbury Hall and the third to fly, after the fighter prototype (W4052), on 10 June 1941. A delay had ensued when the fuselage originally intended for W4051 was used to replace W4050's fuselage, which had fractured at Boscombe in a tailwheel incident. W4051 became the first of three PR versions (the other two were W4054 and W4055) used by the PRU at Benson, Oxfordshire, although it was W4055 which made the first operational Mosquito flight, on 17 September 1941.

Bomber order confirmed

On 21 June 1941, the Air Ministry instructed that, apart from five prototypes (one bomber, one PR and three fighter), 19 aircraft were to be PR models and 176 to be fighters. In July the Air Ministry finally confirmed that 50 more would be unarmed bombers. In addition to the construction totals agreed on 21 June, the Air Ministry further specified that the last 10 aircraft (W4064-72), from the 19 originally ordered on 1 March 1940 as PR versions, could be converted to unarmed bombers also. These 10 aircraft came to be known as the B.Mk IV Series I. W4072, the prototype B.Mk IV bomber, flew for the first time on 8 September 1941. The 50 B.Mk IV Series II bombers differed from the Series I in having a larger bomb bay to increase carriage to four 500-lb (227-kg) bombs instead of the Series I's four of 250 lb (113 kg); this was achived by shortening the tail stabiliser of the 500-lb bomb so that four could be carried. Twenty-seven B.Mk IV Series IIs (W4066 the only PR.Mk IV Series I) were later converted to PR.Mk IV reconnaissance aircraft, with three additional fuel tanks in the bomb bay, while 20 B.Mk IVs were modified by DH, Vickers-Armstrong and Marshalls to carry a 4,000-lb (1814-kg) bomb.

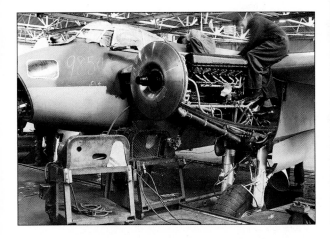

The production lines at Hatfield were joined by a second Mosquito production line at a new factory at Leavesden, Hertfordshire. Standard Motors, too, was later involved in producing Mosquitoes. Eighty Mosquitoes a month were built at Hatfield, while 30 were built by Second Aircraft Group, a widely dispersed shadow scheme first conceived in 1940. With Canadian production included, 110 bombers a month could be produced in 1942. By the end of January that year, de Havilland had orders for 1,378 Mosquitoes of all variants, including 20 T.Mk III trainer versions and 334 FB.Mk VI bombers by the S.A.G. at Leavesden. Another 400 were to be built in Canada.

Into service with the PRU

On 13 July 1941 W4051 was flown to Oxfordshire by Geoffrey de Havilland and handed over to No. 1 PRU at Benson, where it became the first Mosquito to be taken on charge by the RAF. W4054 and W4055 followed, on 22 July and 8 August, respectively. Beginning in September, No. 1 PRU received seven more production PR.Mk Is: W4056 and W4058-63 (W4057 became the bomber prototype, B.Mk V). Four of these (W4060-W4063) were later modified with increased fuel tankage for long-range operations, and two (W4062 and W4063) were tropicalised, leaving the UK for operational use in Malta and Egypt.

During tests on 16 September 1941, W4055's generator packed up over the Bay of Biscay, and with no power to drive the cameras Squadron Leader Rupert Clerke and Sergeant Sowerbutts were forced to abandon the sortie. They were pursued by three Bf 109s but the PR.Mk I easily outpaced them at 23,000 ft (7010 m) and returned safely. Clerke and Sowerbutts made the first successful PR.Mk I sortie the next day, when they set out in W4055 for a daylight photo-reconnaissance of Brest, La Pallice and

Bordeaux, arriving back at Benson at 17.45. On 20 September, Flight Lieutenant Alastair 'Ice' Taylor, DFC and his navigator, Sergeant Sidney Horsfall, successfully photographed Bordeaux, Pauillac, Le Verdon and La Pallice. The third PR sortie was made when Taylor and Horsfall covered Heligoland and Sylt in W4055 (named *Benedictine*). In October the three Mosquitoes carried out 16 successful sorties, all to Norway.

W4051, W4055, W4059 and W4061 were transferred to operate from Wick in Scotland with Squadron Leader Taylor in command. In October 1941 the PR.Mk I Mosquitoes carried out 16 successful sorties to Norway. On 4 December Taylor and Horsfall in W4055 failed to return from a PR sortie to cover Trondheim and Bergen; this, after 88 sorties, was the first loss of a PR Mosquito. By December the unit had moved to Leuchars.

On 15 January 1942, Flight Lieutenant John Merrifield reached Gdynia and Danzig in Poland but his objectives were covered by cloud. On 20 February 1942 W4051 was flown to the Franco-Spanish border, and marshalling yards and airfields at Toulouse in southern France. On 22 February Flight Lieutenant Victor Ricketts and his navigator, Sergeant Boris Lukhmanoff, covered Cuxhaven and Kiel to take photos of the *Gneisenau* in dry dock there. On 2 March Ricketts and Lukhmanoff photographed the *Scharnhorst* undergoing repairs at Wilhelmshaven, while another PR.Mk I photographed the *Gneisenau*. W4060 and W4051 photographed the French coast prior to the commando raid on St Nazaire, and on 3 March Flight Leutenant John Merrifield photographed the Danzig-Gdynia region, successfully this time.

On the night of 3/4 March, 235 bombers of Bomber Command attacked the Renault factory at Boulogne-Billancourt near Paris. An equally spectacular PR sortie was

Above: Wings and fuselages are brought together during the final assembly of bombers at de Havilland's Hatfield plant.

Above left: In order that an aircraft under assembly could be worked upon in a horizontal attitude without raising the aircraft's tail when ceiling space was limited, Mosquitoes were lowered into pits once their undercarriage had been fitted.

Below left and below: de Havilland Aircraft of Canada Ltd undertook Mosquito manufacture at its Downsview, Ontario plant, seen here with production in full swing. Before VJ-Day 1,032 Mosquitoes were completed at the DHC plant.

Benson's PR.Mk Is

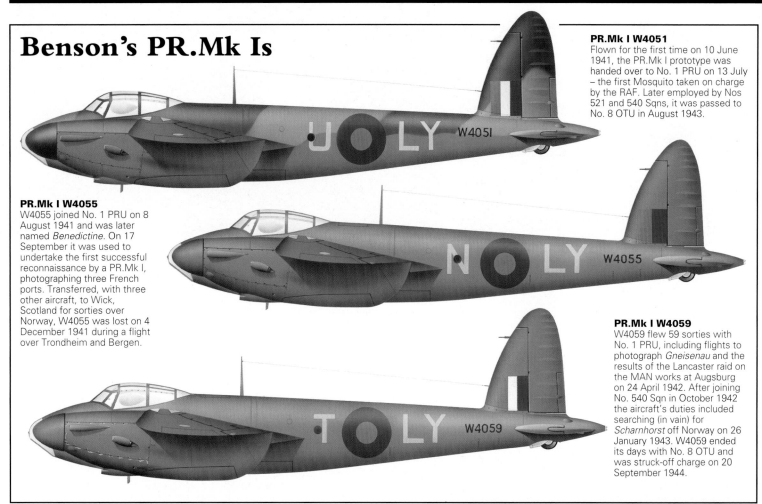

PR.Mk I W4051
Flown for the first time on 10 June 1941, the PR.Mk I prototype was handed over to No. 1 PRU on 13 July – the first Mosquito taken on charge by the RAF. Later employed by Nos 521 and 540 Sqns, it was passed to No. 8 OTU in August 1943.

PR.Mk I W4055
W4055 joined No. 1 PRU on 8 August 1941 and was later named *Benedictine*. On 17 September it was used to undertake the first successful reconnaissance by a PR.Mk I, photographing three French ports. Transferred, with three other aircraft, to Wick, Scotland for sorties over Norway, W4055 was lost on 4 December 1941 during a flight over Trondheim and Bergen.

PR.Mk I W4059
W4059 flew 59 sorties with No. 1 PRU, including flights to photograph *Gneisenau* and the results of the Lancaster raid on the MAN works at Augsburg on 24 April 1942. After joining No. 540 Sqn in October 1942 the aircraft's duties included searching (in vain) for *Scharnhorst* off Norway on 26 January 1943. W4059 ended its days with No. 8 OTU and was struck-off charge on 20 September 1944.

No. 1 PRU

Mosquito Mk Is W4051 (below, coded 'LY-U'), W4055, W4059 and W4061 made up the Mosquito Flight of No. 1 PRU which operated from Wick from May to December 1941 before moving to Leuchars, where it remained until October 1942. W4051 was photographed on 12 May 1942.

No. 1 Photographic Reconnaissance Unit was formed on 16 November 1940 by redesignating the original PRU formed five months earlier to operate Spitfires. Initially stationed at Heston, it moved to Benson on 27 December 1940. Disbanded in October 1942, it was reformed as a wing (No. 106 Wing from July 1943) comprising Nos 540, 541, 542, 543 and 544 Sqns. Of these Nos 540 and 544 Sqns went on to operate Mosquitoes for the duration of the war, principally over northern Europe and the Mediterranean. Initially equipped with Mosquito PR.Mk Is, the need for more PR aircraft saw the unit later add a handful of Mk II fighter and Mk IV bomber conversions. The PR.Mk IV conversions from B.Mk IV standard were a considerable improvement over the earlier standard PR.Mk Is, equipped as they were with extra fuel tankage. Once replaced by later marks those earlier machines that had survived were passed to No. 8 (PR) OTU.

Above: Four PR.Mk Is (W4060-W4063) were fitted with long-range fuel tanks in their redundant bomb bays to allow operations well into occupied Europe. Similar modifications were made to later Mosquito PR marks, notably the Mk 34s.

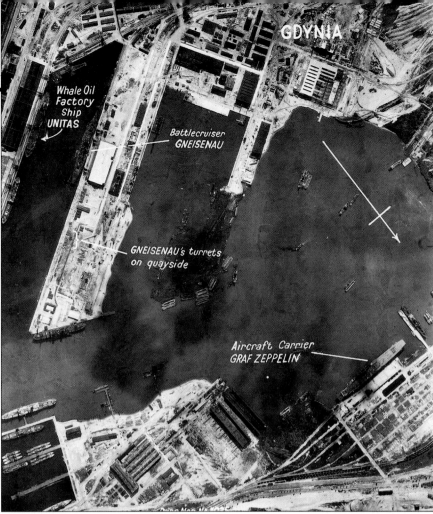

flown by Flying Officer Victor Ricketts and Sergeant Boris Luhkmanoff, to verify the results. On 29 April 1942 Flight Lieutenant Ricketts DFC and Sergeant Lukhmanoff made the first operational flight in a PR.Mk IV, when they covered Augsburg, Stuttgart and Saarbrücken, returning to Benson after five hours.

By spring 1942 the PRU at Benson was in need of additional PR.Mk Is, only nine having been built. During April to June 1942 four NF.Mk IIs – DD615, 620, 659 and W4089, all without long-range tanks – were diverted to the PRU, and in December two B.Mk IV bomber variants – DZ411 and DZ419 – arrived. Ground crew at Benson installed the three vertical and one oblique cameras aboard each of the machines and they were pressed into service.

On 7 May Flight Lieutenant Victor Ricketts made the farthest flight over enemy territory to that time, when he used DK284, a modified Mk IV, to photograph Dresden, Pilsen and Regensburg, returning after six hours. On 14 May Wing Commander Spencer Ring, RCAF, the CO, made the first operational flight in a PR.Mk II when he photographed Alderney using DD615, the first of the modified NF.Mk IIs. On the next day the first PR sortie to the Narvik area was flown from Leuchars by Flying Officer Higson in one of the PR.Mk IVs. On 16 May Flight Lieutenant John Merrifield photographed the *Prinz Eugen* heading southwest, apparently making for Kiel for repairs to damage inflicted by the submarine HMS *Trident*. The day after that, Flying Officer K. H. Bayley and Flight Sergeant Little photographed the *Prinz Eugen* and four destroyers also heading for Kiel. Coverage of Trondheim on 22 and 23 May revealed that the *Tirpitz*, *Admiral Hipper* and *Lützow* were still berthed in fjords.

On 25 May Flight Lieutenant Ricketts used DD615 to photograph targets in France and two days later Flight Lieutenant Gerry R. Wooll, RCAF used DD615 to successfully photograph Saarbrucken and Amiens. (On 24 August, during a PR sortie to Italy, Flight Lieutenant Wooll and Sergeant John Fielden were forced to land in Switzerland during a PR sortie when their glycol pump on the starboard engine began malfunctioning.) On 2 June Pilot Officers Robin Sinclair and Nelson in W4060 used the new 36-in (91-cm) F52 camera to take photos of the German aircraft-carrier *Graf Zeppelin* and the battleship *Scharnhorst* in port at Gydnia. On 10 June Flight Lieutenant Ricketts and Sergeant Boris Lukhmanoff flew a seven-hour sortie from Benson and back to Spezia, Lyons and Marseilles. Ricketts was killed on 11 July when he and Lukhmanoff failed to return from a sortie in W4089 to Strasbourg and Ingolstadt.

On 7 July 1942 Flight Lieutenant Bayley and Pilot Officer Little sighted the German battle fleet at Arno in Langfjord and from 14,000 ft (4267 m) photographed the battleships *Tirpitz*, *Scheer* and *Hipper*, seven destroyers, two torpedo-boats, three E- or R-boats, and one 'Altmark' tanker. They landed at Vaenga in Russia to refuel, and after lunch on the next day took off for Leuchars. They finally landed at 20.50 with their valuable photos, to a huge reception. (A PR detachment was maintained in Russia from mid-August to mid-October 1942.)

No. 1 PRU becomes five squadrons

On 19 October 1942 No. 1 PRU was reformed at Benson as five PR squadrons. Three were equipped with Spitfires, while H and L Flights at Leuchars were merged to form No. 540 (Mosquito) Squadron under the command of Squadron Leader M. J. B. Young, DFC. No. 544 Squadron formed at Benson, equipped with Ansons, Wellington Mk IVs and Spitfire PR.Mk IVs. In the main, No. 540 Squadron photographed German capital ships in Baltic waters and North Germany, and later in the Mediterranean also.

The first PR.Mk VIII sortie was on 19 February 1943 when Squadron Leader Gordon E. Hughes and Sergeant H. W. Evans flew in DZ342 to cover La Rochelle and St Nazaire, although they were unable to take any photos

Above left: On 2 June 1942 P/Os Sinclair and Nelson flew long-range PR.Mk I W4060, fitted with a new 36-in F.52 camera, to photograph the German aircraft-carrier Graf Zeppelin on the banks of the River Oder, at Stettin.

Above: Gydnia is seen here on 1 August 1942, as photographed from a PRU Mosquito. The battlecruiser Gneisenau is undergoing repairs.

Below: DD744 was one of two further conversions (with DD743) from F.Mk II to PR.Mk II standard for use in North Africa. Tropicalised and with camera equipment fitted at RAF Benson, both were painted silver overall and issued to No. 60 Sqn, SAAF in early 1943. Both were struck-off charge in November.

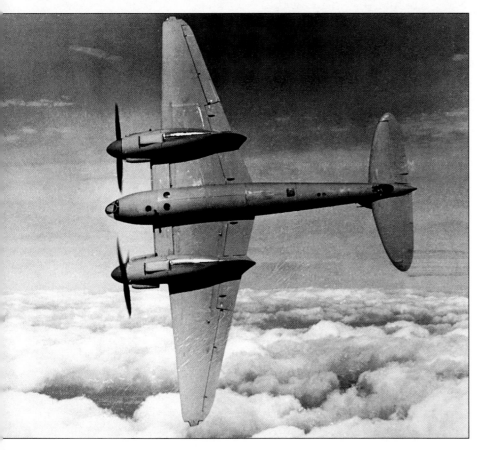

Above: This view of the undersides of a PR.Mk IV reveals the camera ports fitted in the bomb bay doors and beneath the rear fuselage.

Above: DZ383 was among the 27 B.Mk IV Series II bombers converted to PR.Mk IV standard, powered by Merlin 21s and with the same provision for 50-Imp gal (227-litre) underwing drop tanks. '383 joined No. 540 Sqn in 1943 and was finally scrapped in October 1946.

because the mud flap over the camera lens failed to open. (The first of five PR.Mk VIIIs, which began as B.Mk IV Series II aircraft with 1,565-hp (1167-kW) two-stage supercharged Merlin 61 engines, had begun to reach No. 540 Squadron late in 1942. Essentially, the PR.Mk VIII was intended to fill the gap until deliveries of the PR.Mks IX and XVI were made. The PR.Mk VIII had a greatly improved ceiling so that, for the first time, PR Mosquitoes could operate at high altitudes.) The first successful PR.Mk VIII sorties were flown on 27 February when Flight Lieutenant K. H. Bayley, DFC flew DZ364 to Frankfurt on a bomb damage assessment flight, and DZ342 covered Emden and Bremen. On 8 March 1943 the CO, Wing Commander M. J. B. Young, DFC, in Mk VIII DZ364, became the first Mosquito pilot to photograph Berlin.

No. 540 Squadron carried out battle-damage assessment and target reconnaissance at such places as the experimental rocket site at Peenemünde on the Baltic coast. The first five Mosquito sorties to the target revealed nothing, and a sixth sortie on 2 June 1943 brought scant new information. However, on 12 June a sortie by Flight Lieutenant Reggie A. Lenton resulted in the first definite evidence that previously unidentified objects at the site were V-2 rockets. One was photographed laying horizontally on a trailer near a building adjacent to one of the elliptical earthworks. On 23 June Flight Sergeant E. P. H. Peek brought back photos so clear that two rockets could be seen laying on road vehicles inside the elliptical earthwork. The news was relayed immediately to Prime Minister Winston Churhill. PRU Mosquitoes photographed Peenemünde again on 27 June, and 22 and 26 July. It was now virtually certain that Hitler was preparing a rocket offensive against southern England, and it had to be curtailed with all speed.

On 17/18 August 1943, 596 heavies of Bomber Command reduced the experimental site to rubble. Next morning, Flying Officer R. A. Hosking of No. 540 Squadron reconnoitred the target area, and again on 20 August 1943. The Peenemünde raid had set back the production of V-2 rockets by at least two months.

Hunting the V-1 sites

PR also successfully identified the existence and launching sites of V-1 flying-bomb sites. They were spotted on photos of Peenemünde airfield taken on 28 November 1943 by Squadron Leader John Merrifield, DSO, DFC and Flying Officer W. Whalley. The film showed buildings that were similar in size and shape to those which had been photographed at Bois Carr, France, the previous October. The photos of Peenemünde airfield revealed a ski-type ramp identical to ones which had been photographed by PR Spitfires at sites in northern France. The new photographs also showed a "tiny cruciform shape set exactly on the lower end of the inclined rails – a midget aircraft actually in position for launching". The 'midget aircraft' was now revealed to be a flying-bomb (Vergeltungswaffe 1 – Revenge Weapon No. 1 – a small, pilotless aircraft with a

Peenemünde PR.Mk IV

Peenemünde revealed
On 12 June 1943 DZ473 revisited Peenemünde, Flt Lt Lenton bringing back the first real evidence that the previously unidentified objects at the site were V-2 rockets.

PR.Mk IV DZ473
One of 27 B.Mk IV Series IIs in the DZxxx serial range converted to PR standard between December 1942 and March 1943, DZ473 made its 22nd sortie with No. 540 Sqn over railyards at Stettin on 22 April 1943. Its crew, Flt Lts White (RCAF) and Prescott kept their cameras running as they flew down the north coast of Germany and by chance photographed Peenemünde.

TOULON

B-XI-42

Toulon, on the south coast of France, is seen here as it appeared to a Mosquito crew the day after *Operation Torch*, the Allied invasion of North Africa. No. 540 Sqn photographed the port 11 times between 7 and 26 November. About 60 ships were in port, including the Vichy French flagship *Strasbourg*, and 18 submarines. When German forces attempted to seize the French fleet it was scuttled, a No. 540 Sqn aircraft photographing the port once again shortly afterwards as a means of confirmation. By April 1943 No. 4 PRU had received a pair of PR Mosquitoes and was soon flying regular sorties, mainly from Maison Blanche, near Algiers, to ensure that the ships were not repaired.

1,870-lb (848-kg) high-explosive warhead that detonated upon impact.)

On 5 December 1943 bombing of the V-1 sites began. PRU aircraft regularly photographed each site before and after each attack. By the end of the month, the Allies had photographed 42 Noball sites, of which 36 were revealed as damaged, 21 of them seriously. By 12 June 1944 60 weapons sites had been identified. Hitler's 'rocket blitz' began on 13 June, when 10 V-1s, or 'Doodlebugs' as they became known, were launched against London from sites in northeast France. By the end of September 1944, 133 V-1 sites had been identified by PRU aircraft. Only eight ever remained undiscovered by aerial reconnaissance.

No. 544 Squadron, meanwhile, continued to use Ansons, Wellingtons and Spitfire PR.Mk IVs in the PR and night photography roles over Europe, until in April 1943 Mosquito PR.Mk IVs replaced the Wellingtons. In October, PR.Mk IXs completed No. 544 Squadron's re-equipment. This squadron had flown its first PR.Mk IX operation, a night sortie, on 13 September 1943, when Flight Lieutenant R. L. C. Blythe covered Vannes. Production of PR.Mk XVIs began in November 1943, and 435 were eventually built. With 100-Imp gal (455-litre) drop tanks, the PR.Mk XVI had a range of 2,000 miles (3218 km). On 19 February 1944 a PR.Mk XVI brought back photos of Berlin, despite German fighters encroaching at 42,000 ft (12800 m).

In March 1944 No. 544 Squadron received PR.Mk XVI Mosquitoes, while 540 had to wait until July 1944. During 1944 No. 540 Squadron devoted itself solely to reconnaissance of the German rail transportation system in preparation for D-Day.

Some of the first PR.Mk XVI models to come off the production lines were urgently despatched to No. 140 Squadron, 2nd Tactical Air Force, at Hartford Bridge, where they supplemented PR.Mk IXs on reconnaissance and mapping duties as part of the build-up to the June D-Day invasion. 2nd TAF decided that rather than have all its fighter squadrons flying tactical reconnaissance, its three reconnaissance wings should each contain a PR unit. 'B' Flight of No. 4 Squadron in No. 35 Wing (No. 84 Group) and 'A' Flight of No. 400 Squadron, RCAF in No. 39 Wing (No. 83 Group) received PR.Mk XVIs for the role. At the end of May 1944 both flights reverted to Spitfire Mk IXs, but No. 140 Squadron, operating in No. 34 PR Wing (HQ), retained all its PR.Mk XVIs and, equipped with Gee and Rebecca, continued flying long-range blind night-photography operations, first from Northolt, and later, the continent.

No. 544 Squadron had begun receiving PR.Mk XVIs in March 1944, while No. 540 Squadron had to wait until July. On 27 August one of the longest PR flights was flown by Wing Commander John Merrifield, DSO, DFC, the No. 540 Squadron CO, in a PR.Mk XVI. Taking off from Benson at 06.00, Merrifield photographed Gydnia, Danzig, Königsberg and Bromberg in Poland, Gleiwitz in southeast Germany, and oil installations at Bleckhammer, Bratislava and Zarsa on the Dalmatian coast, landing at San Severo, Italy at 12.10. After refuelling, the Mosquito took off at 15.00 to make the return flight to Benson, where it landed at 19.00, having photographed Pola, Trieste, Millstadt in the Tyrol, and Le Havre.

Sink *Tirpitz*!

PR aircraft were responsible for locating the Kriegsmarine's 45,000-ton (45730-tonne) capital ship and they were ultimately responsible for its destruction. In March 1944 *Tirpitz* had left its anchorage in Alten Fjord and was subsequently discovered by a PRU Spitfire operating from Russia. On 3 April *Tirpitz* was attacked by RN aircraft from *Victorious* and *Furious* and was damaged, but the extent of that damage was not known. PR Mosquitoes

Mk VIII stopgap

The Mosquito PR.Mk VIII was the first of the PR variants to benefit from the installation of Merlin engines with two-stage supercharging. Two 1,565-hp (1167-kW) Merlin 61s, as fitted to the Spitfire Mk IX, allowed the Mosquito to operate from higher altitudes for the first time. Five were completed in all, the first (DK324) making its first flight on 20 October 1942. DZ342, '364, '404 and '424 followed and began to join No. 540 Sqn from late 1942. DZ364 became the first PR Mosquito to photograph Berlin the following year, but as a stopgap the type's service was shortlived, Mk IX aircraft becoming available from May 1943.

Hatfield-built B.Mk IV DK324 was converted as the first Mk VIII. In service the variant carried 50-Imp gal (227-litre) underwing tanks.

High-altitude ops

The first PR Mosquito to enter series production with two-stage Merlin engines, the Mk IX differed from the Mk VIII in being powered by Merlin 72s. Though it had the same rating as the Merlin 61, the 72 had a reversed-flow coolant system and was developed specifically for the Mosquito which, in its new guise, was expected to spend long periods at altitude. Ninety PR.Mk IXs were built, No. 544 Sqn completing its re-equipment with the variant in October 1943, having flown its first Mk IX operation on the night of 13 September. The Mk IX was also the first of the PR variants to serve overseas, equipping RAF units in the Middle East, Mediterranean and Far East, and No. 60 Sqn, SAAF in Italy.

Mosquito PR.Mk IX MM230 (top) was at A&AEE Boscombe Down in early 1944 for trials of two types of flame damper (above) neither of which proved satisfactory as with both the aircraft's exhaust remained clearly visible from the rear. Returned to de Havilland for overhaul, MM230 later served with the Fighter Interception Unit before being returned to DH once again and finally being struck-off in October 1946.

carried out a visual and photographic reconnaissance of the west coast of Norway to spot fjords likely to provide suitable anchorage for the ship. On 9 July 1944 Flight Lieutenant Frank Dodd and Flight Sergeant Eric Hill of No. 544 Squadron, in PR.Mk XVI NS504, in a flight lasting seven hours and 44 minutes, carried out a search for the elusive battleship before landing back at Leuchars, with fewer than 10 Imp gal (45 litres) of fuel remaining. On 12 July they finally located *Tirpitz*, in Alten Fjord, and returned to make a night landing at Leuchars, after a total flying time for the sortie of nine hours and 25 minutes. For this outstanding sortie, Flight Lieutenant (later Air Vice Marshal) Dodd was awarded an immediate DSO. In September, Flight Sergeant (later Flying Officer) Hill was awarded the DFM.

On 15 September *Tirpitz* was bombed by Lancasters of No. 5 Group carrying Tallboys and 400- to 500-lb

Johnny Walker mines. Subsequent PR revealed that, although badly damaged and effectively beyond practical repair, *Tirpitz* was still afloat. On 17 October 1944 four PR Mosquitoes of No. 540 Squadron were despatched to Dyce to keep watch on *Tirpitz*. Information from the Norwegian resistance was that the ship had left Kaa Fjord on its way south, at Tromsø. On 18 October Flight Lieutenant Hubert 'Sandy' Powell and Flight Sergeant Joe Townshend in PR.Mk XVI NS641, searching every Norwegian fjord, finally found the elusive battleship 3 miles (5 km) to the west of Tromsø, 215 miles (346 km) inside the Arctic Circle. By this time, the aircraft was at 15,000 ft (4572 m) due to cloud, and they made one photographic run over the ship at this altitude. They encountered some fire from *Tirpitz* and the ground, but it was not accurate. The two tired crew members finally landed at Scatsta at 16.16 with about 15 minutes' fuel left, after a 2,150-mile (3460-km) trip lasting eight hours and 35 minutes. This outstanding feat earned Powell a DFC and Townshend the DFM.

Lancasters finally capsized *Tirpitz* on 12 November 1944. About one hour later, Flight Lieutenant A. R. Cussons and Flight Sergeant Ken Ellis from No. 540 Squadron took photos which showed that the 45,000-ton monster had indeed turned turtle.

Post-war duties

No. 540 Squadron finished the war making a complete PR of the whole of France, starting in March 1945 and finishing in November that year, when the squadron returned to Benson, where it disbanded on 30 September 1946. After VE-Day No. 400 Squadron remained in Germany with BAFO until it disbanded at Lüneberg on 7 August 1945.

Nos 540/544 Sqn Mk IXs

PR.Mk IX LR416
Delivered to No. 540 Sqn on 4 July 1943, LR416 flew its first operation on 10 August, though this was abandoned after problems developed with a wing fuel tank. The following day, unit CO Wg Cdr Lord Malcolm-Hamilton OBE took LR416 to, and successfully photographed, Friedrichshafen before landing at La Marsa, Italy. The aircraft flew 18 sorties during 1943/44, before being wrecked in a crash near Benson on 13 April 1944.

PR.Mk IX LR432
LR432 was delivered to No. 540 Sqn on 4 September 1943, but 11 days later was employed on No. 544 Sqn's first Mk IX operation, being formally transferred to the unit on 8 October. On 29 November 1944 this Mk IX flew its 43rd and last operation, to Hemmingstadt and Heligoland. On 22 January 1944 the veteran was passed to No. 8 OTU, but by September it had been struck off charge.

Prototype at A&AEE

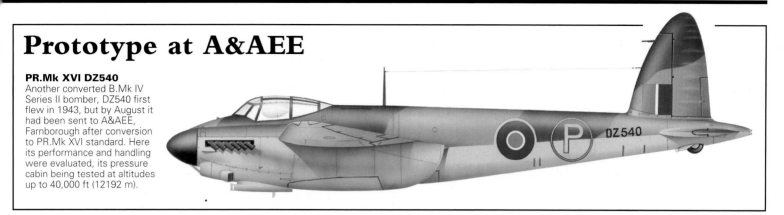

PR.Mk XVI DZ540
Another converted B.Mk IV Series II bomber, DZ540 first flew in 1943, but by August it had been sent to A&AEE, Farnborough after conversion to PR.Mk XVI standard. Here its performance and handling were evaluated, its pressure cabin being tested at altitudes up to 40,000 ft (12192 m).

Pressurised Mk XVI

A pressurised version of the PR.Mk IX, the Mk XVI was developed to enable the PR force to operate at even higher altitudes than the Mk IX had permitted, largely to avoid enemy aircraft. Development of the Mk XVI began with the trial installation of Merlin 67s in a Mk IX (MM229) in December 1943. A second aircraft was then fitted with a Merlin 76/77 combination and Hamilton Standard paddle-bladed propellers, these changes increasing ceiling performance by up to 3,000 ft (914 m) and improving top speed at 35,000 ft (10668 m). In order to photograph V-weapon sites in northern France, eight further Mk IXs were modified to this latter standard, with an F.52 camera installed in each drop tank. Production Mk XVIs had a Merlin 72/73 engine pairing, the latter incorporating a pump for the cabin pressurisation system. Delayed in its introduction by condensation misting its laminated windscreen, the Mk XVI did not enter full service until February 1944, No. 544 Sqn received its first aircraft in March; No. 540 had to wait until July 1944 as deliveries were also made to No. 140 Sqn, 2nd TAF in the run-up to D-Day.

On 13 January 1942 a PR.Mk I piloted by Flying Officer Kelly was sent from Benson to Malta for trials in the Mediterranean, but was written off in a crash-landing upon arrival at Luqa. A second, piloted by Pilot Officer Walker, arrived safely at Malta on 17 January, and after a series of sorties over Italy, was lost on 31 March, on a sortie to Sicily. Badly shot up by Bf 109s, Pilot Officer Kelly and Sergeant Pike nursed the ailing Mosquito to Hal Far, where it crashed and burned out. Both crew survived. Various No. 540 Squadron detachments were made to Malta (on 1 October 1942 Pilot Officer McKay made the first return trip to the island, returning to Benson three days later) and Gibraltar. In addition to undertaking PR of German ships, the squadron carried out BDA and target reconnaissance. Serviceability of aircraft in the winter of 1942-43 was only 50 per cent at times because of water seepage in badly fitted No. 7 bulkheads.

The only Mosquito PR squadron in the Middle East theatre in 1943 was No. 683 Squadron, which formed at Luqa, Malta on 8 February 1943, being equipped initially with Spitfires before adding Mosquito Mk IIs and VIs in May 1943 for a month of operations over Italy and Sicily. Apart from three PR.Mk IXs detached from No. 540 Squadron to the Mediterranean in the summer of 1943, only a few PR Mosquitoes operated in this theatre. 'B' Flight in No. 680 Squadron primarily covered Greece and the Balkans and, later, central and southern Europe, and 'B' Flight in No. 60 Squadron, SAAF made deep penetration sorties to southern Europe and Poland.

Above: With the fitting of a pressure cabin came the need for cockpit canopy strengthening. The bomber-type side blister on either side of the canopy was also replaced by a larger 'blown' side bulge. This comprised a 'dry air' Perspex sandwich and improved visibility considerably. This aircraft, believed to be MM384, was issued to No. 684 Sqn in 1944, but was lost in the sea off India during August.

Above left: In this view of MM384, one of over 100 Mk XVIs supplied to the USAAF and seen here at Watton prior to being repainted in USAAF markings, an oblique camera port – a feature of the Mk XVI – is visible behind the trailing edge of the port wing.

Left: PR.Mk XVI NS705 demonstrates its 'engine out' performance for an official photographer. Of note are the 100-Imp gal (455-litre) external tanks, which helped extend the Mk XVI's range to 2,450 miles (3943 km).

de Havilland DH.98 Mosquito

Above: Seen here in official photographs, NS502/'M' was a No. 544 Sqn machine (see below) and carries 50-Imp gal (227-litre) underwing tanks which allowed a 2,180-mile (3508-km) round trip.

Right: On 22 March 1945 Sqn Ldr Frank Dodd and P/O Eric Hill of No. 544 Sqn flew a 10½-hour round trip in a Mk XVI to photograph Tirpitz in Tromsø fjord, five months after it was capsized by No. 5 Group, Lancasters.

The first PR.Mk XVI to reach the Middle East was MM292, at the end of January 1944. On 17 February the first of nine PR.Mk XVIs for No. 680 Squadron arrived at Matariya, Cairo (the day before No. 680 Squadron received its first PR.Mk IX, LR444). On 7 May 1944 No. 680 flew its first Mosquito PR sortie when Flight Lieutenant A. M. Yelland in MM333 covered ports and airfields in Crete and the Cyclades. Eventually, Mosquito PR.Mk IXs and XVIs, and Spitfire Mk XIs, became the standard equipment. In August 1944 No. 680 Squadron moved to San Severo to range over the Balkans and Hungary, seeing out the war while mapping Italy, a task it finished in February 1945. No. 680 then flew to Egypt to work as a survey squadron, followed by a stint in Palestine to survey that country.

Mk IVs enter service

On 15 November 1941, at the No. 2 (Light Bomber) Group airfield at Swanton Morley, Norfolk, No.105 Squadron finally saw the first of the revolutionary Mosquito Mk IV bombers that Wing Commander Peter H. A. Simmons DFC, the CO, had been promised, to replace his Blenheim Mk IVs. The squadron had almost ceased to exist after terrible losses incurred during a brief day and night bombing campaign and suicidal anti-shipping strikes from England and from Malta. DH Company chief test pilot Geoffrey de Havilland, Jr flew the Mosquito bomber (W4064) and treated crews to an exhilarating display of aerobatics. After the Blenheim, the Mosquito was outstanding. The maximum recommended speed was 420 mph (676 km/h) indicated air

speed but at 20,000 ft (6096 m) this speed was equivalent to 520 mph (837 km/h).

W4064 returned to Hatfield the following day, where the first of the paltry 10 Mosquito Mk IV bombers were coming off the production lines, for adjustments. Not until July 1941 had it been decided to build Mosquitoes as bombers, and then only converted from PR airframes. Another 60 Mosquito bombers were on order but they would not start to arrive until the following February. Initially, No. 105 Squadron had to content itself with W4066 (which arrived on 17 November), the first Mosquito bomber to enter RAF service, and three other Mk IVs, W4064, W4068 and W4071, all of which were delivered at intervals to the squadron.

Early in December 1941 No. 105 Squadron moved to Horsham St Faith, near Norwich. Mosquito spares at this time were non-existent, although No. 105 Squadron was expected to become fully operational with 16-18 crews and a dozen aircraft within a six-month period. Only eight Mosquitoes had arrived by mid-May 1942 but No. 2 Group was anxious to despatch its 'wooden wonders' on the first available opportunity.

On 27 May orders were issued for No. 105 Squadron to prepare four Mosquitoes (W4072, W4064, W4065 and W4071) with bombs and cameras to "harass and obtain photographic evidence" of the 'Thousand Bomber' raid on Cologne, scheduled for the night of 30/31 May. Squadron Leader Oakeshott, followed later by Pilot Officer Kennard, took off from Horsham before the heavies had returned and

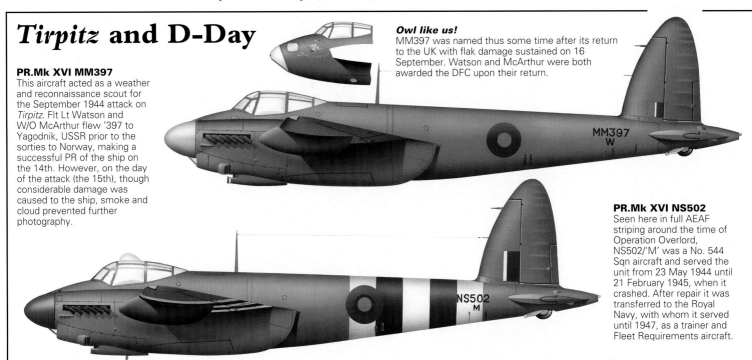

Tirpitz and D-Day

PR.Mk XVI MM397
This aircraft acted as a weather and reconnaissance scout for the September 1944 attack on *Tirpitz*. Flt Lt Watson and W/O McArthur flew '397 to Yagodnik, USSR prior to the sorties to Norway, making a successful PR of the ship on the 14th. However, on the day of the attack (the 15th), though considerable damage was caused to the ship, smoke and cloud prevented further photography.

Owl like us!
MM397 was named thus some time after its return to the UK with flak damage sustained on 16 September. Watson and McArthur were both awarded the DFC upon their return.

PR.Mk XVI NS502
Seen here in full AEAF striping around the time of Operation Overlord, NS502/'M' was a No. 544 Sqn aircraft and served the unit from 23 May 1944 until 21 February 1945, when it crashed. After repair it was transferred to the Royal Navy, with whom it served until 1947, as a trainer and Fleet Requirements aircraft.

2nd TAF operations

During the run-up to D-Day No. 140 Sqn, RAF and No. 400 Sqn, RCAF were tasked with the reconnaissance of northern and central France, using Mosquito Mk XVIs. With support from No. 544 Sqn, both units also kept a watch over the V-weapon sites that appeared to be proliferating throughout the north of the country. 'B' Flight of No. 4 Sqn also operated Mk XVIs briefly over France during early 1944, but in May joined No. 400 Sqn in relinquishing its Mosquitoes for PR Spitfires. On D-Day itself No. 544 Sqn flew day and night sorties covering rail centres and troop movements, while No. 140 Sqn concentrated on tactical targets, often at night using photoflash bombs and Fairchild K.19 cameras with a 6-in, 10-in or 12-in lens fitted. The first Mosquito PR.Mk XVI to fail to return from an operation was a No. 140 Sqn aircraft, MM279, lost on D-Day+1, 7 June 1944. This unit moved from Northolt to Balleroy (A.12), France in September and remained active, with Mk XVIs, until VE-Day.

were followed, shortly before lunchtime the following day, by Pilot Officer Costello-Bowen with Wt Off Tommy Broom, and Flight Lieutenant Houlston with Flight Sergeant Armitage. Oakeshott flew at 24,000 ft (7315 m) over the battered city and added his four 500-lb (227-kg) bombs to the devastation, but with smoke reaching to 14,000 ft (4267 m) his F24 camera was rendered useless. Kennard failed to return, his aircraft being hit by anti-aircraft fire. Cotsello-Bowen and Houlston dropped their bombs from high level into the smoking ruins, and headed back to Norfolk.

In the late afternoon Squadron Leader R. J. Channer, DFC took off from Horsham St Faith and flew in thick cloud to within 60 miles (96 km) of Cologne before diving to low level at almost 380 mph (611 km/h) to take photographs of the damage. Channer quickly realised that this highly successful approach would be particularly effective for future Mosquito bombing operations.

On the evening of 1 June two Mosquitoes returned to Cologne to bomb and reconnoitre the city. One of the

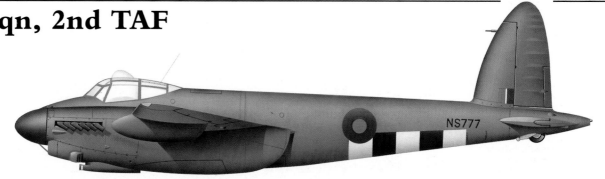

Top: A No. 140 Sqn Mk XVI, NS777, is seen in early 1945, possibly at Melsbroek (B.58). The hangar appears to have been camouflaged to represent a farm building.

Above: This gathering of 2nd TAF PR assets at Melsbroek includes a Wellington Mk XIII of No. 69 Sqn, a Spitfire PR.Mk XI of No. 16 Sqn and a No. 140 Sqn Mosquito Mk XVI. All three units were part of No. 34(PR) Wing.

Left: No. 540 Sqn moved to France in March 1945, remaining for six months. This Mk XVI was at Coulommiers in April.

No. 140 Sqn, 2nd TAF

PR.Mk XVI NS777
Flt Lts Arthur Kirk and A. T. 'Tony' Humphreys flew their first sortie together on 29 December 1944 in this aircraft. They finished their tour in March 1945, the aircraft surviving the war and being passed to the Armée de L'Air on 15 June 1946.

NS777

No. 60 Sqn, SAAF

Record attempt
On 14 December 1944, Col Owen Glynn Davies, a former CO of No. 60 Sqn, and Brigadier Hingeston attempted a record-breaking flight in this aircraft, from Cairo to Pretoria. Damaged on landing at Que Que, Rhodesia, repairs to its undercarriage and propellers were carried out before LR480 was flown on to South Africa. It was later donated to the National Museum of Military History.

PR.Mk IX LR480
Named *Lovely Lady/Anne!*, LR480 served with No. 60 Sqn, SAAF in December 1944, having arrived in the Middle East from Benson a year earlier. Having joined the South African unit at Foggia in June 1944, it flew many sorties over the Balkans and Austria.

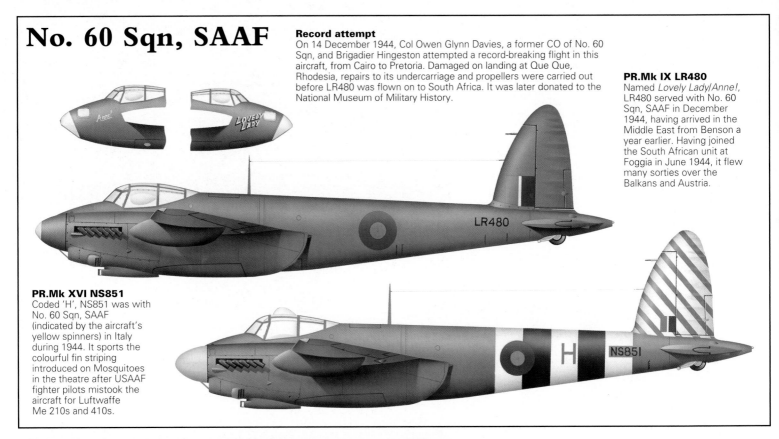

PR.Mk XVI NS851
Coded 'H', NS851 was with No. 60 Sqn, SAAF (indicated by the aircraft's yellow spinners) in Italy during 1944. It sports the colourful fin striping introduced on Mosquitoes in the theatre after USAAF fighter pilots mistook the aircraft for Luftwaffe Me 210s and 410s.

PR.Mk XVI NS644/'G' (right) is a No. 60 SAAF machine. The distinctive tail marking applied to No. 336 Wing's Mosquitoes (later applied to their rudders only) is apparent in this view (above), probably in Italy, of No. 680 Sqn aircraft. The other unit in No. 336 Wing was No. 680 Sqn, RAF. Formed from No. 2 PRU in 1 February 1943, No. 680 Sqn was initially based at Matariyah (LG.219), near Cairo. Then equipped with Spitfire Mk IXs and XIs, and a few Beaufighters, and operating over the eastern Mediterranean and Greece, No. 680 Sqn began to re-equip with Mosquitoes from February 1944, flying its first sortie with the type in May. By the end of the year the squadron had moved to Italy and was photographing targets as far afield as Austria, Bavaria, Czechoslovakia and Germany.

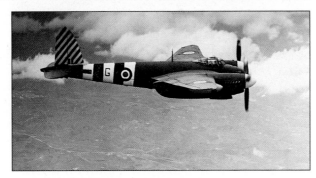

aircraft failed to return. Just before dawn on 2 June, 18 hours after a 'Thousand Bomber' raid on Essen, Squadron Leader George Parry and his navigator, Flying Officer Victor Robson, flew a lone two-hour five-minute round trip to Cologne armed with four 500-lb bombs and a camera. However, thick smoke made photography impossible.

Second bomber squadron

On 8 June, No. 139 Squadron was formed at Horsham St Faith using crews and Mk IVs from No. 105 Squadron. Flight Lieutenant Jack Houlston, AFC, promoted to squadron leader, flew No. 139 Squadron's first operation on 25/26 June with a low-level raid on the airfield at Stade near Wilhelmshaven. He returned after dark just as the RAF 'heavies' were heading for Bremen, in the third of the

1,000 bomber raids. Two of No. 105 Squadron's Mosquitoes flew reconnaissance over the city after the raid and four more went to reconnoitre other German cities to assess damage and bring back photographs.

On 1/2 July No. 139 Squadron bombed the submarine yards at Flensburg in the first mass low-level strikes by Mosquitoes. Group Captain MacDonald and Squadron Leader Oakeshott failed to return. Squadron Leader Houlston came off the target pursued by three Fw 190s, and Flight Lieutenant Hughes was chased by two more fighters after he had been hit by flak over the target. Both pilots made their exits hugging the wave tops and, applying extra boost, they easily outpaced their pursuers.

On 11 July it was the turn of No. 105 Squadron's Mosquitoes to hit the yards at Flensburg, which was laid on as a diversion for the heavies hitting Danzig. Pilot Officer Laston returned with part of his fin blown away by flak, but Flight Lieutenant Hughes's Mosquito failed to return. Sergeant Peter W. R. Rowland, in DK296, borrowed from Squadron Leader Parry, flew so low that he hit a roof and returned to Horsham with pieces of chimney pot lodged in the nose.

High-level raids in clear skies were now the order of the day, and during July the first 29 'Siren Raids' were flown. Involving dog-leg routes across Germany at night at high level, they were designed to disrupt the war workers and their families and ensure they lost at least two hours of sleep before their shifts next day.

Nos 105 and 139 Squadrons moved to RAF Marham, Norfolk in September 1942. On the 19th, six crews flew the first Mosquito daylight raid to Berlin. None of the aircraft was able to penetrate the thick cloud en route, and although Squadron Leader Parry dropped down through the layers he was too low to bomb. He finally turned for home and headed back across the north coast of Germany and into Holland. At 1,000 ft (305 m), just off the Dutch coast, two Bf 109s made two hits on Parry's Mosquito; there was no real damage, and after pulling up into the cloud he finally got down near the sea and outran them.

On 25 September four of the expert low-level raiders in No. 105 Squadron, led by George Parry with 'Robbie' Robson navigating, flew a long overwater mission to Oslo

Reformed at Horsham St. Faith on 8 June 1942, No. 139 Sqn (coded 'XD') became the second Mosquito bomber squadron. These are B.Mk IV Series II machines, with lengthened engine nacelles and shrouded exhausts.

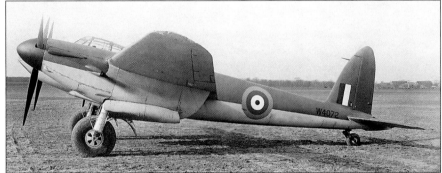

Mosquito bombers

The first Mosquito bombers were a batch of nine 'PR/Bomber Conversion Type' aircraft converted from PR.Mk I to B.Mk IV Series I standard; the first of 292 Series II machines followed. Both types were able to carry 2,000-lb (907-kg) of bombs comprising four 500-lb GP bombs with specially shortened tailfins. The Mosquito remained a secret from the British public until 25 September 1942, when four B.Mk IV Series II aircraft left Leuchars on a sortie to Oslo, to bomb the Gestapo HQ in the city. Though the raid was not an unqualified success (there were problems with bomb fusing and one Mosquito was lost), everyone was now aware of the RAF's new high-speed 'wooden wonder'.

to bomb the Gestapo HQ and also to disrupt a rally of Norwegian Fascists and Quislings. The crews flew from Marham and refuelled and bombed up at Leuchars in Scotland, where the operation came under the control of Wing Commander Hughie Edwards, VC. The raid involved a round trip of some 1,100 miles (1770 km), and an air time of 4 hours and 45 minutes, making it the longest Mosquito mission so far. Bombing would be made at 50-100 ft (15-30 m) with four 11-second delayed-action 500-lb bombs set to explode at low level.

Crews were told there were would be no enemy fighters, but nearing Oslo the Mosquitoes were intercepted by two Fw 190s. Fortunately, the rest of 3./JG 5 did not get off in time. One of the Fw 190s shot down a Mosquito, and although the other chased Squadron Leader Parry, it was unable to bring him down. Parry followed a line southwest over the centre of Oslo for his bomb run and, travelling at 280-300 mph (450-482 km/h), dropped his bombs. Some of the bombs did not explode but at least four entered the roof of the Gestapo HQ, one of which failed to detonate, but the other three crashed through the opposite wall before exploding. It was a remarkably successful assault, the first long-distance raid the Mosquitoes had flown.

Revealed to the public

Parry and the other two crews were debriefed and next morning flew back to Norfolk to rejoin the squadron at Marham. That night, 26 September, listeners to the BBC Home Service heard that a new aircraft, the Mosquito, had been revealed officially for the first time by the RAF and that four had made a daring roof-top raid on Oslo. The next day, 27 September, the first photo of a Mosquito was published,

with a caption indicating that "armament may consist of four 20-mm cannon and four 0.303-in machine-guns".

On 6 December No. 2 Group mounted its biggest operation of the war when 83 Venturas and Bostons and eight Mosquitoes of No. 105 Squadron and two of No. 139 Squadron attacked the Philips radio and valve works at

Far left: Another airframe taken from the first batch of Mosquito PR.Mk Is, W4072 served as the B.Mk IV Series I prototype, first flying as such on 8 September 1941. Seen here the following March, it retains the early style Merlin exhaust system and short engine nacelle, as fitted to the early PR machines. W4072 eventually joined No. 105 Sqn (coded 'GB-D') and led the first operational bombing sortie by Mosquitoes, on 31 May 1942.

Left: B.Mk IV Series II DZ367 peels away from the camera to reveal an underside stained by oil leaks from its Merlin 21s. Note the camera ports in the forward section of the bomb bay doors and a third port in the rear fuselage. Bomber Command Mosquitoes were also tasked with PR of the target in some of their early daylight raids.

Above: No. 139 Sqn aircraft are seen at Marham, in late 1942/early 1943. Both Nos 105 and 139 Sqns moved to the station in September 1942, Horsham St. Faith having been earmarked for use by the USAAF.

Above right: Aircrews from Nos 105 and 139 Sqns pose with a B.Mk IV at RAF Marham. No. 139 Sqn flew its first operation on 2 July 1942, when two aircraft carried out a high altitude raid on Flensburg.

Right: A press day at Horsham St. Faith in early 1942 generated a number of well known views of No. 105's newly delivered Mosquitoes. The aircraft seen here include DZ367/'J', DK336/'P', DZ353/'E' and DZ360/'A'.

On 27 May 1943 DZ467/'GB-P' was on its 19th operation with No. 105 Sqn when it failed to return from the raid on the Zeiss Optical Factory at Jena. P/O R. Massie and Sgt G. Lyster were killed. Only three of the eight aircraft on the raid bombed the target.

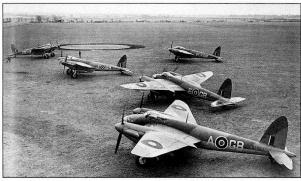

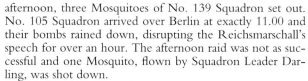

Eindhoven from low level. The Mosquitoes, which cruised at 270 mph (435 km/h), some 100 mph (161 km/h) faster than the other bombers, were forced to slow down to follow the other aircraft to the target. Timings went awry and some crews had to fly through flocks of birds, which penetrated some windscreens. One Mosquito was hit by flak at Den Helder and crashed into the sea, and nine Venturas and four Bostons failed to return; the Philips works was devastated, essential supplies destroyed and the rail network disrupted.

On 27 January 1943 Wing Commander Hughie Edwards, VC, DFC led nine Mosquitoes of No. 105 Squadron in a daring low-level strike on the Burmeister and Wain Diesel engine works at Copenhagen. Edwards found the target only at the last moment and was on the point of returning, but they hit the target and then broke for the sea and home. On 31 January Mosquitoes bombed Berlin for the first time. Both attacks were timed to disrupt speeches in the main broadcasting station in Berlin by Herman Göring in the morning and by Dr Joseph Goebbels in the afternoon. Three Mosquitoes from No. 105 Squadron, led by Squadron Leader R. W. Reynolds and Pilot Officer Ted Sismore, attacked in the morning; in the

afternoon, three Mosquitoes of No. 139 Squadron set out. No. 105 Squadron arrived over Berlin at exactly 11.00 and their bombs rained down, disrupting the Reichsmarschall's speech for over an hour. The afternoon raid was not as successful and one Mosquito, flown by Squadron Leader Darling, was shot down.

The final large-scale daylight raid by Nos 105 and 139 Squadrons was on 27 May 1943 when Wing Commander C. R. W. Reynolds, DSO, DFC and Flight Lieutenant Sismore led an attack on the Zeiss Optical Factory and the Schott Glass Works at Jena. Then they joined Fighter Command and later No. 8 Group (Pathfinder) for operations equipped with Oboe.

In June 1943, Nos 105 and 139 Squadrons were transferred to No. 8 Group (PFF) commanded by Air Commodore (later Air Vice-Marshal) Don Bennett, who was committed to using Mosquitoes for pathfinding, and target-marking with coloured TIs (target indicators), for the main force. Formed originally from No. 3 Group, using volunteer crews, the new organisation had begun as a specialist Pathfinder Force on 15 August 1942, and on 13 January 1943 it became No. 8 Group (PFF). To assist them, No. 8 Group Mosquito navigators used the Oboe high-level blind bombing aid. Oboe was to become the most accurate form of blind bombing used in World War II and, in practice, an error of only 30 seconds was achieved.

No. 105 became the second Oboe squadron, after No. 109 Squadron which moved from Wyton to join No. 105 at Marham in July, and Bennett used No. 139 at Wyton as a 'supporting squadron' for the Oboe squadrons, to go in with the markers. Mosquito bombers of the PFF Group had only one navigational aid – Gee. No. 139 was equipped with the Gee-H bombing aid and, later, with the radar navigational aid, H2S. When the Mosquito force in No. 8 Group was expanded in 1944, No. 139 Squadron led up to 150 of these aircraft in nightly attacks on Berlin.

No. 8 (PFF) Group tries Oboe

Bennett knew that the Mosquito would be ideal for marking duties. Oboe was first used on 20/21 December 1942 when six B.Mk IVs of No. 109 Squadron were despatched to bomb a power station at Lutterade in Holland. The first Oboe-aimed bombs were dropped by the CO, Squadron Leader H. E. 'Hal' Bufton, and his navigator, Flight Lieutenant E. L. Ifould, and two other crews, but the equipment in the three remaining aircraft malfunctioned and they dropped their bombs on targets of opportunity.

On 31 December 1942/1 January 1943, on a raid on Düsseldorf, sky-marking using Oboe was tried for the first time. Sky markers were parachute flares intended to mark a spot in the sky if it was cloudy. Two Mosquitoes of

de Havilland DH.98 Mosquito B.Mk IV Series II
No. 105 Sqn, No. 2 Gp Bomber Command RAF Marham December 1942

DZ360 is an aircraft from a batch of 400 aircraft ordered from de Havilland's Hatfield plant for delivery in late 1942. Of these, 250 were completed as B.Mk IVs like this aircraft, the bulk seeing service with bomber units in Nos 2 and 8 Groups, Bomber Command. However, a significant number of aircraft from this batch were modified, including 27 converted to PR.Mk IV standard, 20 reconfigured to carry a 4,000-lb bomb and at least 27 modified to carry the Highball weapon and operate from aircraft-carriers in the Pacific with No. 618 Sqn.

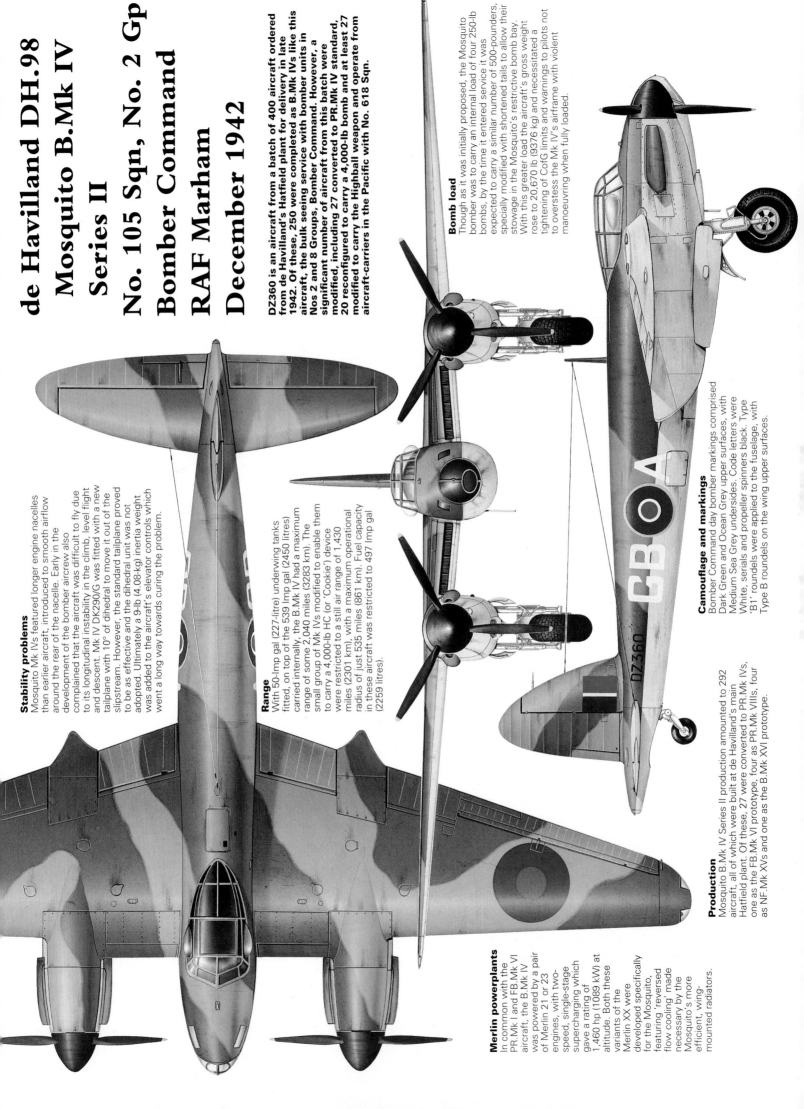

Stability problems

Mosquito Mk IVs featured longer engine nacelles than earlier aircraft, introduced to smooth airflow around the rear of the nacelle. Early in the development of the bomber aircrew also complained that the aircraft was difficult to fly due to its longitudinal instability in the climb, level flight and descent. Mk IV DK290/G was fitted with a new tailplane with 10° of dihedral to move it out of the slipstream. However, the standard tailplane proved to be as effective and the dihedral unit was not adopted. Ultimately a 9-lb (4.08-kg) inertia weight was added to the aircraft's elevator controls which went a long way towards curing the problem.

Range

With 50-Imp gal (227-litre) underwing tanks fitted, on top of the 539 Imp gal (2450 litres) carried internally, the B.Mk IV had a maximum range of some 2,040 miles (3283 km). The small group of Mk IVs modified to enable them to carry a 4,000-lb HC (or 'Cookie') device were restricted to a still air range of 1,430 miles (2301 km), with a maximum operational radius of just 535 miles (861 km). Fuel capacity in these aircraft was restricted to 497 Imp gal (2259 litres).

Merlin powerplants

In common with the PR.Mk I and FB.Mk VI aircraft, the B.Mk IV was powered by a pair of Merlin 21 or 23 engines, with two-speed, single-stage supercharging which gave a rating of 1,460 hp (1089 kW) at altitude. Both these variants of the Merlin XX were developed specifically for the Mosquito, featuring 'reversed flow cooling' made necessary by the Mosquito's more efficient, wing-mounted radiators.

Bomb load

Though as it was initially proposed, the Mosquito bomber was to carry an internal load of four 250-lb bombs, by the time it entered service it was expected to carry a similar number of 500-pounders, specially modified with shortened tails to allow their stowage in the Mosquito's restrictive bomb bay. With this greater load the aircraft's gross weight rose to 20,670 lb (9376 kg) and necessitated a tightening of CofG limits and warnings to pilots not to overstress the Mk IV's airframe with violent manoeuvring when fully loaded.

Camouflage and markings

Bomber Command day bomber markings comprised Dark Green and Ocean Grey upper surfaces, with Medium Sea Grey undersides. Code letters were White, serials and propeller spinners black. Type 'B1' roundels were applied to the fuselage, with Type B roundels on the wing upper surfaces.

Production

Mosquito B.Mk IV Series II production amounted to 292 aircraft, all of which were built at de Havilland's main Hatfield plant. Of these, 27 were converted to PR.Mk IVs, one as the FB.Mk VI prototype, four as PR.Mk VIIIs, four as NF.Mk XVs and one as the B.Mk XVI prototype.

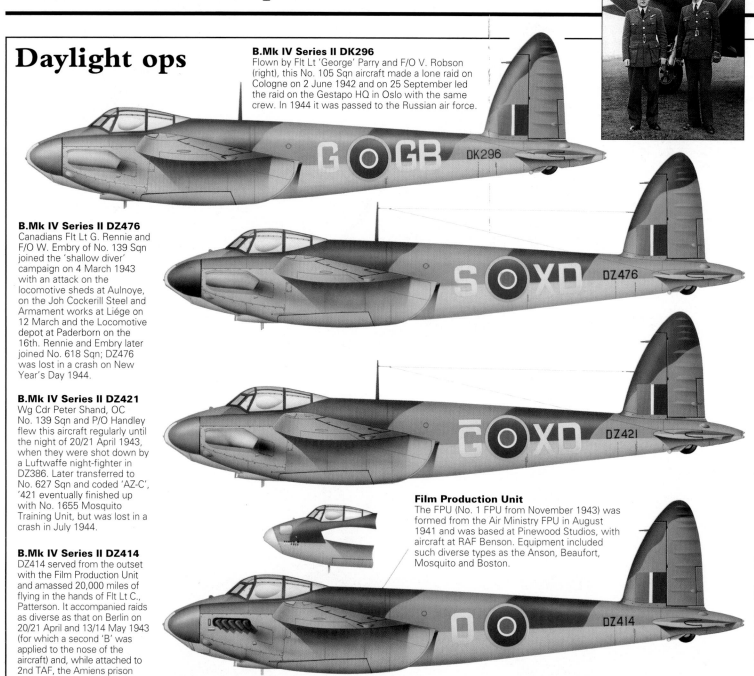

Daylight ops

B.Mk IV Series II DK296
Flown by Flt Lt 'George' Parry and F/O V. Robson (right), this No. 105 Sqn aircraft made a lone raid on Cologne on 2 June 1942 and on 25 September led the raid on the Gestapo HQ in Oslo with the same crew. In 1944 it was passed to the Russian air force.

B.Mk IV Series II DZ476
Canadians Flt Lt G. Rennie and F/O W. Embry of No. 139 Sqn joined the 'shallow diver' campaign on 4 March 1943 with an attack on the locomotive sheds at Aulnoye, on the Joh Cockerill Steel and Armament works at Liége on 12 March and the Locomotive depot at Paderborn on the 16th. Rennie and Embry later joined No. 618 Sqn; DZ476 was lost in a crash on New Year's Day 1944.

B.Mk IV Series II DZ421
Wg Cdr Peter Shand, OC No. 139 Sqn and P/O Handley flew this aircraft regularly until the night of 20/21 April 1943, when they were shot down by a Luftwaffe night-fighter in DZ386. Later transferred to No. 627 Sqn and coded 'AZ-C', '421 eventually finished up with No. 1655 Mosquito Training Unit, but was lost in a crash in July 1944.

B.Mk IV Series II DZ414
DZ414 served from the outset with the Film Production Unit and amassed 20,000 miles of flying in the hands of Flt Lt C., Patterson. It accompanied raids as diverse as that on Berlin on 20/21 April and 13/14 May 1943 (for which a second 'B' was applied to the nose of the aircraft) and, while attached to 2nd TAF, the Amiens prison

Film Production Unit
The FPU (No. 1 FPU from November 1943) was formed from the Air Ministry FPU in August 1941 and was based at Pinewood Studios, with aircraft at RAF Benson. Equipment included such diverse types as the Anson, Beaufort, Mosquito and Boston.

No. 109 Squadron provided the sky markers for eight Lancasters of the Pathfinder Force acting as bombers, but a gale had blown down the mast at one of the Oboe stations and only one Mosquito was able to bomb. Later that night, two of the three Oboe Mosquitoes despatched to the night-fighter control room at Florennes airfield, Belgium, dropped their HE cargoes from 28,000 ft (8534 m) through cloud. Results were unobserved. All Mosquitoes returned safely. (Three types of marking, using names selected by Bennett from the home towns of three of his staff, were later employed. 'Parramatta' in Australia gave its name to the blind ground marking technique, which used H2S only owing to bad visibility or broken cloud. 'Newhaven' was ground marking by visual methods when crews simply aimed at the TIs on the ground, and 'Wanganui' in New Zealand lent its name to pure sky-marking. The use of various plain colours with vivid starbursts of the same or a

No. 105 Sqn aircraft, as were engaged in the first daylight Mosquito operations, formate on a camera aircraft for official photographs. After comparative flights involving Mk IV DK290/G and a captured Fw 190A-3, it was concluded that the Mosquito had a slight edge in terms of speed. However, wing root fillets, ejector exhaust units and a high gloss finish were all tested as possible ways of further improving top speed.

Development airframe

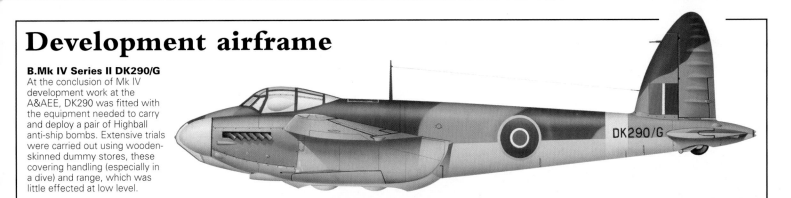

B.Mk IV Series II DK290/G
At the conclusion of Mk IV development work at the A&AEE, DK290 was fitted with the equipment needed to carry and deploy a pair of Highball anti-ship bombs. Extensive trials were carried out using wooden-skinned dummy stores, these covering handling (especially in a dive) and range, which was little effected at low level.

Highball

Amid top security, on 1 April 1943 No. 618 Sqn was formed at Skitten near Wick in Coastal Command for the sole purpose of using modified Mosquito B.Mk IVs to carry a pair of Dr Barnes Wallis' Highball bouncing bombs for use against German capital ships at sea. At 950 lb (431 kg), the Highball was exactly 10 per cent the weight of the 9,500-lb (4309-kg) Upkeep bomb used by No. 617 Sqn's Lancasters to breach the German dams on 16/17 May 1943. By 14 May 1943, the day before a planned No. 618 Sqn attack on *Tirpitz*, only six modified B.Mk IVs were operational, so the raid was abandoned. Late in 1944, 24 Mk IVs (of at least 29 converted) and three PR.Mk XVIs of No. 618 Sqn were shipped to Australia for Operation Oxtail – planned attacks on Japanese shipping in the Pacific. However, before No. 618 Sqn reached Australia, the US Navy had sunk the intended targets, and no Highball operations were flown. No. 618 Squadron finally departed Australia on VE-Day 1945.

different colour prevented the enemy from copying them.)

No. 109 Squadron joined No. 8 Group at Wyton on 1 June 1943. The only other operational Mosquito unit in No. 8 Group at that time was No. 1409 Met Flight, which was established at Oakington on 1 April using Mk Is and crews from No. 521 Squadron, Coastal Command at Bircham Newton. The met flights were known as Pampas and were usually made in daylight because they normally determined the type of weather likely to affect a night bombing raid. They also helped determine whether sky- or ground-TIs should be carried by the marking pathfinders. In July 1943 No. 109 Squadron provided five B.Mk IXs and crews for No. 105 to speed its conversion for Oboe duties. No. 105 Squadron flew its first Oboe operation on

Above: A modified 'Highball Mk IV' is seen during drop testing, probably on Loch Striven, during 1943. Apart from modifications to the bomb bay, the Highball aircraft shipped to Australia were re-engined with Merlin 25s, and fitted with a new windscreen, armour-plating and an arrestor hook.

Far left: G-AGFV is seen, possible at Leuchars, sometime after early 1943. Note the large registration on the upper surface of the wing.

BOAC's first Mossies

For high-speed courier flights between the UK (Leuchars in Scotland) and Stockholm from early 1943 until the end of the war in Europe, the British Overseas Airways Corporation (BOAC) operated a fleet of 10 Mosquitoes. Nicknamed 'ball-bearing' flights, after one of their most important Swedish cargoes, these high-speed dashes across the North Sea also conveyed diplomatic mail and personnel in a pressurised bomb bay. In all 520 round trips were flown between 3 February 1943 and 17 May 1945. Though nine of BOAC's aircraft were unarmed FB.Mk VIs, its first Mosquito was a modified PR.Mk IV.

'Ball-bearing' Mk IVs

B.Mk IV Series II DK301
Finished in overall pale grey, this aircraft was flown by Flt Lt D. A. G. Parry and F/O V. Robson on the first diplomatic flight to Sweden on 4 August 1942, conveying mail and cyphers for the British Embassy.

PR.Mk IV G-AGFV (DZ411)
DZ411 was one of two PR.Mk IVs (converted from B.Mk IV Series II bombers) which joined No. 540 Sqn In December 1942. On the 15th it became the first Mosquito to join BOAC for the Leuchars – Stockholm flights. Returned to the RAF on 6 January 1945, it was finally struck-off charge on 10 October 1946.

No. 8 Group (PFF)

No. 109 Sqn, which had been involved in early trials using the Oboe target marking/bombing aid fitted to its B.Mk IVs and was re-equipping with B.Mk IXs, joined the reformed No. 8 Group (Pathfinder Force) in mid-1943 as one of its first units. On 1 June Nos 105 and 139 Sqns joined the PFF, the latter as the second Oboe unit, followed by No. 627 Sqn in November. The force was further strengthened on 1 January 1944 with the formation of No. 692 Sqn, equipped with the first Mosquito Mk IVs able to carry 4,000-lb HC bombs. Eventually PFF Mosquito units received Mk IXs, XVIs and a few XXs, some equipped with Oboe, as well as defensive systems such as Boozer and Fishpond. As well as pathfinding duties, Nos 139, 627 and 692 Sqns formed the nucleus of the Light Night Striking Force (LNSF), as the PFF's Mosquito force was to be collectively known. No. 139 Sqn was designated the LNSF's marker squadron, its aircraft carrying the Gee-H and, later, the H2S navaid which was used by a Mosquito (Mk XVI) for the first time in February 1944. Other units to join the LNSF before VE-Day were No. 571 (which made the first use of the American Loran navaid in February 1945) and two Canadian squadrons – Nos 608 and 627.

A Mosquito B.Mk IX of the Light Night Striking Force is run-up prior to a sortie.

13 July when two B.Mk IVs attempted to mark Cologne. In September 1943 the squadron began precision bombing of pinpoint targets in western Germany.

Bennett was able expand his Mosquito force and in April 1943 it began 'nuisance' raiding. This does not adequately describe the activities, for the Mosquito could carry a

4,000-lb (1814-kg) 'Cookie' to Berlin, 500 lb (227 kg) more than the US four-engined 'Flying Fortress' (whose bomb bay was too small for a 'Cookie', and which needed an 11-man crew and a much larger load of ammunition for daylight operations). By the summer, 'nuisance raiding' had become so effective that the Mosquitoes in No. 8 Group were now

Mk IVs join the night offensive

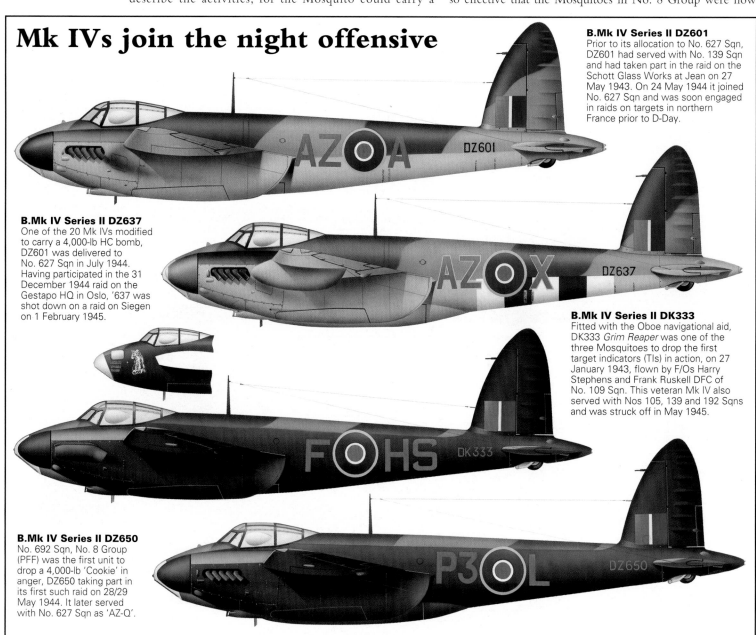

B.Mk IV Series II DZ601
Prior to its allocation to No. 627 Sqn, DZ601 had served with No. 139 Sqn and had taken part in the raid on the Schott Glass Works at Jean on 27 May 1943. On 24 May 1944 it joined No. 627 Sqn and was soon engaged in raids on targets in northern France prior to D-Day.

B.Mk IV Series II DZ637
One of the 20 Mk IVs modified to carry a 4,000-lb HC bomb, DZ601 was delivered to No. 627 Sqn in July 1944. Having participated in the 31 December 1944 raid on the Gestapo HQ in Oslo, '637 was shot down on a raid on Siegen on 1 February 1945.

B.Mk IV Series II DK333
Fitted with the Oboe navigational aid, DK333 *Grim Reaper* was one of the three Mosquitoes to drop the first target indicators (TIs) in action, on 27 January 1943, flown by F/Os Harry Stephens and Frank Ruskell DFC of No. 109 Sqn. This veteran Mk IV also served with Nos 105, 139 and 192 Sqns and was struck off in May 1945.

B.Mk IV Series II DZ650
No. 692 Sqn, No. 8 Group (PFF) was the first unit to drop a 4,000-lb 'Cookie' in anger, DZ650 taking part in its first such raid on 28/29 May 1944. It later served with No. 627 Sqn as 'AZ-Q'.

referred to as the Light Night Striking Force (or, as Bennett preferred, the Fast Night Striking Force).

One of their greatest achievements came during the nine days of Operation Gomorrah, the Battle of Hamburg, 24/25 July-2/3 August 1943, when the PFF and LNSF flew 472 sorties, with the loss of just 13 Mosquitoes. The first raid was led by H2S PFF aircraft and Mosquitoes using Parramatta ground marking, which enabled 728 bombers to rain down 2,284 tons (2321 tonnes) of HE and incendiaries in 50 minutes on the dockyards and city districts of Hamburg, creating a firestorm which rose to a height of 2 miles (3.2 km). RAF losses were light and mainly this was due to Window, which was being used for the first time. (Window was the codename for strips of black paper with aluminium foil stuck to one side, cut to a size (30 x 1.5 cm/11.8 x 0.6 in) equivalent to half the wavelength of the Würzburg ground radar and Lichtenstein AI radar. When dropped by aircraft in bundles of 1,000 at one-minute intervals, Window reflected the radar waves and 'snowed' the tubes.)

Spoof raiding

On 18/19 November 1943 spoof raiding was first tried by No. 139 Squadron and Window was one of the main ingredients used to give the impression of a large bomber force, when in fact it was a mere handful of Mosquitoes. Meanwhile, the true raid by heavies was heading elsewhere. The bundles of Window produced a 'clutter' of blips on German radar screens, prompting German fighter controllers to send up their night-fighters so that, when the heavies did arrive, the Nachtjagdgeschwaders were on the ground refuelling. On 26 November three Mosquitoes of No. 139 Squadron, flying ahead of the main force, scattered Window on the approaches to Berlin and returned to drop bombs. They also made feint attacks on other targets to

This view of B.Mk IX LR500 shows the lengthened engine nacelles necessitated by the use of two-stage Merlins. Note also the intake below the spinner, designed to feed the two-stage engine's intercooler radiator, and the pair of 50-Imp gal (227-litre) underwing tanks. LR500 was later fitted with Oboe and joined No. 105 Sqn.

Mk IX and XVI bombers

Though based on the PR.Mk IX, the first bomber version (LR495) actually flew a month earlier than the former, on 24 March 1943. After company trials it was flown to A&AEE and tested at a maximum all-up weight of 23,000 lb (10432 kg), this including a 500-lb (227-kg) bomb under each wing. The first B.Mk IXs reached No. 109 Sqn in April, Nos 105 and 139 Sqns re-equipping in July and September, respectively. The final Mosquito bomber development of the war years was the B.Mk XVI, like the PR variant of the same mark, a pressurised version of the Mk IX. Mk IV DZ540 was rebuilt as the first B.Mk XVI and flew in July. All Mk XVIs (apart from the first 12 completed) were able to carry a 4,000-lb 'Cookie', deliveries beginning in December to No. 109 Sqn. The first 'Cookie' aircraft (ML937) flew on 1 January 1944 and the first operational use of the variant came on 5/6 March, when No. 692 Sqn took part in a raid on Duisburg.

distract enemy night fighters up to 50 miles (80 km) away from the main stream during an attack.

In November a new Mosquito squadron, No. 627, was formed at Oakington, near Cambridge, from 'C' Flight No. 139 Squadron. During the winter of 1943-44, Bomber Command began its night offensive against Berlin. Sixteen major attacks were mounted but Berlin was not destroyed. By early 1944 suitably modified B.Mk IVs were capable of carrying a 4,000-lb HC, although it was a tight squeeze in the bomb bay. To accommodate this large piece of ordnance, the bomb bay had been strengthened and the bomb doors redesigned. No. 692, which became the fourth Mosquito squadron in No. 8 Group when it formed at Gravely on 1 January, was given the dubious honour of being the first Mosquito squadron to drop one of the 'Cookies', or 'Dangerous Dustbin' as it was known

Above left: B.Mk IV DK594 was the first Mosquito modified to carry a 4,000-lb HC bomb, in November 1943, the conversion taking about seven weeks. The aircraft was tested at A&AEE at an all-up weight of some 25,200 lb (11430 kg) and was eventually issued to No. 627 Sqn in February 1945 and coded 'AZ-X'.

Above: B.Mk IV DZ650 of No. 692 Sqn, seen here at the squadron's Graveley base, was one of 20 Mk IVs modified to carry a 4,000 pounder, more often known by its 'Cookie' nickname. Another unofficial name for the device was 'Dangerous Dustbin'.

Below: The first B.Mk IX (LR495) demonstrates the variant's ability to carry underwing bombs. A handful of Mk IXs were also converted to carry a 'Cookie'.

These well-known Charles E. Brown images of B.Mk XVI ML963 were captured over Hatfield on 30 September 1945. Early B.Mk XVIs were powered by a Merlin 72/73 combination, though most had the later Merlin 76/77 pairing.

'Happy Xmas Adolf' reads the inscription on a 'Cookie' about to be wheeled under and hoisted aboard Mk XVI MM199 'Q-Queenie' of No. 128 Sqn at Wyton in late 1944.

radome under the rear fuselage. Targets had to be carefully selected using H2S and city areas on coastlines or estuaries were picked because of the verifiable distinction between water and land on radar screens. From 1944, H2S-equipped B.Mk IXs of No. 139 Squadron frequently led and marked for other Mosquitoes, and Oboe Mk II-equipped B.Mk IXs of Nos 109 and 105 Squadrons spearheaded the main force bombing raids.

In the 12 months from January to December 1944, apart from No. 692 Squadron already mentioned, five more Mosquito squadrons joined No. 8 Group. On 7 April No. 571 Squadron was formed at Downham Market, a shortage of Mosquitoes meaning that it had to operate at half-strength for a time. On the night of 13/14 April two crews from No. 571, and six from No. 692, attacked Berlin for the first time carrying two 50-Imp gal (227-litre) drop tanks and a 4,000-lb bomb. On 1 August No. 608 Squadron formed in 8 Group at Downham Market, and on 15 September No. 128 Squadron at Wyton joined the LNSF. On 25 October, No. 142 Squadron reformed at Gransden Lodge and that same night flew its first operation, when its only two B.Mk 25s were despatched to Cologne.

Eleventh and final squadron formed

On 18 December No. 162 Squadron reformed at Bourn with B.Mk 25s and soon accompanied No. 139 Squadron on target-marking duties. No. 163 Squadron, the 11th and final Mosquito squadron in No. 8 Group, reformed at Wyton on 25 January 1945, also on B.Mk 25s, under the command of Wing Commander (later Air Marshal) Ivor Broom, DFC and, quite remarkably, flew its first LNSF operation on the night of 28/29 January when four B.Mk 25s dropped Window at Mainz ahead of the PFF force (The other eight

(because of its shape), over Germany. DZ647 released one during a raid on Düsseldorf on 23/24 February. 'Cookies' continued to be carried in modified B.Mk IVs until the B.Mk XVI high-altitude Mosquito, which had first flown in prototype form in November 1943, became operational in the spring.

The B.Mk XVI, with its bulged bomb bay and more powerful two-stage 1,680-hp (1253-kW) Merlin 72/73 or two 1,710-hp (1275-kW) 76/77 engines giving a top speed of 419 mph (674 km/h) at 28,500 ft (8687 m), was a much more acceptable 'Cookie carrier'. No. 692 Squadron first used the B.Mk XVI operationally on 5/6 March, on a raid on Duisburg.

Earlier, on 1/2 February 1944, No. 139 Squadron, which had pioneered the use of Canadian-built Mosquitoes and was now operating a mix of B.Mks IV, IX, XVI and XX, used H2S for the first time, marking the target for a raid on Berlin. H2S provided a map-like image on a cathode ray tube (radar scope screen) which in the Mosquito was connected to a revolving scanner antenna housed in a

Above: The moment of release is captured here as Mosquito B.Mk XVI MM220 drops a 'Cookie'. MM220 served with Nos 692 and 128 Sqns in No. 8 Group.

Bomber Command re-equips

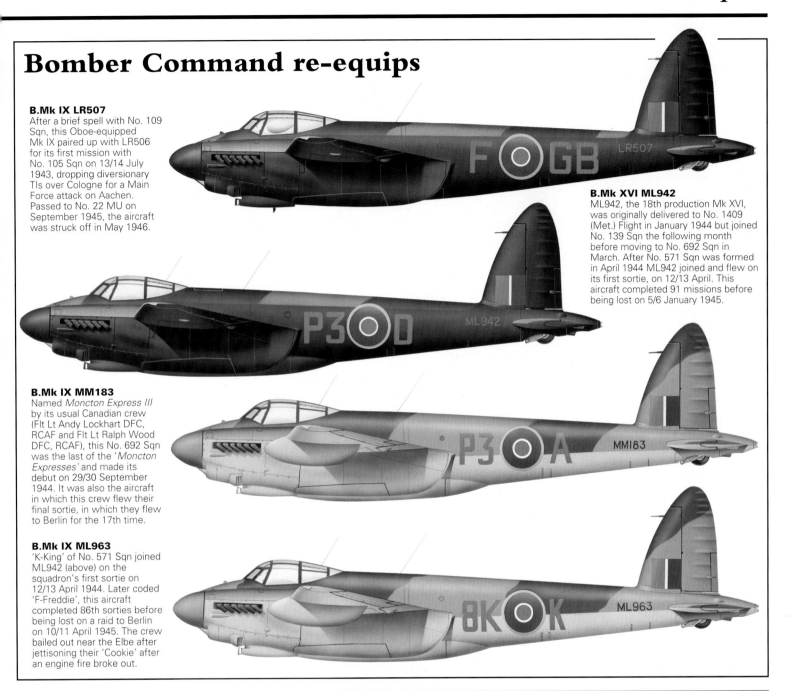

B.Mk IX LR507
After a brief spell with No. 109 Sqn, this Oboe-equipped Mk IX paired up with LR506 for its first mission with No. 105 Sqn on 13/14 July 1943, dropping diversionary TIs over Cologne for a Main Force attack on Aachen. Passed to No. 22 MU on September 1945, the aircraft was struck off in May 1946.

B.Mk XVI ML942
ML942, the 18th production Mk XVI, was originally delivered to No. 1409 (Met.) Flight in January 1944 but joined No. 139 Sqn the following month before moving to No. 692 Sqn in March. After No. 571 Sqn was formed in April 1944 ML942 joined and flew on its first sortie, on 12/13 April. This aircraft completed 91 missions before being lost on 5/6 January 1945.

B.Mk IX MM183
Named *Moncton Express III* by its usual Canadian crew (Flt Lt Andy Lockhart DFC, RCAF and Flt Lt Ralph Wood DFC, RCAF), this No. 692 Sqn was the last of the 'Moncton Expresses' and made its debut on 29/30 September 1944. It was also the aircraft in which this crew flew their final sortie, in which they flew to Berlin for the 17th time.

B.Mk IX ML963
'K-King' of No. 571 Sqn joined ML942 (above) on the squadron's first sortie on 12/13 April 1944. Later coded 'F-Freddie', this aircraft completed 86th sorties before being lost on a raid to Berlin on 10/11 April 1945. The crew bailed out near the Elbe after jettisoning their 'Cookie' after an engine fire broke out.

No. 1409 (Met.) Flight

Weather reconnaissance was one of the unsung, but nonetheless vitally important, tasks the Mosquito was asked to perform. On 1 April 1943, the Mosquito Flight of No. 521 Sqn (which had operated modified Mosquito B.Mk IVs in the WR role since August 1942) was renamed No. 1409 Meteorological Flight and joined No. 8 Group (PFF), Bomber Command. Flying Pampa sorties over Europe for both the RAF and USAAF, No. 1409 Flight operated Mosquito Mk IV, VI and IX aircraft and had trialled (unsuccessfully) a Mk XV before re-equipping with Mk XVIs in early 1944.

squadrons in No. 8 Group were equipped with the Avro Lancaster, two returning to No. 5 Group in April 1944.) In the spring of 1944, No. 627 Squadron moved to Lincolnshire to join No. 617 Squadron at Woodhall Spa in specialised marking operations for No. 5 Group.

No. 5 Group really made its presence felt in three raids, against Brunswick on 22/23 April, Munich two nights later, and Schweinfurt on 26/27 April. After these attacks the Group turned exclusively to support of the bombing campaign against interdiction targets for Operation Overlord. Considerable damage was done to Brunswick

ML897 'D-Dorothy' was from a batch of B.Mk IXs completed at Hatfield in late 1943 and served with Nos 105 and 109 Sqns before joining No. 1409 Flight at Wyton.

Right: LAC Bennet paints the 141st mission symbol on the nose of ML897. The aircraft eventually completed 161 sorties.

ML926/G, the first production B.Mk XVI, was confined to test work with the Telecommunications Flying Unit and A&AEE and was finally struck off in January 1947. Among the equipment tested in this aircraft were Oboe and H2S. The latter was housed in a large radome under the forward fuselage. Operational aircraft so-equipped had a smaller radome under the rear fuselage; those with Oboe fitted often had their nose glazing painted-out, as on this aircraft.

Below: Many PFF Mosquitoes completed over 50 sorties and a handful returned from over 100 raids. B.Mk IX LR503 completed 213 operational sorties and could claim to be the most successful bomber of them all. As 'GB-F' of No. 105 Sqn, the aircraft is seen here after its 203rd mission. Though LR503 survived the war, it was destroyed at Calgary on 10 May 1945, during a goodwill tour of Canada. Sadly its crew – Flt Lt Maurice Briggs DSO, DFC, DFM and F/O John Baker DFC and Bar, themselves veterans of 107 sorties – were killed.

RAAF and Flight Lieutenant L. C. E. De Vigne dropped their marker with such a degree of accuracy that it fell into the water and was extinguished. Only 31 Lancasters bombed before the Master Bomber called for the raid to be abandoned. Better luck was had by the 48 Mosquitoes despatched to Gelsenkirchen on a spoof raid to draw German night-fighters away from the Mittleland attack and a No. 3 Group raid on Koblenz. The Gelsenkirchen raid began as planned, five minutes ahead of the two other attacks, at 19.25. The city was still burning as a result of that afternoon's raid by 738 RAF heavies. From their altitude of 25,000 ft (7620 m) the Mosquitoes added their red and green TIs, and HE, to the fires. A few searchlights and only very light flak greeted the crews over the devastated city.

Efforts to relieve the pressure on the Bulge continued. On a foggy, very cold 27 December, 200 Lancasters and 11 Mosquitoes attacked railway marshalling yards at Rheydt. On New Year's Day 1945, with the Battle of the Bulge still raging in the Ardennes, No. 8 Group's Mosquitoes were asked to fly one of the most remarkable daylight operations of the war. Bomber Command had to cut the railway supply lines through the Eifel region between the Rhine and the Ardennes. While the heavies bombed marshalling yards near Koblenz and Cologne, precision attacks on 14 railway tunnels in the region were carried out by 17 Mosquitoes each carrying a 4,000-lb delayed-action bomb, which they would use to skip-bomb the mouths of the tunnels from 100-200 ft (30-60 m). The only loss was PF411, a No. 128 Squadron B.Mk XVI, which crashed on take-off, killing the crew. Four crews in No. 128 Squadron who bombed achieved mixed results. Six out of seven B.Mk XVIs of No. 692 Squadron bombed tunnels near Mayen, losing PF414 to light flak, while five crews of No. 571 Squadron were more successful. One bomb, dropped by B.Mk XVI ML963 'K-King', crewed by Flight Lieutenant Norman J. Griffiths and Flying Officer W. R. Ball, totally destroyed a tunnel at Bitburg.

Daylight target marking

With the war in Europe reaching a conclusion, the Mosquitoes were repeatedly called upon to mark for the bombers in daylight. One of the most dramatic marking operations of the war occurred on 14 March when a Mosquito of No. 5 Group and eight Oboe Mosquitoes of Nos 105 and 109 Squadrons set out to mark for No. 5 Group Lancasters in attacks on the Bielefeld and Arnsburg viaducts. Although the four Mosquitoes attempting to mark the Arnsburg viaduct for No. 9 Squadron failed in the attempt (with no damage to the viaduct), and three of the Oboe Mosquitoes were unable to mark the Bielefeld viaduct for No. 617 Squadron, B.Mk XVI MM191, flown by Flying Officer G. W. Edwards of No. 105 Squadron, succeeded in getting his markers on target, and more than 100 yd (91 m) of the Bielefeld viaduct collapsed under the

and Munich, and in the case of Munich, 90 per cent of the bombs fell in the right place, doing more damage in one night than had been achieved by Bomber Command and the 8th Air Force in the preceding four years.

The No. 8 Group weather report by Pilot Officers Joe Patient and Norry Gilroy, a No. 1409 Met Flight crew, delayed the Normandy invasion by one day, and D-Day went ahead on 6 June. On the night of 5/6 October six Mosquitoes from No. 692 Squadron, five carrying a 1,000-lb (453-kg) mine and one a 1,500-lb (680-kg) mine, together with four of No. 571 Squadron, mined the Kiel Canal for a second time. Berlin was the most frequent target for the LNSF. The Mosquitoes flew there so often (170 times, 36 on consecutive nights) that the raids were called the 'milk run' or, alternatively, the 'Berlin Express', and the different routes there and back were known as platforms one, two and three.

On 6/7 November, Bomber Command despatched 235 Lancasters to attack the Mittelland Canal at Gravenhorst, the marking being carried out by seven Mosquitoes of No. 627 Squadron. The Mosquitoes eventually found the canal after great difficulty, whereupon Squadron Leader F. W. Boyle,

Above: H2S radar (seen here fitted to a Central Bomber Establishment B.Mk 35 post-war) was fitted to a limited number of No. 8 Group B.Mk XVIs from early 1944.

Bomber Command Mk 25s

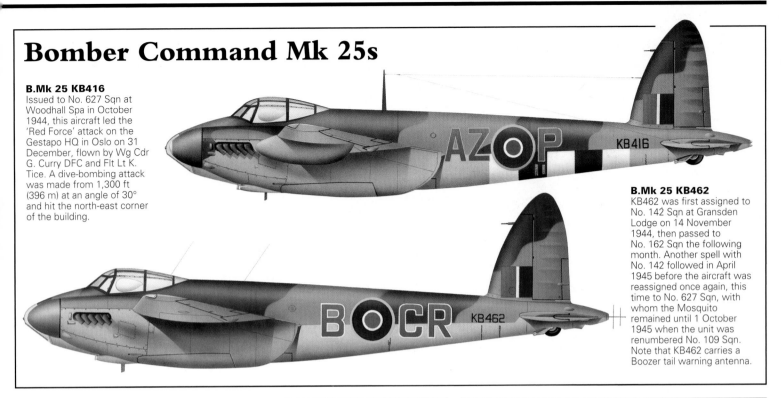

B.Mk 25 KB416
Issued to No. 627 Sqn at Woodhall Spa in October 1944, this aircraft led the 'Red Force' attack on the Gestapo HQ in Oslo on 31 December, flown by Wg Cdr G. Curry DFC and Flt Lt K. Tice. A dive-bombing attack was made from 1,300 ft (396 m) at an angle of 30° and hit the north-east corner of the building.

B.Mk 25 KB462
KB462 was first assigned to No. 142 Sqn at Gransden Lodge on 14 November 1944, then passed to No. 162 Sqn the following month. Another spell with No. 142 followed in April 1945 before the aircraft was reassigned once again, this time to No. 627 Sqn, with whom the Mosquito remained until 1 October 1945 when the unit was renumbered No. 109 Sqn. Note that KB462 carries a Boozer tail warning antenna.

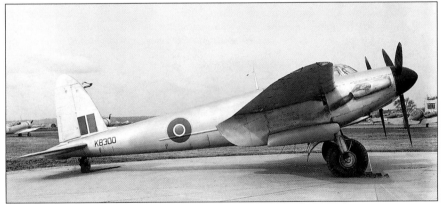

Canadian-built bombers

After the first 25 B.Mk VIIs had been completed, Mosquitoes built by de Havilland of Canada Ltd at Downsview, Ontario were allocated mark numbers from 20 upwards, starting with B.Mk XX. A batch of 245 Mk XXs followed, these incorporating more locally-sourced components and, from the ninth example, Merlin 33 engines and provision for drop tanks. Deliveries to the RAF began in late 1943, No. 139 Sqn receiving its first examples in November and Nos 627, 608, 128 and 142 Sqns following suit shortly afterwards. The USAAF received 34 for conversion by Bell Aircraft to F-8 photo-reconnaissance aircraft. Next came a batch of 400 B.Mk 25s (a proposed high-altitude B.Mk XXIII with Packard Merlin 69s was not built), 343 of which were delivered to the RAF. Powered by Packard Merlin 225s (equivalent to the Rolls-built Merlin 25), Mk 25s began entering RAF service in October 1944; five were fitted with bulged 'Cookie'-type bomb bay doors for use by No. 627 Sqn.

Above left: KB300 was the first of 25 single-stage Packard Merlin 31-engined B.Mk VIIs built in Canada, taking to the air for the first time on 24 September 1942. Most Mk VIIs were retained in Canada and used by the RCAF, but six were transferred to the USAAF and designated F-8 alongside 34 B.Mk XXs.

Above: B.Mk XX New Glasgow, Nova Scotia, Canada (KB162) was one of the first two Canadian-built Mosquitoes delivered to the RAF, arriving at Hatfield on 12 August 1943.

explosions. (Some 28 of the 32 Lancasters despatched carried Tallboy bombs, and one from No. 617 Squadron dropped the first 22,000-lb/9979-kg Grand Slam bomb.)

The biggest No. 8 Group Mosquito operation to Berlin took place on 21/22 March when 142 Mosquitoes carried out two attacks, in which only one aircraft was lost. No. 8 Group made its last daylight raid on 6 March when 48 Mosquitoes led by Oboe leaders in No. 109 Squadron bombed Wesel. The last attack on Berlin by Mosquitoes took place on the night of 20/21 April when 76 aircraft carried out six separate raids on the long-suffering capital.

On 25/26 April 12 Mosquitoes dropped leaflets over PoW camps in Germany. On 29 April flights began to deliver food to the starving Dutch population in German-occupied Holland. The operation, code-named Manna, took place using RAF and USAAF heavy bombers, their bomb bays filled with provisions instead of bombs, the food dropping areas being marked by the Oboe Mosquitoes. Meanwhile, it was feared that the enemy might stage a last stand in Norway when ships laden with troops began assembling at Kiel. Therefore, on the night of 2/3 May three final raids were organised by 142 Mosquitoes from

The Merlin 225s fitted to the B.Mk 25 drove paddle-bladed propellers of the type fitted to the Mk XVIs built in England. Details of KB669's service are unknown, other than that it was struck off RAF charge in 1947.

Tropical tribulations

The first aircraft delivered to the region had suffered at the hands of the humid tropical conditions and insects, both of which attacked the casein glue used to bond their wooden structures. The first Mosquitoes (NF.Mk IIs) arrived in the Far East in February 1943. These four aircraft were followed by a further four, two of which had been assembled using a formaldehyde glue. As the only aircraft in the Far East suitable for long-range PR duties (with No. 681 Sqn), the Mk IIs were converted for the role as a stop-gap until the first PR.Mk IXs arrived in October 1943. These aircraft joined No. 681 Sqn at first, though by November Mosquito PR operations had been handed exclusively to No. 684 Sqn in Burma. Having moved to India, the squadron received Mk XVIs in early 1944 and before VJ-Day had a handful of Mk 34s on strength.

On 22 March 1944 PR.Mk XVI NS688/'Q' made the first sortie by an RAF aircraft over Singapore since the fall of Malaya to the Japanese. Crewed by Flt Lt Robin Sinclair and F/O Reggie Stocks of No. 684 Sqn, the flight from Dum Dum, India to the Malay Peninsula lasted eight hours 45 minutes and covered 2,490 miles (4007 km) – a record for the distance covered. Here the aircraft is seen shortly after its arrival in India in early 1944, bearing the 'SNAKE' appellation that indicated that the aircraft was en route to the Far East and should not be purloined for use elsewhere (i.e. in the Middle East). The significance of the fuselage striping, too early to be AEAF markings, is unknown.

Above right: This photograph, dated 29 March 1945, shows part of the notorious Siam-Burma-Singapore railway – a vital Japanese supply route and typical of the targets photographed by the FEAF's PR Mosquitoes.

eight squadrons in No. 8 Group and 37 Mosquitoes from No. 100 (Bomber Support) Group. In the first raid, a record 126 aircraft from No. 100 Group, including 37 Mosquitoes led by 16 Oboe Mosquitoes, attacked airfields in the Kiel area with napalm and incendiaries. In the second and third attacks, one hour apart, 126 Mosquitoes of No. 8 Group bombed through thick cloud using H2S and Oboe. One Mosquito in No. 100 Group, and two Halifaxes which collided, were lost this night.

In the period January to May 1945, LNSF Mosquitoes had flown almost 4,000 sorties. Altogether, 8 Group's Mosquito squadrons flew 28,215 sorties, yet they had the lowest losses in Bomber Command: just 108 (about one per 2,800 sorties), while 88 more were written off on their return because of battle damage. It was an incredible achievement, even more remarkable when one considers

that well over two-thirds of operations were flown on nights when the heavies were not operating.

SEAC PR Mosquitoes

Among the many problems facing South East Asia Command (SEAC) in India in 1943 was the aerial reconnaissance of Burma and Malaya from its far-flung bases in Ceylon and India. Only the camera-fitted B-25C Mitchells of No. 681 Squadron based at Dum Dum, Calcutta, possessed the range and speed for long-range photo-reconnaissance over the Bay of Bengal and the Rangoon area. At the beginning of April 1943, three Mosquito IIs and three FB.Mk VIs were allotted to No. 27 Squadron at Agartala – three for performance tests and familiarisation, three to be used for weathering trials during the coming rainy season – under the supervision of Mr F. G. Myers, de Havilland's technical representative in India. Late in the month, however, it was decided that the Mosquitoes should supplement the squadron's Beaufighters for intruder operations.

The first Mosquito operation over Burma was a reconnaissance on 14 May. It is reported that Major Hereward de Havilland, visiting No. 27 Squadron, was horrified to find that the Mk IIs were put to operational use and attempted to have them grounded because he considered that the caesin glue with which they were bonded was unlikely to withstand insect attack and the tropical weather. (The Mk VIs, still awaited, were supposedly bonded with 'waterproof formaldehyde adhesive. No. 27 Squadron used the Mk IIs again on only one occasion, and one crashed and another was damaged by ground fire on 5 June.)

Meanwhile, the aircraft situation in No. 681 Squadron at

Above: Mingaladon, Burma was one of No. 684 Sqn's forward bases and is seen here after the arrival of Mosquito PR.Mk 34s in June 1945.

LACs Perry and Smith (right) load a long focus camera into a No. 684 Sqn Mosquito, while LACs Harris and Fisher (far right) check the equipment in another of the unit's machines.

No. 684 Sqn's PR machines

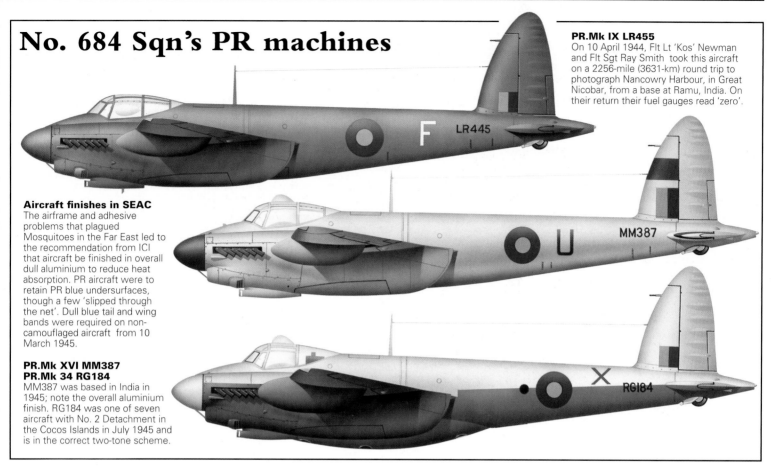

PR.Mk IX LR455
On 10 April 1944, Flt Lt 'Kos' Newman and Flt Sgt Ray Smith took this aircraft on a 2256-mile (3631-km) round trip to photograph Nancowry Harbour, in Great Nicobar, from a base at Ramu, India. On their return their fuel gauges read 'zero'.

Aircraft finishes in SEAC
The airframe and adhesive problems that plagued Mosquitoes in the Far East led to the recommendation from ICI that aircraft be finished in overall dull aluminium to reduce heat absorption. PR aircraft were to retain PR blue undersurfaces, though a few 'slipped through the net'. Dull blue tail and wing bands were required on non-camouflaged aircraft from 10 March 1945.

PR.Mk XVI MM387
PR.Mk 34 RG184
MM387 was based in India in 1945; note the overall aluminium finish. RG184 was one of seven aircraft with No. 2 Detachment in the Cocos Islands in July 1945 and is in the correct two-tone scheme.

Dum Dum was causing great concern. Two serviceable Mitchells had been in use for over 12 months, and there were no aircraft in the command, other than the Mosquito Mk IIs, with equivalent operational range and high speed. After some delay, while Air Ministry approval was sought for their conversion to PR aircraft at No. 1 CMU, Kanchrapara, two Mosquitoes and their flight crews were transferred in August to the twin-engined Flight of No. 681 Squadron, followed by the three newly arrived Mk VIs.

On 23 August Flying Officer Dupee, DFM covered the Mandalay Shewbo-yeu-Monywa-Wuntho area, and on the next day Flight Lieutenant Picknett reconnoitred Akyab Island. During September No. 681 Squadron flew eight PR sorties over vast areas of Burma, and on occasion a Mosquito Mk VI, which had arrived for trials in August, was employed. One of the Mosquitoes became a victim to enemy action but, after a force-landing, it was repaired and returned to Calcutta after three weeks. The feared deterioration of the adhesive did not happen despite the aircraft being continually exposed to high temperature and humidity, so approval was given for the delivery of more Mosquitoes to India.

First Mk IXs in India

In September five PR.Mk IX Mosquitoes arrived in-theatre. In October No. 47 Squadron, which was equipped with the Beaufighter Mk X at Yelahanka, India, began receiving a few Mosquito FB.Mk VIs. On 21 October No. 681 Squadron flew the first of 33 PR sorties over Burma as far as Rangoon and the Akyab trail, before its Mosquitoes were transferred to No. 684 Squadron, which had been formed on 29 September from the twin-engined Flight of No. 681 Squadron, with two Mosquito Mk IIs, three Mosquito Mk VIs and four B-25C Mitchells. The first PR.Mk IX was added to its strength on 18 October and the second followed five days later. On 21 October Flight Lieutenant F. B. McCulloch and Sergeant T. S. Vigers flew a reconnaissance of Rangoon and Magwe. Three days later, McCulloch and Flight Lieutenant Henry

Reeves made a reconnaissance of the Andaman Islands to photograph Japanese shipping and flying-boat activity. Three Nakajima Ki-43 'Oscars' tried to intercept the high-flying Mosquito, but none could reach it. That same day Flight Sergeant Johnson with Sergeant Willis in a Mosquito Mk II returned safely with photos of Rangoon despite another attempted interception, by two fighters, and AA fire at 27,000 ft (8230 m).

The first Mosquito loss on operations from India

Left: No. 681 Sqn, based at Dum Dum, India briefly flew PR.Mk IV and Mk IX aircraft between September and December 1943 before handing them over to No. 684 Sqn. In February 1944, the first Mk XVIs arrived, including this aircraft (NS787/'M'), probably photographed at Dum Dum.

Below: By positioning a detachment of new PR.Mk 34s at a recently completed airstrip on Cocos Island, No. 684 Sqn was able to photograph the Malay capital Kuala Lumpur on several occasions before before VJ-Day.

Aussie PR.Mk 40/41s

de Havilland Pty Ltd began producing Mosquitoes in 1943, using jigs shipped from the UK and Canada and with F.Mk II DD664 as a pattern aircraft. The first FB.Mk 40 (based on the FB.Mk VI) flew on 23 July 1943 and was followed by another 211 examples, the first 100 of which (including the prototype) were powered by Packard Merlin 31s; the remainder had Merlin 33s fitted. Six of these fighter-bombers were completed as PR.Mk 40s, with two cameras in the bomb bay, two oblique cameras in the rear fuselage and a single vertical camera replacing the nose-mounted machine-guns. These became operational with No. 1 PRU (RAAF) and No. 87 Sqn in May 1944, the latter based at Coomalee Creek, Northern Territory for operations over the northwest Pacific, including the photographing of Japanese-held territories and shipping. A batch of PR.Mk XVIs arrived in March 1945 and immediately entered service with No. 87 Sqn in place of the Mk 40s and as a stop-gap until the PR.Mk 41 became available in 1947. Another Mk 40 derivative, the 28 Mk 41s were converted in 1947/48 and serve alongside the Mk XVIs until 1953.

PR.Mk XVI A52-600 is seen at Morotai, off western New Guinea, on 4 August 1945, staging through to Labuan Island on detachment from Coomalee Creek.

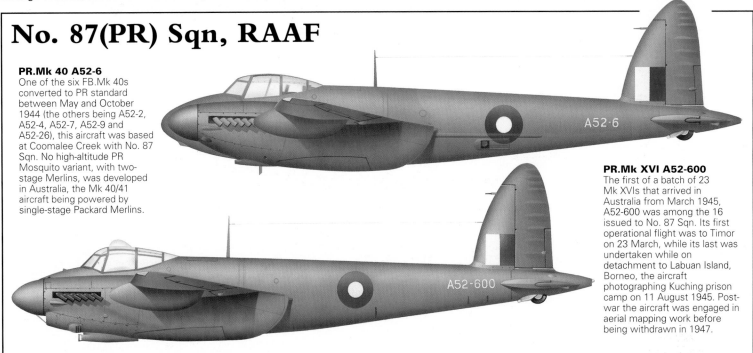

No. 87(PR) Sqn, RAAF

PR.Mk 40 A52-6
One of the six FB.Mk 40s converted to PR standard between May and October 1944 (the others being A52-2, A52-4, A52-7, A52-9 and A52-26), this aircraft was based at Coomalee Creek with No. 87 Sqn. No high-altitude PR Mosquito variant, with two-stage Merlins, was developed in Australia, the Mk 40/41 aircraft being powered by single-stage Packard Merlins.

PR.Mk XVI A52-600
The first of a batch of 23 Mk XVIs that arrived in Australia from March 1945, A52-600 was among the 16 issued to No. 87 Sqn. Its first operational flight was to Timor on 23 March, while its last was undertaken while on detachment to Labuan Island, Borneo, the aircraft photographing Kuching prison camp on 11 August 1945. Postwar the aircraft was engaged in aerial mapping work before being withdrawn in 1947.

occurred on 2 November when Flying Officers Fielding and Turton failed to return from a photo-reconnaissance of the Rangoon area. On 9 December the six remaining Mosquitoes and four B-25Cs of No. 684 Squadron moved to Comilla in East Bengal, where they formed part of No. 171 Wing. Their stay was brief, just one month, and their debut was marred by the loss of two crews. On 10 December a Mosquito Mk II flown by Sergeants Boot and Wilkins was shot down over Rangoon. On 23 December a Mk VI, flown by Flying Officer Orr and Sergeant Johnson, suffered a fatal crash after structural failure. Operations involved distances of over 1,000 miles (1610 km) from base and an eight-hour duration was not uncommon. On 15 December Squadron Leader Basil Jones, the CO, and Flying Officer R. C. Hawson covered Bangkok for the first time, a feat which earned both men the DFC.

Meanwhile, in January 1944, the Air Ministry decided to equip 22 bomber and strike squadrons with Mosquito Mk VI aircraft to replace the Vultee Vengeance and some Beaufighters. De Havilland was to produce replacement airframe components at Karachi. In February No. 684 Squadron, now back at Dum Dum, received nine pressurised PR.Mk XVIs, enabling higher altitudes to be flown. The remaining Mk VIs were retired but were a valuable source of spares, parts being in very short supply. At the beginning of the month No. 684 Squadron had begun a photographic survey of Burma, and reconnaissance flights to islands in the Indian Ocean continued. On 7 February Wing Commander W. B. Murray, who had taken over command in December, with Flying Officer Hawson tussled with a 'Hamp' over Port Blair. Later the same day, another Mosquito was intercepted ove Bangkok and had to abort.

High-altitude Mk 32

Answering the threat posed by enemy fighters, the Mk 32 was lightened and fitted with extended wingtips (giving a span of 59 ft 2 in (18 m) compared to the 54 ft 2 in (16.5 m) of the Mk XVI) for regular operations above 40,000 ft (12192 m). A derivative of the Mk XVI, the Mk 32 featured a pressurised cabin and two-stage Merlins. Of the five examples completed NS589, the prototype (left), was employed by No. 540 Sqn for trials, others serving with this unit and No. 544 Sqn during the latter stages of the war in Europe.

Long-range Mk 34/34A

A development of the PR.Mk XVI, the Mk 34 was intended for long-range work, especially in the Far East. Consideration had been given to the fitting of Mk XVIs with in-flight refuelling equipment, but this was rejected in favour of the Mk 34, which featured new Merlin 113/114 engines with improved altitude performance and an SU fuel-injection pump. To provide the extra range tanks were fitted in the aircraft's enlarged bomb bay which, though it resembled that of a B.Mk XVI, was slightly larger. Underwing 200-Imp gal (909-litre) tanks could also be used, though these imparted a weight and drag penalty. In all 181 were built, the variant entering RAF service shortly before VE-Day and seeing limited use in the Far East. The Mk 34A entered service in the early 1950s and was a conversion of the Mk 34 with minor equipment and engine modifications.

In March No. 684 Squadron made regular flights to the Andamans and reconnoitred the Japanese railway system in Burma. On 22 March Flight Lieutenant Robin Sinclair and Flying Officer Reggie Stocks of No. 684 Squadron made the first sortie by an RAF aircraft over Malaya since the fall of Singapore, when they reconnoitred the Bangkok-Singapore railway line. Five days later, Flight Lieutenant 'Kos' Newman, RNZAF and Flight Sergeant Ron Smith flew a 1,860-mile (2993-km) trip to photograph a stretch of the Burma railway and airfields at Bangkok and Hua Hin. On 31 March Flying Officers Dupee, DFM and McDonnell brought back the first photos of Car Nicobar Island.

In April No. 684 Squadron continued flying long-range flights, with sorties to as far afield as Khun Khaen in central Siam and Vientiane in Laos. On 4 April Sergeant T. Cocks and Flight Sergeant G. Smith brought back photos of the Sittang bridge on the Burma railway, revealing that repairs to earlier bomb damage had been carried out and the rail line was free between Martaban and Rangoon. A few days later the bridge was bombed and further photo-reconnaissance by the Mosquitoes showed that it was again out of commission.

Alipore detachment

In May a No. 684 Squadron detachment began operations from Alipore, a suburb of Calcutta. On 24 May, Wing Commander W. E. M. Lowry, DFC, the CO, and Flying Officer Gerald Stevens flew to Tenasserim and Kra via the advanced landing ground at Kyaukpyu and took high-level vertical photos before dropping to just 50 ft (15 m) for oblique photos of St Luke, St Matthew and the Domel Islands. On 28 May Flying Officer C. G. Andrews and Wt Off H. S. Painter reconnoitred targets in the Siam Valley and observed shipping at Sattahib. This resulted, two days later, in Liberators making attacks on two merchant ships and on 1 June on port installations.

On 4 July 1944 No. 82 (United Provinces) Squadron at Kolar, and No. 84 Squadron at Quetta, India, were to begin conversion to the Mosquito FB.Mk VI from the Vultee Vengeance dive-bomber. (No. 45 Squadron at No. 1672 MCU at Yelahanka near Bangalore had been the first to convert from the Vengeance to the Mosquito, in

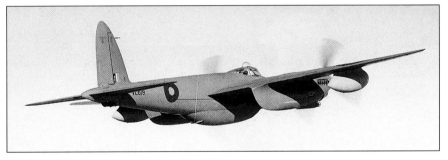

RG176, the first production Mk 34, flew for the first time on 4 December 1944 and was soon despatched to A&AEE for the customary trials. Eventually converted to Mk 34A standard, it went on to serve with No. 540 Sqn, but was wrecked in an accident at Benson in June 1952. In this view the size of the Mk 34's 200-Imp gal (909-litre) underwing tanks is readily apparent.

Left: RG245 peels to starboard for the camera, displaying its eight camera ports. Serving with Nos 540 and 58 Sqns, this aircraft was lost in an accident in 1950.

Below: Mk 34 VL619 was issued to No. 13 Sqn and served in the Middle East post-war.

February 1944.) No. 82 Squadron began conversion at Kolar, 35 miles (56 km) to the east, in July. Heavy monsoons prevented all operations until mid-September, but Nos 45 and 82 Squadrons moved, in turn, to Ranchi, from where No. 45 Squadron flew its first Mosquito sortie on 1 October. No. 47 Squadron moved to Yelahanka on 7 October, followed by No. 110 Squadron three weeks later.

In October No. 684 Squadron Mosquitoes at Alipore were using Cox's Bazaar at the mouth of the Ganges to make long-range flights into Burma. Nos 47, 82 and 110 Squadrons commenced day and night intruder sorties on the Japanese road, rail and river network system. All Mosquito operations came to an abrupt halt on 12 November, when a signal to all units required Mosquito aircraft to be grounded pending inspection. It had been determined that the cause of accidents was supposedly destruction by 'termites' and deterioration of glue. It was presumed that, as the aircraft were left standing in the open, "extreme heat has caused the glue to crack and the upper surfaces to lift from the spar", but it soon became clear that

Mosquito Colours

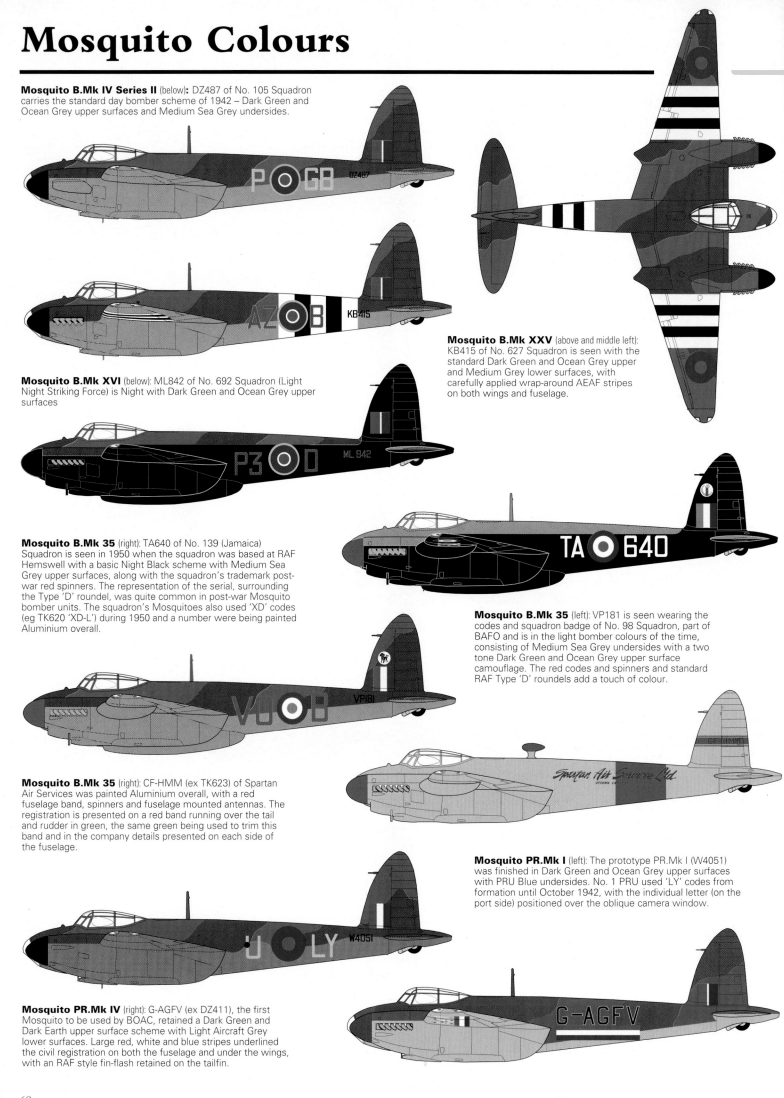

Mosquito B.Mk IV Series II (below): DZ487 of No. 105 Squadron carries the standard day bomber scheme of 1942 – Dark Green and Ocean Grey upper surfaces and Medium Sea Grey undersides.

Mosquito B.Mk XXV (above and middle left): KB415 of No. 627 Squadron is seen with the standard Dark Green and Ocean Grey upper and Medium Grey lower surfaces, with carefully applied wrap-around AEAF stripes on both wings and fuselage.

Mosquito B.Mk XVI (below): ML842 of No. 692 Squadron (Light Night Striking Force) is Night with Dark Green and Ocean Grey upper surfaces

Mosquito B.Mk 35 (right): TA640 of No. 139 (Jamaica) Squadron is seen in 1950 when the squadron was based at RAF Hemswell with a basic Night Black scheme with Medium Sea Grey upper surfaces, along with the squadron's trademark post-war red spinners. The representation of the serial, surrounding the Type 'D' roundel, was quite common in post-war Mosquito bomber units. The squadron's Mosquitoes also used 'XD' codes (eg TK620 'XD-L') during 1950 and a number were being painted Aluminium overall.

Mosquito B.Mk 35 (left): VP181 is seen wearing the codes and squadron badge of No. 98 Squadron, part of BAFO and is in the light bomber colours of the time, consisting of Medium Sea Grey undersides with a two tone Dark Green and Ocean Grey upper surface camouflage. The red codes and spinners and standard RAF Type 'D' roundels add a touch of colour.

Mosquito B.Mk 35 (right): CF-HMM (ex TK623) of Spartan Air Services was painted Aluminium overall, with a red fuselage band, spinners and fuselage mounted antennas. The registration is presented on a red band running over the tail and rudder in green, the same green being used to trim this band and in the company details presented on each side of the fuselage.

Mosquito PR.Mk I (left): The prototype PR.Mk I (W4051) was finished in Dark Green and Ocean Grey upper surfaces with PRU Blue undersides. No. 1 PRU used 'LY' codes from formation until October 1942, with the individual letter (on the port side) positioned over the oblique camera window.

Mosquito PR.Mk IV (right): G-AGFV (ex DZ411), the first Mosquito to be used by BOAC, retained a Dark Green and Dark Earth upper surface scheme with Light Aircraft Grey lower surfaces. Large red, white and blue stripes underlined the civil registration on both the fuselage and under the wings, with an RAF style fin-flash retained on the tailfin.

Mosquito Colours

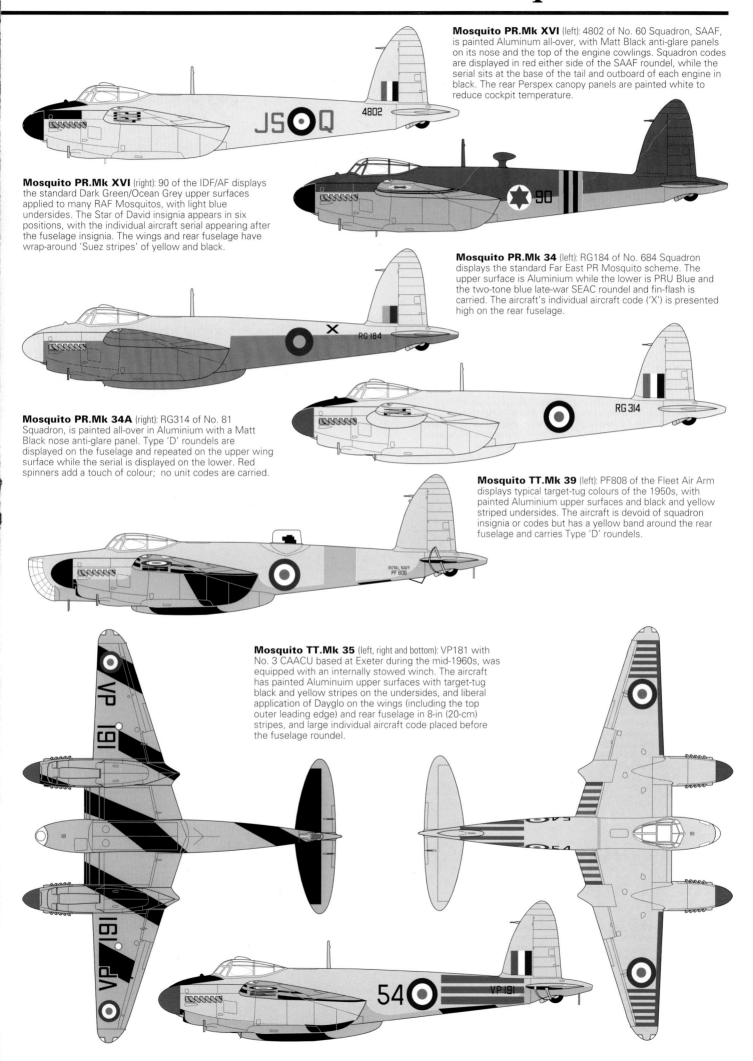

Mosquito PR.Mk XVI (left): 4802 of No. 60 Squadron, SAAF, is painted Aluminum all-over, with Matt Black anti-glare panels on its nose and the top of the engine cowlings. Squadron codes are displayed in red either side of the SAAF roundel, while the serial sits at the base of the tail and outboard of each engine in black. The rear Perspex canopy panels are painted white to reduce cockpit temperature.

Mosquito PR.Mk XVI (right): 90 of the IDF/AF displays the standard Dark Green/Ocean Grey upper surfaces applied to many RAF Mosquitos, with light blue undersides. The Star of David insignia appears in six positions, with the individual aircraft serial appearing after the fuselage insignia. The wings and rear fuselage have wrap-around 'Suez stripes' of yellow and black.

Mosquito PR.Mk 34 (left): RG184 of No. 684 Squadron displays the standard Far East PR Mosquito scheme. The upper surface is Aluminium while the lower is PRU Blue and the two-tone blue late-war SEAC roundel and fin-flash is carried. The aircraft's individual aircraft code ('X') is presented high on the rear fuselage.

Mosquito PR.Mk 34A (right): RG314 of No. 81 Squadron, is painted all-over in Aluminium with a Matt Black nose anti-glare panel. Type 'D' roundels are displayed on the fuselage and repeated on the upper wing surface while the serial is displayed on the lower. Red spinners add a touch of colour; no unit codes are carried.

Mosquito TT.Mk 39 (left): PF808 of the Fleet Air Arm displays typical target-tug colours of the 1950s, with painted Aluminium upper surfaces and black and yellow striped undersides. The aircraft is devoid of squadron insignia or codes but has a yellow band around the rear fuselage and carries Type 'D' roundels.

Mosquito TT.Mk 35 (left, right and bottom): VP181 with No. 3 CAACU based at Exeter during the mid-1960s, was equipped with an internally stowed winch. The aircraft has painted Aluminuim upper surfaces with target-tug black and yellow stripes on the undersides, and liberal application of Dayglo on the wings (including the top outer leading edge) and rear fuselage in 8-in (20-cm) stripes, and large individual aircraft code placed before the fuselage roundel.

Cockpit and crew
The two-man side-by-side cockpit, the layout of which was improved over that of the PR.Mk 34, accommodated the pilot in the left-hand seat. The seat backs were both armoured and the canopy sides were bulged outwards to aid the crew's rearward vision. The bulletproof flat glass windscreen was fitted with an electric wiper and de-icing spray. The cockpit glazing featured a welded steel framework and was fitted with a jettisonable escape hatch. Like the majority of photo-Mosquitoes, PR.Mk 34As were fitted with a bulged Perspex astrodome – used for taking navigational sextant readings – above the navigator's seat. Positioned directly behind the canopy on the top of the fuselage was an equipment hatch, giving access to the rear fuselage, where radio equipment was housed. A two-man dinghy was also carried.

Cameras
The PR.Mk 34A had provision for up to eight cameras. Four were mounted in its bulged bomb bay housing, two F.52s forward of the fuel tanks and two aft for vertical photography. For low-level oblique photography a single Williamson F.24 was mounted in the rear fuselage, aimed through a window in the port side. This could be replaced with an American K.17 camera for aerial survey work. On some post-war PR.Mk 34As, additional forward-facing F.52s could be carried in converted 100-Imp (455-litre) gallon droptanks on the wings. This allowed for accurate taking of low-level photographs, but at the expense of range. For normal vertical photography, the standard bomb sight was used to align the cameras and was operated by the observer, kneeling in the nose. When the oblique cameras were needed, it was the pilot's responsibility to sight the cameras, so calibration marks were provided on the port-side panels of the cockpit and along the wing.

RG177 was the second aircraft of the initial batch of 118 PR.Mk 34s built at Hatfield between January 1945 and January 1946. (These was followed by 13 of another batch of 43 ordered from Hatfield, but cancelled before completion and 50 examples produced by Percival Aircraft at Luton between September 1945 and July 1946.) RG177 appears to have been ready for collection from de Havilland in March 1945 and was immediately despatched to A&AEE Boscombe Down for engine trials – one of six Mk 34s delivered to Boscombe at that time. Production test flying had revealed supercharger surging at high altitude (a problem eventually addressed in the Mk 34A) and Merlin 113/114 reliability on take-off required investigation before clearance for service could be given. The PR.Mk 34/34A was the heaviest of all Mosquitoes, with a gross weight of 25,500 lb (11567 kg), and its single-engine safe speed was 200 mph (322 km/h), which made a crash virtually inevitable in the event of an engine failure on take-off. Trials continued after VE-Day, though by August RG177 was at Rotol Limited, returning to RAF hands (No. 22 Maintenance Unit at Silloth) in November. In storage for the next five and a half years, the aircraft was chosen for conversion to PR.Mk 34A standard and despatched to Marshalls of Cambridge for this work to be carried out in June 1951. There the Mosquito remained for seven months, emerging in January 1952. Sent to No. 38 MU at Llandow, the Mk 34A was again stored until mid-May, when it was allocated to the Far East Air Force. Issued to No. 81 Sqn upon its arrival in Singapore, it served alongside other Mk 34As and Spitfire PR.Mk 19s without incident until 17 March 1955. At 0945 hours the aircraft was landed at Seletar after a routine sortie, only to suffer a brake failure in its starboard landing gear. In order to stop his aircraft careering off the runway, the pilot retracted the landing gear, the aircraft incurring 'Cat. 3R' (repairable) damage. However, the decision was taken not to repair the aircraft and it was recategorised 'Cat. 5' ('write-off') and was struck off charge on 29 March and, most likely, scrapped on site.

de Havilland DH.98 Mosquito PR.Mk 34A
No. 81 Squadron
Far East Air Force
RAF Tengah
May 1953

Construction and loads

The Mosquito's unique wooden fuselage had an oval tapering cross-section and was made of balsa, sandwiched between plywood sheeting. This structure was braced internally with several wooden bulkheads. At first, the Air Ministry was unenthusiastic about the de Havilland Company's proposal for such an aircraft and refused to believe that it could be of any value. The slender one-piece cantilever wing, with an aspect ratio of 7:1, had a wooden-ply skin stretched over two main spars with inter-connecting spruce stringers. The upper skin was double the thickness of the lower, and was exceptionally strong. Ten self-sealing fuel tanks were housed within. The ailerons were made from aluminium and the leading edge, while still of wooden construction, was covered in fabric.

Both the PR.Mk 34 and PR.Mk 34A featured enlarged elevators compared to earlier variants. The extra span was the result of bigger internal balance weights which were incorporated to give more authority to the elevators. Take-off performance of these models was particularly poor and the extra moment on the fuselage was essential for getting the tail off the ground in a timely manner. The tailplane and fir were cantilever one-piece wooden structures, with two box spars covered by a stressed plywood skin. Like the ailerons, the elevator and rudd were made from Alclad, though the rudder was fabric-covered.

With a total fuel capacity of some 1,255 Imp gal (5705 litres), including the two 200-Imp gal (909-litre) tanks and a 310-Imp gal (1409-litre) tank in the bomb bay. PR.Mk 34/34A was the heaviest of all the Mosquitoes, with a maximum loaded weight of 25,500 lb (11567 kg). With fire proofing and armour plate removed a Mk 34 was capable to flying 3,600 miles (5794 km) at 25,000 ft (7620 m), cruising at 300 mph (483 km/h)

Engines nacelles and undercarriage

The intakes beneath the engines were for the carburettor and were covered with an anti-ice guard, while those directly below the propeller spinner fed the supercharger intercooler – a feature of the two-stage Merlin.

The wingroots housed the intakes for the engine oil and coolant radiators. Coolant temperature was maintained by electro-pneumatic ram-controlled flaps in the radiator duct exits.

The main landing gear comprised two interchangeable single-wheel units which retracted backwards into their nacelles under the engines. Two Dunlop pneumatic brakes were used per wheel and the shock absorbers were of the rubber-block compression type. An armoured oil tank was also located in each wheel bay.

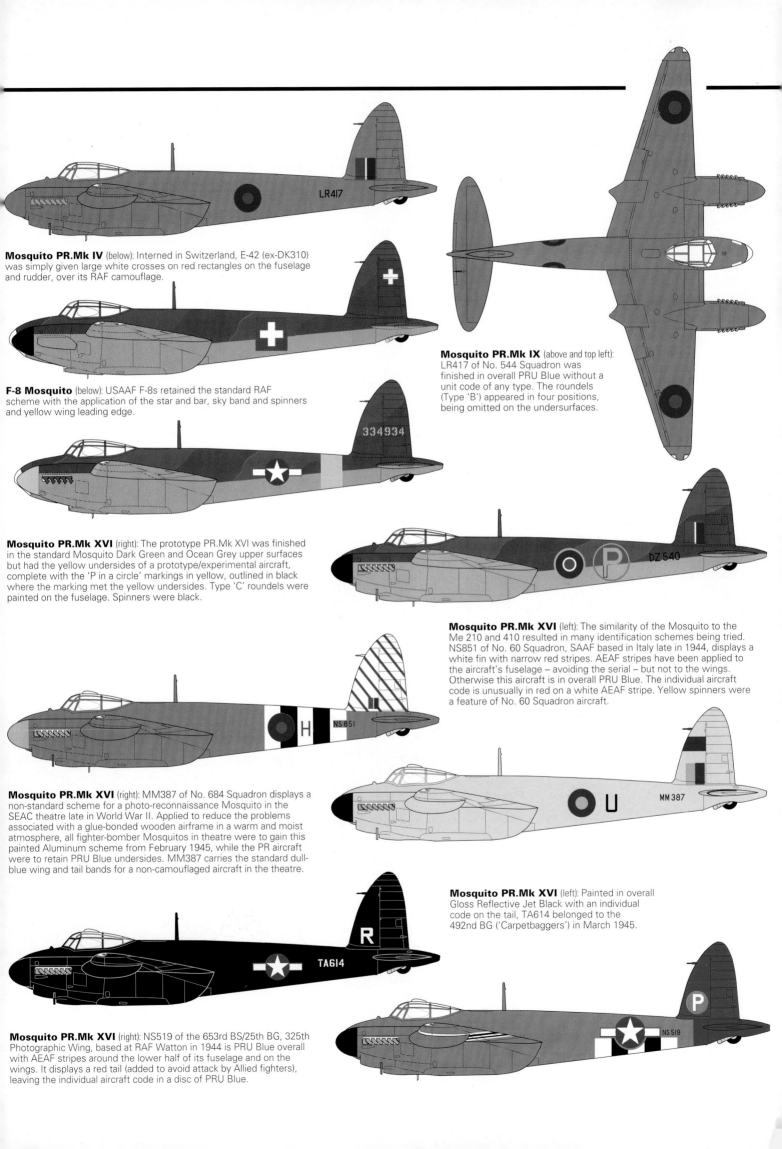

Mosquito PR.Mk IV (below): Interned in Switzerland, E-42 (ex-DK310) was simply given large white crosses on red rectangles on the fuselage and rudder, over its RAF camouflage.

F-8 Mosquito (below): USAAF F-8s retained the standard RAF scheme with the application of the star and bar, sky band and spinners and yellow wing leading edge.

Mosquito PR.Mk IX (above and top left): LR417 of No. 544 Squadron was finished in overall PRU Blue without a unit code of any type. The roundels (Type 'B') appeared in four positions, being omitted on the undersurfaces.

Mosquito PR.Mk XVI (right): The prototype PR.Mk XVI was finished in the standard Mosquito Dark Green and Ocean Grey upper surfaces but had the yellow undersides of a prototype/experimental aircraft, complete with the 'P in a circle' markings in yellow, outlined in black where the marking met the yellow undersides. Type 'C' roundels were painted on the fuselage. Spinners were black.

Mosquito PR.Mk XVI (left): The similarity of the Mosquito to the Me 210 and 410 resulted in many identification schemes being tried. NS851 of No. 60 Squadron, SAAF based in Italy late in 1944, displays a white fin with narrow red stripes. AEAF stripes have been applied to the aircraft's fuselage – avoiding the serial – but not to the wings. Otherwise this aircraft is in overall PRU Blue. The individual aircraft code is unusually in red on a white AEAF stripe. Yellow spinners were a feature of No. 60 Squadron aircraft.

Mosquito PR.Mk XVI (right): MM387 of No. 684 Squadron displays a non-standard scheme for a photo-reconnaissance Mosquito in the SEAC theatre late in World War II. Applied to reduce the problems associated with a glue-bonded wooden airframe in a warm and moist atmosphere, all fighter-bomber Mosquitos in theatre were to gain this painted Aluminum scheme from February 1945, while the PR aircraft were to retain PRU Blue undersides. MM387 carries the standard dull-blue wing and tail bands for a non-camouflaged aircraft in the theatre.

Mosquito PR.Mk XVI (left): Painted in overall Gloss Reflective Jet Black with an individual code on the tail, TA614 belonged to the 492nd BG ('Carpetbaggers') in March 1945.

Mosquito PR.Mk XVI (right): NS519 of the 653rd BS/25th BG, 325th Photographic Wing, based at RAF Watton in 1944 is PRU Blue overall with AEAF stripes around the lower half of its fuselage and on the wings. It displays a red tail (added to avoid attack by Allied fighters), leaving the individual aircraft code in a disc of PRU Blue.

128 Tailplane spar attachment joint
129 Tailwheel leg strut
130 Retracting tailwheel
131 Levered suspension tailwheel forks
132 Fuselage skin fabric covering
133 Identification code lights, white, amber and green
134 Beam approach aerial
135 Camera mounting

136 F.24 camera
137 Tailplane control cables
138 Rear fuselage entry hatch
139 Crew equipment stowage bag
140 Bulged bomb bay tail fairing
141 Bomb door hydraulic jacks
142 Beam approach receiver
143 Oxygen bottles
144 Flap shroud ribs
145 Inboard fuel tank bay ventral access panel
146 Bomb carriers
147 500-lb (227-kg) short-finned HE bombs (four)
148 Port engine nacelle top fairing
149 Main undercarriage hydraulic retraction jack
150 Undercarriage leg rear strut mounting
151 Flap hydraulic jack
152 Nacelle tail fairing
153 Short plain flap segments
154 All-wooden flap construction
155 Port outer fuel tanks
156 Fuel filler cap
157 Retractable landing lamp
158 Aileron tab control linkage
159 Rear spar
160 Aileron hinge control
161 Aileron tab
162 Aluminium aileron construction
163 Resin lamp
164 Port formation lamp
165 Detachable wingtip fairing
166 Port navigation light
167 Leading-edge nose ribs
168 Front spar, box beam construction
169 Wing lower surface single skin/stringer panel
170 Wingrib construction

Badrocke 1999

171 Plywood leading-edge skinning, fabric-covered
172 Port auxiliary fuel tank, capacity 50 Imp gal (227 litres)
173 Fuel filler cap
174 Main undercarriage rear strut
175 Mudguard
176 Mainwheel doors
177 Port mainwheel
178 Mainwheel leg strut
179 Pneumatic brake disc
180 Rubber compression block shock absorber
181 Spring-loaded door guides
182 Main undercarriage pivot fixing
183 Engine oil tank, capacity 16 Imp gal (73 litres)
184 Cabin heater
185 Fireproof bulkhead
186 Two-stage supercharger
187 Intercooler
188 Heywood compressor
189 Rolls-Royce Merlin 72 liquid-cooled 12-cylinder Vee engine
190 Exhaust ports
191 Alternator
192 Engine bearers
193 Carburettor air intake duct
194 Intake guard
195 Intercooler radiator exhaust
196 Intercooler radiator
197 Engine mounting block
198 Coolant header tank
199 Spinner armoured backplate
200 Propeller hub pitch change mechanism
201 Spinner
202 Intercooler radiator intake
203 Port three-bladed de Havilland hydromatic propeller
204 4,000-lb (1814 kg) HC bomb

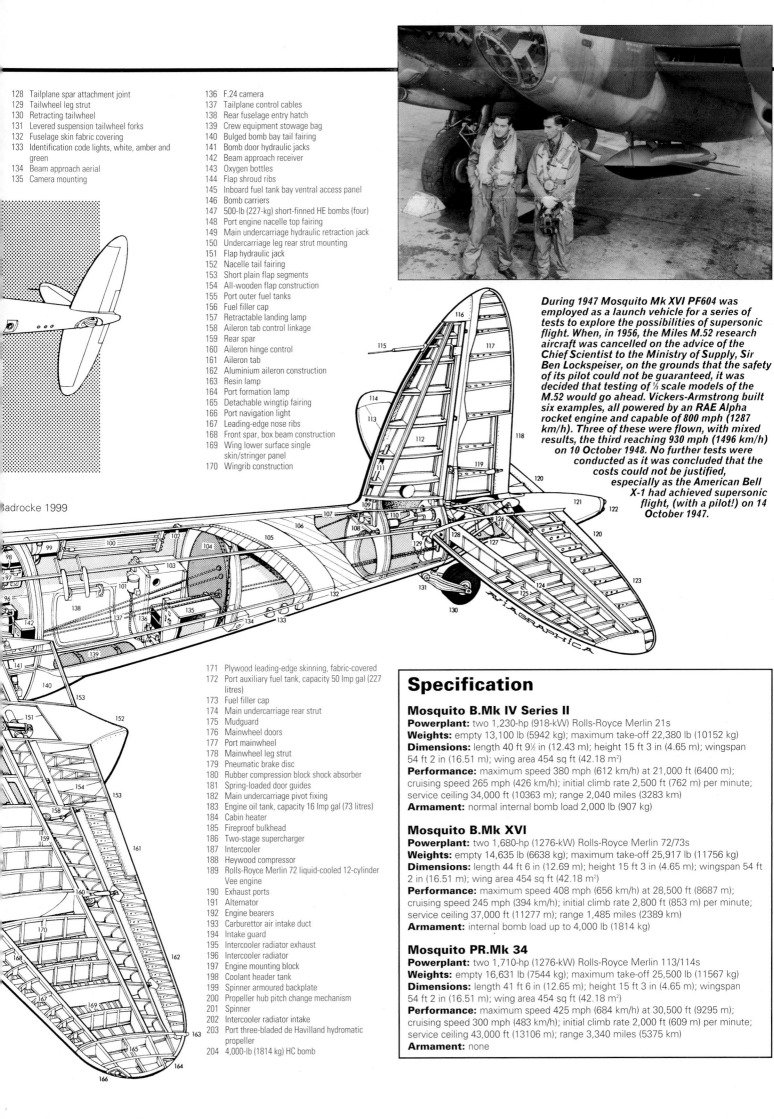

During 1947 Mosquito Mk XVI PF604 was employed as a launch vehicle for a series of tests to explore the possibilities of supersonic flight. When, in 1956, the Miles M.52 research aircraft was cancelled on the advice of the Chief Scientist to the Ministry of Supply, Sir Ben Lockspeiser, on the grounds that the safety of its pilot could not be guaranteed, it was decided that testing of ⅓ scale models of the M.52 would go ahead. Vickers-Armstrong built six examples, all powered by an RAE Alpha rocket engine and capable of 800 mph (1287 km/h). Three of these were flown, with mixed results, the third reaching 930 mph (1496 km/h) on 10 October 1948. No further tests were conducted as it was concluded that the costs could not be justified, especially as the American Bell X-1 had achieved supersonic flight, (with a pilot!) on 14 October 1947.

Specification

Mosquito B.Mk IV Series II
Powerplant: two 1,230-hp (918-kW) Rolls-Royce Merlin 21s
Weights: empty 13,100 lb (5942 kg); maximum take-off 22,380 lb (10152 kg)
Dimensions: length 40 ft 9½ in (12.43 m); height 15 ft 3 in (4.65 m); wingspan 54 ft 2 in (16.51 m); wing area 454 sq ft (42.18 m²)
Performance: maximum speed 380 mph (612 km/h) at 21,000 ft (6400 m); cruising speed 265 mph (426 km/h); initial climb rate 2,500 ft (762 m) per minute; service ceiling 34,000 ft (10363 m); range 2,040 miles (3283 km)
Armament: normal internal bomb load 2,000 lb (907 kg)

Mosquito B.Mk XVI
Powerplant: two 1,680-hp (1276-kW) Rolls-Royce Merlin 72/73s
Weights: empty 14,635 lb (6638 kg); maximum take-off 25,917 lb (11756 kg)
Dimensions: length 44 ft 6 in (12.69 m); height 15 ft 3 in (4.65 m); wingspan 54 ft 2 in (16.51 m); wing area 454 sq ft (42.18 m²)
Performance: maximum speed 408 mph (656 km/h) at 28,500 ft (8687 m); cruising speed 245 mph (394 km/h); initial climb rate 2,800 ft (853 m) per minute; service ceiling 37,000 ft (11277 m); range 1,485 miles (2389 km)
Armament: internal bomb load up to 4,000 lb (1814 kg)

Mosquito PR.Mk 34
Powerplant: two 1,710-hp (1276-kW) Rolls-Royce Merlin 113/114s
Weights: empty 16,631 lb (7544 kg); maximum take-off 25,500 lb (11567 kg)
Dimensions: length 41 ft 6 in (12.65 m); height 15 ft 3 in (4.65 m); wingspan 54 ft 2 in (16.51 m); wing area 454 sq ft (42.18 m²)
Performance: maximum speed 425 mph (684 km/h) at 30,500 ft (9295 m); cruising speed 300 mph (483 km/h); initial climb rate 2,000 ft (609 m) per minute; service ceiling 43,000 ft (13106 m); range 3,340 miles (5375 km)
Armament: none

Colour scheme
This PR.Mk 34A carried the standard post-war reconnaissance colour scheme of a Medium Sea Grey upper fuselage, with Type 'D' roundels. The undersides were Cerulean, more commonly known as PRU Blue. The same scheme also appeared on Spitfire PR.Mk XIXs, Meteors and early Canberras. Heat considerations led to the repainting of the Far East Mosquitoes in a dull Aluminium finish by the time they left service in 1955.

No. 81 Squadr
No. 81 Squadron
war, the squadro
No. 81's acti
the Hurricane an
from Hornchurch
equipped with Sp
1945, No. 123 Sc
1 September 194
The 'Malayar
response was O
PR. Mk 34A
encar

Slipper tanks
The PR.Mk 34A was fitted with a pair of underwing fuel tanks which were significantly larger than those fitted to any other version. The two slipper tanks each housed an extra 200 Imp gal (909 litres). Quite often, these would not be carried operationally due to the weight penalties and resultant drag, but they were extremely useful for long-range ferry flights. Regularly carried by the PR.Mk 34s in the Far East, they were sometimes supplemented by surplus Hurricane tanks which, unlike the slipper tanks, were usually jettisoned in flight.

Mosquito PR.Mk 34 and Mk 34A

The ultimate photo-reconnaissance (PR) version of the Mosquito developed during World War II was the PR.Mk 34 and its derivative, the PR.Mk 34A. Developed with Far East service with the South East Asia Command in mind, the size of the aircraft's wing tanks was doubled, and a large overload fuel tank was installed in the bomb bay, which allowed for a range of over 3,500 miles (5632 km). Powered by a two-stage Merlin 113 and 114 (the latter driving a cabin supercharger), the first production PR.Mk 34 flew on 4 December 1944 and 181 were built at de Havilland's Hatfield factory and at Luton by Percival Aircraft Ltd, before contracts were cancelled at the end of the war.

The PR.Mk 34 entered service with No. 544 Squadron at RAF Benson in April 1944 although the examples delivered saw no active service in Europe before VE-Day, the squadron's PR.Mk IXs and XVIs being used for the few sorties remaining. Post-war, the PR.Mk 34s of No. 58 Squadron flew high-altitude photo-reconnaissance sorties from West German bases over the Soviet-occupied portions of Eastern Europe. In the Far East, the PR.Mk 34 saw a much more active war, photographing railways, airfields, shipping, and potential invasion beaches throughout the Indian Ocean, the first sorties being flown by a detachment of No. 684 Sqn in the Cocos Islands in July 1945. Prisoner-of-war camps became an important target after the atomic bombings of Hiroshima and Nagasaki, as did areas where rebel uprisings were taking place in the vacuum caused by the Japanese surrender.

The PR.Mk 34A was an improved version with Rolls-Royce Merlin 113A/114A engines (with supercharger diffusers to address the surge problem identified during early testing of the Mk 34), the more advanced Gee-H navigation aid (and associated dipoles above and below each wingtip) and, in the prototype at least, an improved undercarriage retraction and locking system. At least 35 aircraft were converted to Mk 34A standard by Marshalls of Cambridge. Visual differences between the two variants were small. The latter had an aerial mast on the rear fuselage with the aerial wire itself leading to a point midway up the fin, and dipole antennas for the IFF system above and below each wingtip.

No. 680 Sqn, which had moved to Palestine after VE-Day and received Mk 34 aircraft in March 1946, was renumbered No. 13 Sqn on 1 September and kept its Mosquitoes until 1952, when they were replaced by Meteor PR.Mk 10s.

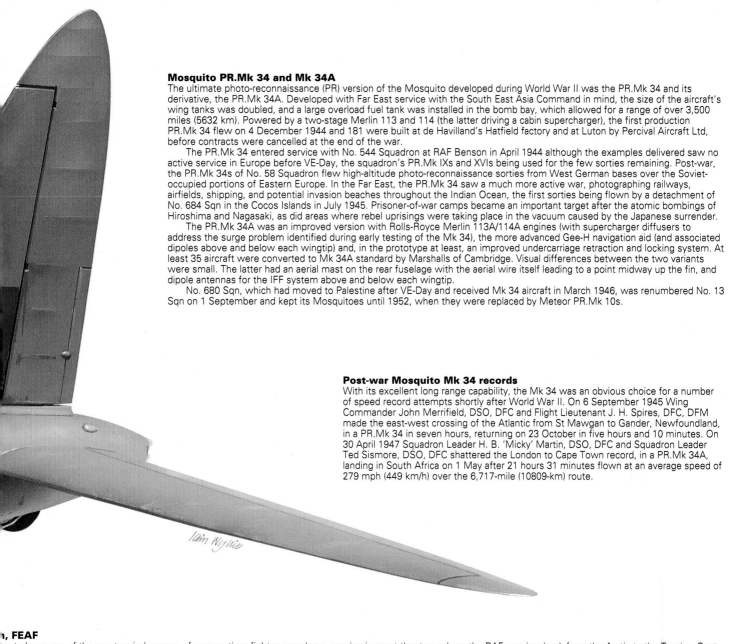

Post-war Mosquito Mk 34 records

With its excellent long range capability, the Mk 34 was an obvious choice for a number of speed record attempts shortly after World War II. On 6 September 1945 Wing Commander John Merrifield, DSO, DFC and Flight Lieutenant J. H. Spires, DFC, DFM made the east-west crossing of the Atlantic from St Mawgan to Gander, Newfoundland, in a PR.Mk 34 in seven hours, returning on 23 October in five hours and 10 minutes. On 30 April 1947 Squadron Leader H. B. 'Micky' Martin, DSO, DFC and Squadron Leader Ted Sismore, DSO, DFC, shattered the London to Cape Town record, in a PR.Mk 34A, landing in South Africa on 1 May after 21 hours 31 minutes flown at an average speed of 279 mph (449 km/h) over the 6,717-mile (10809-km) route.

, FEAF

...as to have one of the most varied careers of any wartime fighter squadrons, serving in most theatres where the RAF was involved, from the Arctic to the Tropics. Post-...was to fly the last operational sorties with three classic British warplanes, the Spitfire, Mosquito and Meteor.

...World War II career began when it was equipped with Hurricane Mk IIs and sent to northern Russia as part of No. 151 Wing in July 1941. After training Soviet pilots on ...ontributing to the defence of Murmansk, it left its aircraft behind and returned to the UK. Adopting the Spitfire Mk V in early 1942, it conducted cross-Channel sweeps ...efore moving to North Africa via Gibraltar at the end of October 1942 followed by action in Sicily and Italy. This nomadic existence continued in late 1943 when, ...ire VIIIs, the squadron was sent to the Far East, flying mostly ground attack missions from various bases in India. At war's end, the squadron was in Ceylon. In June ...dron, a P-47 Thunderbolt unit, was renumbered No. 81 Sqn at Bobbili, India. Post-war, the squadron was soon engaged in operations in the Netherlands East Indies. On ... the squadron again took over the equipment of another unit, with the renumbering of PR Mosquito unit No. 684 Sqn at Seletar in Singapore.
...mergency' began in June 1948 with a full-scale uprising led by the Malayan Peoples' Anti-British Army (formerly the Malayan People's Anti-Japanese Army). The British ...ation Firedog which was to last until 1960. At the beginning of the Emergency, No. 81 Squadron was equipped with two Spitfire PR.Mk XIXs and nine Mosquito ...nd these were soon involved in both tactical and strategic roles. In the former, the aircraft were mainly taking low-level oblique photographs of trails and terrorist ...ments in co-operation with the Army; in the latter, the squadron (primarily the Mosquitoes) photo-mapped the Malayan Peninsula from 16,000 feet (4877 m). In 1953, ...e peak year of operations, the squadron flew 1,335 photo-reconaissance sorties, these including significant mapping surveys of Java and Thailand.

The last operational flight by an RAF Mosquito took place on 15 December 1955 when PR.Mk 34A RG314, flown by Flying Ofiicer A.J. 'Collie' Knox and A.B. 'Tommy' Thompson' from Seletar photographed two suspected terrorist camps .The Mosquitoes were replaced by four Pembroke C(PR).Mk 1s, later supplemented by detachments of Canberras from the UK. In January 1960, the squadron got its own Canberra PR.Mk 7s. The Spitfires had been replaced belatedly by Meteor PR.Mk 10s in November 1955. With the run-down of Britsh forces east of Suez, including Far East Air Force, the squadron was disbanded at Tengah in January 1970.

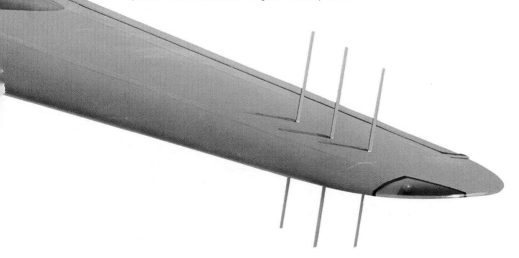

Mosquito details

de Havilland DH.98 Mosquito B.Mk XVI

1 Three-bladed de Havilland type 5000 hydromatic propeller
2 Spinner
3 Starboard engine cowling panels, Merlin 73 engine
4 Exhaust stubs
5 Starboard oil radiator
6 Coolant radiator
7 Radiator air intake
8 Carburettor air intake and guard
9 Fuselage nose skinning
10 Windscreen de-icing fluid nozzle
11 Instrument panel
12 Parachute stowage
13 Junction box
14 Fire axe
15 SYKO apparatus stowage
16 Nose compartment side windows
17 Portable oxygen bottles
18 Mk XIV bombsight
19 Nose glazing
20 Forward navigation/identification light
21 Temperature probe
22 Windscreen de-icing fluid nozzle
23 Optically flat bomb-aiming window
24 Bombsight mounting
25 Bomb selector switches
26 Camera remote control box
27 Bomb aimer's kneeling cushion
28 Signal pistol cartridge racks
29 Rudder pedals
30 Compass
31 Control linkages
32 Oxygen system economiser units
33 Elevator trim handwheel
34 Port radiator ram air intake
35 Oil and coolant radiators
36 Engine throttle levers
37 Ventral entry hatch
38 Control column handwheel
39 Folding chart table
40 Windscreen panels
41 Trailing aerial winch
42 Cockpit roof escape hatch
43 Seat back armour plate
44 Navigator/ bombardier's seat
45 Rearward vision blister fairing
46 Pilot's seat
47 Intercom socket
48 Portable fire extinguisher
49 Cabin pressurisation and heating air ducts
50 Non-return air valve
51 Engine control runs
52 Wingroot rib
53 Centre section fuel tanks (two), capacity 68 Imp gal (309 litres) each; 46 Imp gal (209 litres) port and 47.5 Imp gal (216 litres) starboard with 4,000-lb (1814-kg) bombload
54 Wing upper surface attachment joint
55 Centre fuel tank filler cap
56 ARI-5083 receiver
57 FF transmitter/ receiver
58 Signal pistol aperture
59 Cockpit aft glazing
60 Rear pressure bulkhead
61 Starboard inboard fuel tanks, capacity 78 Imp gal (355 litres) inner and 66 Imp gal (298 litres) outer
62 Fuel filler cap
63 Nacelle fairing
64 Starboard main undercarriage bay
65 Hydraulic retraction jack
66 Outboard fuel tanks, capacity 34 Imp gal (155 litres) inner and 24 Imp gal (109 litres) outer
67 Wing stringers
68 Starboard auxiliary fuel tank, capacity 50 Imp gal (227 litres)
69 Fuel filler cap
70 Plywood leading-edge skinning
71 Wing top skin panelling, double plywood sandwich construction
72 Starboard navigation light
73 Wingtip fairing
74 Formation light
75 Resin light
76 Starboard aileron
77 Aileron hinge control
78 Mass balance weights

79 Aileron tab
80 Underside view showing bulged (increased volume) bomb-bay doors
81 Ventral entry hatch with drift sight aperture
82 Trailing aerial fairing
83 Starboard outer plain flap segment
84 Flap hydraulic jack
85 Nacelle tail fairing
86 Flap inboard segment
87 Oil filler cap
88 Dinghy access panel
89 Two-man dinghy stowage compartment
90 Wing fixing bearer
91 Rear fuselage equipment heater air ducting
92 Long-range oil tank, capacity 10 Imp gal (46 litres)
93 Hydraulic reservoir
94 TR1143 transmitter/receiver
95 Mk XIV bomb sight computer
96 Batteries
97 Hydraulic and pneumatic systems servicing panel
98 Pneumatic system air bottle
99 De-icing fluid reservoir

100 Picketing equipment stowage
101 Camera motor
102 TR1143 aerial
103 Fuselage stringers, between inner and outer skin laminations
104 Heat-conserving canvas bulkhead cover
105 Fuselage half shell sandwich skin construction (plywood/ balsa/plywood)
106 Diagonal graining pattern
107 Centreline fuselage half shell joint strip
108 Rudder control linkage
109 Fin attachment bulkhead
110 Rudder mass balance weight
111 Ferrite aerial rod
112 Tailfin construction
113 Starboard tailplane
114 Elevator horn balance
115 Pitot tube
116 Rudder horn balance
117 Fabric-covered rudder construction
118 Rudder tab

119 Tab operating rod
120 Elevator tab
121 Tailcone
122 Tail navigation lights
123 Fabric-covered elevator construction
124 Tailplane construction
125 Ferrite aerial rod
126 Elevator operating linkage
127 Tailwheel housing

© Mike

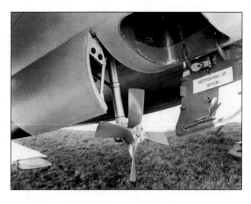

Above: The Mosquito TT.Mk 39 deployed targets from its bomb bay, the hydraulic winch mechanism being driven by this retractable windmill. In the bomber and PR Mosquitos crew access was via a hatch on the starboard side of the forward fuselage.

Above: The original bomber Mosquito variants were able to carry a 2,000-lb (909-kg) load, generally comprising four 500-lb (227-kg) GP bombs.

Top left: Instruments and flying controls aboard a B.Mk IV are shown here, with the engine controls to the left, engine gauges to the left of the instrument panel and flying instruments to the right.

Left: The Perspex 'bomber nose' covering the bomb aimer's position in a Mosquito B.Mk IV Series II was in two pieces. This is the No. 105 Sqn aircraft flown by Flt Lt (later Sqn Ldr) 'George' Parry DFC and F/O (later Flt Lt) Victor Robson DFC during 1942.

Left: PR.Mk 34/34A aircraft carried these extra-large underwing tanks each of 200 Imp gal (909 litre) capacity. Their size imposed something of a drag penalty.

Bottom left: Personnel of No. 684 Sqn service the Merlin 73 powering one of the unit's PR.Mk XVIs. The Merlin 70 series powerplants transformed the Mosquito's performance allowing operations to be carried out at higher altitudes, away from the attentions of enemy fighters.

Bottom: As described in the caption from the period, "the boys with the gen" replenish the oxygen supply aboard aircraft 'W' of No. 613 Sqn, August 1944. The aircraft's oxygen bottles were positioned above the bomb bay and accessed via the hatch illustrated.

Below: Late-production Mosquitoes, like this Mk 35, featured landing gear of Lockheed manufacture, with pneumatic disc brakes.

The USAAF's first Mosquitoes were six B.Mk VII and 34 B.Mk XX bombers converted as F-8 reconnaissance aircraft for use by the 12th Air Force in Italy. In all 120 had been requested by the USAAF, 90 of which would come from Canadian production, though only 40 were completed. Fitted with minimal camera equipment in its nose and hampered by its single-stage Merlins, the F-8 proved a disappointment and was rejected by both the 12th and 8th Air Forces for operational use, the latter having also requested 30 aircraft for weather reconnaissance work. Only 16 examples are believed to have reached Europe, 11 later being passed to the RAF.

The 'Spook'

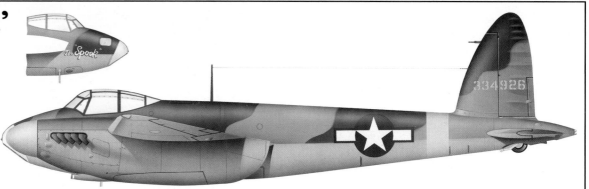

F-8 43-34926 (KB315)
One of the six Canadian-built B.Mk VIIs converted to F-8 standard, *The 'Spook'* found its way to the 12th AF in Italy where it was issued to the 3rd Photographic Group (Reconnaissance) in 1944. The 3rd PG(R), equipped with F-4s and F-5s, and No. 680 Sqn, RAF formed the North African PR Wing in 1943. Whether this or any other F-8 was used operationally in the MTO is unclear.

Top: Seen at an unknown location in the USA, possibly post-war, this F-8 is one of those converted from a Mk XX, as it carries underwing fuel tanks.

Right: Some sources suggest that The Spook saw limited operational use in North Africa and or Italy and that it was shot down behind enemy lines.

Below: In all 145 Mosquitoes are known to have served with the 8th Air Force. The first Mk XVIs were operated in standard RAF PR Blue and retained British markings. NS619 is an example, seen here at Watton after being handed over to the USAAF and in use by the 25th Bombardment Gp (Reconnaissance).

Below right: MM384 lost its port undercarriage in a landing accident at Watton on 4 May 1944.

the adhesive was not the cause of the trouble. The same problems manifested themselves in Australian-built aircraft, while in the UK a series of fatal flying accidents among Mosquitoes of various marks (at the rate of two to four per month from January to June 1944) was attributed to failure of the wing structure.

Indian production cancelled

Plans to manufacture components in India was scrapped and re-equipping of squadrons was delayed. De Havilland still maintained that the failures in India resulted from climatic conditions and ordered the destruction of all parts made with casein glue. Matters reached a head in 1 January 1945 and the Air Ministry forestalled possible loss of confidence in its Mosquito squadrons at home and abroad by holding to de Havilland's assertion that the accidents in India

were caused by "faults largely due to climate". Mosquitoes found to have skin defects were simply struck off charge.

No. 84 Squadron completed conversion to the Mk VI in March 1945, but saw no action against the Japanese, instead being used, along with Nos 47, 82 and 110 Squadrons, in late 1945 against Indonesian separatists. During February No. 89 Squadron at Baigachi had begun converting from the Beaufighter to the Mosquito FB.Mk VI, but they were never used. In March No. 82 Squadron flew some 269 sorties, while Nos 47 and 84 Squadrons were used on bomber support operations for the Army.

Meanwhile, in January 1945, the Mosquitoes of No. 684 Squadron flew over 70 sorties, including survey flights to Phuket Island. A detachment at China Bay near Trincomalee in Ceylon made sorties to the Andaman and Nicobar islands and the tip of Sumatra, almost 1,000 miles (1610 km) across the Bay of Bengal, so each sortie was the equivalent of a transatlantic flight and lasted some eight hours. The detachment commander, Flight Lieutenant Henry Lowcock and Flight Sergeant D. W. R. Lewin had, on 10 February, photographed five Sumatran airfields. Four days later the PR.Mk IXs made low-level photo-reconnaissance flights over the notorious Burma–Siam railway. By March, record-breaking flights of around nine hours were being made to Phuket Island, to reconnoitre possible landing beaches. On 1/2 May Operation Dracula, the seaborne invasion to capture Rangoon, took place. Support was provided by Nos 82 and 110 Squadrons but the PR.Mk IXs of No. 684 Squadron were grounded by bad weather. By the end of May Mosquitoes using Ramree Island as an advanced landing strip were flying regularly over Siam.

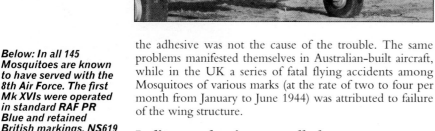

25th BG (Reconnaissance)

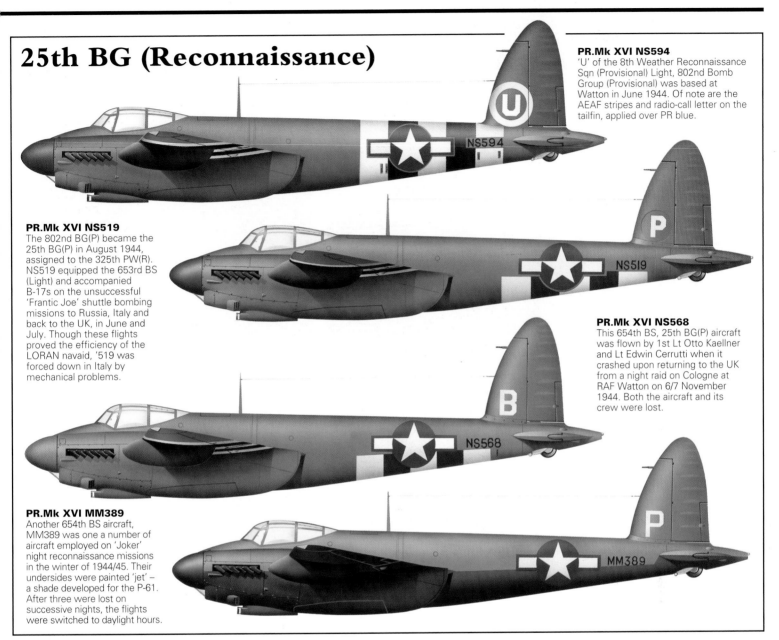

PR.Mk XVI NS594
'U' of the 8th Weather Reconnaissance Sqn (Provisional) Light, 802nd Bomb Group (Provisional) was based at Watton in June 1944. Of note are the AEAF stripes and radio-call letter on the tailfin, applied over PR blue.

PR.Mk XVI NS519
The 802nd BG(P) became the 25th BG(P) in August 1944, assigned to the 325th PW(R). NS519 equipped the 653rd BS (Light) and accompanied B-17s on the unsuccessful 'Frantic Joe' shuttle bombing missions to Russia, Italy and back to the UK, in June and July. Though these flights proved the efficiency of the LORAN navaid, '519 was forced down in Italy by mechanical problems.

PR.Mk XVI NS568
This 654th BS, 25th BG(P) aircraft was flown by 1st Lt Otto Kaellner and Lt Edwin Cerrutti when it crashed upon returning to the UK from a night raid on Cologne at RAF Watton on 6/7 November 1944. Both the aircraft and its crew were lost.

PR.Mk XVI MM389
Another 654th BS aircraft, MM389 was one a number of aircraft employed on 'Joker' night reconnaissance missions in the winter of 1944/45. Their undersides were painted 'jet' – a shade developed for the P-61. After three were lost on successive nights, the flights were switched to daylight hours.

8th Air Force Mk XVIs

General Ira Eaker's request to the Air Ministry in September 1943 for 30 Mosquitoes for weather reconnaissance work led to the offer, later that month, of 30 FB.Mk VIs – the only variant that the RAF could spare at that time. Unhappy with the Mk VI's performance compared with that of dedicated PR aircraft, Eaker elected to wait until the latter were available and was accordingly promised 20 PR.Mk XVIs for February 1944 delivery. By September the 8th AF had 61 Mk XVIs on strength, these aircraft undertaking a range of missions including weather reconnaissance, night and daytime photo-reconnaissance, chaff dispensing and H2X radar scope photography. Two squadrons were equipped within the 802nd Bomb Group (Provisional), later redesignated the 25th BG(R). By VE-Day the 8th AF had 76 aircraft, 62 of which were airworthy, with the rest under repair or overhaul.

Left: CO of the 25th BG between 23 September 1944 and 14 April 1945, Lt Col Leon Gray (left) looks on as Lt Gen James Doolittle, tries his hand at pool. In the background is Major Alvon Podwojski, CO of the 652nd BS, while to the right is the 325th Photographic Wing CO at Watton, Col Elliott Roosevelt, son of the US president.

Mosquito Mk XVI NS569/'N' of the 654th BS is seen at Watton with a 652nd BS (Heavy) B-17 in the background.

Above: NS591/'S' of the 653rd BS lands at Watton in late 1944/early 1945.

Lt Robert A Tunnel and photographer Lt David J. McCarthy were aboard NS569/'N' of the 654th BS on 12 August 1944, accompanying a PB4Y-1 Liberator modified as a flying bomb and packed with 18,000 lb (8165 kg) of explosive. The PB4Y-1 (one of two aircraft converted under Project Anvil), was flown by Joseph P. Kennedy Jr (brother of the future US president) and Lt Wilford 'Bud' Willy and was climbing to 2,000 ft (607 m) where they would hand control over to an accompanying Lockheed PV-1 and bail out. However, before it reached the hand-over point the Liberator exploded without warning, killing its crew and sending Tunnel's Mosquito several hundred feet upwards. Debris showered the Mk XVI, a large piece hitting the port engine. NS569 managed to limp home, landing at Halesworth as the engine cut.

Above: This remarkable photograph of Nippes and Essen was captured during a night 'Joker' sortie on 4/5 October 1944. 700,000 candlepower M46 photoflash bombs, 12 of which could be carried in the bomb bay of a PR.Mk XVI, were used in a technique perfected by the RAF.

On Red Tail missions, 8th AF Mosquitoes carried the command pilots for daylight bombing missions. This 25th BG(R) aircraft is about to leave Attlebridge, Norfolk with 466th BG B-24 Liberators.

In June the PR.Mk 34, a VLR version of the Mk XVI, entered service. Based on the recently completed airfield at Cocos Island, it made reconnaissance missions to Kuala Lumpur and Port Swettenham. The first three aircraft had left the UK for India on 29 May, and on the following day a fourth PR.Mk 34, flown by Squadron Leader Kos Newman, DFC and bar and Wt Off Ray Smith, established a new England-India record of 12 hours and 25 minutes. On 3 July a PR.Mk 34 of No. 684 Squadron crewed by Wing Commander W. E. M. Lowry, DFC and Flight Sergeant Stan Pateman made the first reconnaissance sortie, to Point Pinto via Morib and Port Swettenham area via Gedong and, finally, Sumatra. On the next day, seven runs were made over Kuala Lumpur. By the end of July some 25 sorties had been carried out by PR.Mk 34s from Cocos, with another 13 by VJ-Day.

On 20 August eight FB.Mk VIs of No. 110 Squadron were used to dislodge Japanese troops at Tikedo, east of the Sittang river, who had refused to surrender. It was the final RAF operation of World War II. (No. 110 Squadron had flown the first of the war, when equipped with Blenheims in France.) A more contrite band of Japanese soldiers welcomed Squadron Leader Cliff Andrews, RNZAF and Wt Off H. S. Painter of No. 684 Squadron who put down at Kallang on Singapore Island with engine trouble on 31 August following a reconnaissance of the Palembang oil refineries, rather than risk the long overwater flight back to Cocos Island. They were the first Britons to arrive in Singapore following the Japanese surrender. On 3 September General Itazaki formerly surrendered to Vice-Admiral Lord Louis Mountbatten in Singapore, to bring the war against Japan to an end.

USAAF PR operations

On 20 April 1941 Major General 'Hap' Arnold, Chief of the USAAF, Major Elwood Quesda, General Arnold's aide and the man who later controlled IX Fighter Command in England, plus other senior officers, were present at Hatfield

Col 'Bud' Peaslee used NS519 in the first Chaff dispensing missions flown by 8th AF Mosquitoes. The 653rd BS used the equipment from December 1944, though delivery delays limited its usefulness.

Night photography

The 654th flew 700 varied missions, including 161 night photography flights code-named Joker. These were undertaken at high and medium altitudes at a speed of around 270 mph (435 km/h). In its bomb bay a Mosquito was able to carry 12 60-lb M46 photo-flash bombs of 700,000 candlepower. These were generally dropped at 12,000 ft (3658 m) and burst at 4,000 ft (1219 m).

Colours and markings

The 654th BS's Mosquitoes were initially operated in standard RAF PR colours and markings but, as operations permitted, were gradually given USAF 'stars and bars' and an 18-in (45.7-cm) unit radio call code in white on the tailfin. (On 653rd BS aircraft this letter had a circular white outline). Rudders were painted red after 16 August 1944 as a recognitiom aid; several misidentifications had led to Mosquitoes being shot down by USAAF fighters. This directive was modified to include all tail surfaces on 23 September, further 'bounces' by P-51s having been reported.

Powerplants

After its unhappy experiences with the F-8 (hampered by its single-stage Packard Merlins and limited PR equipment), the 8th Air Force was keen to obtain a Mosquito that was up to the weather reconnaissance role envisaged for the type. The PR.Mk XVIs ultimately delivered were powered by the Merlin 72/73 and were equipped with a pressurised cabin and were therefore able to operate at altitudes up to 37,000 ft (11278 m).

Weights

In standard trim the PR.Mk XVI had an all-up weight of 21,916 lb (9941 kg); with two 100-Imp gal (455-litre) underwing tanks this increased to 23,630 lb (10718 kg). By comparison, a PR.Mk IV had a loaded weight of 18,000 lb (8165 kg).

Flown by Lt Roger W. Gilbert and Lt Raymond G. Spoerl on 20 March 1945, RF992/'R' was one of four Mosquito 'chaff bombers' positioned at 26,000 ft (7925 m), ahead and below a bomber formation bound for Hamburg, in order to dispense chaff ahead of the bombers. Attacked by Me 262s, RF992 was hit by 30-mm cannon fire which blew off the port wingtip and aileron and put its radio out of action. The Mosquito spun out of control, but with a higher power setting on the port engine, Gilbert was able to regain control and nurse the aircraft back to Watton.

Chaff modifications

The lower rear fuel tanks were removed from 12 weather reconnaissance aircraft and replaced with magazines to dispense Chaff (Window in RAF parlance) through metal chutes in the bomb bay doors. Between 1,400 and 1,800 bundles of Type CHA-28 Chaff, weighing 600 lb (272 kg), could be carried.

de Havilland DH.98 Mosquito PR.Mk XVI
654th BS, 25th Bomb Group (R)
325th Photo Wing
8th Air Force
RAF Watton, March 1945

'Mickey Ships' and 'Red Stocking'

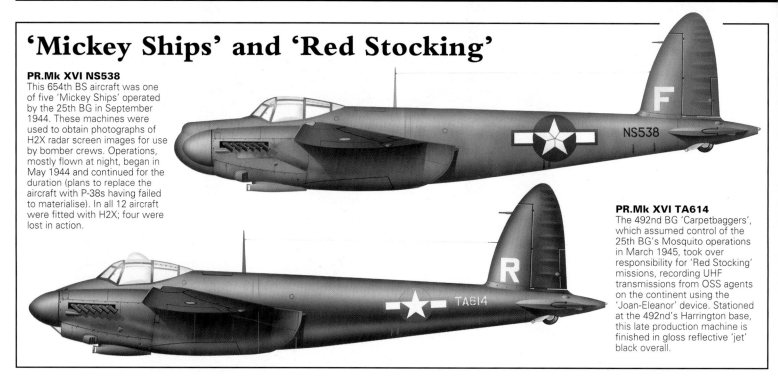

PR.Mk XVI NS538
This 654th BS aircraft was one of five 'Mickey Ships' operated by the 25th BG in September 1944. These machines were used to obtain photographs of H2X radar screen images for use by bomber crews. Operations, mostly flown at night, began in May 1944 and continued for the duration (plans to replace the aircraft with P-38s having failed to materialise). In all 12 aircraft were fitted with H2X; four were lost in action.

PR.Mk XVI TA614
The 492nd BG 'Carpetbaggers', which assumed control of the 25th BG's Mosquito operations in March 1945, took over responsibility for 'Red Stocking' missions, recording UHF transmissions from OSS agents on the continent using the 'Joan-Eleanor' device. Stationed at the 492nd's Harrington base, this late production machine is finished in gloss reflective 'jet' black overall.

Right: Photo Lab personnel Carl Wanka and John Ripley pose with 'Mickey Ship' NS538. Problems arose with the earliest H2X installations as a build up of fuel fumes in the rear fuselage of at least one aircraft caused an explosion. As well as the scanner in the nose, these aircraft carried associated equipment in the nose and bomb bay, the radar's scope being positioned in the rear fuselage. When switched on, the system drew a heavier current than the Mosquito's own electrical system and the 'Mickey' set was known to arc alarmingly.

Greex is a PR.Mk XVI in service with the 492nd BG and engaged in 'Red Stocking' operations over Germany, May 1945.

when the Mosquito prototype (W4050) in the hands of Geoffrey de Havilland, Jr was demonstrated to Lord Beaverbrook, Minister of Aircraft Production. The Americans were greatly impressed by the Mosquito's performance and had long been interested in setting up production in Canada and Australia. However, in America, the Material Division of the AAC placed little importance in the Mosquito, expecting that the F-4 (P-38) Lightning would be capable of carrying out US PR needs.

In the summer of 1942, Colonel Elliott Roosevelt brought two squadrons of F-4 Lightnings and a squadron of B-17F 'mapping Fortresses' to Britain. The President's son was preparing his 3rd PR Group for the invasion of North Africa in November (Torch) and was to work with the RAF until ready. Given a B.Mk IV for combat evaluation, Roosevelt discovered that the Mosquito outperformed his F-4s and had five times the range. General 'Hap' Arnold wanted 200 Mosquitoes to equip all American PR squadrons in Europe. In October 1943 Britain agreed to supply 120 to the USAAF for reconnaissance but, ultimately, only 40 F-8s (six converted from B.Mk VIIs and 34 from B.Mk XXs) ever reached the USAAF. They were to prove very unpopular with the USAAF in England and all, except 11 which were returned to the RAF in late 1944/early 1945, eventually went to the 3rd PR Group in the MTO.

PR for Operation Husky

Planning for Operation Husky, the invasion of Sicily, began in November 1942 and two PR Mosquitoes from No. 544 Squadron were loaned to Roosevelt's PR group at Algiers in December. In February 1943 General Carl Spaatz asked that two PR Mosquitoes be lent to General Eisenhower; they were given by No. 540 Squadron's detachment at Gibraltar, and despite repeated pleas were not returned, being retained in North Africa throughout the winter of 1943. One crashed and, owing to the lack of spares, was not replaced. In March 1943 No. 680 Squadron and the US 3rd Photo Group formed the North African PR Wing, under the unified command of Colonel Elliot Roosevelt. In April General Arnold requested PR Mosquitoes for special tasks but was told that insufficient aircraft were available. Air Marshal Tedder pointed out that Mosquitoes were required for urgent mapping operations and that only aircraft fitted with 36-in cameras could undertake the task. Two more PR Mosquitoes subsequently arrived to join No. 3 PR Group.

For a time the USAAF had to persist with F-5 mapping Lightnings and F-6s (modified P-51s). By March 1944, when American production lines were producing enough PR aircraft for the USAAF, the Mediterranean Theatre of Operations cancelled its requirement for the Mosquito,

Mk 35 – the last bomber

The final Mosquito bomber variant, the Mk 35, first flew on 12 March 1945, but did not see RAF service until 1948, equipping Nos 109 and 139 Sqns in Bomber Command until 1953 and Nos 14, 69 and 98 Sqns with the British Air Forces of Occupation (BAFO). Others were issued to non-operational units such as the Radio Warfare Establishment and the Central Bomber Establishment, the latter including aircraft fitted with H2S. Ten were modified by de Havilland as PR.Mk 35s, intended for night PR operations – four were issued to 'B' Flight, No. 58 Sqn in 1951. In all, 273 Mk 35s were completed, including 65 by Airspeed Ltd at Christchurch. A derivative of the Mk XVI, the Mk 35 was powered by the Merlin 113/114, as fitted to the Mk 34; late production aircraft were equipped with the Merlin 113A/114A. All were pressurised and had enlarged 'Cookie' bomb bays.

Above: Broad-chord 'paddle' propeller blades were a feature introduced in the Mk XVI and perpetuated in the Mk 35. TA638 is an early production example.

Left: Pictured around 1950, these No. 139 Sqn B.Mk 35s are in warmer climes than those normally experienced at their RAF Hemswell base. Of note are the aircraft's night bomber camouflage and 'XD' codes, the latter adopted in 1939 and used until at least 1951. These aircraft were replaced by Canberra Mk 2s in 1952.

choosing to standardise on the F-5 instead. In England, meanwhile, the 8th AF had one reconnaissance group equipped with F-5s and Spitfires while the 9th AF had three groups. Rather than replace any of the aircraft, the decision was taken to organise a group within the 8th using Mosquitoes, and on 22 April 1944 the 802nd Reconnaissance Group (P) was formed at Watton, Norfolk comprising the 652nd Heavy Weather Squadron, equipped with the B-17 and B-24, and two Mosquito squadrons, the 653rd and the 654th, using PR.Mk XVIs delivered from February.

Many personnel who were transferred into the 802nd BG had to be retrained. Mechanics who had never seen a Mosquito night-bomber attended a two-week course at the Rolls-Royce engine school in Derby. Others attended the airframe school at the de Havilland factory in Hatfield. Most of the pilots, many of whom were P-38 Lightning pilots from the 50th Squadron in Iceland and were used to the P-38's contra-rotating propellers, had never experienced the take-off and landing characteristics of the Mosquito, its high landing speed and tendency to swing on take-off. They had also to remember to open the radiator shutters just prior to take off to prevent the engines overheating. PR.Mk XVIs used a two-stage, two-speed supercharger that would cut in automatically at altitude. The superchargers were independent on each engine and a small difference in adjustment caused one to change gears hundreds of feet before the other. The resulting 'bang' and surge of power to one engine could wrest control from the unwary pilot and give the impression that the aircraft had been hit by flak. Several Oxfords and three Mosquito T.Mk IIIs were assigned for training.

Roosevelt's 325th Photo Wing

On 9 August 1944 the 802nd was reactivated as the 25th BG which, together with the 7th Photo Group, became part of the 325th Photographic Wing, commanded by Colonel Elliot Roosevelt. The Mosquitoes in the 25th BG operated from Watton almost all through the war (during the last 50 days of the war, they also operated from Harrington, Northamptonshire). The 653rd Light, Reconnaissance, or 'Light Weather Squadron', flew 1,531

varied missions during 28 March 1944-April 1945, including 1,332 missions known as Blue Stocking, which were associated with weather observation and forecasting. The balance of its missions comprised command flights, target scouting missions and chaff dispensing sorties. Chaff was the American equivalent of Window and was dropped over a wide area to 'snow' German fighter control radar and radar-equipped AA guns, by using an electric dispensing mechanism in the Mosquito's bomb bays. Chaff was dropped over the defence perimeter of a target just before oncoming bombers arrived. Turning and climbing over the bombers, the PR.Mk XVIs then photographed the bomb drop itself in motion picture. They then followed the bombers, taking still photographs of bombardment effectiveness.

The 654th, or the 'Special' Squadron, flew 700 varied types of missions, including 161 night photography flights codenamed Joker, using B-25s, B-26s and PR.Mk XVIs. The Mosquito was much more versatile than the two medium bombers and was employed on medium- and high-altitude night photography missions at an average speed of 270 mph (435 km/h). Each PR.Mk XVI would carry in the bomb bay 12 60-lb Type M46 photo-flash bombs of 700,000 candlepower. They were dropped,

Crews from one of the three Mosquito B.Mk 35 units based at Celle, (Nos 4, 11 and 98 Sqns) make their way to their aircraft parked on the PSP at the West German base during Exercise Agility II in October 1949. RAF Mosquitoes (flying armed reconnaissance and night interdiction sorties), Vampires and Spitfires took part alongside Fleet Air Arm Fireflies and Seafires from the 17th CAG and British, American and Belgian army units.

Post-war RAF PR ops

Post-war the PR.Mk 34/34A became the RAF's primary long-range reconnaissance platform at home and aboard and remained so until a PR variant of the English Electric Canberra became available. In peacetime tasks other than photo-reconnaissance occupied these squadrons. No. 684 Sqn in the Far East operated a high-speed courier service and undertook survey work, while in the Middle East, No. 13 Sqn (still with Mk IX and XVI aircraft) did similar work in Palestine and the Canal Zone until 1952, when it received Meteor Mk 10s. For Nos 58 and 540 Sqns at home, mapping work and the recording of flood damage were major tasks before both units re-equipped with Canberra PR.Mk 3s in 1952/53.

Above: PR.Mk 34A PF662 of No. 540 Sqn (fitted with a fuel tank-mounted camera) lands, possibly at Benson, in the early 1950s. A long-time PR Mosquito operator, No. 540 Sqn adopted a 'DH' code after World War II.

Top right: RG300 is pushed from its hangar at Benson. This aircraft was later sold in the US as N9871F.

Right: PF676 was completed by Percival Aircraft Ltd in 1946, one of a batch of B.Mk XVIs and PR.Mk 34s completed by the Luton-based manufacturer. Here it is seen while with No. 13 Sqn, at an unknown location in the Middle East, possibly Ein Shemer.

Centre right: By the time this photograph was taken RG236, a former No. 540 Sqn aircraft, had been converted to Mk 34A standard and is seen here while allocated to No. 237 (PR) OCU after 1947.

Two No. 13 Sqn Mk 34s, one with underwing tanks fitted, are seen over the Suez Canal in 1949. This unit was formed in September 1946 by renumbering No. 680 Sqn.

normally from around 12,000 ft (3658 m), at eight-second intervals to obtain a 60 per cent running overlap. They were fused to burst at 4,000 ft (1219 m) altitude to illuminate the target below.

Beginning in early 1943, the RAF had attempted night photography missions with PR.Mk IVs, first carrying magnesium flares. By 8 September 1943, 29 sorties had been flown, for the loss of two aircraft, one of them, DZ600, being shot down by a Mosquito night-fighter at Ipsden, near Benson, on 28 July, killing both crew members. Two PR.Mk IXs were then used to perfect the system (once the camera and the flash bombs had been harmonised), using the American flash bombs which were three times brighter than the British equivalents.

The first USAAF Joker mission flown by a Mosquito took place on 28 July 1944, to Lille, by two volunteer airmen, Richard Geary, pilot, and Bill Miskho, navigator, who returned safely after two and a half hours, their mission a complete success. Extensive high-altitude photographic missions deep into enemy territory were carried out at around 22,000 ft (6705 m) with the M-46 flash bombs fused to burst at 6,000 ft (1829 m). Two Type K-19B cameras were installed at a 27° split vertical angle directly over the port holes in the front section of the forward bomb bay. A third K-19B camera was mounted in the rear of the aircraft. The cameras were mounted to tilt to port, starboard and aft.

In addition, 55 missions were daylight still-photography sorties to determine the effectiveness of bombing missions and to observe selected positions, conditions and events. Twenty missions were daylight motion-picture photography flights. Daylight photography flights, both still and motion picture, were codenamed PRU. The other 132 photography missions were made up of chaff-dispensing sorties, command flights, secret OSS operations, and Mickey radar photo-mapping sorties using modified B-17 H2X sets, for it was clear that maps were needed that showed the same image as a radar scope. By this method, the 25th BG prepared photographic records of radar bombing approaches to a number of high-priority targets deep inside Germany. After proper annotation, identification and the exact position of the strategic target had been pinpointed, these Mickey bomb approach strips, or target run-ups, were used to brief the key radar navigator-bombardier of the bomber mission and to sight the bomb target through the overcast in the actual bombing.

'Mickey ships' with H2X

The H2X radar scanner was placed in a bulbous nose, the amplifiers and related equipment in the nose and bomb bay, and the radar scope in the rear fuselage. Before the mission, the observer climbed in through the rear door with a camera (sometimes a motion picture camera) to photograph the details on the radar screen. The observer's

Firedog and the end

It was in the Far East that the RAF's Mosquitoes were to have their swansong. On 1 September 1946, No. 684 Sqn was renumbered No. 81 Sqn and, as the only RAF PR unit remaining in FEAF, was tasked with long-range PR and survey work in the East Indian area. The squadron flew Mk XVIs briefly before converting to Mk 34s, and for shorter range work employed Spitfire PR.Mk 19s. The last Spitfires were retired in 1954, the squadron then soldiering on with its Mosquitoes until 1955. Its last operational sorties were during Operation Firedog, these beginning in 1949 and finally concluding on 15 December 1955, when Flying Officers A. J. 'Collie' Knox and 'Tommy' Thompson completed the final operational sortie in Mk 34A RG314.

only means of escape in an emergency was to crawl over the set and jump through the bomb bay – provided the pilot opened the bomb doors! There was a tendency for the Mickey set to arc or even explode when first turned on. The radar drew a heavier current than the Mosquito's electrical system could handle, and the aircraft were grounded several times in an attempt to overcome the problem.

Much of the effort by the 654th Squadron was directed to improving the strategic value of H2X bombing and to alleviating civilian casualties. Mickey had the highest loss rate, highest abort rate and greatest number of failures of any mission involving USAAF PR.Mk XVIs. Three H2X missions flown at night did not return. There were no losses after December 1944, the month in which Mickey switched to daylight missions with fighter escort. The radar set continued to malfunction. Of 36 missions flown in January, only four were successful, and from 19 February 1945 the 654th switched to light weather missions.

On 24 March, a daylight mission was tried. A Mosquito piloted by Lieutenant C. B. Stubblefield and his navigator-radar operator, First Lieutenant James B. Richmond, flew ahead of the 8th AF bombers, escorted by eight P-51 Mustangs. They would be led to the German fighters as they started their climb to attack the bombers. Unfortunately, the Mosquito was shot down by a 9th AF P-47; Stubblefield was killed and Richmond was made PoW. Later, four P-38 Lightnings were assigned to escort the H2X mission going in at high altitudes.

Blue Stocking weather operations

Meanwhile, in May 1944 the Light Weather Squadron had begun Blue Stocking weather operations, and immediately prior to D-Day, 6 June, gave weather predictions for the invasion. The Special Squadron aided in the search for V-1 sites in northern France that summer, performing Dilly daylight reconnaissance missions over the Pas de Calais in search of Noball sites. The 654th flew day, and night Joker,

photo missions and Scouting sorties just ahead of the main bombing force, transmitting up-to-the-minute weather reports to the task force commander to prevent him leading his bombers into heavy weather fronts. The D-Day invasion was prepared by intelligence gathered on Dilly (night photography missions of coastal defences). Captain Walter D. Gernand, a 654th Squadron pilot, and his cameraman, Sergeant Ebbet C. Lynch, 8th CCU, who carried out a PR of the beachhead, were killed when RS555 hit a railway embankment near High Wycombe on their return.

The US PR.Mk XVIs were used on daylight missions codenamed PRU, using still and motion-picture photography, and on long-range navigation missions using LORAN. When, in the summer of 1944, the US Navy needed data on the range, reception and accuracy of the LORAN overlay, 653rd Squadron PR.Mk XVIs, fitted with the device, accompanied the two 8th AF Frantic shuttle bombing missions to Ukraine, on 21 June and again on 6 August. Late in September 1944 the 654th Squadron flew the first mission to prove the feasibility of reading lines of position (LOP) in the air, on 28 September 1944. The missions proved LORAN's capabilities where all other navigational aids failed. Complete coverage of the continent at all altitudes and in all types of weather was now available.

654th Squadron Mosquitoes carrying an 8th CCU photographer accompanied the USAAF Aphrodite and US Navy Anvil pilotless drone operations, which used war-weary B-17s and PB4Y-1 Liberators, respectively, packed with 18,000 lb (8165 kg) of Torpex, a nitroglycerine compound, and the 26,000-lb (11794-kg) GB-4 Batty glide bombing missions. After the drone or glide bomb was airborne, the 654th Squadron Mosquito would fly close to photograph it in flight and film its effect. These photographs were used to analyse all angles of the flight and to improve methods and equipment of the mission. Each of these missions was preceded by a Blue Stocking weather reconnaissance flight over the target by a 653rd Squadron Mk XVI.

Above: RG314, the last operational Mosquito poses for official photographs during the final weeks of its RAF career, during December 1955.

Above left: F/Os 'Collie' Knox and 'Tommy' Thompson undertake their pre-flight checks before the final sortie on 15 December.

Another of No. 81 Sqn's Mk 34As, RG177, beats up Seletar in May 1953. This aircraft suffered brake failure on landing in March 1955 – a comparatively minor accident that brought about the aircraft's withdrawal for scrap.

RN tugs and others

The post-war Fleet Air Arm received a number of surplus RAF Mosquitoes, including PR.Mk XVIs, B.Mk 25s and PR.Mk 34s, for use in fleet requirements and training roles. In addition, another Mosquito variant, derived from the B.Mk XVI, was specifically developed for target-towing. The TT.Mk 39 was a high-speed shore-based naval target tug developed by General Aircraft Ltd of Feltham, Middlesex, under its designation GAL.59. Intended to fill Royal Navy Specification Q.19/45 (for an aircraft to replace the Miles M.33 Monitor TT.Mk 11), 26 Mk XVIs were converted in all. The Mk 39 was, without a doubt, the least attractive of all Mosquitoes, fitted with an extended, glazed nose (which housed a camera operator) and a dorsal cupola on the rear fuselage. This housed the third crew member, a rear-facing observer/drogue operator. Drogue targets were streamed from a hydraulically-operated winch in the bomb bay, powered by a retractable propeller in the forward bomb bay. A radio altimeter was fitted for radar-calibration purposes. The TT.Mk 39 first entered service with Fleet Requirements Units from 1950 (having been tested by No. 703 Sqn in 1948). No. 728 Sqn FRU at Hal Far, Malta operated the last examples until 1952.

Top: The size of the grossly modified nose of the Mk 39 required that its airscrew blades be cropped. At least one aircraft (PF606, the first 'production' example) was flown with four-bladed propellers. Mk 39s were powered by either a Merlin 72/73 or 76/77 combination.

Above: In this view of PF606, the position of the drogue operator's dorsal cupola is clearly visible, along with the wire guards fitted to the tailplane and tail wheel.

Right: PF489, the 2nd prototype, is seen part way through nose modifications. Photographed at Feltham, the aircraft was en route to Lasham with a dummy nose fitted.

VP191, an Airspeed-built aircraft completed with Merlin 113A/114A engines, was equipped with a Type G winch. Note the undersurfaces were finished in yellow/black stripes in typical target tug fashion, to aid conspicuity. Photographed at the 1958 Biggin Hill Battle of Britain Display, VP191 is a No. 3 CAACU machine.

Bottom: RV365 was a Hatfield-built B.Mk 35 completed in mid-1945 and is seen here in initial TT.Mk 35 condition, without the drogue winch fitted. Coded '6', this aircraft was with No. 233 OCU.

Garden was planned to cut off the Germany Army in the Belgian sector and save the bridges and the port of Antwerp for the American army units and British 30th Corps advancing north from the Dutch border. Bad weather during Market Garden made regular air reconnaissance over the Arnhem bridge impossible, so 25th BG Mosquitoes were despatched on 17, 18 and 22 September to reconnoitre the bridge, or bring back weather reports. One Mosquito and its crew was lost on 17 September, and on 25 September another was lost when it was shot down by a German night-fighter. The crew members baled out and were made PoWs.

Gray Pea chaff dispensing

Some 352 chaff-dispensing sorties, codenamed Gray Pea (after Colonel Leon Gray, who assumed command of the 25th BG on 23 September 1944, and Colonel (later General) Budd Peaslee), were carried out by PR.Mk XVI Mosquitoes of the 653rd and 654th Squadrons using an electric chaff-dispensing mechanism in their bomb bays. A formation of three (later four) PR.Mk XVIs zigzagged ahead of the bomber stream, dropped chaff over the target and then recrossed it to photograph the strike. The Mosquitoes were still able to land before the bombers were over the Channel.

On 20 March 1945, Second Lieutenant Joseph A. Polovick and First Lieutenant Bernard M. Blaum were hit by enemy fire on a Gray Pea mission over Germany and were captured. On 3 April 1945 six Gray Pea Mosquitoes were detailed for chaff-screening for the 8th AF, five scouted for the Fortresses and seven flew weather reconnaissance over the continent and seas around Britain. Lieutenant Colonel Alvin E. Podojski, pilot and Group Deputy Commander, and Captain Lionel A. Proulx, navigator, were leading a flight of four Mosquitoes on a Gray Pea mission over Kiel when they were attacked by German fighters. Their Mosquito received damage but they managed to reach Sweden safely.

The Aphrodite and Anvil missions were less than successful, with several losses, including a Navy PB4Y packed with over 22,000 lb (9979 kg) of Torpex and TNT, which exploded prematurely killing pilot Lieutenant Joseph P. Kennedy, Jr, the eldest son of the former US Ambassador to Britain, and 'Bud' Willy, his co-pilot. This explosion hurled debris into the path of the PR.Mk XVI crewed by Lieutenants Robert A. Tunnel and David J. McCarthy, who just managed to land at the nearest available airfield without further loss. The following day, a Mosquito crewed by First Lieutenant Dean H. Sanner and Staff Sergeant Augie Kurjack was brought down during a glide bombing mission to Le Havre when the Mosquito flew through the bomb blast. Sanner survived and was made a PoW; Kurjack was killed.

In September 1944 the Allies attempted to capture bridges on the Rhine in Holland at Veghel, Grave, Nijmegen and Arnhem using the 1st British and 82nd and 101st American Airborne Divisions. Operation Market

TT.Mk 35 – last of all

With a requirement similar to that of the FAA, the RAF contracted Brooklands Aviation to convert 105 B.Mk 35s to TT.Mk 35 (sometimes referred to as B(TT).Mk 35) standard in 1952/53. Three towed targets could be carried in the aircraft's bomb bay, though a few examples (the first of which was converted by Marshalls Flying Services Ltd) were able to use an ML Type G winch fitted under the closed bomb bay doors. A number of TT.Mk 35s were operated by units supporting gunnery ranges in Germany and Mediterranean. The main operators in the UK were the five Civilian Anti-Aircraft Co-operation Units (CAACUs) – No. 3 CAACU at Exeter (operated by Exeter Airport Ltd) providing target facilities using Mosquitoes until 1963, these becoming the last RAF examples in service. A handful of TT.Mk 35s were also converted for meteorological use as Met.Mk 35s.

Post-war PR exports

The bulk of the surplus Mosquitoes exported after the end of World War II were of the fighter-bomber and photo-reconnaissance marks. The latter comprised Mk XVIs sold to the French Armée de l'Air, South African Air Force Mk XVIs retained after the end of the war and a number of Mk XVIs acquired from a variety of sources by the fledgling Israeli air force. In fact, IDF/AF Mosquitoes were probably the last examples to see combat. Although they had been replaced by jet types in 1955/56, Israel's 'Mossies' were taken out of storage in October 1956 when war with Egypt broke out. Interception, bombing and PR sorties were flown before and during the Sinai (Suez) campaign of 29 October to 2 November. None was lost to enemy action and serviceability rates were comparatively good, given the age of the aircraft.

PR.Mk XVIs of the 25th BG flew 74 Red Tail missions in which they carried the command pilot of 8th AF bombing missions. By accelerating around his formation in a fast Mosquito bomber, the command pilot was provided with an observation platform for greater oversight. He could better monitor the formation and advise key pilots of defects in the assembly pattern. In addition, he was not vulnerable to enemy fighters as he might be in a lead bomber. Despite red tail markings and US stars, the PR.Mk XVIs were often mistaken for Me 262s and Me 410s. Crews were sent to bomber and fighter group bases to display their distinctive aircraft and help prevent identification problems, but the confusion persisted. On 4 April 1945, a 653rd Squadron PR.Mk XVI flown by First Lieutenant T. B. Smith, and carrying Colonel Troy Crawford of the 446th BG was attacked by Me 262s and was shot down by gunners from Crawford's group as the Mosquito moved close to the B-24s for protection. Smith and Crawford parachuted and were taken prisoner.

Three, later five, PR.Mk XVIs were used in a series of top secret spying missions codenamed Red Stocking, so-named to help disguise the true nature of their mission and perhaps persuade the German intelligence services that this was a weather mission similar to Blue Stocking. Their true intent was to detect and record UHF transmissions from OSS agents. For this purpose the bomb bay was fitted with an oxygen system and modified to accept a top-secret and very compact airborne radio receiver connected to a wire recorder, used by an operative who sat on a cramped and uncomfortable drop seat behind the collapsible fuel tank. Entry was through a small hatch on the starboard side of the fuselage just aft of the wing. The Joan-Eleanor device, as it

was called, had been developed by Lieutenant Commander Steve Simpson, a Texan scientist, and DeWitt R. Goddard (taking its name from a major in the WACs and Goddard's wife, respectively), to replace the cumbersome 'S-Phone' device previously carried in a suitcase by agents in France. Joan weighed only 4 lb (1.8 kg) so the agent in the field could carry it easily. It was used to beam transmissions on a radio beam so narrow that it was practically immune to detection. As much information could be passed clearly in one 15- to 20-minute contact as could be passed in days by conventional radio.

'Joan-Eleanor'

The first successful contact was made by Simpson in a Mosquito on 22 November 1944 when, circling at 30,000 ft (10058 m), he recorded the first of eight transmissions with agent Bobbie in Holland. Altogether, the 654th Squadron flew 32 Red Stocking missions for OSS over Germany, Austria and enemy-occupied territory. One of the most daring was flown on 12 March 1945 when a Red Stocking PR.Mk XVI flying at 30,000 ft over Berlin successfully established radio contact with agents who had earlier been dropped from an A-26C Invader. On 15 March the OSS missions moved to the 492nd BG B-24 Liberator base at Harrington, Northamptonshire, but the PR.Mk XVIs (and A-26s) remained at Watton for a while longer because of problems maintaining the aircraft there. Crews flew from Watton to Harrington for briefing and after each mission occasionally eturned to Watton.

All told, the 25th BG flew 3,246 missions, the 653rd Squadron losing 24 PR.Mk XVIs, including 13 on operations, and the 654th losing 27, 16 of them on

Racers and surveyors

Though Spartan Air Services Ltd had by far the largest fleet of civilian-owned Mosquitoes, a considerable number were purchased by other operators and private individuals, mainly in Australia, Canada, the UK and the USA. Four PR.Mk 41s are known to have been registered on the Australian civil register. Two of these were entered in the 1953 London-to-Christchurch, NZ air race, though one was later withdrawn. The surviving entry got as far as Mergui, Burma before crash-landing. In the UK, the first civil-registered Mosquito was G-AOSS, a B.Mk 35 intended to be used by one Roberta Cowell in an attempt to better the South Atlantic speed record, though this came to nought after suitable engines could not be found. In the US, four Mk 35s were registered, the most famous of which was N9919F (ex-VR801). Richard E. Loomis purchased the aircraft for £2,850, insured it for £17,850 and then attempted to persuade James K. Gibbs to wreck the Mosquito in an 'accident'. The deal was to split the insurance pay-out, but Loomis allegedly sabotaged the aircraft so that it crash-landed on 1 July 1957, killing Gibbs. Almost three years later Loomis was charged with murder and, though acquitted in December 1960, was found guilty of conspiracy, destroying insured property and making a false accident report.

This aircraft, serialled 2139, is one of the PR.Mk XVIs acquired by Israel in the mid/late-1950s.

Top left: Ex-FAA PR.Mk XVI G-AOCI was among a batch of 17 Mosquitoes purchased by the IDF/AF and gathered together at Thruxton in the mid-1950s. Only three of these aircraft were overhauled and delivered to Israel; 'AOCI was among those that never left Thruxton.

Below left: N9871F (ex-RG300, a Mk 34) was purchased by Jack Amman Photogrammetric Engineering Inc. in May 1956 and operated by Trans World Aero Surveys for the next three years. After lying derelict for six years, the aircraft was eventually obtained by the Confederate Air Force at Harlingen, it was stripped of useful parts and scrapped.

Bottom: N37878 Wooden Wonder was a Mk 25 (ex-KB377) purchased by Canadian Don McVicar and entered in the 1948 Bendix Trophy Air Race (as CF-FZG). Entered again the following year by American Jesse Stallings (the president of Capitol Airways Inc, who had finished fifth in 1948 in another Mk 25, N66313 Miss Marta), N37878 finished fourth at an average speed of 343.757 mph (553.222 km/h). Modifications made to the aircraft included the fitting of 50-Imp gal (227-litre) underwing tanks and an internal fuel tank in a bulged bomb bay. Note also that the glazed nose of the aircraft has been painted over.

Two round-the-world flights were planned using this aircraft – B.Mk 25 N1203V, ex-KA997. Americans Bob and Dianna Bixby left San Francisco on 1 April 1950, reaching Cairo and Calcutta before engine problems forced the flight to be abandoned. In 1954 a further attempt was planned, this time by Dianna Bixby alone, though she was killed in the crash of a Douglas A-20 before the flight took place. Sold to Clair Waterbury, the aircraft was extensively modified for high-altitude survey work, with a metal forward fuselage and new engines, the latter reportedly salvaged from a pair of P-51s. Sold again, this time to the Flying Tiger Line (sponsors of Bixby's flight) it was employed on survey tasks before being finally written-off in a landing accident in Haiti in 1956.

Below right: A number of surplus ex-RAF Mk 34s and 35s found their way on to civil registers in the 1950s. This Mk 35 (EC-WKH, ex-TK652) was modified by Derby Aviation Ltd and used by Capt Rudolfo Bay Wright for radio emission and reception trials for the Spanish government.

Bottom: British European Airways formed a Gust Research Unit to study clear air turbulence prior to the introduction of new jet airliners like the DH.106 Comet. Two PR.Mk 34s were leased (G-AJZF, ex-RG238 and G-AZJE, ex-RG231) and modified with beam approach and Gee navigation aids and gust research equipment. Cameras were removed and internal fuel capacity reduced, though fixed 100-Imp gal (455-litre) underwing tanks were fitted. High-altitude flights were made between 1948 and 1950, ranging over long distances from Scotland to Spain and the Swiss Alps. Both aircraft were eventually refurbished and returned to the RAF.

operations. With the end of the war in Europe, the 25th BG was expected to be sent to the Pacific, but its PR.Mk XVIs were returned to the RAF and in August the Group returned to the USA, where, on 8 September 1945, it was inactivated at Drew Field, Florida.

In the Royal Australian Air Force, No. 86 Squadron RAAF reformed from No. 1 PRU, RAAF on 10 September 1945, equipped with modified FB.Mk 40s. No. 1 PRU had originally been based in the Northern Territory of Australia to cover the Dutch East Indies, including East Java, Borneo East, the Celebes, the Halmaheras, Timor, Kai Islands and, later, the Philippines, especially Davao Gulf and Leyte Gulf. FB.Mk 40s were modified to carry cameras and the first PR.Mk 40 sortie was flown from Coomalie Creek, 54 miles (87 km) south of Darwin, on 1 June 1944. By 1945, Broome, 1,500 miles (2414 km) from Coomalie Creek, was being used, enabling the Mk 40s and seven British-built PR.Mk XVIs to reach targets in East Java, 2;300 miles (3701 km) distant, on flights lasting up to nine hours.

No. 87 Squadron, RAAF operated 26 PR.Mk 40s and 20 FB.Mk 40s on PR in the northwest area of the Pacific to photograph Japanese-held territories, including Borneo. The first 12 of 16 PR.Mk XVIs were received from Britain during March 1945, when No. 87 Squadron flew a number of sorties to find and successfully photograph the Japanese heavy cruiser *Isuzu* and its three escorts en route to Koepang, Timor Island. The squadron's PR.Mk XVIs were used almost exclusively for the rest of the war, although Mk 40s were still used on sorties to Java and East Borneo. From June 1945, two PR.Mk XVIs and one Mk 40 under the command of Squadron Leader K. J. 'Red' Gray, DFC were detached to Cocus Island to photograph Singapore, but bad weather restricted the unit to just one flight, to Christmas Island. After the war, No. 87 Squadron, RAAF made a large-scale air survey of Australia, before disbanding in 1946.

RAF at home and overseas

The last bomber Mosquito variant built was the B.Mk 35. The type first flew on 12 March 1945, but it did not enter RAF service until 1948, when Nos 109 and 139 PFF Squadrons at Hemswell began receiving the type. Both squadrons re-equipped with the Canberra B.Mk 2 in July 1952 and November 1953, respectively. In Germany, Nos 69, 14 and 98 Squadrons in BAFO (British Air Forces of Occupation) also operated B.Mk 35s. No. 69 Squadron operated the B.Mk 35 until it disbanded on 6 November 1947, and Nos 14 and 98 Squadrons operated them until February 1951 when they were replaced by Vampire FB.Mk 5s.

PR.Mk 34s operated with the RAF at home and abroad in the late 1940s and early 1950s. After VJ-Day No. 684 Squadron used its PR.Mk 34s as a high-speed courier service in the Far East, before moving to Bangkok, Thailand in January 1946 for survey duty. On 1 September No. 684 Squadron disbanded at Seletar, Malaya, renumbering as No. 81 Squadron, now the only PR unit in FEAF, responsible for long-range PR and survey in the East Indian area. No. 13 Squadron, which had disbanded in Greece in April 1946, reformed on 13 September; operating PR.Mk IXs and PR.Mk XVIs, it carried out PR and photo-survey work in Palestine and the Canal Zone from April 1946 until February 1952, when the Mosquitoes were replaced by Meteor PR.Mk I0s.

No. 540 Squadron, which had disbanded at Benson on 30 September 1946, reformed there on 1 December 1947 with PR.Mk 34s. They were used on PR and survey duties until December 1952 when Canberra PR.Mk 3s took over. No. 58 Squadron, which had reformed at Benson on 1 October 1946 in the PR role using Ansons and PR.Mk 34s, was used for the Ordnance Survey of Great Britain. In 1953 the Ansons and PR.Mk 34s were also superseded by Canberras.

Spartan Air Services

One of the biggest civil users of the Mosquito was Ottawa-based aerial survey company Spartan Air Services Ltd, which purchased 10 new Mk 35s (nine B.Mk 35s and the PR.Mk 35 prototype RS700) from storage for C$1,500 each in 1955. After overhaul, by Derby Aviation Ltd, all were flown across the Atlantic. Modifications made upon arrival in Canada included the fitting of blown nose glazing, a forward-hinged upper canopy panel, the fitting of wooden covers in place of the bomb doors, and cameras in the fuselage, forward and aft of the bomb bay. These were operated by a camera operator seated in the rear fuselage. New radio gear and a D/F loop were installed and the crew was provided with an oxygen system, as the airframe modifications rendered the Mk 35s' pressurisation system unusable. A further five Mk 35s were obtained in 1955, and although it was intended to fly these to Canada, they were eventually stripped of useable parts and scrapped in the UK. By 1962, when Spartan wound up its Mosquito operations, the company had just three aircraft still in use.

This view of Spartan's CF-HMQ (ex-VP189) over one of the more inhospitable parts of the Canadian landscape shows the extent of the modifications made to these aircraft. The blown nose glazing and camera ports are particularly evident.

Left: An immaculate CF-HMT (ex-RS711) is seen prior to its delivery flight across the Atlantic.

Bottom left: Seen at Luton in December 1971, RS709 is seen prior to its departure for the United States and new owners, the Confederate Air Force. Note the N9797 registration applied in place of its RAF serial number and the unusual three-port exhaust on the Merlin engine.

The UK's last two airworthy Mosquitoes were RR299/G-ASKH (a T.Mk III, sadly written-off in a fatal accident on 21 July 1996 while in the ownership of British Aerospace) and RS712/G-ASKB, a Mk 35. The latter was sold in 1981 to American collector Kermit Weeks, overhauled and flown to Florida in September 1987. Flown only briefly (as N35MK), RS712 has since been loaned to the Experimental Aircraft Association (EAA) and is displayed in Oshkosh, WI.

In February 1953, at Wyton, No. 58 Squadron's PR.Mk 34s and PR.35s (including four in 'B' Flight converted for night photo-reconnaissance using flashlights), and No. 540 Squadron's PR.Mk 34s at Benson, photographed the torrential floods which paralysed the east coast of Britain. For eight days they chronicled the devastation, taking over 100,000 photographs which were used to help aid the rescue and repair efforts. In mid-1953 No. 58 Squadron's PR.Mk 34s were replaced by Canberra PR.Mk 3s, 540 having begun re-equipment with the jet in December 1952.

The last RAF Mosquitoes in RAF service were PR.Mk 34As of No. 81 Squadron at Seletar, on 1 April 1954. In 1946-47, No. 81 Squadron had carried out an aerial survey of the country. A state of emergency in Malaya was declared on 17 June 1948 when an all-out Communist uprising began, and No. 81 Squadron's PR.Mk 34As reverted to their PR role as part of Operation Firedog, which began in July 1949. By the end of 1952 No. 81 Squadron's Mosquitoes had made in excess of 4,000 sorties and had photographed 34,000 sq miles (88053 km²). No. 81 Squadron flew some 6,619 sorties during eight years of operations in Malaya. The honour of flying the very last RAF Mosquito sortie went to RG314, when Flying Officers A. J. 'Collie' Knox and 'Tommy' Thompson returned from a Firedog reconnaissance sortie against two terrorist camps in Malaya on 15 December 1955.

Martin Bowman

Mossies in the movies

633 Squadron, filmed in the summer of 1963 and relating the story of a fictitious wartime RAF FB.Mk VI squadron (commanded by Cliff Robertson), utilised TT.Mk 35s just retired by No. 3 CAACU. Three were given the civil registrations G-ASKA (ex-RS709), G-ASKB (ex-RS712) and G-ASKH (ex-TA719) and, along with the rest of the unit's aircraft, were modified to represent Mk VIs. In 1966, Mosquito Squadron (starring David McCallum) was produced using four of the aircraft employed in the earlier picture, namely RR299, RS709, RS712 and TA634. In both films the aircraft carried 'HT' codes (actually used by No. 154 Sqn – a fighter unit – during the war years, and No. 601 Sqn, RAuxAF in 1949. Apart from RR299, the above named aircraft have all survived.

Mosquito Operators

Such was the success of the Mosquito design that it had a remarkably long career in the post-war RAF and surplus aircraft proved popular with foreign air forces. The greater versatility of the fighter-bomber Mosquito variants made them more attractive, though PR aircraft found a few customers. Bombers were confined to service in the countries of their manufacture.   Martin Bowman and John Heathcott

United Kingdom
Royal Air Force

The following is a listing of the front-line reconnaissance and bomber units equipped with Mosquitoes during World War II, plus the major second-line units, as well as units equipped with Mosquito PR and bomber aircraft and their derivatives post-war.

Wartime RAF PR units

unit	theatre/group	dates	variants employed
No. 1 PRU	UK	Sep 41 – Oct 42	PR.Mk I/II/IV
No. 4 Sqn ('B' Flt)	2nd TAF	Dec 43 – May 44	PR.Mk XVI
No. 140 Sqn	2nd TAF	Nov 43 – Nov 45	PR.Mk IX/XVI
No. 521 Sqn	UK	Aug 42 – Mar 43	PR.Mk IV (Met?)
No. 540 Sqn	UK	Oct 42 – Sep 46	PR.Mk IV/IX/XVI
No. 543 Sqn	UK	Jun 43 – Oct 43	PR.Mk IV (training)
No. 544 Sqn	UK	Apr 43 – Oct 45	PR.Mk IV/IX/XVI/32/34
No. 618 Sqn	Australia	Jul 44 – Mar 45	PR.Mk XVI (five)
No. 680 Sqn	Middle East/Med	Feb 44 – Aug 46	PR.Mk IX/XVI
No. 681 Sqn	Far East	Aug 43 – Nov 43	PR.Mk II
No. 682 Sqn	North Africa	May 43 – Jul 43	PR.Mk IX
No. 683 Sqn	Malta	May 43 – Jun 43	PR.Mk IV
No. 684 Sqn	India/Burma	Sep 43 – Aug 46	PR.Mk II/IX/XVI/34, FB.Mk VI
No. 8 (PR)OTU	UK	Nov 42 – Jul 47	PR.Mk I/IV/VIII/XVI/34
PR Development Unit/APDU		Dec 43 – Mar 50	PR.Mk IV/XVI/32/34/B.Mk 35

Wartime bomber units

unit	group	dates	variants employed
No. 105 Sqn	No. 2 Gp/No. 8 Gp	Nov 41 – Jan 46	B.Mk IV/IX/XVI
No. 109 Sqn	No. 2 Gp/No. 8 Gp	Oct 45 – Jul 52	B.Mk IV/IX/XVI/35
No. 128 Sqn	No. 8 Gp	Sep 44 – Apr 46	B.Mk 25
No. 139 Sqn	No. 2 Gp/No. 8 Gp	Sep 42 – Nov 52	B.Mk IV/IX/XVI/XX/25/35
No. 142 Sqn	No. 8 Gp	Oct 44 – May 45	B.Mk
No. 162 Sqn	No. 8 Gp	Dec 44 – Jul 46	B.Mk 25
No. 163 Sqn	No. 8 Gp	Jan 45 – May 45	B.Mk 25/XVI
No. 571 Sqn	No. 8 Gp	Apr 44 – May 45	B.Mk IX/XVI
No. 608 Sqn	No. 8 Gp	Aug 44 – May 45	B.Mk XX/XVI
No. 618 Sqn	Coastal Command	Apr 43 – Jun 45	B.Mk IV/PR.Mk XVI
No. 627 Sqn	No. 8 Gp/No. 5 Gp	Nov 43 – Aug 45	B.Mk IV/XVI/XX/25/IX
No. 692 Sqn	No. 8 Gp	Jan 44 – Sep 45	B.Mk IV/XVI
No. 1474 Flt.	No. 100 Gp (ELINT)	Nov 42 – Jan 43	B.Mk IV
No. 192 Sqn	No. 100 Gp (ELINT)	Jan 43 – Aug 45	B.Mk IV/PR.Mk XVI
No. 1317 Flight	No. 5 Gp	Jun 45 – Jun 45	B.Mk IX/XVI/PR.Mk IX
No. 1409 Met. Flt	No. 8 Gp	Apr 43 – May 45	B.IV/IX/XVI
PFF Navigation Training Unit (PFFNTU)		Dec 44 – Jun 45	B.Mk IV/XX
No. 1655 MCU/TU	No. 8 Gp	Aug 42 – Dec 44	B.Mk IV/XVI/XX/25
No. 13 OTU		?	B.Mk IV
No. 16 OTU		Jan 45 – Mar 47	B.Mk IV/XVI/XX/25

Post-war Mosquito units (PR, bomber, TT)

unit	location	dates	variants employed
No. 13 Sqn	MEAF	Sep 46 – Feb 52	PR.Mk 34
No. 14 Sqn	BAFO	Apr 46 – Feb 51	B.Mk XVI/35
No. 58 Sqn	UK	Oct 46 – Jan 53	PR.Mk 34/34A/B.Mk 35
No. 69 Sqn	BAFO	Apr 46 – Nov 47	B.Mk XVI
No. 81 Sqn	FEAF	Sep 46 – Dec 55	PR.Mk XVI/34/34A
No. 98 Sqn	BAFO	Jan 46 – Feb 51	B.Mk XVI/35
No. 180 Sqn	BAFO	Sep 45 – Apr 46	B.Mk XVI
No. 527 Sqn	UK (calibration)	Sep 52 – Jan 56	B.Mk 35
No. 540 Sqn	UK	Dec 47 – Aug 53	PR.Mk 34/34A
No. 1 CAACU	UK	?	TT.Mk 35
No. 2 CAACU	UK	?	TT.Mk 35
No. 3 CAACU	UK	? – 1963	TT.Mk 35
No. 4 CAACU	UK	Aug 51 – ?	TT.Mk 35
No. 5 CAACU	UK	Sep 51 – ?	TT.Mk 35
Central Bomber Establishment		Sep 45 – Dec 49	B.Mk XVI/35
No. 237 (PR) OCU	UK	Jul 47 – Dec 51	PR.Mk 34/B.Mk 35
No. 229 OCU	UK	Dec 54 – June 56	TT.Mk 35
No. 231 OCU	UK	Mar 47 – Dec 49	B.Mk XVI
No. 233 OCU	UK	Jun 55 – Aug 56	TT.Mk 35
No. 236 OCU	UK	Sep 52 – Sep 54	TT.Mk 35
No. 237 OCU	UK	Jul 47 – Aug 51	PR.Mk 34/B.Mk 35
No. 238 OCU	UK	Oct 53 – Feb 54	TT.Mk 35
Towed Target Flight, Gibraltar		May 53 – ?	TT.Mk 35
Towed Target Flight, Schleswigland		Mar 53 – May 58	TT.Mk 35
Towed Target Flight, St Eval		Sep 53 – Sep 55	TT.Mk 35
Radio Warfare/Central Signals Estab.		Jul 45 – ?	B.Mk XVI/34/B.Mk 35

Fleet Air Arm

The Royal Navy's post-war Mosquito fleet included surplus ex-RAF PR.Mk XVIs, Mk 34s and B.Mk 25s, used largely for training and fleet requirements duties, as well as the TT.Mk 39 target tugs.

In 1945, about 70 Mk 25s were handed over by RAF Bomber Command for use by No. 771 Sqn, a Fleet Requirements Unit. These were operated until 1947. The following year PR.Mk 34s joined the unit's existing Sea Mosquitoes though by early 1950 these had been replaced with TT.Mk 39 target tugs. The other FAA target tug unit was No. 728 Sqn, another FRU based at Hal Far, Malta until 1952.

PR.Mk 16s were operated by Nos 703, 728, 770, 771, 772 and 778 Sqns; PR.Mk 34s equipped Nos 771 and 772 Sqns; B.Mk 25s served with Nos 704, 728, 733, 762, 770, 771, 772, 777, 778, 790 and 797 Sqns.

Above: No. 139 Squadron was the second unit to receive Mosquito B.Mk IVs, flying daylight sorties within No. 2 Group.

Below: NS787 is one of No. 684 Squadron's Mk XVIs, operated from bases in India and Burma from 1944 until VJ-Day.

Above: No. 81 Sqn, operator of the RAF's last Mosquitoes, was active during Operation Firedog. Mk 34A RG314 was its last active aircraft.

Below: Firestreak AAM trials were behind the modifications made to B.Mk 35 TH988, including the fitting of a radar scanner in a ventral pod and a large circular window in its nose (for a camera or IR emitter?).

Below: This unusual Fleet Air Arm PR.Mk 34 (PF664) was photographed on Gibraltar and sports some unusual excrescences, including a small Perspex cupola at the extreme rear of the bomb bay and a long whip aerial under the starboard wing. Its unit is unknown, though this may have been No. 751 Sqn, a Radio Warfare Unit based at Watton.

Australia

Royal Australian Air Force use of PR Mosquitoes began in May 1944 when No. 87 Sqn (based at Coomalee Creek, NT and Parkes, NSW) received the first PR.Mk 40s modified from locally-built FB.Mk 40s. From March 1945 the squadron operated 12 of the more capable PR.Mk XVIs received from Britain (of 23 in all, serialled A52-600/-622) almost exclusively for the rest of the war. The squadron disbanded in July 1946.

No. 1 PRU, RAAF (at Coomalee Creek, NT) received PR.Mk 40s in June 1944, operating these until September 1945, when the PRU became No. 86 Sqn (having moved to Broome, WA). By then, seven PR.Mk XVIs had entered service. This

Above: A No. 87 Sqn, RAAF PR Mosquito demonstrates its single-engined capability during a 'beat up' of its Northern Territory base.

squadron also disbanded in 1946.

In 1947 the first of 28 PR.Mk 41s (A52-300/-327) became available, and were employed in an aerial survey of the whole of Australia, with the remaining Mk XVIs, from 1946 until 1953.

This was undertaken in conjunction with the Australian Survey Corporation (and its fleet of Ansons and Hudsons). The Survey Flight was renamed No. 87 Survey Squadron in 1951 and disbanded in 1953, two thirds of the continent having been mapped.

Right: PR.Mk XVI A52-611 enjoyed only a brief RAAF career. Received by No. 87 Sqn on 9 June 1945, it was wrecked in a take-off crash just nine days later. Here it seen after being stripped of useful components. Prior to VJ-Day the RAAF Mk XVIs were finished in PRU Blue.

Survey Squadron Mosquito

PR.Mk 41 A52-306
Converted from FB.Mk 40 A52-197, this aircraft was delivered to the Survey Flight in 1947/48.

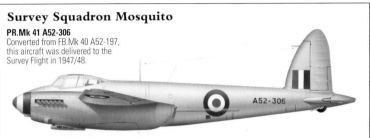

Canada

In Europe 'A' Flight, No. 400 Sqn was equipped with PR.Mk XVIs in 2nd TAF from December 1943 until VE-Day.

In Canada, a few locally-built Mosquitoes equipped No. 13 (Photographic) Sqn (later 413 Photographic Sqn) at Patricia Bay,

British Columbia. Secondary units with Mosquito bombers included No. 7 OTU (formed as No. 31 OTU, RAF) at Debert, Nova Scotia, No.8 OTU (ex-No. 36 OTU at Greenwood, Nova Scotia and No. 124 (Ferry) Squadron.

Switzerland

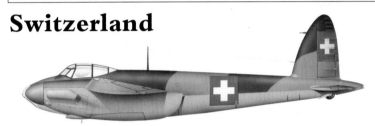

Switzerland's Mosquitoes were aircraft that crash-landed in the country during World War II. PR.Mk IV DK310 (above) arrived on 24 August 1942 after suffering engine problems and was eventually sold to the Swiss government in July 1944. Coded 'E-42' it had previously been evaluated by

Swiss Army pilots, this process being completed in October 1944. Then handed over to Swissair (as HB-IMO), the aircraft was used to train pilots for night mail runs, though this came to nought and it was returned to the Army as B-4 and flown until August 1946.

France

Among the Mosquitoes obtained by the Armée de l'Air after World War II were 29 ex-RAF PR.Mk XVIs. These served with the Groupe de Reconnaissance 1/20 'Lorraine', formed at Dijon in 1945. This unit served

primarily in North Africa, moving to Agadir and Rabat and finally back to Tours in 1952. GR 1/20 disbanded in June 1953, most of surviving its Mosquitoes being scrapped, though a few were sold to Israel.

USSR

Details of any use of the Mosquito by the USSR during World War II has not emerged, though a batch of ex-B.Mk IVs

(including DK296, below) was taken from storage in late 1943 and prepared for delivery in August 1944.

Israel

In 1948, two ex-Royal Navy Mk XVIs (NS511 and NS512) were obtained from the UK via an intermediary, despite the fact that an embargo on arms sales to the Jewish state was in place.

A number of ex-Armée de l'Air Mk XVIs were also acquired in 1952 and these were

augmented by three further ex-FAA aircraft, purchased after the lifting of the sales ban in 1956.

PR Mosquitoes were among the aircraft brought out of mothballs by the IDF/AF during the 1956 Suez Crisis.

Mosquito PR.Mk XVI 2190 was written off in this accident on 22 November 1956. Note the 'Suez stripes' applied to the rear fuselage of this aircraft.

United States

Though Canadian-built F-8s were flown to the UK for use by the 8th Air Force, they were never used operationally. At least one aircraft was flown to Italy, though whether it saw service with the 15th Air Force is unclear and seems unlikely.

The 8th Air Force's PR.Mk XVIs were initially operated by the 802nd Reconnaissance Group (Photographic) from February 1944, this becoming the 25th Bomb Group (Reconnaissance) in August and joining the 7th PRG as part of the 325th Photographic Reconnaissance Wing.

Within the 25th BG two squadrons, the 653rd BS and the 654th BS, were tasked primarily with weather reconnaissance and photo-reconnaissance, respectively.

A handful of aircraft were also employed by the 492nd BG 'Carpetbaggers' after it assumed control of the 25th operations in March 1945. These aircraft recorded UHF transmissions from OSS agents on the continent.

The USAAF's Mosquito fleet (which included three T.Mk III aircraft for training) was returned to the RAF after VE-Day.

South Africa

No. 60 Sqn, South African Air Force, operated a pair of modified Mk IIs fitted with cameras. These were only operated for a few months from May 1943, initially in North Africa, before being replaced by PR.Mk IXs and XVIs as the unit moved to Italy. Post-war, 14 aircraft were taken back to South Africa, No. 60 Sqn operating these aircraft in the survey role for a number of years.

Ground crewman Les Deadfield poses in front of BANCVIRNLES, one of No. 60 Sqn's aircraft at San Severo, Italy in 1944.

Right: PR.Mk XVI NS590/'B', is seen around late 1944, its AEAF stripes having been partially painted out. The 8th AF returned about 70 aircraft to the RAF after VE-Day.

Pencils of flame
Bristol's Type 188

Way back in 1962 when the author was very young, he was given a book on aircraft. Besides all the old stories it included a painting of the forthcoming Bristol 188 supersonic research aircraft screaming across the skies at very high speed and very great height. If ever anything looked futuristic and just what a child might imagine as a space-age supersonic aircraft, this was it.

Illustrations such as this, produced before the 188's first flight, heightened public expectations that the aircraft would be a 'world beater'. Despite its looks, the 188 never quite lived up to its potential.

Reality, of course, proved quite different. As a result of a structure fabricated from stainless steel, the construction of the Type 188 proved really tough and, because it never had suitable engines, it was never able to fly anywhere near the required speeds or soak at these speeds for anything like long enough; some important information was gained but the return for the large amount of money spent on the project seemed small. Today, many historians and enthusiasts turn their backs on it,

but the Type 188 remains an aircraft of great interest, and still looks incredible. It was in some ways a remarkable achievement, not least since it actually survived the swathing cuts brought about by the 1957 Defence White Paper.

Specification ER.134T

In 1952 the Ministry of Supply, having accepted transonic and supersonic fighters as the way forward, now considered even higher speeds and at the end of the year issued

specification ER.134T for a 'Research Aircraft for Mach Number 2'. The programme was designed to explore the design problems associated with the next step in high speed flight beyond that of the Fairey Delta 2: the minimum top speed in level flight was Mach 2, a speed which had to be sustained for at least 10 minutes.

Ten designs were tendered in May 1953, in the forms of the Armstrong Whitworth AW.166, Boulton Paul P.128 and Bristol Type 188 all with a slim-fuselage, a straight wing, and two engines in wing-mounted nacelles; three English Electric P.6 contenders including two 'Lightning' derivatives and a third with wing-mounted engine nacelles; the Hawker P.1096 and P.1097 with swept wings and single engines; the Saunders-Roe P.163 with combined jet and rocket propulsion; and the

Top: The second Bristol 188, XF926, is seen about to land at Boscombe Down, probably in early July 1963. The fin of its Hunter chase plane, a single-seater, appears above the fuselage.

Left: Supermarine's single-engined Type 553, seen here in model form, was among the designs competing for the ER.134T contract.

Supermarine Type 553 with a swept wing and single engine. After consideration, the AW.166 was declared the narrow winner over the Type 188, but as Armstrong Whitworth was then building the Gloster Javelin in quantity, the Type 188 was chosen instead on 16 December 1953.

The Royal Aircraft Establishment Farnborough felt that a straight wing with nacelles was the optimum configuration for such an aircraft. But the ministry's C. B. Baker wrote that the "opinion of the top level organisation at Bristol is not high", and noted the Type 176 research aircraft to E.8/47 where "the firm lost interest and the project was cancelled at the firm's request". Nevertheless, a contract for two aircraft went to Bristol in February 1954. In the event the tailplane, fin, rudder, outer wings, ailerons and cockpit canopy were all built by Armstrong Whitworth at Coventry.

Soon flight between Mach 1.8 and 2.5 was being planned with an emphasis placed on supersonic intakes and kinetic heating. At these speeds steel began to take over from Dural (aluminium alloy) as the optimum airframe material for high stiffness and resistance to deterioration at elevated temperature, as a result largely of kinetic heating, so the need for steel construction was fixed, and this then opened the possibility of a full investigation into design and fabrication aspects of this material ahead of any service requirements. Specification ER.134D of 11 March requested a minimum top speed of Mach 2.5 but acknowledged that the plan to fit afterburning Rolls-Royce Avon RA.24 turbojets was an initial step only for Mach 2 pending the availability of new lightweight medium-thrust engines.

The Type 188 promised to be an exceptional machine. Its expected performance reached across the heat barrier and exceeded, by a factor of nearly two to one in speed and altitude, the performance of any aircraft then in service. Furthermore, the design had been arranged on such simple and adaptable lines that it lent itself readily to the testing and development of many new types of engine, armament and equipment.

Politics and a new appearance

The Type 188's structure was designed for Mach 1.2 at sea level rising to Mach 2.5 above 35,000 ft (10670 m), and extensive instrumentation, featuring paper and magnetic tape recorders and continuous telemetry to ground receivers, was built into the aircraft to facilitate the rapid acquisition of data on aerodynamics (stability and control), low-level turbulence, structural loads and distortion, kinetic heating, and engine and systems behaviour. Extensive strain gauging would be used for the first time and several hundred transducers formed part of the 'payload'. There was even a possibility for fitting moderate-size ram jets, studies having shown that a 16-in (40.6-cm) ram jet could be pylon mounted for a useful Mach number and endurance. During February the wing was reassessed by RAE and on 19 February Bristol completed a new planform much nearer to what

XF923 is seen on 3 April 1962 prior to taxi trials. The fire extinguisher fairings were added during the first aircraft's short career. These and the positioning of the brake parachute housing were the only differences between the two 188s.

With its comparatively small wing area the Type 188 had a fairly high landing speed, but employed an efficient brake 'chute to limit its landing roll.

was eventually built. There was no provision for the Type 188 to be a combat aircraft, a fact for which Bristol was far from happy.

Once the programme was under way the real difficulties became clear, and those associated with heat, steel construction and aerodynamics stood out as the most difficult. In February 1956 it was felt that the flutter problems of the Type 188 would be as great as on any previous British aircraft, while the fact that the machine would take-off on its own power, unlike the American X-planes dropped from mother

Javelin F(AW).Mk 1 XA552 was converted by de Havilland to use twin Gyron Junior engines with reheat. It was painted overall blue and had a new nose with a long instrumentation boom. Godfrey Auty, who was to be the chief test pilot on the 188, flew this Javelin many times.

Bristol Type 188 concepts

General arrangement of the Avon-powered Bristol 188 as tendered to ER.134T; drawing dated 20 April 1953

General arrangement of the Bristol 188 as built with Gyron Juniors. Note changes to wing, nacelle and fin shape, and to the tail position from the 1953 original.

Artist's concept of the 188 powered by four Bristol Orpheus B.OR.12 turbojets.

Artist's concept of the 188 powered by six Bristol Orpheus B.OR.12 turbojets.

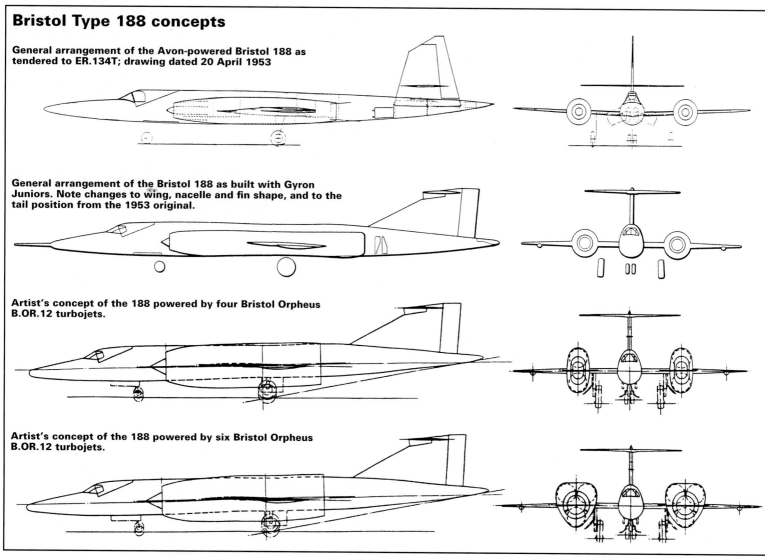

Two of the models built for use in the 3-ft (0.91-m) x 3-ft (0.91-m) wind tunnel at RAE Bedford are displayed here. On the left is a ⅛th scale supersonic half-wing model for measurement of aileron hinge moments. Next to it is a ⅛₈th scale airframe model, complete with air brakes.

aircraft, made ER.134 an even more exacting requirement. A plan to fit the first aircraft with aluminium alloy wings was rejected in January 1954 as a needless duplication of effort, but the delivery time for stainless steel was quoted in years. A Type 188 mock-up was inspected on 24 November, at which time the first flight was planned for June 1957.

In 1955 Avro received a contract to produce its Type 730 high-altitude supersonic strategic reconnaissance bomber with Armstrong Siddeley P.176 engines. In addition the F.155T requirement for a supersonic successor to the Javelin was being assessed and, in consequence, three more Type 188 aircraft were ordered to accelerate the programme and provide manufacturing experience for the steel-built Type 730. As the P.176 engine could fit into the Type 188, it was decided to adopt this engine for these additional aircraft as flying test beds, and while the serials for the first two aircraft were XF923 and XF926, those for the latter three were XK429, XK434 and XK436. The P.176 was also the only engine likely to permit the Type 188 to attain its specified performance. Discussions on alternative engines had begun in March 1954, but only the Rolls-Royce RB.106 and RB.115 and the Bristol BE.30 were then available, and all of these were but paper studies. Seven other turbojet types were examined before the P.176 was selected.

Then the 1957 Defence White Paper revealed that no new strategic supersonic bombers or defensive supersonic fighters would be built for the RAF, this decision leading to the cancellation of the Type 730 bomber and the F.155 fighter requirement, together with the P.176 engine. This necessitated a full review of the Type 188 in the light of this policy and the project's cost. In February 1954 the estimate for constructing two prototypes to first flight, excluding engines, had been £2.5 million; it was now obvious that this original figure had been unrealistic. The figure for five Type 188 aircraft had, by the end of 1956, reached £10.5 million and was still rising. It was decided therefore to continue the project but only with the original pair of aircraft: the other three could not be justified and were accordingly cancelled. However, the ministry still regarded the Type 188 concept vital for the future of British aviation: as the UK's only aircraft capable of Mach 2.5, it was "indispensable". No other aircraft was capable of undertaking the Type 188's programme – the Lightning, for example, would be unstable when fitted with advanced intakes.

The powerplant situation was difficult since the P.176 would be too costly for development as the engine of the Type 188 alone, but its cancellation deprived the Type 188 of the engine required for Mach 2.5 performance. The only British unit that could give reasonable flight durations at Mach 2+ was the de

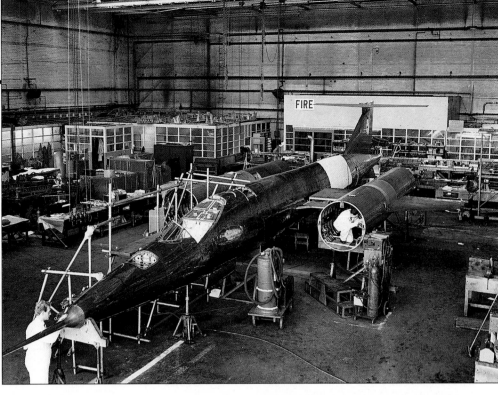

Havilland Gyron Junior, of which a higher-thrust PS.50 version was under development for the Saro P.177 hybrid rocket/turbojet fighter. On 15 April 1957 Bristol completed a study in favour of substituting the Gyron Junior, which fitted the wing structure but required a new nose and tail section for the nacelle, and this was adopted despite the later cancellation of the P.177. Rejected alternatives were the Armstrong Siddeley Sapphire ASSa.7 and Rolls-Royce RB.133, the latter a relatively minor development of the Avon RA.24 but providing a substantial thrust increase, though it still only offered Mach 2.4 for 2.5 minutes and was also 700 lb (318 kg) heavier. In June it was decided

not to fly with the Avon powerplant since deterioration of its performance prevented speeds in excess of Mach 2.1 at 50,000 ft (15240 m), but to convert the intake and systems to suit the Gyron Junior immediately. Nevertheless, spending on PS.50 development was cut to a minimum, and this contributed to an overall delay. Maximum endurance with the PS.50 at Mach 2.5 and 50,000 ft (15240 m) was predicted to be about 1.5 minutes.

Development difficulties continue

Following the White Paper, the Type 188 emerged as a pure research project with PS.50 engines and fully variable afterburning, but airframe and systems problems continued. By March 1958 it was hoped that more advanced engines, which in fact never became available, would allow four minutes at Mach 2.5 in the altitude band between 40,000 ft (12190 m) and 70,000 ft (21335 m) with decelerating controlled flight up to 80,000 ft (24385 m); the continual trend for exploiting the airframe for yet higher Mach numbers brought further proposed developments of the inlet temperature

Above: XF923 is seen on 22 July 1960 during manufacture. Completion was still nine months away and the first flight was not to take place for another year after that.

Left upper: The engine nacelles of the 188 were over 30 ft (9.1 m) long and fractionally wider than the fuselage itself.

Left lower: The Gyron Junior was a tight fit, even in the large nacelles of the 188 as shown in this view of the installation of the number one unit.

to make possible a level speed of Mach 3. At the opposite end of the scale buffet, particularly at low speeds, would be investigated. The PS.50 had a design limit of Mach 2.7 at 70,000 ft (21335 m), but the cost of improving it to withstand Mach 3 was prohibitive and since there appeared little research benefit from achieving this extreme speed, it was concluded in December 1959 that developing the Type 188 beyond Mach 2.7 was not worth the cost. Hence, after initial flight clearance to Mach 2,

A third Type 188 airframe was constructed for static test purposes and is seen here upon arrival at RAE Farnborough (below left) and during testing (below).

Above: *In this head-on view the aysymmetric mounting of the single-shot fire extinguishers on the engines may be discerned. The 10 EGR (engine ground running) doors are open to improve air flow on the ground.*

Above right: *Engine running takes place at Filton, probably of XF923. Almost a year elapsed between the roll out of the first Type 188 and its first flight.*

Right: *XF923's engines underwent further ground testing on 13 December 1961. Fire extinguisher fairings had, by then, been added to the upper forward nacelles, a feature that did not appear on XF926.*

there was to be a short extension programme to Mach 2.5 before fitting an advanced intake and new reheat nozzles for Mach 2.7. Auto-stabilisation would also be introduced.

Several suppliers of steel alloys were consulted for a suitable airframe material before Firth-Vickers' REX448 stainless steel, already in production for jet engine parts, was developed for sheet manufacture. However, achieving an acceptable standard of flatness, surface finish and thickness tolerance proved exacting. Two years were spent on different fabrication techniques, heat treatment, machining and polishing methods before, early in 1956, it was possible to order a quantity of material for aircraft use, and this was delivered in September. However, defects were found in this material which, coupled with welding problems, caused more delay. The need for new close-tolerance high strength stainless steel bolts, rivets and fasteners was another difficulty and, in service, the bolts

The original brake 'chute housing had the appearance of an afterthought. It was also useable as a spin 'chute. On one flight it was inadvertently deployed at supersonic speed.

were found to have hairline cracks – these were not serious, but nonetheless needed fixing.

The Puddle (argon-arc fusion spot welding) process was selected because in large-scale applications there was a problem of expansion and contraction during welding and this was the best solution for main jointing throughout the Type 188's structure. Perfected by Bristol, this technique was extremely flexible in allowing welds to be made in locations inaccessible by other methods but, for a satisfactory job, the skills had to be learnt thoroughly and this took time. To combat kinetic heat, a powerful refrigeration system was installed in the Type 188 to protect both pilot and instrumentation, and special transparent materials were developed for the cockpit windows.

Type 188 described

The Type 188 was a single-seat mid-wing aircraft conforming to the area-rule concept, and had its engine nacelles mounted centrally on a thin wing. The landing gear was orthodox, and hydraulic power controls were used. In cross-section the fuselage was oval, with the

lower portion basically semi-circular and faired into an upper section of smaller radius, and the structure was conventional with stressed skinning over stringers and frames. There were five fuselage fuel tanks, three forward of the wing and two to the rear of it, while part of the nose forward of the cabin was pressurised to house instrument recorders. When retracted, the main wheel struts lay in the wing with the wheels housed in the fuselage. In order that they would be brought into the correct position, the wheels were mounted on stub axles which rotated through 86° before main part of the retraction movement began. Two cascade-type air brakes were mounted on each side of the rear fuselage.

The wing between the fuselage and nacelles was unswept but had triangular leading-edge strakes added to each end. Tunnel testing had established the existence of 'long bubble' type airflows separating from the leading edge if the inboard wing and the strakes were to reduce the rate of chordwise growth of the bubble and ensure that take-off and landing performance would not be dictated by low speed buffet. Outboard of the engines the leading edge was

Right: The design called for the 16-ft (4.9 m) diameter drag 'chute to be housed in the tail, but both Type 188s flew with an external unit mounted on the port side of the rear fuselage.

Below right: Although the Bristol 188 was created to explore high speeds for long periods to investigate heat soaking of airframes, it only ever reached Mach 1.9 (and then only for two minutes) before fuel considerations forced its pilot to land. Five years earlier in the USA, the Douglas X-3 Stiletto was built to explore the same high-temperature regime. It too suffered from being powered by engines that produced insufficient power.

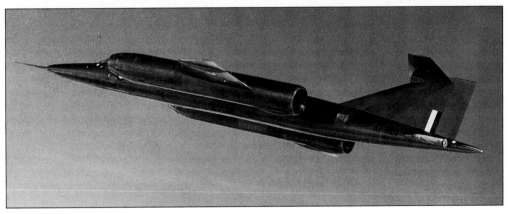

swept 38°, while the tip was formed by the balance area of the aileron forward of its hinge, the leading edge of which was swept 64°; extending the ailerons from the nacelles formed, in effect, all-moving tips specifically to reduce peak control hinge moments in super and subsonic flight to about the same magnitude. Skin thickness tapered from 0.28 in (0.71 cm) at the root to 0.06 in (0.15 cm) at the tip.

The wing box was enclosed by front and rear spars with intermediate spars formed by corrugated webs welded to angles attached to the skins. Conventional trailing-edge flaps of the plain type were fitted to the inner wing, and these could be continuously operated down to 55° depression. The mix of unswept inboard sections and swept outboard panels was aimed at combining low wave drag at supersonic speeds with good transonic characteristics.

The tail unit comprised a swept fin with orthodox trailing-edge rudder and an all-moving tailplane mounted on two bearings and hinged to the top of the fixed fin structure. The fin leading-edge sweep angle was 65°, and the rudder was of constant chord without aerodynamic balance. Below the tailplane, forward of the hinge, was a vertical blade which moved in a slot at the top of the fin. The fin was of multiple frame structure bolted to the rear fuselage, while the tailplane was of multi-spar construction like the wing. The T-tail was essential to keep the tailplane clear of the jet efflux and to ensure low-speed static longitudinal stability with the trailing-edge flaps deflected. Tunnel tests showed a lower tail position led to instability and pitch-up at moderate angles of attack; the greater thickness/chord figure of 4.5 per cent was to prevent tail flutter.

The nacelles, made in four sections, were detachable to permit the fitting of alternative engines that might require a larger-diameter nacelle. The air intake was removable so that alternative intakes could be easily installed for flight test; for the Gyron Junior there was a retracting centrebody for shock wave control with a set of controllable valves and flaps to let air in or out. Next came the forebody shell, which carried the front and rear engine suspension, and then the cylindrical centre body formed by three forged and machined rings, which was attached to the inner and outer wing spars as part of the wing structure. The afterbody contained the main landing gear support structure, the afterburning unit front attachment and, at the rear, the afterburner pipe.

It was appreciated that construction entirely in steel would delay the Type 188's completion, but the difficulties proved more complex than had been predicted. As a result the scheduled date for the first flight was regularly pushed back; in July 1958 it was expected in April

1960, a year later this had become July 1960, soon after this a time in December 1960 was proposed, and in January 1961 the date had become the following April. Ever-rising costs even brought proposals to move assembly to either Hawker or de Havilland. Many models were used to examine aerodynamic and flutter aspects, some being launched by rocket from the Royal Aircraft Establishment Aberporth in Wales for free-flight investigation. A static test airframe was delivered by road to RAE Farnborough in May 1960 before going to RAE Bedford later in the year. XF923 was finally rolled out on 26 April 1961, but it still did not fly for another year. The metal finish was, however, one of the smoothest ever seen on any aircraft.

Into the air

Engine bench testing revealed surge and afterburner problems with, consequently, much alteration of the intakes and their centrebodies. Thus taxiing did not start until February 1962, but then bad weather prevented further progress for two months. The Type 188's pilot was to be Godfrey Auty, who in July 1959 was instructed to get some experience on the Lightning as well as the Supermarine Swift and Hawker Hunter;

Auty's preparations eventually covered the Avro Type 707A, Fairey Delta 2, the American Convair F-102 and Lockheed F-104, the Lightning and, lastly, a Gloster Javelin Mk 1 used to flight test the PS.50 Gyron Junior with its afterburner unit.

These problems were hidden from the general public while publicity suggested that a truly spectacular machine was forthcoming. On 5 December 1960 the *Daily Express* newspaper announced that Auty was to fly the 'Flaming Pencil', as the Type 188 had been nicknamed and whose outside skin temperature of 350° F (177° C) would be "hot enough to cook the Sunday joint". Just before first flight the *Daily Mirror* newspaper called it the "Hottest new plane in Britain"; public interest was great indeed. The Type 188 was, in fact, to be the only turbojet-powered aircraft to be built by the Bristol Aircraft Company, those which followed being completed under the aegis of the British Aircraft Corporation in which Bristol was a component.

XF923, the first Type 188, made a 22-minute maiden flight on 14 April 1962. Auty reported that the take-off from Filton was somewhat shorter than forecast with a 5-kt (9.3-km/h) tail wind and, using the brake para-

Above: The second 188 departs Filton on 25 July 1963. This view shows the complex undercarriage folding arrangement, designed to enable the main wheels to fit inside the fuselage.

Both 188s are seen together in the Filton hanger on 24 October 1963. Nearest is XF926 being prepared for another flight; behind is XF923 already 'withdrawn' and about to go into official store with the nacelles sealed up. Further back can be seen Hunter F.Mk.6 XF509, a Valiant bomber, a de Havilland Heron transport and what appears to be a Britannia airliner.

Olympus engine, but a further disadvantage was that no other demand existed for the Type 188's engines and, in consequence, little background support could be provided. By May 1962 it was known that PS.50 performance would limit flight at Mach 2 to just three minutes and, with an advanced intake, offered little more than two minutes at Mach 2.2.

Because of slow progress with flight trials and engine clearance, it became doubtful in the autumn of 1962 that implementation of the planned programme, including advanced intake development, was still justifiable. The value of the programme was questioned, in terms of its future as a research tool in its own right and in support of the Concorde SST. As a result, XF923 was grounded as an economy measure.

Second aircraft

XF926 first flew on 29 April 1963 and was the only Type 188 to get the full high-speed research instrumentation. Engine problems had postponed this flight from August 1962 but by 5 June 14 flights had been made with Mach 1.64 achieved above 40,000 ft (12190 m). Ten flights were supersonic and two flights a day proved

chute, the landing at Boscombe Down required less than half the runway. The No. 2 hydraulic system failed during landing gear retraction, leaving the landing gear in a partially extended state, but the No. 1 system functioned satisfactorily and the flying controls worked perfectly on the half power available. Despite the loss of power to the controls, good handling was achieved, and the pilot reported on this most favourably and asked for no alterations. A separate equipment failure caused a loss of communication with both the Hunter chase aircraft and the ground controller.

XF923 completed its 19th sortie on 30 November for a total of 9 hours 51 minutes flying, including four appearances at the September SBAC Farnborough Show, where the afterburning PS.50 engines left their mark on spectators' ears. The machine then began ground resonance tests at Filton in early 1963. After that it went into store as the flight programme passed to XF926. XF923 had purposely been restricted to subsonic speeds and moderate altitudes, but within this envelope the flight characteristics and engineering systems were very good. In fact XF923 never flew again. It had reached a top speed of Mach 0.86 (on its last flight) and, although achieving successful test results on most trips, suffered afterburning troubles on three occasions plus surging and double flame-outs several times. Stall speed with flaps up was 170 kt (315 km/h) with buffet from 195 kt (361 km/h); with 30° flap the figures were 154 kt (285 km/h) and 160 kt (296 km/h), and for 50° flap 143 kt (265 km/h) and 160 kt (296 km/h). In the climb there was no marked change in stability

with change in centre of gravity, and in general the aircraft was not difficult to trim. During the SBAC Show buffet from normal acceleration was experienced while flying at low altitude (at 300 kt/556 km/h and 3g, and 350 kt/649 km/h and 4g).

The full Boscombe-based XF923 flight programme was never achieved because of the unscheduled removal of both engines on two occasions, problems with the afterburning system before Farnborough, continual failures of the ADC (air data computer) just before flight, and then the onset of bad weather. But Auty could report in December 1962 that the Type 188 was extremely easy and pleasant to fly in instrument meteorological conditions, with visibility in rain better than on any other aircraft not fitted with a windscreen wiper that he had flown. Asymmetric handling both on the ground and in the air was good, and it was felt that a maximum 165-kt (306-km/h) ground speed would be safe in all headwind or crosswind conditions. Auty concluded that with improved engine performance, ADC reliability and functioning, the Type 188 could achieve its required research task without difficulty.

The first Type 188 engines were limited to Mach 1.6. It was expected that Mach 2 units would be available in November 1962 but, in the event, test-bed trials revealed unexpected shortcomings culminating in a mechanical failure in August. The proposed design remedies imposed a deterioration of performance while clearance to Mach 2 would be delayed until the spring of 1964 because test facility time was not available. This was the result primarily of the priority given to development of the Bristol

Specifications

Bristol Type 188 (as tendered May 1953)
Powerplant: two Rolls-Royce Avon RA.14R turbojet engines each rated at 8,850 lb st (39.30 kN) dry and 11,300 lb st (50.26 kN) with afterburning

Maximum speed:	Mach 2.0 above 50,000 ft (15240 m)
Maximum take-off weight:	30,000 lb (13608 kg)
Wing span:	35 ft 8 in (10.87 m)
Length:	68 ft (20.73 m)
Gross wing area:	358.00 sq ft (33.29 m²)

Bristol Type 188 (as built and flown)
Powerplant: two de Havilland Gyron Junior PS.50/DGJ.10R turbojet engines each rated at 10,000 lb st (44.48 kN) dry and 14,000 lb st (62.28 kN) with afterburning at sea level, and 20,000 lb st (88.96 kN) with afterburning at Mach 2 and 36,000 ft (10975 m)

Maximum speed achieved:	Mach 1.88 at 36,000 ft (10975 m)
Weights:	no data available
Wing span:	35 ft 1 in (10.69 m)
Length (with probe):	77 ft 8 in (23.67 m)
Length (without probe):	71 ft (21.64 m)
Height:	11 ft 11²⁄₅ in (3.65 m)
Tailplane span:	15 ft 6 in (4.72 m)
Gross wing area:	396.85 sq ft (36.85 m²)
Gross tailplane area:	71.25 sq ft (6.63 m²)

Bristol Type 188 cutaway

1 Pitot head
2 Yaw vane
3 Front pressure bulkhead
4 Air data computer
5 Fuel system management computer
6 Trace recorder
7 Electrical panels, port and starboard
8 Dual silver-zinc batteries
9 Ballast weights
10 Rudder pedals
11 Control column
12 Instrument panel
13 Optically flat laminated windscreen panels
14 Sliding canopy cover, electrically actuated
15 Pilot's Martin-Baker Mk 4 ejection seat
16 Cockpit conditioned air supply ducts
17 Side console panel with engine throttle levers
18 Sloping rear pressure bulkhead
19 VHF communications antenna
20 Twin nosewheels, forward retracting
21 Hydraulic retraction jack
22 Fuel flow recorder

23 Flight instrumentation pack
24 Electrical equipment panels, port and starboard
25 Anti-g suit air bottle (port) and oxygen bottle (starboard)
26 Emergency hydraulic pump, electrically driven
27 Pilot's air-ventilated suit air bottle
28 Starboard side air-driven turbo-generator
29 Tape recorder can
30 Telemetry can
31 Electrical system AC/DC controller
32 Air conditioning equipment pack
33 Ground power and intercom sockets
34 Electrical system relays
35 Fan-driven cooling air ducting
36 Forward three-bay fuel tank, capacity 630 Imp gal (2864 litres)
37 Fuel/air heat exchanger
38 Fuel/hydraulic fluid heat exchanger
39 Starboard main landing gear unit, articulated axle keeping wheel vertical on retraction

40 Hydraulic retraction jack
41 Engine bleed air ducting to conditioning system and turbo-generator
42 Starboard engine installation
43 Engine fire extinguisher housing (first prototype only)
44 Aileron hydraulic actuator
45 Starboard aileron
46 Nacelle afterburner housing with internal titanium heat shield
47 Starboard plain flap
48 No. 1 hydraulic reservoir
49 Mainwheel door hydraulic jack
50 Mainwheel, retracted position
51 Flap hydraulic jack and interconnecting torque shaft
52 Fuel cocks and flowmeter transmitters
53 Rear two-bay fuel tank, capacity 370 Imp gal (1682 litres)
54 No. 2 hydraulic reservoir
55 Airbrake actuating interlinkage
56 Starboard airbrake panels
57 All-moving tailplane

58 Tailplane hydraulic actuator
59 Pivot mounting
60 Rudder
61 Brake parachute installation, initial position (retained as anti-spin parachute)
62 Rudder hydraulic actuator and autostabiliser jack
63 Brake parachute housing, later modified installation
64 Tailplane autostabiliser jack
65 Flight control system hydraulic accumulator
66 Parachute release actuator nitrogen bottle

67 Structural instrumentation pack
68 Power supply pack
69 Port airbrake panels
70 Airbrake hydraulic jacks and accumulator
71 Variable-area afterburner nozzle
72 Nozzle control unit
73 Afterburner duct
74 Port plain flap
75 Engine fuel feed lines
76 Port aileron
77 Aileron aerodynamic horn balance
78 Hydraulic actuator in ventral fairing
79 Port mainwheel
80 Main landing gear leg telescopic radius strut

81 Jetpipe passing through nacelle structural barrel, machined steel forging
82 Afterburner fuel pump
83 Engine bleed air manifold
84 Port de Havilland Gyron Junior afterburning turbojet engine
85 Variable inlet guide vane and first stage stator actuator
86 Oil tank
87 Engine fuel control units
88 Intake overpressure spill ducts, mechanically actuated via air-driven motor
89 Intake suction relief doors, spring loaded
90 Fixed-geometry intake conical centrebody

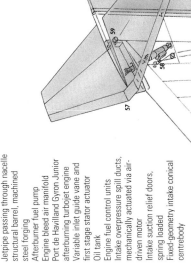

Below: This close-up of the forward section of the engine nacelle shows suction relief doors, mechanically actuated via an air-driven motor and positioned behind the spring-loaded intake suction relief doors.

Below right: This view of the inboard wing shows its extremely thin section (maximum seven inches/17.78 cm) and the 'cascade'-type speed brakes on the rear fuselage.

This photograph, taken by the late Charles Hollis, a Filton employee, shows Godfrey Auty in the cockpit of a 188. Believed to have been taken at Filton, it probably shows XF926 in the summer of 1963. The small size of the cockpit is most evident. Godfrey Auty became Chief Test Pilot at Bristol in 1960. Glass was used for the transparencies as the temperatures were too high for plastics. Cooling during deceleration brought its own stresses, however. Construction of the, mainly steel, cockpit canopy was sub-contracted to Armstrong Whitworth.

XF926 is seen during a test flight on 31 July 1963. Note that the suction relief doors (or flaps) circling the forward nacelle are closed in flight.

Left: The second Bristol 188 XF926 departs Filton for its maiden flight on 29 April 1963, accompanied by a Hawker Hunter chase plane (the first production two-seat Hunter T.Mk.7 XL563).

possible on four occasions. No handling difficulties were reported, but there were no high-speed manoeuvres except a 3-*g* turn at Mach 0.9 at 25,000 ft (7620 m). Engine surging was experienced on flights 9 and 10, and afterburning was lost but successfully relit at Mach 1.4 and 36,500 ft (11125 m) and at Mach 1.45 and 38,000 ft (11580 m) respectively. A defective afterburner nozzle control system caused fluctuations in nozzle position above Mach 1.5, and on flight 11 afterburning on the starboard engine was lost with two unsuccessful relights, so the high-speed programme was suspended for three weeks to change the engines. In due course it was planned to move XF926 to RAE Bedford for an extensive research programme.

Engine problems

The PS.50 engine was not a happy choice. There was a tendency to surge outside a narrow range of incidences, while blade vibration required the implementation of many

XF923's brake parachute was housed in an external fitting on the port side of the tailcone; XF926's parachute was eventually placed in the tailcone itself for one of only two major external differences to the first machine (the other was the lack of nacelle fire extinguisher fairings), but this early view of XF926 shows that the external housing was used initially.

modifications. Pressure of work on de Havilland prompted the firm to suggest ending PS.50 development, but this would stop the whole Type 188 project. Thus a more modest programme was planned in May 1963 based on an aircraft cleared to Mach 1.6, which would provide the time for engine clearance to Mach 2, but this was rejected as the Type 188's present low performance reduced its value so much that the return would be too small in relation to the effort involved. The costly and time-consuming work necessary to get the Type 188 and its engines to a reasonable performance was just not worth it, while the technical effort for the firms would be an embarrassment because of other commitments. Options were cancel immediately or introduce a controlled rundown of effort to get a maximum return from the remaining expenditure; it was eventually proposed to close the programme by the year's end. The ministry stated that the Type 188 had been a considerable achievement for the firms concerned.

A limited intensive flying programme was drawn up for XF926. The Mach 1.6 engines were still fitted, but a concession allowed operation at Mach 1.8 for short periods with the intake spill doors closed and locked. Mach 2 engines were to be fitted in August and the research was to include flight load measurement from pressure plotting and a limited

investigation of techniques of derivative measurement, flight flutter clearance, digital recording, and skin temperature measurement. The latter was requested by the RAE, and arrangements were made for RAE pilots to fly the aircraft. By the end of June 1963, XF926 had completed 21 flights but further afterburner nozzle problems limited progress, and flight clearance was confined within a narrow boundary by the powerplant's surge characteristics. No signs of aileron buzz had been encountered, but flutter testing had been restricted by the lack of endurance at higher Mach numbers: the fuel consumption of the PS.50 had been far higher than expected, and some had felt even before the first flight that there would be insufficient fuel for prolonged high speeds. XF926 would now use high-density kerosene fuel (AVCAT), which would raise fuel load by about 500 lb (227 kg), and during September the continuance of flight testing up to the end of December was approved.

Flight with Mach 1.6 engines continued until 31 July, and 15 sorties were made in the month with a maximum speed of Mach 1.83, but operation was still restricted to a narrow band of speed and altitude conditions. A double flame-out occurred on one flight by an RAE pilot who inadvertently strayed outside the prescribed climb routine, but both engines relit satisfactorily. The main problem was still afterburner malfunction, which occurred on nine flights, but by careful selection and adjustment, combinations were found which appeared to work rather better. Just 12 of the 22 flights during June and July went supersonic.

XF926 was grounded in August for the installation of Mach 2 engines, and flying

resumed on 4 October with 11 flights (including seven supersonic) completed by mid-December. Much trouble was experienced with inlet guide vane operation and the starboard engine surged supersonically six times before the system was modified. Apart from this no major problems arose, the cause of afterburner malfunction having been traced and an effective modification introduced, but an inadvertent streaming of the brake parachute occurred during one supersonic flight. The highest speed so far reached was an indicated Mach 1.88 at 36,000 ft (10975 m) on flight 47 in mid-November, while the limited performance checks confirmed the low aircraft drag estimated from earlier results. A top speed of Mach 2.2 and a duration of 1.5 minutes at Mach 2 were predicted, but insufficient time remained to complete the limited pressure plotting, kinetic heating and digital recording programme agreed in September.

Bad weather and the need to find the causes of some intake control malfunctions forced a postponement of the last four flights, so flying did not end until 16 January 1964. After 51 flights all told, Bristol offered a further programme with XF926 of about 60 flights more from Filton aimed at finding techniques for detecting buzz on Concorde and the kinetic heat testing of some borderline Concorde components by attachment to the Type 188 of structurally representative specimens, but by 10 September 1964 the firm was concerned about availability of technical manpower and was no longer happy it could supply the effort needed to sustain the Type 188 programme. This amounted to a withdrawal of the proposal, which was finally rejected in February 1965 and the programme closed.

Both airframes went into official store at Filton, XF923 in November 1963 and XF926 in March 1964. They were struck off charge on 7 November 1966 and despatched to the Proof and Experimental Establishment at Shoeburyness for use as gunnery targets for testing the resistance of modern airframes to damage. But before destruction, XF926 was salvaged and restored for preservation at the Cosford Aerospace Museum, where it arrived in 1974 as ground instruction airframe 8368M.

Was it worth it?

A large portion of the money spent on the Type 188, amounting to £20 million pounds of which only 60 per cent fell on the defence budget with the other 40 per cent coming from research funds, covered basic development work not normally chargeable to a specific aircraft. For example, introducing steel sheet manufacturers to aircraft standards of thickness control and flatness led to a high scrap rate, and it became necessary to place orders much in excess of the needs of just two aircraft. Basic developments in high-temperature tyres, fuel tank sealant, and advanced instrumentation were also charged to the Type 188 bill. Thus, in these and other areas of development, there was a substantial return on the investment, and this proved beneficial to future programmes, particularly that of the Concorde. Proving the practicable use of real-time telemetry, allowing data to be evaluated as it happened, was also extremely valuable. However, a final cost of £20 million is still difficult to justify.

With just 1,000 Imp gal (4546 litres) of fuel available, the Type 188 never had sufficient endurance to give the long soak at Mach 2 required for the supply of worthwhile data. Average flight time was around 20 to 25 minutes, although one trip did last 48 minutes, but as Auty pointed out, by airline standards of fuel reserve he was in an emergency situation even at take-off. The PS.50 lacked power and was never fully developed, but the Type 188 still became one of the fastest conventionally powered aircraft in the world, though by 1962 Lightning fighters were regularly achieving Mach 2 for short periods. It appears that the Type 188 was, in aerodynamic terms, a fine aircraft but its Achilles heel was a powerplant that was both unreliable and very thirsty. On a lighter note, at the 1962 Empire Test Pilots School dinner, Auty was voted the 'man most likely to eject in the coming year'; fortunately he never had to.

Tony Buttler AMRAeS

Top: The fairings to the rear of each engine nacelle covered the exhaust nozzle controls.

Below left: Among the rarer views of the Type 188 is this of XF923 at altitude with its gear down.

The two 188s were cocooned and stored at Filton. The shape of the fire extinguisher fairings under the brown paper reveals this to be XF923. The date was 20 March 1964, the month that XF926 joined '923 in storage.

Avro Canada CF-100
Variant and Operator Briefing

The RCAF's requirement for the aircraft which eventually became the CF-100 stemmed from its desire to take an active role in the defence of Canadian airspace. The Permanent Joint Board on Defence had been formed by Canada and the United States in 1940 but, following the end of World War II and the beginning of the Cold War, Canada chose not to hand over responsibility for its air defence to the Americans. It was, however, recognised that close co-ordination and some degree of integration of American and Canadian air defence resources would be required if an attack took place. The result was NORAD: initially known as the North American Air Defence Command ('Defense' in the USA), this was later changed to North American Aerospace Defence Command. The agreement provided for the Commander-in-Chief NORAD (CINCNORAD) to be a USAF officer with the Deputy Commander always to be a Canadian. NORAD was established on 1 August 1957, with the official signing taking place on 12 May 1958.

It was determined that the RCAF needed a capable, modern aircraft that was fast, possessed a high rate of climb to a high service ceiling, long range, all-weather capability, substantial armament, two crew members, and the best possible navigation and weapons control systems. Existing types, including the English Electric Canberra, Gloster Meteor, and Lockheed F-94 Starfire (a development of the F-80 Shooting Star and T-33A 'T-Bird') were studied, and the conclusion was quickly reached

that none met the RCAF's requirements. Before and during World War II, Canada had produced few aircraft of local design, most being manufactured under licence and many of those being obsolete. It was a courageous decision to award Avro Canada the contract to design, develop and produce the RCAF's new fighter.

During 1942, Canada's Air Council had recommended that a technical mission be sent to Britain to study gas turbine engines (as jets were then known). A group of Canadians travelled to the UK in late 1942 and returned in early 1943. They proposed the creation of a cold-weather station for test and development of British designs and further recommended that a gas turbine research and development establishment be set up in Canada to design and build engines of independent, Canadian design.

Both recommendations were acted upon, beginning with the establishment of a cold-weather testing station at Stevenson Field in Winnipeg (now shared by Winnipeg International Airport and 17 Wing/CFB Winnipeg.) Cold-weather testing was necessary as a means to simulate the conditions encountered at the high altitudes at which jet engines would operate. The station was initially set up by the National Research Council. As it had done for the United States for the Bell XP-59A Airacomet programme, Britain gave Canada a Whittle W.1 engine for study.

Turbo Research Limited (note that some sources hyphenate the company's name) was formed as a Crown Corporation in July 1944.

Its design office was co-located in Leaside, Toronto with another Crown Corporation, Research Enterprises Limited, and the company took over the cold-weather station. In January 1945, the RCAF formally requested that Turbo Research design a jet engine for its future aircraft.

Turbo's initial design studies were three axial-compressor types, designated TR1, TR2 and TR3, and differing from Whittle's centrifugal-flow designs. (Note that some sources list the designations as TR-1, TR-2, TR-3, TR-4 and TR-5.) Work on the TR3, which was to have produced some 4,200 lb (18.67 kN) of thrust, was abandoned in favour of development of the TR4, primarily because it was felt to be too ambitious at that stage. The TR4, later named Chinook, was an axial-flow turbojet designed to produce about 2,600 lb (11.56 kN) of thrust and first ran on 17 March 1948. Enough parts were made for six engines, although only three complete Chinooks and one test compressor were actually built. The engines ran for some 1,000 hours over a period of 20 months, and all reached a thrust of 3,000 lb (13.34 kN).

Turbo Research was taken over and moved to Malton by A. V. Roe Canada on 4 May 1946. In November 1946, the power house and associated facilities at Nobel, Ontario (near Parry Sound) were acquired as an engine test site. The facilities had previously belonged to D.I.L. (Defence Industries Limited), a Crown Corporation, which had produced explosives during World War II.

The only Canadian-designed and -built jet fighter to achieve operational status, the CF-100 had its beginnings in January 1945, when the Royal Canadian Air Force issued a set of specifications for what would be its major post-war fighter aircraft. This was later formalised in October 1946, when the government issued a proposal, AIR Spec 7-1, to A. V. Roe Canada Limited.

Main picture: 'Clunk' in its element: a No. 410 'Cougar' Squadron CF-100 Mk 5 climbs to height while operating from Harmon Field, Newfoundland in 1957. The Mk 5 was the last of three service variants, with extended wings and weight-savings for extra altitude performance.

Above: Though poor in quality, this rare colour photograph shows the first CF-100 Mk 1 prototype at Boston in 1950.

Below: The ill-fated second prototype took to the air in July 1950, but was lost in unknown circumstances the following April. A fault in the oxygen supply is thought to have caused the pilot to fall unconscious.

Above: This is how the XC.100 mock-up appeared in June 1947. Although superficially similar to the eventual machine, it has a fin fillet and slightly swept wings. The latter were discarded later as being too technologically demanding. The original armament specification called for four 20-mm or 30-mm cannon in the nose.

The TR4 was followed by the TR5, later named Orenda, with the first contract issued in April 1947. (The name Orenda was that of an Iroquois spirit whose presence in a person or object conferred power.) The new engine was first run on 10 February 1949. It ran for the remarkable total of 477 hours before its first rebuild and reached 750 hours in 8½ months. The prototype Orenda came very close to the 1,000-hour milestone, but was destroyed in a freak accident. A technician who had entered the test cell to top up the oil reservoir had his

RATO (Rocket-Assisted Take-Off) tests began with one of the Mk 2Ts (18105/VC-FBH) in August 1952, followed by trials with other variants. Here the Mk 2T blasts off in October with all six bottles. RATO was another concept proven but not adopted for the CF-100.

Above: 18105, a Mk 2T, demonstrates that the 'Clunk' could carry bombs although it was never called upon to do so operationally. In RCAF service the wing hardpoints were only used much later for the carriage of chaff dispensers.

lab coat pulled off and sucked into the intake. In one of the pockets was a package of razor blades and these were, so to speak, the final straw. Nevertheless, the first three TR5s reached nearly 2,000 hours of running time in the first year, doubling the typical achievement of contemporary, foreign engine programmes.

Origin of the CF-100 Canuck

On 3 November 1945, Avro Canada concluded an airframe agreement with the government, although this was not formally executed until 31 October 1946. At that time, Avro Canada agreed to "design, manufacture, sell, supply and deliver" prototype aircraft that met Department of National Defence AIR Spec 7-1, which set demanding requirements. No

aircraft anywhere then existed which met them, and none would for several years. It was clear to all involved that if the requirements could be met, they would have the best aircraft of its kind anywhere, as well as a substantial lead on its competitors.

According to AIR Spec 7-1, "The aeroplane shall be powered by two gas turbine jet propulsion engines and shall provide for a crew of two. It shall be of all metal construction with a pressurised cabin. The aeroplane shall be designed for satisfactory operation over an ambient temperature range of −57°C to +45°C. The range in still air with built in fuel tankage at maximum gross weight shall be sufficient to permit the following operation: Taxi and run-up 4 minutes, climb to 40,000 ft at takeoff RPM, cruise to a radius of action of 650 nm, combat 15 minutes at 490 kt at 40,000 ft, return cruise 650 nm, descent 10 minutes from 40,000 ft, approach 7 minutes at idling RPM. The operational ceiling shall not be less than 50,000 ft. The sea level rate of climb shall not be less

than 10,000 ft per minute. The maximum true air speed in level flight at 40,000 ft altitude shall not be less than 490 kt (0.85 Mach)." This was a very challenging set of requirements for any aircraft builder, let alone a new one.

Three designs were submitted in August 1946 in response to what was, at first, a rather vague specification. The RCAF was not particularly enthusiastic about any of the three, but it was serious about its need for a new, modern fighter aircraft. In October 1946, when the RCAF had a better idea of what it wanted and issued a preliminary specification, three more designs were proposed, and one of these was selected.

The early drawings and mockups revealed a very conventional design. Other than the engine nacelles tucked in close to the fuselage, the design retained a late World War II look. Much time was spent debating the pros and cons of straight wings versus swept wings but, in the end, it was decided that they did not have enough information to build the CF-100 with swept wings. As well as being more expensive and taking longer to produce, another factor in the decision was the need to get aircraft into RCAF service as soon as possible. Its principal opponent would be the Russian copy of the Boeing B-29 Superfortress, the Tupolev Tu-4 'Bull', which would be easy prey for an aircraft in the CF-100's class. Finally, almost all of its contemporaries were straight-winged, including the F-84 Thunderjet, F2H Banshee, F9F Panther, Seahawk, Canberra and F-89 Scorpion. At that time, only the MiG-15 'Fagot' and F-86 Sabre were introducing swept wings to modern combat aircraft.

Specifications

Avro Canada received a contract for two prototypes and one static test airframe. The value of Contract Demand CD 187 is unknown. The CF-100's chief design engineer for military projects at Avro Canada was John

The CF-100 Mk 3B was the first front-line variant, although it only reached three units before it was supplanted by the Mk 4. No. 440 Squadron was the last to equip with the variant, from October 1953.

Frost, who had worked for such companies as Airspeed, Blackburn and Slingsby, before going to de Havilland where he worked on the Vampire. He then became the project engineer for the DH.108 research aircraft. By the end of 1946, cockpit and forward fuselage mockups had been built and, in May 1947, detail design of components began. In January 1948, tooling and the manufacture of components for the prototypes began. Both Mk 1 prototypes were powered by Rolls-Royce Avon RA 2 engines, rather than the Orenda TR5 engines specified for production aircraft, the reason being that, although testing of the Orenda was proceeding well and showing it to be an excellent engine, it was not yet ready for flight. Also, the Rolls-Royce Avon was a more proven design and its use meant that Avro Canada would not be testing simultaneously both a new airframe and a new engine when the CF-100 first flew.

It was around this time that the company designation XC.100 (some sources list it as XC-100 and XC100) was adopted. Avro Canada's British parent company was by then assigning company model numbers in the 500s, so the Canadian company began with 100, prefixed with 'C' for Canada.

In August 1948, the RCAF changed its requirements from the British Mk 9A-1 search radar to the American AN/APS-19A. This would have no effect on the prototypes and other early aircraft and was but one of many changes to the weapons systems over the next few years. The air force itself was busy preparing for the introduction of the CF-100, setting up a major training programme in which an operational training unit would be established first, followed by front-line squadrons.

Post-war air defence capabilities differed little from the war years, with the Royal Canadian Air Force equipped with North American Mustangs and the Royal Canadian Navy operating the Hawker Sea Fury. The latter, along with the small number of Supermarine Seafires that were being retired in 1948, operated from HMCS *Magnificent* and from the

Right: This trio of CF-100 Mk 3Ts represent the first three aircraft delivered to the RCAF. As with most Mk 3/3As, they were assigned to crew training duties with No. 3 AW(F) OTU at North Bay, Ontario.

Below: The prototype CF-100 was subsequently used for various armament trials, and is seen here on rocket tests over the Point Petre range over Lake Ontario. The first prototype survived its test programme but was sadly scrapped.

Naval Air Station at Shearwater, Nova Scotia. On 10 January 1949, No. 410 Squadron converted to de Havilland Vampires F.3, becoming in the process Canada's first jet fighter squadron. With the first flight of the Soviet Union's first jet-powered bomber, the Ilyushin Il-28 on 8 July 1948, it was clear that neither piston-engined fighters nor the Vampires were sufficient to protect Canadian cities from attack. (At that time, RCAF fighter squadrons were based in Toronto, Winnipeg, Edmonton and Vancouver. They were later supplemented, even replaced, by Auxiliary squadrons, with additional cities receiving their limited protection.)

Of the three XC.100s ordered under CD 187, the first was to be for test flying, the second for static testing (it did not receive an RCAF serial or an Avro Canada constructor's number), and the third for additional test flying with modifications as they were developed, and was later to undertake proving trials.

The Orenda's initials trials showed it to be a successful design but, as mentioned, it was not ready in time for the two prototypes. Instead, they were fitted with Rolls-Royce RA.2 Avon engines, which produced 6,500 lb (28.91 kN) of thrust. In many respects, the Orenda programme was a much greater technical challenge than the CF-100, Canada having far fewer designers and engineers for jet engines than it did for airframes. The Orenda would be developed through several versions and the experience gained would, in turn, lead to the mighty PS-13 Iroquois for the ill-fated CF-105 Arrow. It has been argued that the cancellation

of the Iroquois was a greater loss than that of the Arrow itself. France was interested in using the engines in its Dassault Mirage IV and there was talk of using them in both the Republic F-105 Thunderchief and the Boeing B-52 Stratofortress, both of which would have been significant sales.

First flight

By the time the CF-100 first flew, approximately C$140 million had been spent on the project; converted into today's dollars, that is a staggering sum of money. The first prototype, 18101, was rolled out at the end of 1949 and began ground handling trials almost immediately. It made its first taxiing trials on 17 January 1950 and the first flight followed on 19 January. Don Rogers and Mike Cooper-Slipper were the Avro Canada test pilots at that time. Rogers had been checked out on the Vampire and both men had flown the Avro Canada Jetliner, but neither had fast jet experience. Consequently, the chief test pilot at Gloster in the UK was sent over to fly the CF-100. Bill Waterton, a Canadian, had his first jet experience flying Meteors late in the war. The chase planes for this flight were a Mitchell 2U (KL136), flown by Flight Lieutenant Barlow of the RCAF, and a Vampire F.3 (17051), flown by Avro Canada's Don Rogers.

Due to the combination of cold weather and a light fuel load, the prototype was airborne in just 1,500 ft (457 m). The first flight test programme was simple, with Waterton not venturing above 5,000 ft (1524 m) or 180 kt (97 km/h). After 40 minutes, he brought 18101 back in for a landing at Malton. A second flight took place on 25 January 1950. On its third

Avro Canada CF-100

Above: The Mk 4 represented a major improvement over the interim Mk 3: better radar and fire control system, more power and rocket armament. This aircraft was built as a Mk 4A but converted to Mk 4B standard with Orenda 11s.

Left: This Mk 4A tested a brake 'chute, attached to the tailplane joint but housed in an extended tailcone. It was not adopted for production.

flight, a serious problem was discovered. Waterton experienced difficulty with the controls and a post-flight inspection revealed that the outer skin on the centre-section next to the wings was seriously buckled. The cause of this damage was the excessive flexing of the wing spar at its joint to the nacelle, which was not strong enough to absorb the full design loads.

Discovering the cause of the problem did not take long. In their original design, Avro Canada's engineers had positioned the engines above the wing/centre-section structure. Although the RCAF had seen the mockup in that configuration, the design was later altered to move the engines forward where they would be clear of the main spar structure, in part to make lowering them for servicing much easier. However, as design work progressed, it became obvious that this new arrangement introduced

A Canadian-designed and -built fighter, with Canadian engines, flies over Niagara Falls. Significantly, the land at left is the United States, which jointly controlled the CF-100s (through NORAD) and provided the all-important fire control system and radar. The CF-100 Mk 4B was from No. 423 'Eagle' Squadron.

its own problems, such as having the centre of gravity too far forward (causing pitching moment problems) and also obstructing the crew's view with the big nacelles on either side of the cockpit. The CF-100's chief design engineer, John Frost, made the decision to move the engines back and lower. This required that a section of the top of the spar had to be cut away, or 'dipped', to allow the jet pipe to go straight back from the engine.

The initial solution to the cracked spar was to move the engines back again, but that introduced yet another problem. The engine's centre line was left unchanged but the main spar was cut out to accommodate the engines. The spar was then strengthened with doubler plates. Nevertheless, problems with cracking at the joint continued, each one accompanied by a loud crack clearly heard by the crew, much to their consternation. The airframe's structural ring around the engines also supported the outer skin, but it was insufficient to withstand the continuous flexing of the main spar, typically failing at the spar-to-ring joint. Additional doubler plates were fitted, but failed to resolve the problem. As more RCAF crews began

exploring the aircraft's capabilities as a fighter, the problem worsened. One even occurred during an aerial demonstration at Andrews AFB, Maryland for the USAF and another happened at the annual air show in Toronto on 20 September 1952. On that occasion, a 500-mph (804-km/h) pass followed by a steep pull-up overstressed the wings. The wing fillets scraped the engine nacelles and the bullet fairings on the starter motors were canted downward at some 30°. Avro soon realised that the fate of the entire programme was at risk and work on a solution began in earnest.

Flight testing continued. Waterton was pleased overall with the aircraft, but he criticised the solid dive brakes and approved of a proposed slotted version. On the prototype's eighth flight, the chief design engineer, John Frost, flew as a passenger, something few in his position are able to do.

Competition

On 9 May 1950, 18101 was flown to Andrews AFB at an average speed of 575 mph (925 km/h), with Bill Waterton as pilot and Mike Cooper-Slipper as navigator. On 27 May 1950, the Permanent Joint Defence Board toured the Avro Canada plant and was impressed with the project. The problem of wingroot cracks reared its ugly head, but at least it did not affect the outcome of the competition. Also around this time, a record speed of 638 mph (1026 km/h) was set for the Toronto–Montréal route.

Both Mk 1 prototypes were painted in an overall-gloss black colour scheme with white lightning bolts along the fuselage and engine nacelles. 18101 wore the individual registration letter 'D' and the 'FB' unit codes of the Central Experimental and Proving Establishment. Although the FB-D codes were not changed, they could have been, and the aircraft is much more accurately identified by its serial. Canada is believed to have been the only country to adopt ICAO codes for its military aircraft, in which RCAF aircraft codes began with VC- and RCN aircraft wore VG- codes. The system proved cumbersome and costly, because

every time an aircraft was transferred between units it had to be re-registered. The system's use was discontinued by Canada on 19 November 1951.

Bill Waterton ended his secondment to Avro Canada in February 1951 and returned to Gloster to conduct test flying on the Javelin, an aircraft that would one day compete against the CF-100 and lose. Waterton was replaced by Flight Lieutenant Bruce Warren. He and his twin brother, Douglas, had flown Spitfires together while with Nos 66 and 165 Squadrons, RAF. Bruce Warren had attended the Empire Test Pilots' School in 1959 and was then seconded to Avro Canada from the RCAF.

The second prototype (18102; coded FB-K), first flew in July 1950 and was transferred to CEPE in October for service evaluation. Most such trials were conducted at RCAF Station Rockcliffe, where CEPE was located, but 18102 was twice flown to Wright-Patterson AFB, Ohio for speed calibration trials. Several USAF pilots were checked out on the aircraft and all were reportedly impressed with it.

Additional fuel

18102 was most often photographed with wingtip fuel tanks, as it was engaged in their testing. The tip tanks contained approximately 290 Imp gal (1318 litres) of fuel each and gave the CF-100 a still-air range of 2,500 miles (4023 km). Initially, the added weight of the tanks and their contents caused the wings to twist, which affected the controls and the wings' fatigue life, but the addition of fins at the outer rear of each tank solved that problem. In addition, the tanks with fins increased the stability of the aircraft compared to operating without the tanks installed. Concerns about the tip tanks causing wing flutter led to taxiing trials along the runway with a flight test engineer riding on the wing. The windy and noisy ride showed no evidence of flutter and the tanks were cleared for flight.

The second prototype crashed near London, Ontario on 5 April 1951, the cause believed to

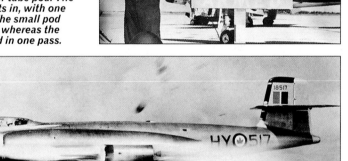

The 2.75-in FFAR Mighty Mouse rocket (right, being loaded) was the primary armament of the Mks 4 and 5, carried in 29-tube wingtip pods. The pod had a frangible nosecone (seen flying from the aircraft below) and after the rockets had fired the main pod section was jettisoned by a burst of compressed air. The pod can be seen falling away from the aircraft above. Both were on the strength of the WPU (Weapons Practice Unit) at Cold Lake. In addition to the operational 29-tube pod, CF-100s employed a simple three-round rack for training or, from 1959, a seven-tube pod. The latter usually had only six rockets in, with one tube empty for safety reasons. The small pod allowed two passes for training, whereas the three-round racks had to be fired in one pass.

be due to a fault in the crew's oxygen system, likely the pilot's mask. Flight Lieutenant Bruce Warren and his observer, Robert Ostrander, were killed. They had been conducting a series of flights at high altitude when the aircraft dove straight in. The accident caused the cancellation of Avro Canada's plans to demonstrate the CF-100 at that year's Farnborough air show, although there had been lingering pressurisation problems that also would have had to be resolved before undertaking the flight. The decision not to send the first prototype was a lost opportunity for publicity and, as it turned out, the CF-100 would not attend the air show of the Society of British Aircraft Constructors until September 1955.

The flight to Britain would have been the first-ever transatlantic crossing by a jet-powered aircraft, an honour that was subsequently claimed by an English Electric Canberra B.Mk 2 (WD932) on 21 February 1951 en

route to a demonstration and competition held at Andrews AFB by the USAF, that also included the CF-100. 18101 competed against the Canberra, Martin XB-51, and North American's AJ-1 Savage and B-45 Tornado for a USAF requirement for a Douglas B-26 (as it was then designated) Invader replacement. While it impressed its intended audience, it lost the competition to the Canberra due to its limited ground attack capabilities.

Once more, attention was turned to the problem of wingroot cracks, which, by then, posed a serious threat to the entire programme. Avro Canada engineer Waclaw Czerwinski was assigned the task of not only devising something that would prevent new aircraft from suffering the problem but would also be capable of being retrofitted to those aircraft already assembled. Czerwinski began his aeronautical career in his native Poland, later working in France and England; his Avro career started with a job as

No view better illustrated just why the CF-100 was called the 'Clunk'. Like the similar Northrop F-89, the CF-100 had a huge fuselage to allow the carriage of heavy fire control equipment, a second crew member, two powerful engines and sufficient fuel for its long-range mission.

effective than required, so the wing was redesigned to replace the air brakes with spoiler-like panels with serrated edges located forward of the flaps. 18101 was fitted with the new wing and made its first flight with it in October 1950, but it is not clear if 18102 had been similarly upgraded prior to its crash.

Initial plans called for the armament to be four 30-mm cannon, but their development had not progressed enough to allow their use, so the aircraft was redesigned to have a pack of eight 0.50-in machine-guns in its belly.

Orenda flies

The Orenda made it first flight on 13 July 1950 following a highly satisfactory series of ground tests. A Victory Aircraft-built Lancaster Mk X (FM209) was modified with an Orenda jet engine and its nacelle replacing each of the two outer Merlins of the Lancaster. The crew on this first flight consisted of pilot Don Rogers and two engineers, Walter Bellian and Bill Wildfong. The Orenda testbed was redesignated as a Lancaster 10.O (sometimes written as 10O) and was capable of flying comfortably with the two inboard Merlin engines shut down. With all four engines working, it became a difficult high-speed target for the New York Air National Guard's Republic F-47 Thunderbolt squadron, the 136th FIS, based across Lake Ontario at Niagara Falls, New York. The half-hour first flight ushered in a busy and hard-working career for the aircraft, which ended abruptly on 22 March 1955, when Avro Canada's Hangar H5 burned down. Also lost that day were two CF-100s (a Mk 3T, 18111, and a Mk 4B, 18348) and a Sabre 5 (23024).

An Orenda was installed in a North American F-86A Sabre following a visit to the Los Angeles facility in mid-1950. This benefited both Avro Canada as well as Canadair, which was then building General Electric J47-powered Sabre 2s, but was planning an improved version fitted with an Orenda engine. The USAF Sabre (49-1069) was redesignated as F-86AO. It was test flown by R. A. 'Bob' Hoover, the project test pilot, for the first time on 5 October 1950 at Los Angeles International Airport. Although the Orenda was bulkier than the J47, Hoover reported that it had much less vibration and was pleasant to fly. Later test flights were conducted at Edwards AFB (renamed as such from Muroc AFB on 27 January 1950) initially and then moved to Malton.

18101 was taken on strength by the RCAF on 23 June 1951 and was not struck off strength until 31 May 1965, an unusually long period of service for a prototype. Unfortunately, this aircraft was scrapped. Formal agreement was reached on 17 May 1949 for 10 pre-production CF-100s powered by Orenda engines, 30 spare engines, other spares, publications, ground handling equipment, etc. In July 1949, AIR

Above: 18222 was one of two Mk 4s converted for target-tug duties with CEPE, receiving an all-over red scheme which led to nicknames such as the 'Red Dragon' and 'Pink Lady'.

group leader in the stress office and he subsequently became project engineer and head of the preliminary design office. His solution to the cracking problem was to modify former 13A, redesigning the junction of the former, the wing fittings and the main spar to use a pin joint, and to add more doubler plates where the main spar had been dipped or cut away to lower the centreline of the engines. This solution allowed the aircraft to be flown to its design limits without the fear of major structural damage. The modification was tested and approved and, by late 1952, it was being applied to all CF-100s both on the production line and to those already built. This averted the potential cancellation of the programme, which had been feared since the problem was discovered.

The original design of the air brakes consisted of split trailing edges but they proved to be less

Having originally intended to exhibit the CF-100 at the 1951 SBAC show at Farnborough, Avro Canada eventually dispatched two Mk 5s to the 1955 show. One of them is depicted here flying over Tennyson Down on the Isle of Wight.

Spec 17-8 was issued for a new version of the CF-100, calling for 10 pre-production Mk 2s to be powered by Orenda 2s. Contract Demand CD 469 covered the design, tooling and manufacture, which began immediately, although the prototypes had not yet made their first flights. In September 1950, the contract was amended from 12 aircraft (two Mk 1s and 10 Mk 2s) to a total of 124, the balance being production Mk 3s.

At the same time, Avro Canada was looking even further ahead, beginning work on the CF-103, which was a largely standard CF-100 fuselage with swept wings. It was intended to fill the niche between the CF-100 and a completely new, supersonic aircraft at some point in the future. (The latter eventually became the CF-105 Arrow.) It is worth noting that, at that time, no operational aircraft was supersonic other than in a power dive. The only 'straight and level' supersonic aircraft were pure research designs such as Bell's X-1 and X-2 and Douglas's D-558 Skyrocket.

Pressure from government

With some justification, Avro Canada has been accused of considering itself to be nothing less than an arm of the RCAF. Its president and general manager, Fred Smye, once stated, "Avro and Orenda were the industrial arm of the RCAF and servants of the government, as is any purely defence contractor. The companies had fulfilled this role solely from their inception and for a period of 15 years." After the Arrow's cancellation, then-Prime Minister John Diefenbaker said that "the company seemed horror-struck at ever having to compete in a normal marketplace situation".

The CF-100 programme had encountered problems with the government from early on. Although turned over to the RCAF on 17 October 1951 with great fanfare and publicity, the first example, 18104, was quickly back at Malton undergoing further work and

Although nowhere near as agile as the Sabre, the Canuck had range aplenty, a vital attribute in the defence of the Canadian north. The type eventually gave way the the McDonnell CF-101B, following the cancellation of the CF-105 Arrow.

In late 1956 the first of four Mk 4B squadrons (No. 445) deployed from Canada to Europe, replacing one Sabre squadron at each of the four bases. RAF-style green/grey camouflage was adopted, as was the Red Ensign fin marking. At right is a 'Wolverines' aircraft seen prior to the move, while above a No. 445 aircraft displays its new camouflage.

modifications. On 12 November 1951, the Minister of Defence Production, the Honourable C. D. Howe, informed Avro Canada that "this letter is to advise you that all work in connection with new development is to be suspended, at least until the problems involved in the production of airframes and engines now on order have been resolved and deliveries made at a satisfactory rate. Personnel and facilities that are now engaged in new development work should be directed to the redesign of the engines and airframes on order to improve machine ability or to overcome other production problems. I do not wish at this time to issue a formal notice of termination in respect of development contracts, but I am determined that the full resources of your company be devoted to the all-important problem of getting actual production from the investment that has been made in the programme"; Howe toned down his approach when the Minister of National Defence, the Honourable Brooke Claxton, intervened on

behalf of the CF-100 programme. Howe's reaction to the CF-100's early problems pales in comparison to his statement about the CF-105 – "a programme of development that frankly gives me the shudders" – although he also said that "those weapons [the Arrows] are certainly required as soon as they can be produced" and "we have never missed yet". Once CF-100s began to be produced in quantity, Howe's opinion of Avro Canada improved markedly.

Part of the problem lay with the RCAF's desire for nothing but the best. The Chief of the Air Staff, Air Marshall Wilf Curtis, had been in the embarrassing position during World War II of having been denied Hurricanes for his Home Defence squadrons. As CAS, his determination that this would never happen again led first to the CF-100 and then to the CF-105. There were uniquely Canadian requirements for the aircraft to fulfil, the sheer size of the country being the most important one.

In early 1951, Avro Canada received

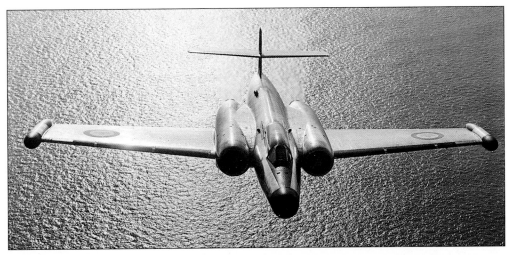

Above: The Mk 5 was the final major incarnation of the CF-100, the ungainliness of its wingtip extensions offset by a much cleaner profile thanks to deletion of the gunpack. This machine wears the lark badge of No. 425 'Alouette' Squadron, which was based at St-Hubert.

In the late 1950s NORAD mounted a powerful defence of the North American mainland. The Convair F-102 was the primary USAF interceptor while the CF-100 Mk 5 (this example from No. 409 Sqn) handled the Canadian contribution. Between them is the Boeing IM-99 Bomarc SAM.

'authority' for the production of 400 CF-100s. (An authority would appear to be the next best thing to a contract.) On 21 March 1951, 'clarification' was given to the company with a revised total of 718 aircraft and 738 engines. In June 1951, a firm order was issued for 70 Mk 3 aircraft, down from the original 124. The 'lost' aircraft would be accounted for later as Mk 4 versions. Based on a purchase of 718 airframes and 738 engines, Avro Canada estimated that the cost would be C$360,000 and C$60,000, respectively, for a flyaway unit cost of C$480,000.

Although the second contract was for 10 Mk 2s, only the first, 18103, was actually built as such. The next four, 18104 to 18107, were converted – somewhat hurriedly, according to some sources – as dual-control trainers and were redesignated Mk 2T. Four more, 18108 to 18111, became Mk 3Ts (also trainers) and the 10th, 18112, became the prototype Mk 4 (and is described later). 18103, the first Mk 2, was also the first CF-100 to be powered by Orenda engines. As noted above, it made its first flight on 20 June 1951, marking the first flight of an aircraft wholly designed and built in Canada (i.e., the airframe and engines). Design layout of the engine had begun on 3 September 1946 and the first one was delivered to the test house on 8 February 1949. Its first run took place there on 10 February 1949. By most standards, this was a rapid development time.

Test pilots reported few differences between the Orenda-powered CF-100s and the two Rolls-Royce Avon-powered prototypes. One change was that the Orenda offered minor improvements at high altitude. Avro Canada opened a large engine factory next to its Malton facility on 29 September 1952.

18104 had its pre-acceptance test flight with CEPE on 13 October 1951 and was flown to Rockcliffe on 17 October 1951 for handling trials and a demonstration. Its official hand-over to the RCAF took place back at Malton later that same day. The majority of the Mk 2s were converted to dual-control versions in order to hasten the transition of pilots to the new jet aircraft.

Rocket assist

A series of trials using Aerojet RATO 'bottles' was conducted at RCAF Station Uplands between 8 and 15 August 1952. 18105 made a number of assisted take-offs using both two and six bottles, comparing the results with not using any at all. Although the 1,000-lb (4.45-kN) thrust RATO bottles were found to provide considerable additional take-off power, the concept was not used operationally.

During the RATO trials, two bombs were carried on the CF-100's underwing pylons. Two pylons could be fitted under each wing, all capable of carrying a 1,000-lb bomb. In 1954, 18105 was modified aerodynamically as a Mk 3 and was used in a series of bomb-dropping trials. In the course of 14 flights, a total of 21 1,000-lb bombs and 20 100-lb practice bombs was dropped into Lake Ontario, but the conclusion reached was that the airframe did not possess sufficient g capacity. It could sustain $7g$, but 10-$12g$ was considered to be the minimum required for a ground attack capability. The four underwing hardpoints were retained, however, giving a future capability to carry bombs, air-to-ground rockets or air-to-air rockets. None of these was used operationally and the hardpoints' only operational use was to carry pylons on which were mounted chaff dispensers.

18107 was used to test the powered controls of the Avro Canada C.105, later to become the CF-105 Arrow. On 25 November 1952, 18107 carried out the first air firing of the gunpack, which contained eight 0.50-in Colt-Browning M3 machine-guns, each with 200 rounds. The trials were held at RCAF Station Trenton. Over a 20-day period, eight air firings and 54 ground firings were conducted, consuming more than 83,000 rounds. Apparently, 18107 was only used for the first air firing, with 18129 used thereafter as it was the first CF-100 fitted with the full Mk 3 weapons system.

One proposal that reached the testing stage involved the use of four T160 20-mm rotary-breech cannon, a design originating with a German World War II weapon and produced by Ford. Avro Canada's work began in November 1952; a year later, they had 16 T160 Type E3 cannon. The test programme began with ground firing a cannon from a test stand, then ground firing an unknown number mounted in a CF-100, followed by air firing. Using 18103, air firing began on 21 May 1954 and continued until 22 April 1955. Serious reliability problems with a wide range of components led to the abandonment of the programme. Other gun pack trials were conducted using 18143 at RCAF Station Namao between October 1953 and March 1954 with a series of cold-weather tests at Fort Churchill.

First deliveries to the RCAF were made in 1952, with the first front-line squadron equipping in April 1953. The aircraft had a long career defending not only Canada, but also (from November 1956) the southern half of West Germany, flying with the 1st Canadian Air Division. The CF-100's operational career is recounted in the operators section, while details of the individual variants are described in a subsequent section.

Record-setting flight

To reap some favourable publicity from its new long-range interceptor, Avro Canada and the RCAF organised a long-range endurance flight in November 1953. 445 Squadron, the first operational CF-100 squadron, supplied a

The Mk 5 served exclusively on NORAD duties, and none was sent to Europe. The Mk 4B's better low-level manoeuvrability and gun armament were more appropriate to the low-altitude environment which prevailed in Europe, where interceptors operated underneath a SAM belt.

Above: CF-100s regularly practised high-altitude intercepts against SAC bombers. Here a No. 428 'Ghost' Squadron Mk 5B formates on a 7th Bomb Wing B-36H after intercepting the monster.

crew (Flight Lieutenant Mike Kobierski was the pilot and Flight Lieutenant Doug Turner was the navigator) and a Mk 3B (18136). The aircraft was ferried from Ottawa to Vancouver, British Columbia on 5–6 November 1953. Military and Avro Canada support teams made every effort to prepare the aircraft, including cooling the fuel with dry ice to increase its density, which enabled them to load more fuel on board than if it had been at its usual temperature.

On 16 November 1953, 18136 departed Vancouver en route for Halifax, Nova Scotia: from west to east across the entire country. By taking advantage of high-level winds and pressure ridges, the aircraft made good progress, despite minor engine difficulties over northern Ontario. Unfortunately, Halifax's weather had deteriorated and the airport was closed, as was Montréal's. Ottawa was also closed, so, at that point, 18136 turned back and landed at North Bay, Ontario. Total flight time was 4 hours and 30 minutes, although it was reported in *Avro Canada News* as being 3 hours and 50 minutes, with the note that it was a routine flight, not one attempting to set a record.

In mid-1954, the Royal Canadian Air Force held Operation Prairie Pacific, a trans-Canada air pageant on a rather grand scale. Its three major objectives were: to stimulate interest in the RCAF, especially among the young; to acquaint Canadians with their new jet aircraft; and to test the efficiency and mobility of a task force composed of elements from different jet and transport units. The aircraft were reportedly formed into a composite squadron, but its designation (if it had one) is unknown. No fewer than 19 aircraft were involved: three heavy transports (type, serials and units unknown), a Canso (serial and unit unknown), five Sabre 2s (serials unknown) from 431 Squadron, five Silver Stars (serials unknown) from the Central Flying School, and five

CF-100 Mk 3Bs (18148, 18149, 18164, 18170 and 18177) from 423 AW(F) Squadron.

The first show was on 15 August 1954 at Winnipeg, Manitoba. Other shows followed at Saskatoon, Regina, Calgary, Lethbridge, Victoria, Vancouver and Port Arthur, with a final series at the Canadian National Exhibition in Toronto, ending on 11 September 1954. Approximately 80,000 miles (128744 km) were flown, with routes planned to overfly many small communities. Contemporary estimates of the number of people who saw some aspect of Operation Prairie Pacific reached 2 million.

Bristol Aerospace was awarded a contract for the Calendar Aircraft Inspection and Repair (CAIR) programme. (Some cynics referred to CAIR as 'Canadian Aircraft Industry Relief'.) This encompassed 21 Mk 3Ds, 43 Mk 4s and 32 Mk 5s and continued until February 1961. The last CF-100 to go through Bristol's CAIR programme was 18156. Bristol also carried out repairs to 12 CF-100s of various marks following B Category accidents. Avro Canada also performed a great deal of CAIR work, including installing new modifications on CF-100s straight out of the factory, overhauling aircraft, and repairing damaged aircraft. Depending on the extent of the damage, the repairs were either carried out at its base or the aircraft transported back to Avro Canada by rail.

Velvet Glove

During the late 1940s, Canada began the Velvet Glove air-to-air guided missile project,

Despite its attributes, the CF-100 only found one overseas customer – Belgium. The FAB/BLu operated 53 Mk 5s between 1957 and 1963, the aircraft being funded by Canada (25 per cent) and the US (75 per cent). All were scrapped following replacement by the Lockheed F-104G.

part of a joint Canada/US/UK programme. Canada's portion of the work was largely carried out by the Canadian Armament Research and Development Establishment (CARDE), part of the Defence Research Board (DRB) located at Val Cartier, Québec. Its personnel were a mix of civilian and military. On 18 September 1950, the Minister of National Defence recommended to the Cabinet Defence Committee that approval be given for the development of an air-to-air missile in Canada. Work commenced formally on 1 April 1951 at CARDE. Full-scale test firings began in the autumn of 1951 and 20 firings took place in 1952. By 1953, half of CARDE's work was devoted to the Velvet Glove.

A total of 28 ground launchings took place between December 1951 and December 1953 at a newly-opened range at Point Petre, Ontario. The first air launch was from an F-86E (serial unknown) on 27 August 1953. Testing was also performed at the range at RCAF Station Cold Lake. The latter location was used in parallel initially, only taking over exclusively for the final few months. Over 300 missiles were produced and fired.

A primary concern in the design of Velvet Glove was simplicity. It was intended for one

Avro Canada CF-100

The Velvet Glove missile programme was an ambitious one for Canada. Not only the development of the missile itself, but also the provision of the sophisticated test facilities required to evaluate aspects of the weapon. The first air launch (from a Sabre) was on 27 August 1953 and by the end of the programme over 300 had been fired. The vital statistics of the missile were: length 10 ft 8 in (3.25 m); wingspan 3 ft 2 in (0.96 m); body diameter 8 in (20 cm); launch weight 318 lb (144 kg); speed Mach 2.3; and range up to 2.55 miles (4.11 km). The solid fuel rocket motor was provided by Aerojet and gave a thrust of 7,600 lb (33.82 kN) over a burn time of approximately 1.9 seconds. The seeker was a semi-active radar homing type.

These two photos show Mk 3A 18117 engaged in captive carry and jettison trials with the Velvet Glove missiles carried under the nacelles.

kind of threat, which had a specific, limited operational requirement. The goal of high reliability was sought along with the greatest possible economies of effort in research, development, manufacturing, handling, operational use, servicing and repair. The rocket motors were purchased from the United States but the rest of the missile was wholly Canadian. Velvet Glove was designed to be launched from behind a target by a pursuing aircraft, thereby classifying it as a semi-active

Left: The front cockpit of this Mk 4 has been modified with the addition of two launch control modules (marked 'V.G. Missile Control' and 'V.G. Exp. Pylon') for the Velvet Glove weapon.

Below: Various aircraft carried and launched Velvet Gloves. This Mk 4B has the missiles on the underwing hardpoints.

homing missile. Mid-1950s' plans called for it to be armed with a fragmenting warhead controlled by a proximity fuse. Avro Canada's proposed to equip a CF-100 Mk 4 with four of the missiles, supplemented by the standard wingtip FFAR pods. A simple modification to the MG-2A fire control system was all that was required to employ the weapon on the CF-100. The proposal also called for the deletion of the ventral gun pack.

Development proceeded until 1956, but the design was superseded by British and American guided missile developments. Velvet Glove was not going to be effective against a manoeuvring target and the days of the straight-and-level massed bomber stream were long over. Simply put, the requirements for a missile in 1951 were no longer valid. With jet bombers replacing Tu-4 'Bulls' in the Soviet air force, there was

no place for a missile designed for a fighter that was closing on a bomber at high speed from the rear. Avro suggested an interim, unguided design employing a 'king-sized' warhead and proximity fuse, but it went no further. It was decided to discontinue development of Velvet Glove and acquire rights to the American Sparrow 2 missile.

Ejection trials

In February 1955, an internal windshield was installed in production aircraft to provide the navigator with protection from windblast following the jettisoning of the canopy. It had become clear that the force of the windblast was such that the navigator's arms would be forced above his head and held there, preventing him from activating his ejection seat. Tests soon proved the new windshield to be effective at speeds up to 500 kt (922 km/h).

Only one live test ejection was made. This occurred on 26 May 1955 at Camp Borden, Ontario (now CFB Borden) and was designed to test both the Martin-Baker Model 2E seat and the internal windshield. A CF-100 Mk 4, 18262, was used, flown by Avro Canada's Jan Zurakowski. In the rear seat was Martin-Baker's Sqn Ldr 'Pat' Fifield and the test was observed by James Martin of the same firm. The test run was made at 1,500 ft (457 m) above ground level at a speed of 300 kt (553 km/h). The canopy separated when signalled, followed one second later by the seat, which cleared the aircraft's tail by some 17 ft (5.2 m). Five seconds later, Fifield separated from the seat and descended safely by parachute.

The Avro Canada C.102 Jetliner, CF-EJD, served as the chase plane, carrying four movie and two still cameras. 18262 carried four movie cameras and there were another five cameras on the ground to record the test.

Further ejection seat trials were conducted on 26 and 27 May 1955, once again employing 18262. For these tests, a dummy (named George) was used rather than a live subject. Experiments with settings of the automatic sequencer resulted in a successful ejection at an altitude of 50 ft (15 m) and a speed of 400 kt (737 km/h). However, the report noted that "at this altitude the timing is so critical that it is difficult to assess the ejection from a safety aspect".

Following the cancellation of Velvet Glove, the RCAF turned to the Sperry Sparrow 2D missile, which was extensively tested by several CF-100s designated Mk 5M. This aircraft is actually the 'Mk 5/6', with a trial installation of the extended engine nacelles intended for the reheated Orenda 11R engines of the proposed Mk 6.

RCAF CF-100s were used in several research programmes in association with the United States, one such – Operation Lookout – beginning in 1960. Phase 1 measured the infra-red emissions from re-entering missile nosecones, Phase 2 measured rocket plumes from launch to burnout, and Phase 3 continued the measurements begun in the first two phases. From April to June 1961, three other CF-100 Mk 4Bs (18434, 18439 and 18453) were based at Patrick AFB, Florida, to track launches in Phase 2 of Operation Lookout. Phase 3 began in September 1961, with the aircraft based at Patrick again, as well as from Eleuthera, Mayaguana and San Salvador in the Bahamas. The CF-100s worked as part of a team with USAF Fairchild C-119 and Lockheed U-2 sensing aircraft. Operation Lookout continued in Florida for three years. The IR signatures of approximately 150 missiles were measured, including those of the first manned US space mission and at least four later Mercury missions. (There were six manned Mercury launches, two sub-orbital and four orbital.) Although not widely publicised due to security considerations, the information gained by the Canadian CF-100s played a major role in gathering data used to develop missile launch detection systems carried on satellites.

Jets on Ascension

In January 1960, two CF-100 Mk 4Bs, 18439 and 18453, accompanied by a Canadair North Star and a Fairchild C-119 (serials unknown), left the CEPE Detachment at Québec for the 7000-mile (1126-km) flight to Ascension Island in the Atlantic Ocean. Eight days after leaving Canada, the two CF-100s became the first jets ever to land at Ascension, later to become famous as the staging point for the British during the Falklands War. The CF-100s were chosen for their payload, short-field capability, range and stability. Special instrumented pods were installed on the left wingtip and a fuel tank was carried on the right. They remained at Ascension for 11 months.

From August 1962 to June 1963, 86 flights in three sessions were flown in support of Operation Blind Twinkler, which measured IR radiation as part of the development of the Ballistic Missile Early Warning System (BMEWS). Two CF-100s (serials unknown) were involved in this programme, based at Thule, Greenland.

Another research flight was carried out on 20 July 1963, when a CF-100 (serial unknown) was used to chase a solar eclipse over Québec.

In 1964, a CF-100 (serial unknown) was used to conduct airborne tests of the infra-red scanner under development for NASA's Nimbus weather satellite. A pod containing the prototype scanner was installed by the University of Michigan and was subsequently

Between 1967 and 1982 this aircraft, on loan to engine manufacturer P&W Canada, tested different versions of the JT15D small turbofan. The stalky undercarriage of the 'Clunk' made it the natural candidate for this task.

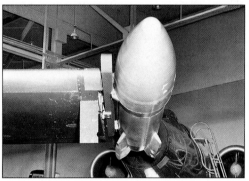

The Douglas MB-1 Genie unguided nuclear rocket was proposed as wingtip armament for the CF-100 Mk 5.

Hughes GAR-8 Falcons were also proposed, being lighter than the Sparrow 2D. This trial installation was undertaken on a No. 432 Sqn jet.

tested over Florida, the Caribbean, and the deserts and mountains of southern California.

In August 1955, Avro Canada decided to participate in that year's Society of British Aircraft Companies' 16th Flying Display and Exhibition, better known by its location, Farnborough. 18321 and 18322 were brought out of storage and made ready for the event, arriving on 3 September 1955. The flying programme commenced on 5 September and the two CF-100s returned to Langar one week later. Contemporary reports make clear the impressive performances of the CF-100 flown by Avro Canada test pilot Jan Zurakowski.

A demonstration tour of Canadian fighter bases in Europe by 18321 began on 25 September 1955 at Grostenquin. It ended on 28 September 1955. The return flight to Canada - codenamed Random Westbound – was made by 18321 between 4 and 10 November 1955.

Less than a year after the CF-100's tour of the Air Division, it was decided to replace one Sabre squadron in each wing with a CF-100 Mk 4B squadron as a result of increasing

Avro Canada CF-100

The CF-100 enjoyed a new lease of life when it was chosen to act as an electronic warfare training aircraft. This is a Mk 5D, with underwing chaff dispensers and numerous onboard jammers.

tensions in Europe, particularly the Hungarian Revolution, and the Suez Crisis.

Avro Canada made many proposals for further development of the CF-100, described in detail in the variants section. Other proposals not assigned a designation included arming Mk 4 and 5 aircraft with four Falcons (model unknown) or two Genies or four Sidewinders, all in addition to their regular FFAR armament. Any interest shown by the RCAF in these and other proposals was overtaken by the CF-105 Arrow programme.

United Aircraft of Canada (which was renamed as Pratt & Whitney Aircraft of Canada on 1 May 1975 and then as Pratt & Whitney Canada on 26 October 1982) requested the loan of a CF-100 during 1967 to serve as a flying testbed for its JT15D turbofan. The RCAF supplied 18760 (later reserialled 100760), which arrived at the company's St Hubert test centre on 22 November 1967. Its high ground clearance was a particularly useful characteristic, as was its ability to cruise at Mach 0.8 at up to 48,000 ft (14630 m). Its first flight with UACL was on 22 July 1968 and its first flight with a test engine was on 14 August 1968. The first air-start of a JT15D took place on 22 August 1968.

The loan was extended numerous times while 100760 logged a total of 1017.6 flying hours in over 400 flights with the company. The initial loan period was from 1 September 1967 to 31 December 1970, this being authorised on 14 November 1967. On 4 January 1971, the loan period was extended to 31 December 1971. Further extensions were authorised, usually for a period of one year, but occasionally for two, and the aircraft never again served in a CAF unit. It made its final flight on 28 June 1982, was struck off strength by the CAF on 8 July, and was placed on a pylon at CFB Montréal (St Hubert) on 19 April 1983. During its testing career, it was involved in trials of the JT15D-1, JT15D-1A, JT15D-4, JT15D-4A, JT15D-4B and JT15D-4C.

Specifications

	Mk 1	Mk 3	Mk 4	Mk 5
Length	52 ft 6 in (16.00 m)	52 ft 3.7 in (15.94 m)	54 ft 2 in (16.51 m)	54 ft 2 in (16.51 m)
Wingspan	52 ft 0 in (15.85 m)	52 ft 0 in (15.85 m)	53 ft 7 in (16.33 m)	58 ft 7 in (17.86 m)
Wingspan (rocket pods)	n/a	n/a	55 ft 10 in (17.02 m)	60 ft 10 in (18.54 m)
Wing area	540 sq ft (50.17 m²)	540 sq ft (50.17 m²)	540 sq ft (50.17 m²)	591 sq ft (54.90 m²)
Chord (root)	unknown	12 ft 2.9 in (3.73 m)	13 ft 11 in (4.24 m)	13 ft 11 in (4.24 m)
Chord (tip)	unknown	6 ft 11 in (2.11 m)	7 ft 2.5 in (2.19 m)	7 ft 2.5 in (2.19 m)
Tailplane span	21 ft 0 in (6.4 m)	21 ft 0 in (6.4 m)	21 ft 0 in (6.4 m)	25 ft 0 in (7.65 m)
Height (fin)	15 ft 1 in	15 ft 6.4 in (4.73 m)	14 ft 6 in (4.42 m)	14 ft 6 in (4.42 m)
Engines (two)	RA.2 Avon	Orenda 8	Orenda 9 (Mk 4A) Orenda 11 (Mk 4B)	Orenda 11
Armament	none	eight 0.50-in M3	eight 0.50-in M3 and 58 FFARs	58 FFARs

Conclusion

Due both to the cancellation of the CF-105 Arrow and its use as an electronic warfare trainer, the CF-100 Canuck served much longer than had ever been expected. It was the only Canadian-designed and -built fighter aircraft to reach operational status, a remarkable achievement for a relatively small nation, and would have been overshadowed completely as a mere stepping-stone had the CF-105 Arrow programme not been cancelled. With both the airframe and engine designed from scratch, a production run of 692 aircraft (including prototypes and pre-production examples) was nothing short of a major success, all the more so considering that there was only one small sale to a foreign country. **Jeff Rankin-Lowe**

No. 414 Squadron, successor of the Electronic Warfare Unit, put up this fine formation in about 1980, one of the last flying CF-100 Mk 5Ds being accompanied by an EW CE-117 Falcon and two CT-133s. The CF-100 was retired in 1981, but in 1983 No. 414 acquired another old warrior in the form of the single EF-101B EW Voodoo, which was flown until 1987.

Preserved 'Clunks'

A total of 34 CF-100s has been preserved, comprising two Mk 2Ts, three Mk 3Ds, two Mk 4As, one Mk 4B, 12 Mk 5s, 13 Mk 5C/Ds and one Mk 5M. Their current locations are as follows:

18104 (CFB St Jean), **18106** (Military Memorial Museum, Campbelford, Ontario), **18126** (Aero Space Museum, Calgary, Alberta), **18138** (Canadian Museum of Flight and Transportation, Langley, BC), **18152** (Nanton Lancaster Museum, Alberta), **18194** (CFB Borden), **18241** (Belleville, Ontario), **18393** (Imperial War Museum, Duxford, England), **100472** (Air Defence Museum, CFB Bagotville), **100476** (Alberta Aviation Museum, Edmonton), **18488** (Centennial Park, Moncton, New Brunswick), **100493** (CFB Borden), **100500** (22 Wing Museum, CFB North Bay), **100504** (Castle Air Museum, Atwater, California), **18506** (Canadian Warplane Heritage Museum, Mount Hope, Ontario), **18534** (Royal Military Museum, Brussels, Belgium), **18602** (Royal Canadian Legion, Haliburton, Ontario), **18619** (Malton, Ontario), **18626** (Lee Park, North Bay, Ontario), **18731** (Royal Military College of Canada Museum, Kingston, Ontario), **18746** (CFB Montreal), **100747** (Atlantic Canada Aviation Museum, Halifax, Nova Scotia), **18752** (CFB Uplands, Ottawa, Ontario), **100757** (National Aviation Museum, Rockcliffe, Ontario), **100759** (Reynolds-Alberta Museum, Wetaskiwin), **100760** (Musée de l'Aviation du Quebec, St-Hubert), **18761** (CFB Cold Lake Air Park, Alberta), **18764** (Western Canada Aviation Museum, Winnipeg, Manitoba), **18773** (Trenton Air Cadet Camp, **100774** (RCAF Memorial Museum, Trenton), **100779** (Edward J. Peterson Air and Space Museum, Peterson AFB, Colorado), **100784** (Heritage Park, 1 CAD Headquarters, CFB Winnipeg), **100785** (Canadian Warplane Heritage Museum, Mount Hope, Ontario), **100790** (Comox Air Force Museum, BC).

Above: 18602, Mk 5, Royal Canadian Legion, Haliburton, Ontario, displayed in No. 413 Sqn marks
Below: 18104, Mk 2T, Saint Jean garrison, CFB Montréal, oldest surviving CF-100 (fourth aircraft built)

Above: 18106, Mk 2T, Military Memorial Museum, Campbelford, Ontario, carries 'B-615' serial

Above: 18619, Mk 5, Malton, Toronto, Ontario. Preserved at site of former Avro Canada factory

Above: 18626, Mk 5M, Lee Park, North Bay, Ontario, displayed in No. 414 Squadron marks (with Bomarc)

Above: 18138, Mk 3D, Canadian Museum of Flight and Transportation, Langley, British Columbia

Above: 100476, Mk 5D, Alberta Aviation Museum, Edmonton, restored in No. 440 Squadron markings

Above: 18488, Mk 5C, Centennial Park, Moncton, New Brunswick, on display in Electronic Warfare Unit markings

Above: 100774, Mk 5, RCAF Memorial Museum, CFB Trenton, painted to resemble prototype
Left: 100500, Mk 5D, 22 Wing Museum, CFB North Bay
Right: 100779, Mk 5, on display at NORAD Headquarters, Peterson AFB, Colorado

Avro Canada CF-100 Variants

CF-100 Mk 1

Two prototype CF-100 Mk 1 aircraft were built, serials 18101 and 18102, plus a third example for static tests (which received neither an RCAF serial or an Avro Canada constructor's number). They were powered by Rolls-Royce RA.2 Avon engines. 18101, which wore VC-FBD codes, made its first flight on 19 January 1950, having been rolled out in December 1949 and first conducting taxiing trials on 17 January 1950. 18102, with VC-FBK codes, first flew in July 1950 and was delivered to the Central Proving and Experimental Establishment for service trials in October of that year. It was engaged primarily in trials while the first prototype carried out demonstrations in addition to its trials work.

The second prototype was most often

fitted with 290-Imp gal (1318-litre) tip tanks, which extended its still-air range to 2,500 miles (4023 km). Both were painted gloss black with a white lightning bolt along the fuselage. 18101 wore 'CF-100' below the windscreen, but this was replaced by the RCAF's heraldic crest on 18102. The latter was expected to be flown to the 1951 SBAC show at Farnborough, but was lost in a crash on 5 April 1951. As a result, the CF-100 had to wait until September 1955 to attend the show. 18101 survived until 1965, an unusually long life for a prototype, but was, unfortunately, scrapped that year, even though it had once been earmarked for possible museum display as long ago in 1956.

The first CF-100 is seen in January 1950 during an early test flight. The aircraft took to the air for the first time on 19 January, piloted by Bill Waterton, chief test pilot of Gloster. The aircraft remained powered by the Rolls-Royce Avon throughout its long career, although it was later upgraded to Mk 3 equivalent and was used for various armament tests. The codes 'FB-D' were derived from the full serial VC-FBD.

The second prototype, VC-FBK, is seen fitted with a nose-mounted pitot and tip tanks. The latter were fitted for much of the aircraft's short test career, and soon gained fins to overcome stability problems. From October 1950 it was sent to CEPE at Rockcliffe for initial RCAF evaluation, although it also made trips to Wright-Patterson AFB for speed calibration.

CF-100 Mk 1

Nose pitot occasionally mounted for tests

Rolls-Royce RA.2 Avon turbojet engines

No armament fitted

300-gal tip-tanks fitted to second prototype

Tail bumper to avoid damage on over-rotation

CF-100 Mk 2

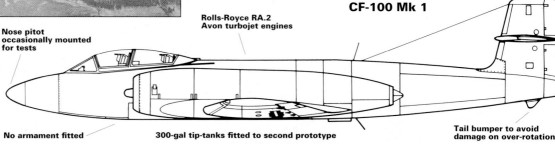

Described at the time as being pre-production aircraft, five CF-100 Mk 2s were ordered, all of which were powered by Orenda 1 engines, but only the first, 18103, was built as a straight Mk 2. It made the first flight of an Orenda-powered Canuck on 20 June 1951. It was used for icing trials in April and May 1953 and for trials of the T160 E3 20-mm cannon (which eventually became the M61 Gatling gun still in use today) between May 1954 and April 1955. All Mk 2s had a natural metal finish. 18103 wore VC-FBN codes. In reality, the Mk 2 and 2Ts were closer to being prototypes powered by Orendas than true pre-production models.

CF-100 Mk 2P: Proposed photographic reconnaissance conversion of Mk 3 18112. Not accepted and 18112 became the prototype for the Mk 4 (see below).

CF-100 Mk 2T: The remaining four CF-100 Mk 2s were built as Mk 2T variants with dual controls, although they were all employed by CEPE and/or Avro Canada for various trials in addition to helping to train the air force's first CF-100 pilots. They were all powered by Orenda 1 engines. 18104 was flown to RCAF Station Rockcliffe on 17 October 1951, returning the same day to Malton for the pomp and ceremony of an official hand-over to the RCAF. It was subsequently employed on handling trials. It survives today on display at the former CFB St-Jean, where it wears '100104'. 18105 was used for RATO trials in August 1952, went to Hughes in Minnesota with CEPE for autopilot trials in December 1952, bomb-carrying and -dropping trials in 1954, and conducted early wingtip rocket pod evaluations. It was converted to a training aid, A611, in April 1955, and was not struck off strength until November 1974. 18106

also survives, residing in the Military Memorial Museum in Campbellford, Ontario (where the CF-100's Martin-Baker ejection seats were built under licence). 18107 carried out the first air-firing of the gunpack on 25 November 1952, was used for icing

trials between January and June 1954, and was later modified for trials of the CF-105 Arrow's powered elevator controls.

18103 (above) was the only true Mk 2, the remainder of the batch being completed as Mk 2Ts (left). The aircraft depicted, 18104, was the first to be handed over to the RCAF, although the ceremony was entirely symbolic as the Mk 2s were, in effect, prototypes of the production fighter.

CF-100 Mk 2

Orenda 1 engines

Structural improvements to prevent wing cracks

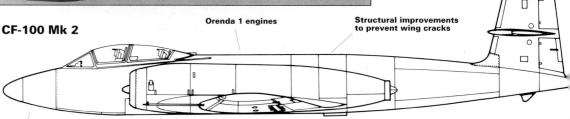

'Solid' metal nose fitted for gun-firing trials

Gun pack not fitted here, first carried by 18107

CF-100 Mk 3

The first five Mk 3s, 18108 to 18112, although intended for squadron service, were actually pre-production aircraft also. All but the first were built as Mk 3T trainers, while the fifth was later modified to serve as the Mk 4 prototype. The remainder of the Mk 3s were either the Mk 3A or Mk 3B, depending on the version of the Orenda installed (Orenda 2 and Orenda 8, respectively, although one source states that only the first Mk 3 and 11 of the Mk 3CTs had the Orenda 2). 18108 was the first CF-100 delivered to the RCAF for operational use. It was delivered to the OTU at North Bay on 22 July 1952.

Some confusion exists in various sources regarding when Mk 3s entered service, due to four Mk 2s being converted to Mk 3Ts. The first 'true' Mk 3 was 18113. The early Mk 3 aircraft left much to be desired, suffering from poor detail design and inadequate quality control, and they possessed little standardisation. One frequent problem was the failure of the nose gear to retract. The chief flying instructor, Squadron Leader R.D. Schultz, was one day briefing a sceptical senior engineer form Avro Canada when he simply pointed out the window; upon seeing the CF-100 flying circuits with its nose gear extended, the doubter at last understood the problem. When the gear did retract, it often caused problems with an already-unreliable VHF radio.

The hefty control column obscured the compass, a problem solved when the then-commanding officer of 423 Squadron, Wing Commander R. J. 'Pop' Lawlor, had the top cut off and remounted so it was canted to the right. Other CF-100-equipped units soon followed suit.

Another problem was caused by the

18132 was the last of the Mk 3As, seen here in OTU service with gun pack fitted. Some confusion exists as to whether all or some Mk 3As were fitted with the Orenda 2 engine.

aircraft not having been equipped with a fuel flow control, instead regulating fuel flow to the engines directly with the throttle setting. As few pilots, let alone students, had a great deal of jet time, it was easy to induce compressor stalls, which frequently burned out the turbine when the engine temperature went out of control.

The unreliable, complex, solenoid-operated fuel system frequently caused other trouble. Some pilots reportedly joked that the system required an engineering degree before learning to fly the CF-100. Six fuel gauges ranged across the top of the pilot's instrument panel, calibrated in Imperial gallons, and reading them and converting those readings so as to calculate the fuel and time remaining, added much to the pilot's workload. Other problems included landing gear oleos that leaked in cold weather, hydraulic pump failures, and high tyre consumption. The latter was solved with the installation of Maxaret anti-skid brakes. The lack of nosewheel steering was yet another problem. Considering the howls of outrage when a modern aircraft has relatively minor teething problems, one can scarcely imagine what would have been made of the CF-100's early troubles today.

Sixty Mk 3s were to be modified to other configurations, including the Mk 3CT production dual-control gunnery trainer and Mk 3D production dual-control trainer. Eleven became Mk 3CTs on the production line and it was planned to convert 49 Mk 3As and 3Bs as Mk 3Ds. However, two were lost before they were converted and were not replaced. Some Mk 3s eventually became ground instructional airframes, while others went to Air Defence Command squadrons as 'hacks' or to the Electronic Warfare Unit. Later, the nine surviving Mk 3CTs were converted to Mk 3Ds.

18112 was used to test the belly pack of rockets, which was located to the rear of the gun pack. It contained 48 of the 2.75-in FFARs. A similar, 24-tube pack was a feature of the North American F-86D Sabre and was considered by Avro Canada as early as October 1951. On 10 February 1953, AFHQ sent the company a letter requesting the development of the system. The belly pack was developed in parallel

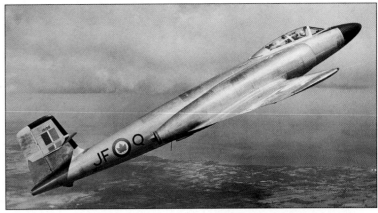

18108 was the first CF-100 Mk 3, differing primarily from the Mk 2s by having Orenda 2 engines and operational systems. It was the first aircraft to be delivered to the RCAF, arriving at North Bay in July 1952.

with the wingtip rocket pod system.

A test firing example of the belly pack was tested in July 1953 and a full pack was tested in September of that year. 18112 (the prototype Mk 4) was transported to Point Petre, near Picton, Ontario, for ground firing trials in November 1953. The wings were removed and the aircraft placed on jacks (to avoid shooting off its own nose gear). Flight trials began in January 1954 to test the effects on handling of the massive belly pack in the lowered position. Flights were conducted at Mach 0.85 at higher altitudes and 460 kt (848 km/h) at lower altitudes. A strong buffeting began at around 300 kt (553 km/h) and it progressively worsened at higher speeds. The first air firing was carried out on 11 February 1954. Test launches began with six and progressed through 12, 30 and 48 rockets in a salvo.

It was also found during the trials that the nose of the aircraft pitched up as the rocket pack was lowered, for which Avro suggested adding a pitch compensation device to the auto-pilot. Other trials connected with the programme included assessing the damage that could be done if a rocket ignited inside the retracted pack. 18112 was lost near Ajax, Ontario during a

test flight on 23 August 1954. Despite the installation of the pitch compensation device, the aircraft sill was severely buffeted when the rocket pack was extended. An explosion occurred, followed by another, which pilot Jan Zurakowski thought was the ejection of his observer, John Hiebert, so 'Zura' ejected, suffering minor injuries. In fact, Hiebert had not ejected and he was killed in the crash. The cause of the accident was believed to have been the ignition of fuel leaking from a fuel line that had been ruptured by the sever buffeting.

Although it took less than a second for the belly pack to extend, fire all of its missiles, and retract, the problems with buffeting led to the cancellation of the belly pack for the Mk 3 in September 1954. The ventral gun pack was retained and FFARs would be housed in wingtip pods. These minimised FOD damage to the engines,

This Mk 3A, 18117, was used by CEPE for tests with the Velvet Glove missile programme, carrying four of the weapons on underwing pylons. A nose pitot was fitted for providing accurate air data during carriage trials. Adorning the nose is the bear badge of CEPE's Namao detachment.

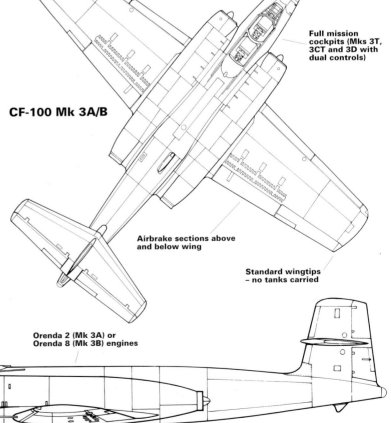

CF-100 Mk 3A/B

Wing-mounted pitot

Full mission cockpits (Mks 3T, 3CT and 3D with dual controls)

Airbrake sections above and below wing

Standard wingtips – no tanks carried

Hughes AN/APG-33 radar

Orenda 2 (Mk 3A) or Orenda 8 (Mk 3B) engines

Ventral gun pack housing eight Colt-Browning M3 0.50-in (12.7-mm) machine-guns

Avro Canada CF-100 Variants

Fitted with gun packs, a pair of Mk 3Bs take off from the Malton facility (above). The Mk 3 saw only limited RCAF service, most operating with the OTU in a training function. Only the Mk 3B reached the front line, equipping Nos 423 (right), 440 and 445 (below) Squadrons. The latter became the first front-line user of the type, acquiring its first CF-100s in May 1953.

were more quickly reloaded to hasten combat turnarounds, and did not interfere with the pilot's forward vision.

By late 1953, Avro Canada was studying having up to 52 FFARs in each wingtip pod, but the RCAF settled on 29 per pod. It was felt that launching more than 60 in one salvo did not result in increased effectiveness. By contrast, the USAF's Northrop F-89D Scorpion carried a total of 104 FFARs. The CF-100's wingtip pods incorporated frangible fibreglass front and rear covers which provided improved aerodynamics prior to firing the rockets, and were simply

shot away when the FFARs were fired. The proposed change in armament from the Mk 3's eight 0.50-in M3 machine-guns to the Mk 4's rockets reflected a change in theory by the RCAF. Like many other air forces over the next 20 years, it was felt that the days of the close-in guns-only dogfight were over. However, unlike most aircraft, the CF-100 retained its gun pack when rockets were added rather than substituted.

CF-100 Mk 3T: Although described as being production aircraft, in view of their many problems and limited capabilities the

Mk 3s really were service test aircraft, perhaps even pre-production aircraft, even though built in some quantity. The first five Mk 3s were part of the Mk 2 pre-production aircraft order, but the first four of these were built from the start as Mk 3T variants with dual controls and powered by Orenda 2 engines. Their serials were 18108 to 18111, with 18112 becoming the hand-built prototype for the Mk 4 (described later). The early Mk 3s differed from the definitive Mk 3As and Bs by retaining the nosecone of the Mk 2. 18111 was lost in a hangar fire at Avro Canada's Malton facility on 22 March

1955, but the other Mk 3Ts all served with No. 3 AW(F) OTU at RCAF Station North Bay from the summer of 1952.

CF-100 Mk 3A: A total of 70 CF-100 Mk 3s was built, not including those built as Mk 3Ts (described above). Of the 20 ordered as Mk 3As – 18113 to 18132 – 11 were converted on the production line as Mk 3CT dual-control trainers (18114 to 18116 and 18118 to 18125, see below). 18113 was powered by Orenda 2s, with the rest being fitted with the improved Orenda 8. The Mk 3A was equipped with the Hughes AN/APG-33 radar, the same as installed in the USAF's Northrop F-89A Scorpion. Armament consisted of a belly pack of eight 0.50-in Colt-Browning M3 machine-guns. 18129 was the aircraft used in the gun pack's trials. Later, five Mk 3As were converted to Mk 3Ds - 18126 and 18128 to 18131 (see below). Mk 3As equipped No. 3 AW(F) OTU. 18117 was employed in trials of the Velvet Glove long-range missile, carrying the missiles in pairs under the engine nacelles.

CF-100 Mk 3B: Powered by the Orenda 8, 50 CF-100 Mk 3Bs were built, 18133 to 18182. Forty-four were converted to Mk 3D dual-control trainer variants (see below) by MacDonald Bros (now Bristol Aerospace): 18133 to 18136, 18138 to 18140, 18142 to 18145, 18147 to 18153, 18155, 18156, 18158, 18159, and 18161 to 18182. The Mk 3B's armament and radar were the same as the Mk 3A's. The Mk 3B equipped the OTU as well as 423, 440 and 445 AW(F) Squadrons, and were operated by CEPE. One source states that 18149 and 18173 were later modified as Mk 5C ECM Phase 2 aircraft, but this is unconfirmed.

CF-100 Mk 3CT: Eleven Mk 3As were converted on the production line to become Mk 3CT dual-control trainers - 18114 to 18116 and 18118 to 18125. This rather hurried conversion was designed to hasten the introduction of the CF-100 to No. 3 AW(F) OTU at RCAF Station North Bay. Production delays forced by the government so that Avro Canada would solve problems with the airframes and engines adversely affected deliveries, training and the formation of operational squadrons. Nine Mk 3CTs were later upgraded by Bristol as Mk 3Ds - 18114, 18116, 18118 to 18121, and 18123 to 18125 (see below).

CF-100 Mk 3D

Once Mk 4 production and deliveries were well underway, there was a surplus of Mk 3s and it was decided to convert 49 Mks 3A and 3B to Mk 3D dual-control trainers. The contract was awarded to MacDonald Brothers of Winnipeg. The first to arrive was 18140 on 20 November 1954 and the conversion programme was scheduled to begin in February 1955. By that date, MacDonald Brothers had been renamed Bristol Aircraft (Western) Ltd following its take-over by the Bristol Aeroplane Co., although when Bristol's British operations were themselves taken over by Rolls-Royce, the name of the Canadian branch did not change.

The conversion programme involved four Mk 3As (18126, 18128, 18129 and 18131) and 43 Mk 3Bs (18133, 18134, 18135, 18136, 18138, 18139, 18140, 18142, 18143, 18144, 18145, 18147, 18148, 18149, 18150, 18151, 18152, 18153, 18155, 18156, 18158, 18159, 18161, 18162, 18163, 18164, 18165, 18166, 18167, 18168, 18169, 18170, 18171, 18172, 18173, 18174, 18175, 18176, 18177, 18178, 18179, 18180, 18181 and 18182). Two of the scheduled 49, 18177 and 18180, were lost in crashes with No. 3 AW(F) OTU and were not replaced, resulting in a total of 47 machines. The conversion called for the removal of all equipment used in the fighter role including

radar, the gun sight, the guns, and the navigator's equipment. Full flight controls were then installed in the rear cockpit and the front cockpit was updated somewhat. When the initial contract was completed, Bristol was awarded a follow-up covering the conversion of nine Mk 3CTs to Mk 3D standard, these being 18114, 18116, 18118, 18119, 18120, 18121, 18123, 18124 and 18125. This contract was completed by

June 1957.

Those converted from the Mk 3CT were powered by the Orenda 2, while those converted from Mk 3As and 3Bs had the Orenda 8.

18125 was originally built as one of the Mk 3CTs, but was later upgraded to Mk 3D standard. It carries the black witch insignia of No. 3 AW(F) OTU, the CF-100 training unit

CF-100 Mk 4

The final pre-production Mk 3, 18112, was hand-built by Avro Canada as the prototype Mk 4. At the time, the company was expecting to develop the type at least as far as the Mk 6, and the USAF and USN were moving towards all-missile armament with a sophisticated, automatic fire control system. Both influenced the design of the new CF-100 variant and the original intent was for the Mk 4 to have only missiles for armament. The Mk 4 prototype, 18112, made its first flight on 11 October 1952 and exceeded Mach 1 in a dive on 4 December 1952. (The speed indicated on 18112's Mach meter was not backed up by a calibrated instrument, so the speed was unofficial.) This no doubt played a major part in the RCAF's lack of interest in Avro Canada's proposed swept-wing development, to be designated CF-103. 18112 was to have been the last of the pre-production Mk 2 aircraft. On 16 December 1952, it was flown to Ottawa for flights with a calibrated Sabre, but it repeatedly outran its chase plane. Testing returned to Malton and, on 18 December 1952, 18112 reached Mach 1.06 in a dive, in the hands of Avro Canada test pilot Jan Zurakowski, a noteworthy accomplishment for a straight-winged, heavy aircraft. Avro Canada engineers had placed a Mach 0.85 limit on the aircraft and were working on the CF-103 swept-wing, transonic development of the CF-100. As this design offered little improvement over the CF-100, work did not proceed past the mock-up stage. As recounted under the Mk 3 heading, the Mk 4 prototype was lost in a crash on 23 August 1954.

The first production Mk 4, 18183, was delivered to the RCAF on 2 November 1953, having made its first flight on 4 October 1953. Mk 4s entered RCAF service in July 1954 when 18198 and 18199 joined the OTU at North Bay. The Mk 4 featured a Hughes AN/APG-40 radar and MG-2 fire control system, a retractable ventral pack housing 48 folding-fin aircraft rockets (FFARs) replaced the eight gun ventral pack, and wingtip-mounted rocket pods were introduced.

The new model differed from its predecessors in numerous ways. Most noticeable was the longer, blunt nose which housed the Hughes AN/APG-40 radar and the MG-2 fire control system (which also equipped the USAF's F-89D Scorpion), the combination of which allowed for lead collision course interceptions in place of the previous curve of pursuit approaches from the target's rear. Other changes included a new one-piece canopy with a higher profile and a slightly changed engine nacelle. The engines were Orenda 9s which, while essentially similar to the earlier Orenda 8, featured small anti-icing vanes in the bullet fairing protruding from the engine nacelles. Another marked addition to the Mk 4 was the internal windscreen for the navigator, which deflected the windblast following canopy ejection (or loss, not unknown to the CF-100) which had caught the arms of the navigator, pinning them over and behind his head and preventing him from pulling the

ring handle to initiate his ejection. The first 219 CF-100s had a tail bumper under the rear fuselage, but it was discontinued thereafter.

The MG-2 had three modes: auto search, manual search and auto track. It could also be used as a beacon and had ground-mapping capability. An Avro Canada innovation was the ability to exchange the entire nose section without the need to realign the radar with the weapons system. Until Belgium acquired 53 CF-100s, Canada was the only country other than the United States to receive the AN/APG-40 or MG-2, due to its advanced capabilities and state-of-the-art technology.

The Mk 4 also came in A and B versions powered by the Orenda 9 and 11, respectively. There were 135 Mk 4As, serialled 18183 to 18319, the first 50, 18183 to 18232, being delivered without autopilots. Later, 18300 and 18301 were converted to Mk 4Bs. Production of Mk 4Bs totalled 145, serialled 18320 to 18512. The Orenda 11 produced 7,000 lb (31.13 kN) of thrust, compared with 6,500 lb (28.90 kN) for the Orenda 9. Quite a few Mk 4Bs were converted to Mk 5s: 18341, 18342 and 18464 to 18512. (Note that some sources incorrectly state that the latter range of serials commences with 18364.) The first Mk 4B was delivered in January 1955. There were no dual-control Mk 4s produced, either as new-build aircraft or conversions.

Some other Mk 4s were later converted to Mk 5C and 5M configuration and one became a 'hybrid' Mk 5/6.

The Mk 4As were initially assigned to squadrons in Air Defence Command. Once all squadrons were up to strength, the aircraft were replaced by Mk 4Bs, the As being transferred to the OTU. Only Mk 4Bs were assigned to the Air Division's CF-100 squadrons in Europe, until they were

disbanded in 1961 through 1962. In Canada, Mk 4s remained in operational use until replaced by Mk 5s in 1956.

CEPE conducted flight trials of the CF-100 autopilot in Minneapolis, US beginning in December 1952 using 18105. Trials continued through February 1953. Eventually, the autopilot was coupled to the MG-2 fire control system for another test programme.

Right: 18112 was originally ordered as a Mk 2, but was hand-built as the prototype Mk 4. Here it undertakes trials of the belly-mounted rocket pack, during which the aircraft was lost. The pack was not adopted.

Below: 18188 was the sixth CF-100 Mk 4A. The fairings on the nose housed cameras for trials work.

The Mk 4 can be regarded as the first true operational version, seeing service with all 13 front-line units to operate the 'Clunk'. This aircraft, a Mk 4B, is seen in the colours of No. 445 Squadron, which became the first unit to go to Europe (under Nimble Bat 1) to bolster the Air Division's night-fighting capability.

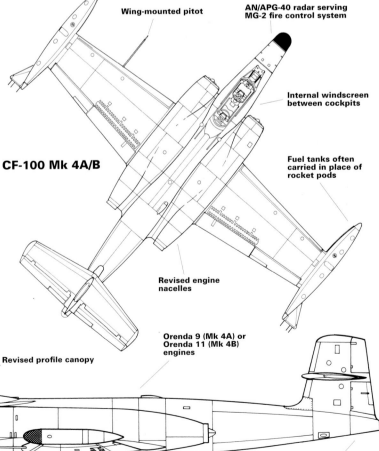

CF-100 Mk 4A/B

Wing-mounted pitot

AN/APG-40 radar serving MG-2 fire control system

Internal windscreen between cockpits

Fuel tanks often carried in place of rocket pods

Revised engine nacelles

Orenda 9 (Mk 4A) or Orenda 11 (Mk 4B) engines

Revised profile canopy

Bulged radome

Eight-gun ventral pack retained

Wingtip pods for 29 2.75-in Folding Fin Aircraft Rockets (FFARs)

Tail bumper fitted to early production aircraft: removed from 18300 onwards

The Mk 4 introduced the CF-100's distinctive rounded nose, the radome covering the state-of-the-art APG-40 radar which allowed lead-collision intercepts. Tip tanks were a regular feature in place of rockets.

two Mk 4As were converted later, 18300 and 18301. Of these, 49 were converted to Mk 5s – 18341, 18342 and 18464 to 18512 – of which eight may have been converted to Mk 5C ECM Phase 2 configuration (18465, 18480, 18482, 18486, 18488, 18501 to 18503 and 18506). Six were converted to Mk 5D ECM Phase 3 configuration (and some of these might have first been Mk 5Cs, but this is unconfirmed), 18472, 18474, 18476, 18493, 18500 and 18504. (Of the latter, all but 18474 were later reserialled in the 100xxx range.) The Mk 4B's armament, radar and fire control system were unchanged from that of the Mk 4A. Both the Mk 4A and 4B equipped all of the home-based ADC squadrons (409, 410, 413, 414, 416, 425, 428, 432 and 433) as well as one squadron in each of the four wings in 1 Air Division in Europe (419, 423, 440 and 445). Under four phases of Operation Nimble Bat, CF-100 Mk 4Bs were flown to Europe, where they each replaced one Sabre 6 day fighter squadron. Those units returned to Canada and were re-equipped with CF-100 Mk 5s and assigned to Air Defence Command (and, soon after, to the newly-formed NORAD).

Three Mk 4Bs – 18434, 18435 and 18439 – carried special instrumentation in redesigned wingtip tanks for Operation Outlook, a joint project of the RCAF, CARDE (Canadian Armament Research and Development Establishment) and ARPA (Advanced Research Projects Agency) of the US Department of Defense. The aircraft deployed to Ascension Island (becoming the first jet-powered aircraft to land there) and Patrick AFB, Florida to measure infra-red emissions of missile nose cones re-entering the atmosphere and of exhaust plumes of missiles being launched, respectively. The programme, carried out between January 1960 and the spring of 1964, was connected with the development of an early warning system for ICBMs. A similar programme, Operation Blind Twinkler, with two CF-100s (serials unknown), was conducted from Thule, Greenland. 18229 was employed in trials of the Velvet Glove missile and carried them in pairs on the underwing hardpoints. A Mk 4B, 18393, was acquired by Ormond Haydon-Baillie and registered as G-BCYK, but his premature death in 1977 put an end to hopes for it to be restored to flying condition.

CF-100 Mk 4C: This appears to be either an unofficial or interim designation for trials conducted in the summer of 1955 to determine the absolute ceiling of the Mk 5 in comparison with the Mk 4B at various weights and with different modifications. The aircraft used were 18201 and 18301.

CF-100 Mk 4X: Proposed 'thin wing' version of Mk 4B.

As with interceptor units south of the 49th parallel, RCAF ADC units adorned their natural metal mounts with bright squadron markings. These CF-100 Mk 4Bs flew with No. 428 'Ghost' Squadron, which applied its death's head badge to the intake sides.

CF-100 Mk 4A: After the teething problems and other problems with the preceding variants, the Mk 4A was a true production, all-weather interceptor for the RCAF. It was powered by Orenda 9s and equipped the RCAF's nine Air Defence Command squadrons: 409, 419, 423, 425, 428, 432, 433, 440 and 445. As production switched to the Mk 4B (see below), the older Mk 4As were passed to the OTU. The CF-100 Mk 4As included 137 examples – 18183 to 18319. Of these, 18183 to 18232 were not fitted with autopilots, while the rest were so equipped. 18299 was the last CF-100 built with a tail bumper to prevent damage if the aircraft was over-rotated during take-off. 18300 and 18301 were converted to Mk 4Bs. 18221 and 18222 (plus a Mk 5, 18508) were modified as target tugs and wore a garish, bright red colour scheme. They were not redesignated after being converted. The first Mk 4A rolled off the assembly line on 30 September 1953. One source states that 18225 was converted as a Mk 5C ECM Phase 2 aircraft, but this is unconfirmed. Also unconfirmed is whether 18301 was converted as a Mk 5M trials aircraft. Because of problems with the belly rocket pack, the gun pack containing eight 0.50-in machine-guns was retained, supplemented by wingtip rocket pods containing 29 2.75-in FFARs each. The prototype Mk 4's AN/APG-40 radar and MG-2 fire control system were also installed in the Mk 4A.

CF-100 Mk 4B: Differing from the Mk 4A by having Orenda 11 engines, 193 Mk 4B aircraft were built – 18320 to 18512 – and

A six-bottle RATO pack was available for the CF-100, and tested by various aircraft, including this Mk 4. Despite conferring astounding take-off performance, it was not adopted.

CF-100 Mk 5

Avro Canada first proposed the Mk 5 in June 1952. It was to feature a new, refined wing and mid-section to permit a higher Mach number, an improved fire control system, and the capability of employing newer missiles. More powerful engines were also proposed to increase the service ceiling. The RCAF was not interested in what it considered to be costly changes for small improvements, but it was interested in a high-altitude version, so Avro Canada pushed back its ideas for a potential Mk 6.

A total of 281 Mk 5s was built as such and 49 Mk 4Bs were converted to the improved variant. 18341 and 18342 were converted from Mk 4As to Mk 5s to serve as prototypes for the high-altitude variant. The first Mk 5 prototype made its first flight in September 1954, with the first production model making its first flight on 12 October 1955. In essence, the Mk 5 was a lightweight, high-altitude version of the Mk 4. The wing was extended with constant-chord, 44-in (112-cm) extensions

18516 was the fourth production Mk 5, evaluated by CEPE in 1956/57. The standard radome was replaced by an instrumented nosecone for research into shock waves and aspects of the new variant.

lacking any sweep at all and the tailplane received a 24-in (61-cm) extension. (Unlike the tailplane extensions, the wingtip extensions were a bolt-on item and were later removed from the ECM variants.) The Mk 5 shared the Mk 4B's Orenda 11s, but the gun pack was deleted, leaving the variant armed solely with the wingtip rocket pods. Also deleted (or removed from the converted Mk 4Bs) were the wing leading-edge de-icing boots, RATO bottle fittings, gun sight, and all other gun pack-related items. The service ceiling was increased from the Mk 4B's 47,000 ft (14325 m) to 53,000 ft (15154 m) for the Mk 5.

Mod 1000 included the removal of engine anti-icing, the installation of a map table for the navigator, and of a fire extinguisher for the pilot. Several weight-

saving modifications were also introduced under Mod 1071.

In 1955, Contract Demand CD 501429 was issued for the acquisition of 180 CF-100 Mk 5s at a unit cost of C$525,000 each. (One source states that this price only applied to the first 60 examples. Also, it appears that this Contract Demand was

issued for the purchase of Mk 3A, 3B, 4A and 4B aircraft and then amended to cover the 180 Mk 5s mentioned here.)

18514 was lost on 20 October 1955 during unauthorised low-level aerobatics by a company pilot. The first Mk 5 to be handed over to the Royal Canadian Air Force was 18515, on 9 December 1955.

Left: *The extended wingtips of the Mk 5 are illustrated well in this view of a No. 428 Squadron aircraft cavorting near its Uplands base.*

Above: *A three-engined CF-100 – 100760 was the aircraft used by Pratt & Whitney Canada as a flying testbed for its JT15D turbofan.*

The contract also called for Avro Canada to convert 48 Mk 4Bs to Mk 5 configuration at a cost of C$2,484,437. Later, CD 562026 would cover an additional 100 Mk 5s.

There were early problems with some of the wingtip extensions, including one incident when they departed the aircraft during an air show. Its disintegration was captured on film and the detailed analysis that followed led to an improved training programme covering the flight envelope and the dangers of gust loads added to manœuvre loads, both of which were frequently encountered in hot weather and at low level. Restrictions were placed on manœuvres at low altitude and/or high speeds.

The RCAF's evaluation of the Mk 5 began on 1 April 1955 with 18516. Between September 1956 and April 1957, trials were conducted with wingtip extensions and rocket pods, wingtip extensions without rocket pods, and with wingtip fuel tanks. Later in 1957, further tests were carried out to investigate the effects of using vortex generators in combination with the wingtip extensions and rocket pods. The service ceiling was increased from 37,000 to 40,000 ft (11277 to 12192 m), but the take-off and landing distances were increased, too. Stall speed went up by 3 to 4 kt (5.5 to 7.4 km/h). The CEPE test report recommended the use of more powerful engines if vortex generators were to be adopted, but they were not.

Along with a pair of Mk 4As, 18221 and 18222, a Mk 5, 18508, was converted to serve as a gunnery target tug and was painted bright red.

CF-100 Mk 5s for the Belgian Air Force (Force Aérienne Belge/Belgische Luchtmacht; FAB/BLu) were serialled AX-1 to AX-53 (RCAF 18685 to 18730 and 18732 to 18738; 18731 was damaged in a pre-delivery fire and was retained in Canada). All surviving FAB/BLu CF-100s were scrapped when retired, so 18534 was obtained for C$1.00 and shipped to the Musée Royal de l'Armée et d'Histoire Militaire/Koninklijk Legermuseum in Brussels, where it is displayed in Canadian markings.

A CF-100 Mk 5, 100767, was modified with a variety of cameras and infra-red line-scanning sensors for the Canadian Forces Airborne Sensing Unit, where it served with two Dakotas and, later, a Dassault CC-17 Falcon. The CFASU was assigned to Air Transport Command, making 100767 that command's only fighter aircraft. When the unit was transferred from the Department of National Defence to the Department of Energy, Mines and Resources, the CF-100 was retired. Another Mk 5, 18760 (later 100760), was loaned to Pratt & Whitney Canada as an airborne testbed for its then-new JT15D engine. P&WC needed an aircraft that had room for a test engineer and was capable of carrying the test engines. After considering mounting the JT15D on a wingtip or under the nose, it was decided that the fairing over the gunpack was the best location., the CF-100's high landing gear contributing to that decision. A set of clamshell doors that shielded the test engine's inlet from runway debris was designed to retract to form part of its nacelle's outer skin. The loan agreement was extended numerous times until the aircraft was finally retired in 1982, making 100760 the last flying 'Clunk'.

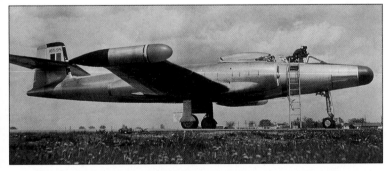

The Mk 5 was based closely on the Mk 4, but with an accent on weight reduction. Visible here is the internal blast screen which protected the navigator in the event of an ejection or canopy loss.

This Mk 5 demonstrates the use of the 'Clunk' as a target-tug. The aircraft carries two Del Mar Radop targets, deployed from the wingtips. Under the wing hardpoints are the wind-driven winches for the system. Only a handful of CF-100s were used as target-tugs, most of this work being undertaken at the Weapons Practice Unit by CT-133 Silver Stars.

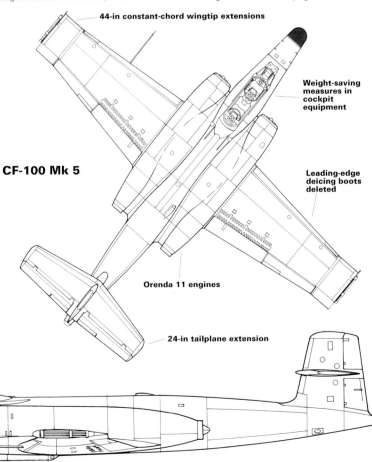

CF-100 Mk 5

44-in constant-chord wingtip extensions

Weight-saving measures in cockpit equipment

Leading-edge deicing boots deleted

Orenda 11 engines

24-in tailplane extension

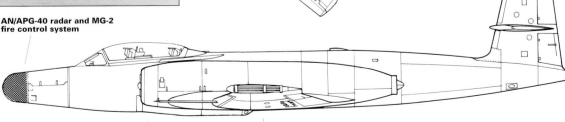

AN/APG-40 radar and MG-2 fire control system

Gun pack deleted

Optional wingtip rocket installations: operational 29-round pod, 7-round training pod or 3-tube training pack (illustrated)

CF-100 Mk 5C/D

In the CF-100's later years, Mk 5s were also modified for service with the Electronic Warfare Unit, these being designated as Mk 5C and 5D. The first EW conversion had been a Mk 4A (18225) in late 1956. The Mk 5C conversion, also known as Phase 2, involved the installation of radar jammers and chaff dispensers mounted on wing pylons. Most 5Cs were later upgraded to Mk 5D, or Phase 3, configuration. Other 5Ds were converted directly from Mk 5s.

The Mk 5D was modified to meet AIR Spec 17-14, Issue 3, dated 15 March 1963. Its external differences were the cooling pack in place of the ventral gun pack and the removal of the wingtip extensions (but

not of the tailplane extensions). Improved EW equipment was installed that added communications jamming capabilities to the 5C's radar jamming capability. The EW gear weighed about 1,000 lb (454 kg) and was located in the ventral gun pack bay. The Mk 5D also carried about 6,000 lb (2721 kg) of additional fuel.

CF-100 Mk 5C: An unknown number of aircraft were converted to ECM Phase 2 configuration as the Mk 5C. Those believed to have been converted include 18149 and 18173 (Mk 3Bs), 18225 (Mk 4A), 18465, 18472, 18474, 18480, 18482, 18486, 18488, 18493, 18500 to 18504, and 18506 (Mk

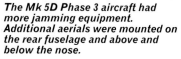

4Bs), 18513, 18525, 18551, 18556, 18614, 18650, 18661, 18662, 18670, 18673 to 18675, 18677, 18680, 18746, 18757, 18772, 18775, 18778 to 18780, 18782 to 18784, 18785 to 18792. 18225, converted in 1956, was the first Mk 5C conversion. Aircraft believed to have been upgraded from Mk 5C to Mk 5D configuration (see below) include 18513, 18757, 18778, 18784, 18785, 18786, 18788, 18789, 18790 and

Left: The Mk 5D was the last CF-100 variant in use, receiving tactical camouflage in its later years. The aircraft soldiered on in the EW role until October 1981.

The Mk 5D Phase 3 aircraft had more jamming equipment. Additional aerials were mounted on the rear fuselage and above and below the nose.

18792. (Note that some of these aircraft were later reserialled in the 100xxx range.)

The Mk 5C could jam airborne radar and drop chaff, a large dispenser for the latter function being carried under each wing, finally making operational use of the underwing hardpoints originally intended for bombs or guided missiles. The wingtip extensions were removed and fuel tanks were fitted in place of the rocket pods to improve range and endurance. Several sensors and antennas were fitted above and below the rear fuselage. Mk 5Cs first served with 104 Composite Unit, then the EW training function was split off and, along with modified Fairchild C-119 Flying Boxcars, formed the Electronic Warfare Unit, although the 'Clunks' were flown by crews from 425 and 416 Squadrons. Later, 414 Squadron was reformed to take over the duties of the EWU and it became the last military operator of the CF-100.

CF-100 Mk 5D: One official document refers to 15 CF-100 Mk 5D ECM Phase 3 conversions, but other evidence suggests that the number was at least 16: 18472, 18474, 18476, 18493, 18500, 18504, 18513, 18757, 18778, 18784 to 18786, 18788 to 18790, and 18792. (Note that most of these aircraft were reserialled in the 100xxx range.) The Mk 5D could be distinguished from the Mk 5C by its cooling air inlets in the area where the Mk 4s had their machine-gun muzzles. Like the Mk 5C, the Mk 5D had its wingtip extensions removed and carried fuel tanks in place of the standard Mk 5's wingtip rocket pods.

A CF-100 Mk 5C wears the colours of No. 414 Squadron. The underwing pods are for laying chaff, with a dispenser aperture on the underside.

CF-100 Mk 5M

Other than the Mks 5C and 5D, few aspects of the CF-100 appear to create as much confusion as determining which aircraft were modified as Mk 5M variants. One official document entitled "Royal Canadian Air Force Air Matériel Command Headquarters AMC Experimental Project 58/21 for Engineering Evaluation of the Douglas 1242D [Sparrow 2D] Missiles on the CF-100 Mk 5M" lists 18626, 18638, 18639, 18653, 18664, 18671 and 18672. Some sources state that three CF-100s (18300, 18301, and 18323) which had been used for Mk 6 development trials were redesignated Mk 5M, as were seven others (18626, 18638, 18639, 18653, 18664, 18671 and 18672) used as part of the CF-105 Arrow development programme. Other sources list various serials (18626, 18627, 18628, 18629, 18630, 18631, 18632, 18633, 18634, 18635, 18636, 18637, 18638, 18639, 18653, 18664, 18671 and 18674) as being Mk 5Ms. However, further research has revealed the following: 18301, 18626, 18638, 18639, 18653, 18664, 18671 and 18672 were Mk 5Ms. 18508 was also used, but only as a chase plane and was definitely not a Mk 5M.

One thing that remains unclear is whether some of these aircraft were

unmodified Mk 5s used in support of the programme which was conducted by the Air Armament Evaluation Detachment of the Central Experimental and Proving Establishment at its RCAF Station Cold Lake location and also at its 'Ultra West' location at NAS Pt Mugu, California. At one point, it had been proposed to designate the trials

aircraft as Mk 6s but, because of the small quantity and the cancellation of the Mk 6 programme, the RCAF chose to designate them as a sub-type of the Mk 5. The USN cancelled the Sparrow 2 programme, and although the RCAF tried to continue it for the CF-105 Arrow, the latter's cancellation finished the missile once and for all.

18300 was one of three Mk 5s used as part of the initial Sparrow 2 missile trials, but is unlikely to have received the Mk 5M designation. The aircraft is seen here with dummy missiles during aerodynamic carriage trials.

CF-100 Mk 5/6

Whether or not it was ever officially a Mk 5M, 18323 became a hybrid Mk 5/6. Beginning as a Mk 4B, it was modified with the Mk 5's extended wingtips and tailplane for trials of the high altitude version in 1955. A notation on 18323's aircraft record card states "peculiar a/c in that it is not a complete 5 and has some 6 work incorporated". The reference to a Mk 6 most likely means a Mk 5M.

18323 was one of the 'odd' CF-100s, and is usually referred to as a Mk 5/6 on account of its configuration. It was originally built as a Mk 4B, but was given most of the Mk 5's features, including the extended wingtips and tailplane, and deletion of the gun pack and associated equipment. It also had several features intended for the Mk 6. It was used for various Sparrow 2 missile trials, as illustrated, although it is not thought that it received the full Mk 5M modification.

CF-100 Mk 6

This designation covered a number of proposals including an early high-altitude version and then the trials aircraft for the Sparrow 2. In 1955-56, Avro proposed a CF-100 Mk 6 as a high-altitude interceptor, armed with the Sperry Sparrow 2D missile. The 17 major modifications included the deletion of de-icing boots on the wing and tail, addition of both fixed and removable Sparrow 2D missile fittings, a modified MG-2 fire control system, installation of Orenda 11R afterburning engines, a redesigned tail and elevator, weight-saving modifications,

and strengthening modifications. The Mk 6 was to operate at 50,000 ft (15240 m) and engage targets at 60,000 ft (18288 m).

Later, the Mk 6 was to be a Mk 5 with simple afterburners added to its engines (to be designated Orenda 11R) and either Sparrow or Falcon guided missiles. The latter, being lighter, gave a 1,600-ft (487-m) ceiling and 7-kt (13-km/h) performance advantage over the former. Further study and analysis indicated that this version would not be sufficient to meet the threat and that the service ceiling would be raised and that the CF-105 Arrow, then under development, would be much better suited to the task. The cancellation of the Mk 6 came in October 1957.

CF-100 Mk 7

This proposal returned to the wingspan of the Mk 4B, but with a new, thinner wing having a larger area. The thickness to chord ratio was to be 6 per cent, compared with the original (1952) Mk 5 high-altitude version proposal (see above). It would have been equipped with the Hughes E-9 fire control system armed with Sparrow missiles.

CF-100 Mk 8

In June 1959, Avro Canada issued a proposal for the CF-100 Mk 8, which it called the 'Long Range Missile Version'.

External differences would include a much bigger nose containing a radar dish of 32-36 in (81-91 cm) in diameter, modified wingtips carrying Eagle air-to-air missiles, underwing fuel tanks holding 200 Imp gal (909 litres), and either upgraded Orenda 11 engines on a standard Mk 4 wing or Bristol Orpheus BE61 or Armstrong Siddeley Sapphire engines with a new, thinner wing. The Canadian government was not at all interested, as it had already selected the combination of the McDonnell F-101B Voodoo and Boeing BOMARC for the air defence of the country following the cancellation of the Avro Canada CF-105 Arrow.

CF-100 Mk X

In May 1956, Avro Canada proposed a four-engined CF-100 Mk X, to be fitted with Orenda engines in the usual positions and Bristol Orpheus turbojets in a new wingtip installation. The Orpheus was a small engine (111 in/282 cm long; 850 lb/385 kg in weight) that produced 4,850 lb (21.57 kN) of thrust. The company suggested that this could be a conversion of existing CF-100s and that the service ceiling would be raised to well above 50,000 ft (15240 m), requiring at least partial pressure suits for the crew. Like so many other development proposals, nothing came of the Mk X. (The X in the designation was for 'unknown' or 'experimental', not a roman numeral 10.)

STOVL CF-100

In 1958, Avro Canada's project research group under Mario Pesando proposed a short take-off and vertical landing (STOVL) variant of the CF-100. (It should be remembered that Avro Canada's corporate parent was the Hawker Siddeley Group, which created the Hawker P.1127.) The engines were to be the Bristol Orpheus BE 53/2. The crew would be reduced to just the pilot, and additional underwing hardpoints would be fitted. From the start, Avro Canada appears to have considered the whole idea little more than a design exercise, acknowledging in a company memo that it was "unlikely to be more than 12-18 months ahead of operational Hawker P.1127s ... with first flight late in 1960", adding that at "27,000/30,000 lb gross the CF-100 STOVL is a much bigger vehicle than NATO, for example, requires for the ground attack role ... Moreover, the CF-100 STOVL ... does not appear to have any more capability than the P.1127 with which to justify the larger size. In some respects it does not equal the P.1127 capability."

CF-103

In 1950, Avro Canada's design office proposed its Model C.103, soon dubbed CF-103, a swept-wing development of the CF-100. It was an extensive redesign of the Canuck, with a thinner, slightly swept-back wing, with swept-back vertical and horizontal tail surfaces. The wing's area was also increased in size. The intent was to allow a diving speed of Mach 0.95, but other performance figures were expected to be reduced. The proposal, which reached the full-scale mockup stage and underwent wind tunnel tests, was unknown to the flight test section and its test pilots. When Jan Zurakowski's flight in the Mk 4 prototype broke the sound barrier (officially on 18 December 1952, unofficially on 4 December), any RCAF interest in the CF-103 evaporated and the design office was considerably less than pleased (although it should be noted that wind tunnel data was not promising).

Rather than leading to increased co-operation with the flight test section as the latter hoped, the design office instead began to control the flight test programme closely.

Avro Canada CF-100 Operators

Royal Canadian Air Force/Canadian Armed Forces

The first production Mk 3, 18113, made its first flight in October 1952. It was delivered by Squadron Leader Paul Hartman to No. 3 All Weather (Fighter) OTU at RCAF Station North Bay, Ontario on 14 November 1952. The first CF-100 for use by the RCAF, other than in test roles with CEPE, was 18108, which was delivered to the OTU on 22 July 1952. 18109 and 18110 soon joined it there. These deliveries helped to quell what had been a rising tide of criticism in the press and in Parliament against the inevitable delays as the CF-100 and the Orenda – both complex examples of high technology – were perfected.

Prior to the introduction of the CF-100 into service, observation and training had been undertaken with foreign operators of similar types. Two members of the OTU staff had visited Britain in May 1950 to observe the RAF's training and operational all-weather fighter organisation. The Royal Air Force was then using the Gloster Meteor NF.Mk 11 as its all-weather fighter and was developing the Gloster Javelin to replace it. The Meteor NF.Mk 11 was the RAF's first-jet-powered night-fighter. The Javelin would be its first delta-winged interceptor, its first purpose-built all-weather interceptor, and the world's first twin-engined, delta-winged fighter.

In August 1950, RCAF personnel visited the USAF's 317th All-Weather Fighter Squadron, which flew the Lockheed F-94B Starfire. It was the USAF's first turbojet-powered, all-weather interceptor in service with its Air Defense Command. The prototype YF-94, 48-536, had made its first flight on 1 July 1948. The F-94 series was developed from the T-33, in turn a development of the F-80. (Several sources also state that some RCAF personnel were involved in the flight testing of the Lockheed F-94C Starfire.)

Between September and November 1950, eight pilots were sent to Moody AFB, Georgia for an instrument flying course and eight navigators went to James Connally AFB (formerly Waco AFB), Texas for a radar course. The latter employed TB-25Ks and Ms equipped with AN/APG-33 radars and E-1 and E-5 fire control systems, respectively. In December 1950, the pilots and navigators came together at Tyndall AFB, Florida for further training using North American B-25 Mitchells and T-28 Trojans and Lockheed F-80 Shooting Stars, T-33s and F-94 Starfires. They returned to North Bay in March 1952 to establish the training syllabus for the students who would soon join them.

The OTU initially used T-33A Silver Stars (borrowed from the USAF to supplement 20 T-33A Silver Star Mk 1s while awaiting delivery of T-33AN Silver Star Mk 3s from Canadair), Mitchell 3AIs and 3AIAs, and Expeditor 3Ns and 3NMs (which served as utility 'hacks' and as targets for the navigators training on the Mitchells). Pilot training began on the Silver Stars (30 to 40 hours), followed by conversion to the CF-100 (approximately 50 hours of dual and solo flying). Navigators trained on the 3AI and 3AIA versions of the Mitchell, also converting later in the course to the CF-100. The Mitchell 3AIs were equipped with AN/APG-33 'curve of pursuit' gun-laying radar, while the 3AIAs had AN/APG-40 radars.

The instructors assigned to No. 3 AW(F) OTU were a highly qualified group, most having had recent night-fighter combat experience, and students were highly motivated. Nevertheless, problems arose as they tried to master an unproven and underdeveloped aircraft that was much faster than anything they had flown before. One pilot, noting the lack of a simulator at that time, commented that one was not necessary as there was an emergency "every second flight".

In 1953-54, No. 3 All-Weather (Fighter) OTU had nine A Category accidents. In total, throughout the course of its existence, the OTU lost 22 CF-100s in A Category accidents and another seven suffered B Category damage but were written off rather than repaired. The OTU also lost two Mitchells and one Silver Star in A Category accidents.

OTU moves west

To make room for operational units at North Bay, the OTU moved to the then-new base at Cold Lake, Alberta in April 1955. As at North Bay, the Instrument and Conversion Flight used T-33As and CF-100 Mk 3s, while the Crew Training Flight used Mitchell 3AI and 3 AIAs. Before long, the latter flight also used Mk 4As, which by then had joined the OTU. Every six weeks, 20 crews arrived to begin a new course. The navigators arrived three weeks after the pilots, who spent the time doing the instrument phase. That aspect was transferred to RCAF Station Saskatoon, Saskatchewan in the spring of 1956, so the OTU was reorganised into three flights: Basic Flight had Mitchells, Conversion Flight had CF-100 Mk 3 dual-control aircraft, and Advanced Flight had Mk 4As. Twelve crews arrived every three weeks. After six months, it dropped to eight crews every three weeks. Another change had the navigators arriving concurrently with the pilots.

In late 1957, the Mitchells and Expeditors were phased out of the OTU, replaced by the CAE training and tactics simulator. The Ground Instruction School had Lecture Staff in one section and Simulator Staff in another, and there was a Special Duties Flight. Between six and nine crews were arriving, with pilots coming from the Advanced Flying Schools (2 AFS at RCAF Station Portage la Prairie, Manitoba and 3 AFS at RCAF Station Gimli, Manitoba) and navigators from 2 Air Observer School (at RCAF Station Winnipeg, Manitoba). By then, the syllabus had become 13 weeks divided into three phases. Phase I was the Ground Instructional School, which introduced the pilots to airborne interception techniques and navigators to the MG-2 fire control system. This lasted approximately 150 hours, with crews being 'married' during the last week.

Phase II saw the pilots converting to the CF-100 Mk 3 dual-control aircraft, and the

A CF-100 Mk 3B cruises over its birthplace at Malton, Ontario. The Avro Canada Aircraft Division is the plant under the aircraft's rear fuselage, while the Gas Turbine Division (Orenda) is to the right, under the nose. Visible on the ramp are CF-100s, a Lancaster and the C-102 Jetliner.

As one would expect, the training unit was the first service recipient of the new fighter. Initially based at North Bay, No. 3 AW(F)OTU, embarked on a major training programme from 1952. In addition to its CF-100 Mk 3s, the unit employed the Lockheed T-33 for initial jet pilot training and the Mitchell 3AI and 3AIA for initial radar instruction for the navigators. CF-100 Mk 4As were added when they became available.

navigators undertaking high-level navigation and Air Defence Command flight procedures. Together, the pilots and navigators were taught the rudiments of crew co-operation. The pilots' Conversion Flight course comprised approximately 23 hours of day flying and a further eight hours at night. There followed a return to the Ground Instruction School for two days of familiarisation with the Mk 4, including about three hours of simulator time. Next, during their time with the Advanced Flight, the crews progressed to the Mk 4. For the first three weeks, they flew in the morning and had simulator exercises during the afternoon. After completing 12 simulator exercises (which took approximately 14 hours of 'flying' time), they progressed to the final three weeks, flying both in the afternoon and at night.

During the six-week Phase III, 35 exercises totalling 42 hours of day flying and 17 hours of night flying were achieved. Each crew received a minimum of 15 additional hours to compensate for aborted flights earlier in their training.

In July 1962, 3 AW(F) OTU moved again, this time to RCAF Station Bagotville. By that time, the CF-100 had less than six months of front-line service remaining and the OTU's role increasingly became one of preparing students for the CF-101 Voodoo. Pilots graduated from the Advanced Flying Schools qualified on the Silver Star, then went to the OTU to convert first to the CF-100 Mk 3D for type conversion and to qualify for solo status, and then on the Mk 5 for a total of 30-40 hours of general fighter tactics training. As there were no dual-control Mks 4 or 5, the OTU retained various sub-types of the Mk 3s throughout its CF-100 era. The unit remained at Bagotville until it became the CF-101 Voodoo OTU in December 1964, finally relinquishing its CF-100s at that time.

Introduction to operational squadrons

The first operational CF-100 squadron, 445, formed on 1 April 1953 at RCAF Station North Bay. On 1 June 1953, 423 All-Weather (Fighter) Squadron followed at St Hubert and 440 Squadron formed on 1 October 1953 at Bagotville. Other than dual-control 'hacks' assigned to front-line squadrons equipped with later marks, the CF-100 Mk 3 was only in service with 445 Squadron for a year and with 423 and 440 Squadrons for two years.

Although the government had given strong indications of planning substantial future orders, the fact remained that the last formal order received by Avro Canada had been for 70 Mk 3s in June 1951. However, in January 1953, a new contract was negotiated covering 59 Mk 3 fighters, 11 Mk 3CT trainers, 300 Mk 4 fighters, and 30 "CF-100 aircraft or other variants as may be directed". The contract's value was not to exceed C$188.7 million but it was renegotiated after the first 120 aircraft had been delivered. A second contract was issued, worth C$121 million, for 1,600 Orenda engines. Of the 300 Mk 4s, the first 50 were to have only guns, with the remainder having both guns and rockets. It is believed that the Contract Demand for these 400 aircraft was CD 501429. If so, it was later amended to include 180 Mk 5s. (The engine contract's number is unknown.)

By late 1954, the RCAF had selected the name Canuck for its new fighter, in keeping with its practice of identifying aircraft by name rather than type number (a system still in use with the RAF today). Avro Canada had proposed naming the Mk 4 as 'Jaeger', but wiser heads prevailed. The RCAF was, apparently, not very keen about 'Canuck' and eventually stopped using it, referring to the aircraft only as the CF-100. A resolution was passed at one of the RCAF Association's national conventions urging the RCAF to adopt the name Thunderbird for the CF-100, obviously without success (and, perhaps, to the disappointment of 426 'Thunderbird' Squadron, even if it was a transport unit).

Air Defence Command

Air Defence Command had nine 16-aircraft CF-100 Mk 4 all-weather fighter squadrons by November 1954, comprising:

Squadron	Base	Date Formed
445	Uplands, Ontario	1 April 1953
423	St Hubert, Québec	1 June 1953
440	Bagotville, Québec	1 October 1953
419	North Bay, Ontario	15 March 1954
428	Uplands, Ontario	21 June 1954
425	St Hubert, Québec	1 October 1954
432	Bagotville, Québec	1 October 1954
409	Comox, British Columbia	1 November 1954
433	Cold Lake, Alberta	15 November 1954

Entering service at the start of 1954, the Mk 4 was built at a rapid rate, enabling Air Defence Command to build up a sizeable force. Four of these squadrons, with Mk 4Bs, were subsequently dispatched to Europe for service with the Air Division (1st CAD), for which RAF-style camouflage was adopted. This pair is from No. 440 'Bat' Squadron, which flew from Zweibrücken in West Germany.

In addition, No. 3 All Weather (Fighter) Operational Training Unit, the Weapons Practice Unit, and the Central Experimental and Proving Establishment (later AETE) all flew CF-100s. The OTU later used the CF-100 as an interim trainer leading to the CF-101 Voodoo. In mid-1964, it became an all-Voodoo unit and, in March 1968, it became 410 Operational Training Squadron at CFB Bagotville. Later, 414 was reformed as an electronic warfare training squadron, operating CF-100s along with CT-133s and CC-117s, and the Airborne Sensing Unit also had one CF-100. Early plans had called for the Auxiliary squadrons (tasked with the air defence of specific Canadian cities) to receive CF-100s, but the aircraft's complexity was eventually deemed to be too great for part-time fliers and maintainers.

From 12 March 1955 to 16 May, under Operation Gloat, 433 AW(F) Squadron carried out intensive flying trials with the Mk 4B and its Orenda 11 engines. The aircraft were fitted with wingtip fuel tanks and many long-range or long-duration flights were made, most of two to four hours. The purpose of the trials was to determine range and fuel consumption at different altitudes. Load conditions, climb rates and handling characteristics under various rates of turn were all established. The results were averaged and supplied to all Air Defence Command CF-100 units as reliable operational performance data.

Target-towing 'Clunks'

During 1959, CF-100s joined Silver Stars in the target-towing role. The same Del Mar Radop target was used (similar in size and appearance to a 1,000-lb bomb), attached to 8,000 ft (2438 m) of cable, but the Canucks could work at 40,000 ft (12192 m), doubling the altitude reached by the Silver Stars. Their undersides were painted bright red (to remind their customers that the tug is in front towing and not behind pushing, as one pilot put it). N9 cameras were used to film the radar scope, rocket trajectory and target, with the film used to determine the results. (One source says that CEPE found the concept was not feasible.) 18221, 18222, and 18508 were the three aircraft so modified.

Five types of scrambles were regularly practised: Ground scramble against unknown target; Ground scramble against known target; Ground scramble against ECM; Airborne scramble against unknown target; and Airborne scramble against known target. Targets included a wide variety of aircraft types, including other CF-100s, B-36s, B-47s, B-52s, DHC-2 Beavers, Mosquitoes (from Spartan Air Services), C-119s, Cessnas, and Seabees, among many others. Between November 1956 and August 1957, the RCAF's Air Defence Command (ADC) was fully integrated into NORAD, increasing joint training and operations. N9 cameras fitted to the attacking CF-100s filmed the radar scope, the rockets' (frequently erratic) paths, and the Del Mar Radop target itself.

Early on, there was a shortage of rocket pods but training continued at the OTU. An annual Rocket Meet at Cold Lake tested the skills of the operational units. Initially, training sorties used the 29-tube wingtip pods, which was an expensive proposition as there were no reusable pods. The staff of the Weapons Practice Unit at Cold Lake rewired the pods for a two-pass capability, with three rockets per pod per pass, allowing 10-15 uses before the pod became unserviceable. It was found that flying with unfaired pods (i.e. without the frangible nosecone) caused serious vortices around the ailerons, so they resumed flying with faired pods, but at C$10,000 for each combat pod this practice could not continue. Avro Canada then supplied three-tube pods as an interim solution, leading to seven-tube pods in time for the 1960 Rocket Meet. These were normally armed with six rockets to allow a two-pass capability as before.

The Weapons Practice Unit was formed on 1 April 1956, hosting its first customers – 419 and 440 Squadrons – in June. Typically, a squadron sent half of its aircraft and crews for two weeks, then the other half for two weeks. The WPU was disbanded on 1 April 1961 due to the impending introduction of the CF-101 Voodoo. As a side note, when a CF-100 was placed on display at CFB Cold Lake in 1969, no rocket pods remained in the supply system to equip it; however, the base commander was a former officer in charge of the Weapons Practice Unit and he knew exactly where to find some. Many had been jettisoned over a particular area of the range, so several were retrieved using one of the Base Flight's helicopters.

A 'Bat' Squadron CF-100 Mk 4B taxis past a shepherd and his unconcerned flock at Zweibrücken. Sheep were found to be a more cost-effective way of keeping the grass down at the Air Division's airfields than mowing.

The European counterpart to the WPU was 1 Air Division's Air Weapons Unit at Decimomannu, Sardinia, although it did not have any CF-100s. Instead, it had several Silver Stars to tow banners for aerial gunnery and rocketry training. During a three-week deployment, crews would get one and two weeks, respectively. Later, gunnery was dropped from the training, although it was a superb platform. The CF-100 was equipped with a yaw damper that kept the aircraft on a precise attack course without the need for either rudder or rudder trim tab correction. The Sabres that equipped the other squadrons in the Air Division not only required pre-trimming for the direction of the turn but also for the amount of *g* that their pilots expected to be pulled. 445 Squadron was the AWU's first customer, arriving on 23 November 1957.

Nimble Bat – Transatlantic deliveries

Four fighter wings comprised the RCAF's No. 1 Air Division, with each wing consisting of three squadrons. Initially, all 12 squadrons were equipped with Canadair Sabres, these being Sabre 2s, succeeded by 4s, 5s and 6s. ('Mk' was not used with the Sabres, although it was with the CF-100s.) Three CF-100 Mk 4Bs were flown to Britain in March 1955 for evaluation and trials by the RAF's Central Fighter Establishment, marking the first time a Canadian-designed fighter had flown across the Atlantic Ocean. These aircraft, 18320, 18321, and 18322, took a short break from the trials and participated in the Paris air show. They were then flown to RCAF Station Langar and placed in storage.

In order to get the four CF-100 squadrons operational in Europe in the shortest time, it was decided to transfer the first four ADC units formed on the type. The aircraft were ferried across the Atlantic in operations named Nimble Bat 1 through 4. The CF-100 squadrons and the Sabre squadrons they replaced were:

CF-100 Squadron	Base	Sabre Squadron	Wing	Base	Dates	Exercise no.
445	Uplands	410	1 Wing	Marville	1–4 November 1956	1
423	St Hubert	416	2 Wing	Grostenquin	12–16 February 1957	2
440	Bagotville	413	3 Wing	Zweibrucken	11–12 May 1957	3
419	North Bay	414	4 Wing	Baden-Soellingen	5 August 1957	4

Only one aircraft was lost during the deployment: 445 Squadron's 18395 had to be abandoned over Scotland during Nimble Bat 1 when the controls locked, but the crew was rescued safely. The route flown by 445 Squadron was Uplands (Ottawa) to Goose Bay to Keflavik to Marville in a flying time of 8 hours and 50 minutes.

The RCAF only operated Mk 4Bs in Europe, unlike the Belgians with their Mk 5s. However, the 4B's *g* limit was 7.3 compared with the Mk 5's 5*g*. The Canadians were better able to mix it with other NATO fighters and were rarely the easy prey they had been expected to be.

No. 1 Air Division was part of the 4th Allied Tactical Air Force. This also included USAFE's 12th Air Force and the French Tactical Air Force, and had as its mission the defence of central Europe. Alert duty was generally held by the CF-100s during the night, while the Sabres handled the daylight hours. Two aircraft with complete air and ground crews were able to scramble within two minutes of receiving the alert.

Until 1963, Air Division CF-100 squadrons had two three-week armament practice camps each year. They were held at an Italian base – Decimomannu, in Sardinia – the home of the RCAF's Air Weapons Unit (AWU). The Air Division's CF-100s all operated in camouflage. The upper surfaces were painted in a disruptive pattern of dark sea grey and dark green and the undersides were painted medium sea grey. In addition, the usual RCAF fin flash was replaced by the Red Ensign. The rest of the RCAF's aircraft adopted the flag as a tail marking beginning in 1958. Two-letter squadron codes were used until 1959 (although some squadrons did not wear them on their aircraft), at which time 'RCAF' replaced the unit codes. Other than the target-tugs, home-based CF-100s operated in bare metal with a black radome and anti-glare panel.

The four Sabre squadrons replaced by CF-100 units returned to Canada and converted to the CF-100 and were assigned to air defence duties.

Squadron	Base	Date Reformed
410	Uplands	1 November 1956
416	St Hubert	1 February 1957
413	Bagotville	1 May 1957
414	North Bay	5 August 1957

No. 445 'Wolverine' Squadron was one of the four Air Division squadrons, resident at Marville. A new style of squadron badge presentation was adopted in the later years of the CF-100's service, with the markings being applied to the rudder.

Avro Canada CF-100 Operators

At least 27 CF-100s can be seen in this photo, as well as two CT-133s, a DC-4 and a USAF C-54. The aircraft in the foreground are freshly painted CF-100 Mk 4Bs destined for service with No. 445 Squadron.

The four Nimble Bat ferry operations were not the only transatlantic CF-100 flights, as many aircraft were flown to and from the Air Division before and after maintenance, and for other reasons. Crews for these came from both 1 Overseas Ferry Unit and regular squadron personnel.

Major overhauls and repairs were carried out under contract by Scottish Aviation Limited (SAL) at Prestwick, which later handled similar work for the Air Division's CF-104s.

The cancellation of the CF-105 Arrow meant an end to plans to replace both Sabres and CF-100s with the advanced interceptor, and required quick action to find an alternative. During July 1959, the government announced that the four CF-100 squadrons in the Air Division would be disbanded and that the remaining Sabre squadrons would be replaced by the Lockheed F-104 Starfighter. This would change Canada's role in NATO from day and night air defence to tactical nuclear strike and reconnaissance. The CF-100 squadrons had been disbanded by 31 December 1962, with most of the aircraft going to Scottish Aviation for scrapping. The final CF-100 to leave 4 Wing was 18327, departing on 9 January 1963.

The Electronic Warfare Unit began as part of 104 Composite Unit at RCAF Station St Hubert, becoming the EWU on 1 April 1959. In addition to CF-100 Mk 5Cs, it had several Fairchild C-119 Flying Boxcars, with the latter equipped with emitters and serving as targets. The CF-100s were generally flown by crews from the co-located 425 AW(F) Squadron. EWOs (Electronic Warfare Officers) were often sent to the USAF's EW course that trained

B-52 EWOs which, at the time, was conducted at Keesler AFB in Biloxi, Mississippi and employed TC-54Ds and T-29Bs. The course relocated and re-equipped several times before being conducted by the US Navy, at which time no non-US students were permitted to enrol.

In July 1962, de Havilland Aircraft of Canada took over Avro Canada and assumed responsibility for servicing CF-100s. The final CF-100, 18692, was rolled out on schedule on 4 December 1958, past the nose of the CF-105 Arrow prototype (25201). The last batch included those converted to Mk 5C configuration for ECM work. From that point, all CF-100 servicing and other maintenance was carried out at Trenton by No. 6 Repair Depot (later AMDU and now ATESS).

Most CF-100 squadrons had either been disbanded or were converting to the CF-101 Voodoo. CF-100 phase-out dates were as follows: WPU – 1 April 1961; 425 Squadron – 1 May 1961; 428 Squadron – 1 June 1961; 433 Squadron – 1 August 1961; 416 Squadron – 1 September 1961; 432 Squadron – 15 October 1961; 410 Squadron – 11 November 1961; 413 Squadron – 30 December 1961; 414 Squadron – February 1962; 409 Squadron – March 1962; 419 Squadron – 31 December 1962; 423 Squadron – 31 December 1962; 440 Squadron – 31 December 1962; 445 Squadron – 31 December 1962; 3 AW(F) OTU – December 1964; AETE – February 1973; ASU – 3 March 1975; 414 Squadron – October 1981; P&WC – 28 June 1982.

Most surplus CF-100s were ferried by CEPE and 129 T&FF crews to Mountain View, where the aircraft were then cut up and melted down. Others went to steel mills in Hamilton, Ontario, with one source reporting the following aircraft there on 27 October 1963: 18176, 18433, 18491, 18511, 18522, 18526, 18530, 18532, 18538, 18539, 18545, 18550, 18576, 18607, 18621, 18623, 18627, 18633, 18634, 18635, 18641, and 18681.

Three CF-100s – 18493, 18504, and 18779 – were designated as Lead the Force aircraft and subjected to more intensive flying and inspections. The LTF programme served to monitor the condition of the airframe and components and to discover any problems that occurred well before they were encountered in a large portion of the fleet at once. It also permitted the end-of-service date to be put back and still be within an acceptable safety margin. The Lead the Force programme was terminated on 3 January 1973.

New serial numbers

Following first integration, then formal unification on 1 February 1968, the Canadian Armed Forces became the country's military, replacing the Royal Canadian Air Force, Canadian Army, and Royal Canadian Navy. Subsequently, designations and serial numbers were changed under a new scheme. For the CF-100 Canuck, the original 18xxx serials became 100xxx. This took effect on 1 November 1970 and applied to all active CF-100s, but not all training aids. In early 1968, it had been proposed to renumber all surviving CF-100s in a new range starting with 10001, with no relation to their original serials (i.e., not leaving gaps for written-off aircraft). Similar proposals were put forward for all other CAF fleets, but only the CC-129 Dakotas were so numbered and that was because of the wide variety of RCAF serials (three, four and five digits, and two letters/three digits). In theory, reserialling was to be completed within 30 days, but one official document refers to a completion date of 30 April 1971, some five months after the effective date.

AETE retired its last CF-100, 100747, in February 1973. The only remaining CAF operator was 414 (Electronic Warfare) Squadron, which had moved to CFB North Bay in mid-1972. 414 Squadron officially retired its CF-100s in October 1981, ending 28 years of RCAF/CAF service. The last-ever operational flight of a CF-100 took place on 8 December 1981.

The last transatlantic CF-100 flight was on 17 December 1981, when 100784 was delivered to CFB Baden-Soellingen for preservation. This Canuck returned to Canada, but not under its own power, when it was shipped to Winnipeg to join the Heritage Park outside Air Command (now renamed as 1 Air Division) Headquarters. The final CAF Canuck flight was on 10 February 1982, this being the delivery flight of 100785 to the National Aviation Museum at Rockcliffe.

Right: The CF-100 was given a new lease of life when it adopted the electronic warfare training role. This grew in importance throughout the late 1950s/early 1960s, resulting in the Electronic Warfare Unit being redesignated as No. 414 Squadron in 1967. This is a CF-100 Mk 5D.

Below: When the CF-100 finally bowed out of service in 1981, the 'Black Knights' of No. 414 Squadron took the opportunity to paint of its aircraft (Mk 5D 100785) in the black scheme and white cheatline as worn by the prototype. Over 31 years had elapsed since the type's first flight.

409 AW(F) Squadron 'Nighthawk'

Codes (CF-100 era): 'LP'
Callsign (CF-100 era): CUDGEL (HOTEL GOLF after May 1960)
Motto: 'Media Nox Meridies Noster' (Midnight is Our Noon)
Badge: In front of a cloak, a crossbow

Formed as No. 409 (Night Fighter) Squadron on 17 June 1941 at Digby, Lincolnshire, this unit flew Defiants, Beaufighters and Mosquitoes during World War II. It was reformed as No. 409 All-Weather (Fighter) Squadron on 1 November 1954 at RCAF Station Comox on Vancouver Island, British Columbia. Previously, it had been planned to reform the squadron as No. 409 (Fighter)

The 'Nighthawk' squadron was ADC-assigned, and carried a large crossbow badge on the nose.

Squadron (Auxiliary), to be located at Victoria, also on Vancouver Island. That administrative order was dated 1 January 1947, but it was subsequently cancelled. 409 AW(F) Squadron flew the CF-100 Mk 4A from February to June 1955, the Mk 4B from May 1955 to September 1957, and the Mk 5 from February 1957 to March 1962 (although one source reports the first Mk 5 arrived in July 1957). 409 All-Weather (Fighter) Squadron also operated the Silver Star (T-33AN licence-built by Canadair), receiving its first examples before it was assigned any CF-100s.

The unit temporarily relocated to RCAF Station Namao (Edmonton, Alberta) between 5 February and 13 March 1962 to undergo conversion training on the CF-101 Voodoo with 425 Squadron, which was then

the Voodoo OTU. It returned to Comox, where it operated both the CF-101B and F

variants. It became the first operational CF-188 squadron in 1984.

410 AW(F) Squadron Cougar'

Codes (CF-100 era): 'AN'
Callsign (CF-100 era): HAMLET
Motto: 'Noctivaga' (Wandering by Night)
Badge: In front of a decrescent, a cougar's face

Formed at Ayr, Scotland on 30 June 1941, No. 410 (Night Fighter) Squadron operated Defiant Mk IF, Beaufighter Mk IIF, Spitfire (F.Mk IIA, F.Mk IX and LF.Mk IX), Mosquito (NF.Mk II, T.Mk III, NF.Mk XII, NF.Mk XIII, and NF.Mk 30), and Harvard Mk IIB aircraft during World War II. On 1 December 1948, it was reformed at RCAF Station St Hubert, Québec as No. 410 (Fighter) Squadron. It was the first RCAF fighter squadron to be formed after the war, the first equipped with the Vampire, the first equipped with the Sabre and, later, the first assigned to No. 1 Air Division. 410 Squadron moved to RCAF Station North Luffenham on 15 November 1951, remaining there until 14 November 1954, when it relocated to

Baden-Soellingen, West Germany and joined No. 4 (Fighter) Wing. Later, it was transferred to No. 1 (Fighter) Wing at Marville, France. When it was decided to replace one Sabre day fighter squadron in each wing with a CF-100 all-weather squadron, 410 was one of those selected to be returned to Canada and it was deactivated on 2 October 1956. 410 All-Weather (Fighter) Squadron flew the Vampire 3 between December 1948 and May 1951, followed by the Sabre 2 (May 1951 to November 1954), and the CF-100 Mk 5 between November 1956 and November 1961.

The unit was reactivated at RCAF Station Uplands (Ottawa, Ontario) as 410 All-Weather (Fighter) Squadron on 1 November 1956. In September 1957, the squadron temporarily relocated to Harmon AFB near Stephenville, Newfoundland while the resident USAF unit, the 61st FIS, converted

A No. 410 Squadron CF-100 is seen in formation with a 61st FIS F-102A during the period the CF-100s held the alert at Harmon AFB.

from the F-89 Scorpion to the F-102 Delta Dagger. 410 was one of the squadrons selected to receive the Avro Canada CF-105 Arrow Mk 2 (in the first half of 1961), but the type's cancellation on 20 February 1959

ended those plans. 410 squadron went to RCAF Station Namao for CF-101 Voodoo conversion training on 11 November 1961 and was disbanded at Uplands on 1 April 1964.

413 AW(F) Squadron 'Tusker'

Codes (CF-100 era): 'AP'
Callsign (CF-100 era): JUMBO
Motto: 'Ad Vigilamus Undis' (We Watch the Waves)
Badge: In front of a maple leaf, an elephant's head affronté

No. 413 (General Reconnaissance) Squadron formed on 1 July 1941 at Stanraer, Scotland, to operate the Short S-23 Empire flying-boat and Consolidated Catalina (Mk I, Mk IB and Mk IV) during World War II. It had a dual existence between 1947 and 1950 as a mapping unit flying the Canso A, Lancaster 10.P, Norseman Mk VI, Dakota (Mk II, 3CFP, and 4M), Mitchell (Mk II and 2PT), and Harvard

As befitted a unit known as the 'Tuskers', No. 413 carried an elephant badge on the intake of its CF-100 Mk 5s.

Mk II. The unit was reformed as No. 413 All-Weather (Fighter) Squadron on 1 August 1951. On 8 November 1951, this title was amended to No. 413 (Fighter) Squadron. Under Operation Leap Frog III (7 March to 6 April 1953), it flew its Sabre 2s across the Atlantic to join No. 3 (Fighter) Wing at Zweibrücken. 413 (F) Squadron flew the Vampire 3 from August to December 1951, the Canadair Sabre 2 from November 1951 to June 1954, the Sabre 5 from June 1954 to September 1955, and the Sabre 6 from September 1955 to April 1957. 413 also had some Silver Star 3s on charge. It was deactivated at Zweibrücken on 7 April 1957, then reactivated at RCAF Station Bagotville

as 413 All-Weather (Fighter) Squadron on 1 May 1957. It was stood down on 30 December 1961. It flew the CF-100 Mk 5

and had some Mk 3Bs and Ds on hand as trainers and hacks, and, for a time, had CF-100 Mk 4Bs.

414 AW(F) Squadron/414 (EW) Squadron 'Black Knight'

Codes (first CF-100 era): 'AQ'
Callsign (AW(F) era): HALFBACK;
(EW era): KNIGHT
Motto: 'Totis Viribus' (With All Our Might)
Badge: Over a cloud, a knight on a charger

Formed on 13 August 1941 as No. 414 (Army Co-operation) Squadron at Croydon, Surrey, the unit flew the following types during World War II: Lysander Mk IIIA, Hurricane Mk IIC, Tomahawk (Mk I, Mk IIA, and Mk IIB), Fairey Battle Mk I, Tiger Moth (Mk I and Mk II), Miles Magister Mk I, North American Mustang Mk I, and Spitfire (F.Mk VB, LF.Mk VB, F.Mk IX, FR.Mk IX, LF.Mk IX, F.Mk XIV, F.Mk XIVE, FR.Mk XIV and FR.Mk XIVE). Like No. 413, it later operated as a

mapping unit equipped with Dakotas (Mk III, 3P, Mk IV, Mk IVM, Mk IVP and 4P) and the Lancaster 10.P, and was employed on charting and mapping duties in Canada's northern regions. It was disbanded on 1 November 1950.

Two years to the day later, the unit was reformed as 414 (Fighter) Squadron at RCAF Station Bagotville. Between 24 August and 3 September 1953, it moved under

Operation Leapfrog IV to Europe, where it joined 4 (Fighter) Wing at Baden-Soellingen, Germany. It flew the Sabre 4 from November 1952 to November 1953, the Sabre 5 from November 1953 to August 1955, and the Sabre 6 from July 1955 to July 1957. It was deactivated on 14 July 1957 and was reactivated at RCAF Station North Bay, Ontario as 414 All-Weather (Fighter) Squadron on 5 August 1957.

414 operated the CF-100 Mk 3B (as hacks and trainers) and the CF-100 Mk 5. Plans called for 414 to receive the CF-105 Arrow 2 beginning in the second half of 1962. With the Arrow's cancellation, 414 All-Weather (Fighter) Squadron re-equipped with the CF-101 Voodoo. It was disbanded on 30 June 1964. On 15 September 1967, the Electronic Warfare Unit at CFB St Hubert was redesignated as 414 (Electronic Warfare) Squadron, reuniting 414 with the 'Clunk'. It moved to CFB North Bay in August 1972. 414 (EW) Squadron operated the CF-100 Mk 5C and 5D variants, along with the CC-117 Falcon (unofficially referred to as 'EC-117'), EF-101B Voodoo (plus one CF-101F as a proficiency trainer), CC-144A Challenger-600, and CE-144A Challenger-EST. It became the world's last 'Clunk' and last Voodoo operator, in 1981 and 1987, respectively.

The knight badge was perhaps the best-known CF-100 marking due to the longevity of 414's EW aircraft.

416 AW(F) Squadron 'Lynx', 'Black Lynx'

Codes (CF-100 era): (not worn)
Callsign (CF-100 era): PUNCHBOWL
Motto: 'Ad Saltum Paratus' (Ready for the Leap)
Badge: In front of a maple leaf, a lynx leaping

No. 416 (Fighter) Squadron was formed at Peterhead, Scotland on 22 November 1941 and operated the following marks of Spitfire (in varying quantities): F.Mk IA, Mk IIA, Mk IIB, Mk VB, LF.Mk VB, Mk VC, Mk VC (Trop), F.Mk IX, LF.Mk IX, LF.Mk IXB, LF.Mk IXC, F.Mk XIV, FR Mk XIV, F.Mk XVI, LF.Mk XVI, and LF.Mk XVIE. It was reformed as No. 416 (Fighter) Squadron on 8 January 1951 at RCAF Station Uplands, and was initially equipped with the Mustang IV. In

preparation for its conversion to the Sabre, the unit received some Lockheed Silver Star 1s (ex-USAF T-33As). Between 28 September and 11 October 1952, under Operation Leapfrog II, 416 Squadron moved to join No. 2 (Fighter) Wing at Grostenquin, France. It operated the Sabre 2 from March 1952 to March 1954, the Sabre 5 from March 1954 to May 1955, and the Sabre 6 from April 1955 to January 1957.

As a result of the decision to replace one Sabre day fighter squadron in each of the four Air Division wings with a CF-100 all-weather fighter squadron, 416 was selected to return to Canada, being replaced by 423 All-Weather (Fighter) Squadron. It was deactivated at Grostenquin on 31 January 1957, then reactivated as 416 All-Weather (Fighter) Squadron on 1 February 1957 at RCAF Station St Hubert. It operated a small number of Mk 3, Mk 3D and Mk 4B Canucks, but was officially equipped with the CF-100 Mk 5. It was deactivated on 1 September 1961, soon resurfacing as a CF-101 Voodoo operator within Air Defence Command.

Three CF-100 units used big cats as their badges, No. 416 being the 'Lynx' unit and adorning its aircraft with a lynx's head on the intake. This is a Mk 5, seen flying from the base at St Hubert.

419 AW(F) Squadron 'Moose'

Codes (CF-100 era): 'UD'
Callsign (CF-100 era): CHOPSTICK
Motto: 'Moosa Aswayita' (Beware of the Moose)
Badge: A moose attacking

Formed as No. 419 (Bomber) Squadron at RAF Mildenhall, Suffolk, the squadron operated the Wellington (Mk IC and Mk III), Halifax (B.Mk I, B.Mk II, and B/GR.Mk II), and Lancaster B.Mk X during World War II. It was reformed at RCAF Station North Bay on 15 March 1954 as 419 All-Weather (Fighter) Squadron. In early 1955, 419 was involved in a series of tactical trials to minimise the threat of multiple targets such

'Beware of the Moose' warned No. 419's motto, and in the Air Division the CF-100 units built a reputation for excellence in air combat. No. 419 was at Baden-Soellingen.

as bomber streams. Rather than control every CF-100 that launched, only the lead aircraft would be dealt with; those that followed took off at 20-second intervals and used their radar to lock onto the aircraft in front. Phase I of Harlequin ended on 23 June 1955 and, the following year, 419 was again chosen to be the project leader of Harlequin II, which was judged to be even more successful than Phase I. 419 AW(F) Squadron transferred to Europe under Operation Nimble Bat 4 in August 1957, when it replaced 414 (F) Squadron in 4 (Fighter) Wing at Baden-Soellingen. It

disbanded there on 31 December 1962. The unit operated the CF-100 Mk 4A from March 1954 to May 1955 and the Mk 4B from May

1955 to December 1962. It also had a few Silver Star 3 assigned, but it is unclear if it had any CF-100 Mk 3 hacks.

423 AW(F) Squadron 'Eagle'

Codes (CF-100 era): 'NQ'
Callsign (CF-100 era): HANDCUFF
Motto: 'Quaerimus et Petimus' (We Search and Strike)
Badge: A bald-headed eagle volant

No. 423 (General Reconnaissance) Squadron formed on 18 May 1942 at Oban, Argyllshire and operated the Sunderland (Mk II and Mk III) and the Liberator C Mk VIII during World War II. The unit was reformed as 423 All-Weather (Fighter) Squadron at RCAF Station St Hubert on 1 June 1953. Under Operation Nimble Bat 2, it flew across the Atlantic between 12 and

15 February 1957, joining 2 (Fighter) Wing at Grostenquin, France, where it replaced 416 (F) Squadron. It was equipped with the CF-100 Mk 3B (and at least one Mk 3A) from July 1953 to May 1955. It then flew the CF-100 Mk 4B between February 1955 and December 1962. While its Mk 4Bs were being painted in camouflage and otherwise readied for service in 1 Air Division, 423 AW(F) Squadron temporarily re-equipped with Mk 5s between April and December 1956. It was disbanded on 31 December 1962.

The striking eagle intake badge identifies No. 423 Squadron which operated this Mk 4B from Grostenquin. It had earlier operated the Mk 3B.

425 AW(F) Squadron 'Alouettes'

Codes (CF-100 era): ('BB'; not worn)
Callsign (CF-100 era): FROGMAN, BLACKSHEEP
Motto: 'Je Te Plumerai' (I Shall Pluck You)
Badge: A lark volant

On 25 June 1942 No. 425 (Bomber) Squadron was formed at Dishforth, Yorkshire and went on to operate the Wellington (B.Mk III and B.Mk X), Halifax (B.Mk I, B/A.Mk III, B/A Met.Mk III, and B/Met.Mk III) and Lancaster X. On 1 October 1954, it was reformed at RCAF Station St Hubert as 425 All-Weather (Fighter) Squadron. It flew the CF-100 Mk 4A and 4B from October 1954 to April 1958 and the CF-100 Mk 5 from March 1956 to April 1961. It also had a few Mk 3B and 3D

models on hand as trainers and hacks. From 1955 to 1956, 425 Squadron was involved in the development and evaluation of standard operating procedures for the Rho Theta

computer. This was a Canadian-invented device that gave CF-100 navigators a continuous indication of ground position in terms of distance and bearing in nautical

miles from a designated point. 425 squadron was deactivated at St Hubert on 1 May 1961, and reactivated in October to become the CF-101 OTU.

Presentation of the Alouette (lark) badge varied throughout No. 425's CF-100 history, this being a late variation as seen on a Mk 5.

428 AW(F) Squadron 'Ghost'

Codes (CF-100 era): 'HG'
Callsign (CF-100 era): DAVENPORT
Motto: 'Usque ad Finem' (To the Very End)
Badge: In a shroud, a death's head

Formed at Dalton, Yorkshire as No. 428 (Bomber) Squadron on 7 November 1942, the unit was equipped during wartime with the Wellington (B.Mk II and B.Mk X), Halifax (B.Mk II, B/GR.Mk II, B/Met.Mk V, and B/A.Met Mk V), and Lancaster (B.Mk II and B.Mk X). It was reformed on 21 June 1954 as 428 All-Weather (Fighter) Squadron at RCAF Station Uplands and was equipped with the CF-100 Mk 4A from June 1954 to April 1955, the Mk 4B from February 1955 to August 1956, and the Mk 5 from March 1956 to May 1961. In October 1957, the squadron temporarily relocated to Harmon AFB near Stephenville, Newfoundland while the resident USAF unit, the 61st FIS, converted from the F-89 Scorpion to the F-102 Delta Dagger. 428 AW(F) Squadron was selected to become the first CF-105 Arrow 2 squadron, to receive its first six aircraft in the first half of 1961, but with the

cancellation of the Arrow on 20 February 1959 it retained the CF-100 until it was

disbanded at Uplands on 1 June 1961, and has not been reformed.

The skull badge identified No. 428 'Ghost' Squadron from Uplands.

432 AW(F) Squadron 'Black Cougar'

Codes (CF-100 era): 'DL'
Callsign (CF-100 era): RHINO
Motto: 'Saeviter ad Lucem' (Ferociously Towards the Light)
Badge: In front of a full moon, a cougar leaping down

No. 432 (Bomber) Squadron was formed at Skipton-on-Swale on 1 May 1943. During World War II it flew the Wellington B.Mk X,

Lancaster B.Mk II and Halifax (B.Mk III, B/A Mk III, B.Mk VII, and B/A Mk VII). It was reformed on 21 June 1954 as 432 All-Weather (Fighter) Squadron at RCAF Station Bagotville and flew the CF-100 Mk 4A from December 1954 to May 1955, the Mk 4B from April 1955 to August 1956, and the Mk 5 from June 1956 to October 1961. 432 also had some Mk 3Bs and some Silver Star 3s on strength as trainers and hacks. It was disbanded on 15 October 1961 and has not been reformed.

While 410 Sqn used a red cougar on their CF-100s, No. 432's was in black. The unit was ADC-assigned, based at 'Bagtown' (Bagotville).

433 AW(F) Squadron 'Porcupine'

Codes (CF-100 era): 'FG'
Callsign (CF-100 era): GIGOLO
Motto: 'Qui S'y Frott S'y Pique' (Who Opposes It Gets Hurt)
Badge: In front of a hurt, a porcupine

Having initially been formed as No. 433 (Bomber) Squadron at Skipton-on-Swale, Yorkshire on 25 September 1943, the unit undertook bombing missions for the remainder of the war, and flew PoW repatriation missions immediately after. It was reformed at RCAF Station Cold Lake as 433 All-Weather (Fighter) Squadron on 15 November 1954 and moved to RCAF

Station North Bay on 17 October 1955. 433 AW(F) Squadron was selected to convert to the CF-105 Arrow 2 in early 1962, but the Arrow programme was cancelled on 20 February 1959. The squadron was disbanded at North Bay on 1 August 1961. It flew the CF-100 Mk 4 between February 1955 and September 1957 and the Mk 5 from September 1956 to July 1961. It also had some Silver Star 3s, an Expeditor 3T and a couple of Harvards on strength as trainers and hacks. From 12 March to 16 May 1955 under Operation Gloat, 433 conducted many long-distance flights to establish range and fuel consumption data at different altitudes and loads, climb rates, handling characteristics under various rates of turn, and maximum and optimum engine relight altitudes.

This 433 Sqn CF-100 Mk 5 displays the three-round rocket dispenser used for weapon practice.

440 AW(F) Squadron 'Beaver', 'Bat', 'Red Bat'

Codes (CF-100 era): 'KE'
Callsign (CF-100 era): RHUBARB
Motto: 'Kaganawaitak Saguenay' (He Who Protects the Saguenay)
Badge: A bat in front of clouds

No. 440 Squadron's heritage reaches back to the formation of No. 11 (Army Co-operation) Squadron (Auxiliary) on 5 October 1932 at Vancouver. In 1937 it was renumbered as No. 111 (Coast Artillery Co-operation) Squadron (Auxiliary) and later reformed as No. 111 (Fighter) Squadron, moving to Britain in 1944 to fly the Typhoon. On 1 October 1953, it was reformed as 440 All-Weather (Fighter) Squadron at RCAF Station Bagotville. 440 received its first Mk 3, 18155, on 14 October, but it took several months to build up to its full strength of aircraft and crews. Under Operation Nimble

Bat 3, the unit relocated to Europe, where it replaced 413 (Fighter) Squadron in 3 (F) Wing at Zweibrücken. On 16 June 1962, it transferred within 1 Air Division to 4 (Fighter) Wing at Baden-Soellingen, where it was disbanded on 31 December 1962. It

had a small quantity of CF-100 Mk 3CT, Mk 3A and Mk 4A aircraft assigned, but its primary types were the CF-100 Mk 3B between October 1953 and September 1955, and the Mk 4B between February 1955 and December 1962.

A green and white teardrop pattern was No. 440's marking scheme for its first CF-100s, which were Mk 3Bs. Later a bat emblem was adopted to reflect the squadron's name.

445 AW(F) Squadron 'Wolverine'

Codes (CF-100 era): 'SA'
Callsign (CF-100 era): UKELELE, DALTON
Motto: 'Strike as Lightning'
Badge: A wolverine rampant holding in its dexter paw a lightning flash

Formed as 445 All-Weather (Fighter) Squadron at RCAF Station North Bay on 1 April 1953, this was the first squadron formed post-war that had not served in World War II. It was the first CF-100 unit assigned to Air Defence Command. In October 1953, the squadron moved to RCAF Station Uplands. 445 Squadron became the first CF-100 unit to deploy to the new Val d'Or detachment base. A forward operating location, Val d'Or was very basic with one short runway, no taxiways, and only a beacon as a landing aid. Between 1 and 4 November 1956, it

relocated to Europe under Operation Nimble Bat 1, joining 1 (Fighter) Wing at Marville, France where it replaced 410 (F) Squadron. It was disbanded there on 31 December

1962. 440 All-Weather (Fighter) Squadron flew the CF-100 Mk 3B from May 1953 to June 1954 and the Mk 4B from June 1954 to December 1962, when it was disbanded.

445 notched up two notable 'firsts': it was the first CF-100 unit, and the first to deploy to Europe (illustrated).

3 AW(F) OTU

Codes (CF-100 era): 'JF'
Callsign (CF-100 era): BLACK BALL

Formed at RCAF Station North Bay on 3 November 1952, No. 3 All-Weather (Fighter) Operational Training Unit moved to RCAF Station Cold Lake on 22 May 1955, then to RCAF Station Bagotville on 25 September 1961. (One source states the move was in July 1962.) It was disbanded there in December 1964. It operated the following types: Expeditor 3NM, Dakota, Mitchell (2PT, 3AI and 3AIA), CF-100 (Mk 2T, Mk 3T, Mk 3CT, Mk 3A, Mk 3B, Mk 3D, Mk 4A, Mk 4B and Mk 5), and Silver Star 3. After

completing its role as the CF-100 OTU, it became the CF-101 Voodoo OTU and operated the CF-101B and F models before turning over the Voodoo conversion course to 425 All-Weather (Fighter) Squadron at RCAF Station Bagotville. The OTU started instrument-rated Silver Star pilots in the CF-100 Mk 3D for check rides leading to solo status, the pilots then moving to the Mk 5 for 30 to 40 hours of general fighter tactics training, and finally to the Voodoo.

The witch badge of the OTU adorned many CF-100s, and almost all of the Mk 3s, like this aircraft. Mks 4 and 5 were assigned for the final operational training phase.

Weapons Practice Unit

Codes (CF-100 era): 'HY'
Callsign (CF-100 era): BAGGAGE

Formed at RCAF Station Cold Lake on 1 April 1956, this unit's original name was to have been the Weapons Training Unit. All CF-100 squadrons rotated through the WPU to conduct live-fire exercises against aircraft towing Del Mar Radop targets. The WPU's aircraft included several CF-100 Mk 4Bs and Mk 5s, as well as some Silver Star 3s. At least two of the Canucks were painted bright red. The Weapons Practice unit was disbanded on 1 April 1961 following the introduction into RCAF service of the CF-101 Voodoo.

This immaculate Mk 5, complete with three-round rocket launchers on the wingtips, wears the 'HY' codes of the 'Cool Pool'-based WPU. This unit parented live-fire exercises and also undertook trials work with the 2.75-in rocket armament.

Electronic Warfare Unit

Codes (CF-100 era): (none known)
Motto: 'Mens et Memoria'
Badge: A crow superimposed over red lightning bolts

The EWU was formed on 1 April 1959 at RCAF Station St Hubert from 104 Composite Unit, which had originally begun as No. 1 Communications Flight, and was redesignated as No. 104 Communications Unit in 1954 and then became 104 Composite Unit. In 1955, 104 CU began its involvement with electronic warfare training. It was equipped with Harvards (Mk II and 4), Dakotas (Mk 3 and 4MSR), C-119, Silver

Star 3, CF-100s (Mk 3D, Mk 4A, Mk 4B, Mk 5, Mk 5C and Mk 5D), and Expeditor (Mk IMN, 3NM, 3NMT and 3TM), but not all of these were used in the EW training role. On 1 November 1959, the EWU moved to RCAF Station Bagotville, but its modified C-119s remained at St Hubert. Its CF-100s were actually flown by crews from 425 All-Weather (Fighter) Squadron. A small detachment was later established at RCAF Station Comox. On 15 September 1967, the Electronic Warfare Unit was redesignated as 414 (Electronic Warfare) Squadron. It moved to CFB North Bay during August 1972. (See above for the rest of the story.)

Best-known for its use of the Mk 5C/5D, the Electronic Warfare Unit also used Mk 3Ds as 'hacks' and for training.

Central Experimental and Proving Establishment/Aerospace Engineering Test Establishment

Codes (CF-100 era): 'FB', 'FC', 'PX'
Motto: 'Experto Crede' (Believe One Who Knows from Experience)
Badge: Hercules in combat with Hydra

This unit's history began as the Test and Development Flight, which was formed in 1931. It became the Test and Development Establishment in 1940, then the Experimental and Proving Establishment in 1947. In 1951, it was redesignated as the Central Experimental and Proving Establishment. On 15 May 1957, CEPE moved from RCAF Station Rockcliffe to Uplands (both in Ottawa, Ontario), then later to Cold Lake. It had detachments at Arnprior (Ontario), Suffield (Alberta) and at Scottish Aviation in Prestwick, Scotland. Prior to its move there, CEPE had a detachment at RCAF Station Cold Lake called the Air Armament Evaluation Detachment and the CEPE Climatic Detachment (which had begun as the Winter Experimental Establishment Flight and was disbanded on 30 August 1960 when CEPE took over that role at Uplands) was at RCAF Station Namao. On 4 May 1967, CEPE, 448 (Test) Squadron, 129 Test & Ferry Flight, and the Royal Canadian Navy's VX 10 were amalgamated and renamed the Aerospace Engineering Test Establishment. 448 (Test)

Squadron continued to exist as AETE's flying component until it was disbanded on 1 September 1971, at which time AETE took over its flying duties. The above-named units have operated a huge variety of aircraft, but only the CF-100s flown by them are listed here: CF-100 (Mk 1, Mk, 2, Mk 3, Mk 3A, Mk 4A, Mk 4B, Mk 5 and Mk 5M).

Above: CEPE's codes were briefly applied to many of the prototype and early CF-100s. 18112 was the Mk 4 prototype, the first aircraft with the definitive nose shape.

Right: In later years most AETE aircraft were marked with a large red 'X' on the fin to denote their experimental status. AETE use of the CF-100 ended in 1973.

Top and above: CEPE was heavily involved in the test work for the Velvet Glove guided missile programme. Early captive-carry and jettison trials were performed using Mk 3CT 18117, seen here with the unique intake-mounted pylons originally developed (service aircraft would have used wing-mounted pylons). At top the aircraft is seen with the 'PX' codes associated with the Air Armament Evaluation Detachment, while above is the aircraft still bearing the 'JF' codes from its 3 AW(F) OTU past. Note the Namao Detachment polar bear badge.

Air Armament Evaluation Detachment

The Air Armament Evaluation Detachment was a component of the Central Proving and Experimental Establishment and was formed at RCAF Station Cold Lake on 1 July 1954 to evaluate rocket armament for the CF-100. It operated Lancaster 10.DC drone controllers, Firebee drones, a Mitchell 2PT, Sabre 6s, a Canadair Argus 1, and CF-100s (Mk 4A, Mk 4B, Mk 5, and Mk 5M). AAED's aircraft wore 'PX' codes.

Winter Experimental Flight

The Winter Experimental Establishment Flight had its beginnings as part of the Test and Development Establishment at RCAF Station Rockcliffe as early as 1933. This evolved into No. 1 Winter Experimental and Training Flight, which was formed in 1943 in Kapuskasing, in northern Ontario. It moved to RCAF Station Gimli, Manitoba in March 1944, then to Namao on 1 October 1945,

when its named changed to Winter Experimental Detachment. It became part of the Central Experimental and Proving Establishment in mid-1951, at which time it was renamed the CEPE Climatic Detachment. WEE conducted trials with and/or for the RCAF, RCN, RAF, FAA, USAAF, USAF and USN, and, over the

years, had an astonishing variety of aircraft assigned to it. Its Naval Detachment was operated by VX 10. Its assigned code letters were 'FC', but some of its aircraft wore CEPE's 'FB' codes instead. At least one CF-100 Mk 4B is known to have been assigned to WEE Flight. It was disbanded in 1960.

Airborne Sensing Unit

The federal Department of Energy, Mines and Resources was interested in high-altitude photography and approached the Canadian Armed Forces in 1970 for the use of a CF-100. 18767, a Mk 5, was assigned and its previous owner, the Aerospace

Engineering Test Establishment, installed a variety of cameras and other sensors. These included both nose- and belly-mounted items, comprising Vinten F95 70-mm cameras, Wild Heerbrugg RC 10 9?9 camera, and HRB Singer Reconofax single-channel line-scan imaging system. The latter was used to measure infra-red radiant energy. A closed-circuit video camera was also installed.
   Successful tests led to the July 1971

formation of the Airborne Sensing Unit as part of Air Transport Command (giving ATC its one and only fighter), based in Ottawa. The ASU was also equipped with two Dakotas and a Dassault-Breguet Falcon 20 (117508). The CF-100 and one of the Dakotas were transferred from AETE, with the other Dakota coming from the Crown Assets Disposal Corporation's facility at Saskatoon, Saskatchewan. 'Customers' for the aircraft's new abilities included three

branches of EMR (Inland Waters, Surveys & Mapping, and Geological Surveys), as well as Agriculture Canada, the Forest Management Institute, and the Department of National Defence. The unit was transferred from the military to a civilian agency, the Canada Centre for Remote Sensing, which retired 100767 to Canada's 'mini-AMARC' at CFD Mountain View on 3 March 1975. It had amassed a total of 1,903 hours.

RCAF Air Weapons Unit

Activated on either 1 March 1957 or 26 June 1957 at Decimomannu, Sardinia, this unit had no CF-100s of its own, but hosted Canuck squadrons from 1 Air Division for

both gunnery and rocketry training. The first to arrive was 445 AW(F) Squadron on 23 November 1957. The AWU had several Silver Star 3s and at least one Expeditor. It

was disbanded on 1 September 1970, having also hosted Sabre and CF-104 Starfighter squadrons.

Planned CF-100 Operators:

Operational Proving Unit

This unit was formed sometime during 1959, probably in January or early February, to evaluate the CF-105 Arrow for service. It was to be equipped with several Arrows as well CF-100 Mk 5s, Sabre 6s and Silver Star 3s. They were to serve as chase aircraft and for what is today known as dissimilar air combat training.

Auxiliary Squadrons

Very early plans called for the Auxiliary squadrons, then equipped with Mustangs, Vampires or Sabres, to operate the CF-100 Canuck as part of Air Defence Command. These units included 400 and 411 at RCAF Station Downsview (Toronto), 401 and 438 at RCAF Station St Hubert (Montréal), 420 at RCAF Station London (Ontario), and 442 and 443 at RCAF Station Sea Island (Vancouver). It was even suggested that they would eventually re-equip with the Avro Canada CF-105 Arrow. It was soon acknowledged that both types were too complex to be flown and maintained by part-time personnel. 420 Squadron was disbanded and the others reroled and re-equipped with Expeditors. Other Auxiliary squadrons had flown Mitchells rather than fighters and were never scheduled to receive CF-100s.

Belgian Air Force

Only one foreign customer was found for the CF-100, that being Belgium. NATO was concerned about the country's all-weather fighter capability and Belgium was keen to improve its situation; in 1957, its only all-weather fighters were the survivors of 24 ex-RAF Gloster Meteor NF.Mk 11s, obtained between 1952 and 1956, which had supplanted de Havilland Mosquito NF.Mk 30s. To replace these obsolete aircraft, the Belgians evaluated the Gloster Javelin FAW.Mk 7, Sud-Aviation Vautour IIN, Northrop F-89 Scorpion, and Avro Canada CF-100 Mk 5. (They also considered, but did not test, the Saab Lansen.) The Javelin appeared to be the front-runner, but the Vautour could not be overlooked given the ties between France and Belgium. Also, the F-89 Scorpion was viewed as a strong contender. Few, apparently, can have considered the CF-100 as having much of a chance of winning the competition.

Fortunately for Avro Canada, the decision was left to the Belgian Air Force rather than the politicians, as there was a considerable amount of lobbying going on. The air force wanted a combination of the best fire control system with the best performance. The FCSs of the Javelin and Vautour were no match for the CF-100's and, while the F-89's FCS was better, the aircraft's performance was not. Initially, the Americans had been reluctant to let Canada have the MG-2 FCS for the CF-100, not even permitting the RAF to use it in its Javelins, so including it in the Belgian CF-100s took some persuading. Avro Canada, with the assistance of C. D. Howe, convinced the US Secretary of the Air Force to release the MG-2 and its associated AN/APG-40 radar to Belgium, and the deal was done.

Operational suitability tests were required by the United States before it would fund the Belgian CF-100s, these being conducted under Operation Banana Belt. During November 1955, four brand-new Mk 4s (18494, 18495, 18496 and 18497) were flown to RCAF Station Cold Lake. Until 16 December 1955, the aircraft fired many salvoes of rockets on the Primrose Lake Range in an evaluation of the weapons systems. Early in January 1956, the aircraft were flown to Eglin AFB, Florida for further evaluation, this time by a joint Canadian/US team. Fifty RCAF personnel were joined by members of the 3241st Test Group (Interceptor), a component of the USAF Operational Test Center. The project's eight flight crew were evenly divided between the two air forces. (Some sources seem to imply that the four USAF personnel were all pilots. However, it should be remembered that as late as the mid-1960s, it was USAF policy to put two rated pilots in the F-4 Phantom II, only later adopting the idea of a specialist Weapons System Operator.) Operation Banana Belt concluded on 2 May 1956 with the CF-100 being deemed eminently suitable for the Belgian Air Force.

The 53 CF-100s for Belgium were purchased on its behalf by the RCAF, delivered from RCAF stocks, and all were assigned RCAF serials prior to delivery. Twenty-five per cent of their cost was paid by the Canadian government, with the balance by the United States through the Military Assistance Program (MAP); they were not, strictly speaking, 'sold' to Belgium. The deal included a large stock of spares, manuals, and training. All of these aircraft were officially taken on strength and then officially struck off strength by the RCAF on 7 October 1957, not 27 October as has been published numerous times previously. The RCAF serials were 18685 to 18738, but 18731 received B Category damage in a fire at the Avro Canada factory in Malton, and it was not delivered and was replaced by 18738. The Belgian aircraft received the serials AX-1 to AX-46 (RCAF serials 18685 to 18730) and AX-47 to AX-53 (RCAF serials 18732 to 18738). 18731 underwent controlled cannibalisation, became a training aid, and is now displayed at the Royal Military College in Kingston, Ontario.

Training Belgian crews

The first five Belgian crews reported to 3 (AW) OTU on 8 August 1957 and commenced training the very next day. Three crews began with a 20-hour course using Mitchell 3AI and 3AIA trainers, while two others started with the flight simulator programme. 24 September 1957 brought the beginning of flying training using CF-100 Mk 3Ds, followed by the Mk 4A from 11 October. The Belgians' training did not include gunnery or rocket firing. Next on the schedule for the 10 Belgians was a three-day visit to Malton for familiarisation with the Mk 5, but this did not include flying.

The ferrying flights across the Atlantic were carried out by RCAF crews and were known as Operation Jump Moat. The first of these, with 15 aircraft, departed Canada on 5 December 1957 and ended at RCAF Station Marville, France, from where FAB/BLu crews continued on to Beauvechain (also known as Bevekom), arriving on 20 December for the acceptance ceremonies. Jump Moat 2, with 16 aircraft, followed on 3 March 1958. Jump Moat 3 departed on 7 May 1958 with 11 aircraft. Jump Moat 4, also consisting of 11 aircraft, left Canada on 25 June 1958. The later ferry flights were made directly to Belgium without the intermediate stop in France for Belgian crews to complete the flights.

Above: Belgium's CF-100s were Mk 5s, unlike those operated during the same time period by the RCAF in Europe. Belgium's aircraft were considered to be all-weather interceptors like those assigned to NORAD, a task for which the lengthened wingtips (and reduced g limits) and lack of gun armament were more appropriate.

Above right: This Mk 5 is from No. 350 Squadron, the intake marking being a stylised helmet of Ambiorix the Gaul.

Right: Two No. 350 Squadron aircraft are seen in typically European surroundings. The CF-100 had a relatively short career in Belgium before replacement by the Mach 2 F-104 Starfighter.

Beauvechain was the home of 1 All-Weather Wing, which consisted of 11, 349 and 350 Squadrons. Official BAF acceptance of the CF-100s was on 20 December 1957. On that date, 1 Wing was renamed as No. 1 (All-Weather) Wing, which was rendered as 'Alle-Weder' and 'Tous Temps' in Belgium's two official languages, the word squadron becoming Smaldeel and Escadrille. 11 Squadron began its conversion from Gloster Meteor NF.Mk 11s on 25 January 1958. All of this unit's crews had trained in Canada and they became responsible for training crews from the other two squadrons. 349 Squadron began its conversion on 17 March 1958, followed by 350 Squadron on 15 September. Both 349 and 350 Squadrons had previously flown Hawker Hunters.

Interestingly, the Belgian crews included NCOs as well as officers. This had no apparent effect on the type's safety record, which was fairly good. Only seven A Category accidents occurred between 30 July 1959 and 13 March 1963: three wheels-up landings, one engine flame-out on finals, one crash during a low-level navigation exercise, another crash, and one, the first accident, broke up at low altitude during a mock dogfight. A total of seven aircrew was killed in these accidents.

In 1959, the Belgians flew four CF-100s (AX-1, AX-12, AX-23 and AX-44) to Kamina in the south central Belgian Congo (later Zaire and now the Democratic Republic of Congo), ostensibly to celebrate the 10th anniversary of the training base there but also to act as a show of force to rebel groups in the area. Departing Beauvechain on 4 July 1959, they arrived at Leopoldville on 6 July, and arrived at Kamina Airfield on 8 July. Logistic support came in the form of two Fairchild C-119G Flying Boxcars. With the impending independence for the Belgian Congo, the CF-100s served to remind the various factions in the colony that Belgium wanted a peaceful transition. The aircraft participated in a number of displays throughout the Belgian Congo, before departing on 13 July. They arrived back at Beauvechain on 16 July, each having flown approximately 35 hours in the course of the deployment. Other than a few inadvertent border crossings along the Iron Curtain, this was probably the closest that any CF-100s, Canadian or Belgian, came to any form of serious confrontation.

The Belgian Air Force (Force Aérienne Belge/Belgische Luchtmacht, to give it its official bilingual title) operated the CF-100 until the early 1960s. 11 Squadron disbanded in November 1960, with its crews going to 349 Squadron and its aircraft shared between 349

Ground crew lift a rocket pod on to the wingtip of a No. 349 Squadron CF-100 Mk 5. The squadron's badge consisted of two maces, crossed, the weapon being known locally as the Goedendag. The unit's motto was 'Strike Hard, Strike Home'.

and 350 Squadrons. A few also went to the range at Solenzara, Corsica, as target tugs. 350 Squadron retired its CF-100s in April 1963, followed by 349 Squadron in August. Both units re-equipped with the F-104G Starfighter (built by SABCA in Belgium under licence from Lockheed) and, later, with F-16 Fighting Falcons. They retained the interceptor role they had performed with their CF-100s, unlike the RCAF squadrons that changed roles when they re-equipped with CF-104s.

All of the Belgian Air Force's surviving CF-100s were flown to Koksijde (Coxyde) and sold as scrap. One contractor took 20 of the 46 survivors, with the rest being accounted for by a variety of other scrap merchants. So quickly were they gone that the Musée Royal de l'Armée et d'Histoire Militaire/Koninklijk Legermuseum at the Palais du Cinquantenaire in Brussels had to obtain an ex-CAF Mk 5, 18534, in May 1971. The Canadian Department of Trade and Commerce sold it to Belgium for C$1.00. It was loaded aboard the Belgian troopship Godetia on 18 November 1971, arriving in Ostend on 24 November. It is still displayed in its RCAF markings, not having been repainted to represent one of Belgium's 53 CF-100 Canucks.

In Belgian service, the CF-100s wore a camouflage scheme comprising the same dark green and dark sea grey upper surfaces with medium sea grey undersides that was applied to the RCAF aircraft assigned to 1 Air Division. Unit markings were carried on the intakes. 11 Squadron's badge was a grey and black bat, usually on a yellow triangle. 349 Squadron used a pair of spiked and chained maces in blue with either silver or white outlines. 350 Squadron's badge consisted of a large red symbol with yellow outline, based on the winged helmet of Ambiorix the Gaul. These markings were often referred to as moustaches due to their appearance when viewed from the front. The Belgian roundels were outlined in a non-standard narrow blue band, but it was not a remnant of the RCAF roundels as they were smaller.

Other operators

United Aircraft of Canada/Pratt & Whitney Canada

In 1967, United Aircraft of Canada Ltd (later known as Pratt & Whitney Aircraft of Canada Ltd and then as Pratt & Whitney Canada) submitted a request to the government for the loan of a CF-100 Canuck Mk 5 as a flying testbed for its JT15D turbofan engine. The manufacturer required a two-seat aircraft so that a test engineer could accompany the flight, one with performance matching that of the engine's intended users. The CF-100 was a natural as its weapons bay offered a good place to mount the test engine and the tall landing gear gave sufficient ground clearance.

(Other locations investigated but rejected included mounting the test engine on the wingtip, under the nose, and over the wing. The only drawback to mounting it under the weapons bay was the risk of ingesting FOD, so clamshell doors were developed for its nacelle. The doors opened as the nosewheel lifted off the runway and they formed the outer skin of the front end of the nacelle.) At that time, the only remaining CF-100 operator was the Electronic Warfare Unit, and it shared the airfield with P&WC, easing logistical concerns. The aircraft was delivered to UACL on 22 November 1967. Its first flight with the company was on 22 July 1968 and its first flight with a test engine took place on 14 August 1968. The

first air-start was on 22 August. It made its final flight with P&WAC on 28 June 1982 and was struck off strength by the CAF on 8 July. The aircraft logged a total of 1,017.6

flying hours in over 400 flights while with the company. It is now displayed at St Hubert (now known as CFB Montréal), where it was unveiled on 19 April 1983.

This view highlights the tall undercarriage of the CF-100, which made it ideal for testing of the JT15D turbofan.

Malta
1940-1943
'The Fighter Pilot's Paradise'

When recounting the history of Malta during World War II, it is the fortunes of the fighting forces which operated from the island, and the suffering of its civilian population, that are most often recorded; it is less frequently emphasised that Malta was a vital base for offensive operations against the Axis, and a real threat to the enemy's ambitions in North Africa and the Middle East.

Above: As an FAA pilot buckles his flying helmet, naval groundcrew prepare to swing the prop of Gloster-built Hurricane Mk IIA BG766, armed with a pair of 250-lb bombs for another offensive sweep.

Left: Four Gloster Sea Gladiators formed the initial fighter defence of the island when Italy unleashed its bombing offensive in June 1940. This aircraft is N5520 Faith, one of three christened by a Maltese newspaper.

So effective were the Allied offensive operations that the enemy, in an attempt to render the island impotent, tried every means at its disposal – except outright invasion and capture (though this was certainly considered at one time) – from aerial bombing, naval attack, blockade and starvation. The tiny island's ordeal lasted from mid-1940 until the final Allied victory in North Africa in May 1943, a longer period of investment and assault than that suffered by a similar garrisoned objective in World War II.

After a turbulent history of religious, political and military intrigue, spanning some 2,000 years, the island of Malta, with its Grand Harbour at Valletta, was captured by Britain from France in 1801. For more than a century after that, it came to represent an important naval and military staging base in the central Mediterranean, laying as it did roughly half-way between the great bastions of British Empire communications at Gibraltar and Alexandria. As long as Britain and Italy remained allies, Malta's security was never seriously at risk, and its garrison forces remained relatively small. In 1917, during World War I, the Royal Naval Air Service established a seaplane station at

Air Chief Marshal Sir Arthur Tedder, C-in-C Mediterranean Air Command (above, at right) is greeted by Air Vice Marshal Sir Keith Park on his arrival in Malta during a visit paid to the island. While AOC No. 11 Group during the Battle of Britain, Park had famously used Hurricane 'OK-1' as his personal mount. On Malta another Hurricane, coded 'OK-2', was employed.

Kalafrana, from where British aircraft flew regular anti-submarine patrols, on watch for submarines of the Central Powers which occasionally broke out from enemy ports in the Adriatic. After the amalgamation of the RFC and RNAS to form the Royal Air Force in April 1918, Kalafrana became an RAF Station, later also administering a new airfield at Hal Far, which opened in March 1929. Reverting to its original spelling of Kalafrana in 1936, the seaplane base was often visited by RAF flying-boat squadrons between the wars, particularly during the Spanish Civil War, while Fleet Air Arm carrierborne aircraft and warship-borne seaplanes were held in reserve as replacements for the Mediterranean Fleet. Scant attention was paid before World War II to the air defence of the island, despite its importance to the Royal Navy – although a couple of home-based RAF fighter squadrons were detached to Hal Far during the Abyssinian crisis of 1935-36, as Italy broadcasted thinly disguised signals of its imperial ambitions in East Africa.

Italy enters the war

Upon Italy's entry on 10 June 1940 into World War II as an Axis partner, two more airfields were being completed at Ta Kali and Luqa, although no established fighter defences existed. True, four fighter squadrons had been planned during the previous 30 months but, owing to the priorities at home, they had not materialised when the first few Italian reconnaissance aircraft appeared in the Maltese skies. Nor had the recommended 172 anti-aircraft guns been delivered for the defence of the island. The general attitude at home was that if Italy displayed any determination to seize the island, there was precious little that Britain could do. The only aircraft on the island were five naval Swordfish and a Queen Bee radio-controlled target aircraft, as well as eight Sea Gladiator biplane fighters in crates (intended as replacements for Royal Navy carrier aircraft in transit through the Mediterranean). A few days prior to Italy's entry into the war, four of the latter were assembled and manned by several

volunteer pilots from the gunnery flight and three pilots of the RAF Headquarters staff, headed by Air Commodore Forster Herbert Martin Maynard, AFC. One vital piece of equipment had been set up on the island, an AMES (an acronym standing for Air Ministry Experimental Station) Mk 1 Type 6 radar which had been erected late in 1939 at Fort Ta Salvatur as No. 241 Transportable Radio Unit (TRU), capable of providing fairly reliable surveillance in all directions up to a distance of

Above: This Ju 88A-4, seen while en route to Malta on 9 April 1942, carries an SC1000 'Hermann' GP bomb. Its nose insignia appears to be that of either II. or III./KG 77. As well as being tasked with attacking the island itself Ju 88s also made anti-shipping strikes.

Above left: The Regia Aeronautica opened hostilities against Malta in June 1940. A pair of Cant Z1007Bis Alciones, believed to be of either the 210ª or 211ª Squadriglia, 50° Gruppo, 16° Stormo BT, is seen releasing bombs over the Grand Harbour, Valletta.

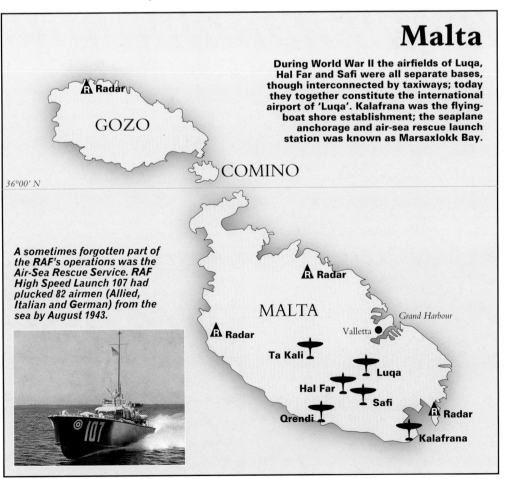

Malta

During World War II the airfields of Luqa, Hal Far and Safi were all separate bases, though interconnected by taxiways; today they together constitute the international airport of 'Luqa'. Kalafrana was the flying-boat shore establishment; the seaplane anchorage and air-sea rescue launch station was known as Marsaxlokk Bay.

GOZO

36°00' N

COMINO

A sometimes forgotten part of the RAF's operations was the Air-Sea Rescue Service. RAF High Speed Launch 107 had plucked 82 airmen (Allied, Italian and German) from the sea by August 1943.

MALTA

Grand Harbour

Valletta

Ta Kali

Luqa

Hal Far

Safi

Qrendi

Radar

Kalafrana

Left: Unmolested by fighters, the gunner of an Italian Junkers Ju 87 (Picchiatello or 'Little Woodpecker' in Italian service) photographs the results of another sortie over Malta.

Above: Introduced late in 1941, the Macchi MC.202 initially gave the Maltese defenders a hard time. This 378ª Squadriglia, 151ª Gruppo, 51° Stormo CT Serie III aircraft was shot-down by Flt Lt George F. 'Buzz' Beurling on Gozo during August 1942. Its pilot, Sergente Maggiore Faliero Gelli had two kills to his name and was taken prisoner.

about 100 miles (160 km) above 8,000 ft (2438 m). A second radar, No. 242 TRU, was in the process of completion.

When, on 11 June, fewer than a dozen Italian SM.79 bombers appeared over Malta, three Sea Gladiators rose in defence, their pilots under orders to harry the raiders to upset their bombing aim, rather than risk prolonged combat. This pattern continued for several days, and at least one Italian aircraft was destroyed. The Italians were apparently convinced that at least two squadrons of RAF fighters were resident on the island, a view almost certainly prompted by the bombers' reports of encountering Hurricanes. Four such aircraft arrived on Malta early in the morning of 14 June, their arrival being the culmination of an instance of sheer determination in the face of repeated setbacks. On 10 June, following the personal intervention of Winston Churchill, 12 Hurricane Mk Is (fitted with long-range fuel tanks) had set off from Boscombe Down in the company of a 'navigating' Blenheim, their pilots being ordered to land in the south of France where arrangements had been made for their refueling. Arriving at the prescribed airfield, they found that, fearing reprisals from the Luftwaffe,

the local people had placed obstructions on the field. The Blenheim and eight Hurricanes crashed on landing and were unable to continue. The surviving four fighters were successfully refuelled (by their pilots, using petrol cans) and took off the following morning, landing on a coastal road in Tunisia, where they again refuelled, with the help of the local civilians. Airborne once more, these four Hurricanes succeeded in finding Malta, where they landed safely, only to learn that their guns had not arrived (being brought from England in a Hudson, which had been delayed at Gibraltar).

Under orders from Cairo, the pilots took off once more for Egypt, where it was intended to fit the Browning guns. No sooner had they arrived than news was received that the Hudson had landed on Malta and could not proceed further, owing to an unserviceable engine. The Hurricanes were refuelled at Abu Sueir and ordered back to Malta where, with their guns at last fitted and tested, they joined the island defences within six hours of their eventual arrival. Within a week their pilots had destroyed nine Italian aircraft – a high proportion of the aircraft despatched. Many months later, as the result of journalistic licence, the names Faith,

Hope and Charity appeared in a Maltese newspaper, to refer to three Sea Gladiators which had flown 'alone' against the might of the Regia Aeronautica – it made a good story, and entered service mythology. Who, in wartime, would dare to denigrate the efforts of the gallant islanders?

Additional aircraft sought

Aware that not only was Malta bound to assume much greater strategic naval importance to the Royal Navy in the near future, but that it also lay squarely across the Italian supply routes to Marshal Graziani's armies in Africa, Maynard sought to obtain additional aircraft with which to strike against the Italians. In addition to a squadron of Swordfish (No. 830 of the Fleet Air Arm), a Hudson and a French Latécoère seaplane, two Sunderlands of Nos 228 and 230 Squadrons of the RAF began flying from Kalafrana. The immediate effect of these steps was evident on 28 June when Flight Lieutenant William Weir Campbell of No. 230 Squadron sank the Italian submarine Argonauta in the central Mediterranean, and followed this feat the very next day by sinking the submarine Rubino in the Ionian Sea – returning with four survivors to provide evidence of his success.

Despite the obvious value of the island as a base for offensive operations – particularly reconnaissance over the Italian mainland – the Air Ministry decided to strengthen Malta's fighter defences yet further before committing bombers and other aircraft. On 2 August the carrier HMS Argus sailed to within 200 miles (320 km) of

The pounding that the island received was extensive and concentrated. RAF Ta Kali in April 1942 (left) was a mass of bomb-craters revealing the chalky undersoil of the island and pinpointing the airfield for other Axis bomber pilots. Only the craters obstructing continued operations on the aerodromes were filled.

Far left: A huge cloud of debris and dust swells skyward after an ammunition dump on Malta receives a direct hit.

Above: With little in the way of hangarage, most maintenance was undertaken outdoors. The crew of this No. 185 Sqn Hurricane Mk II (with black night-fighter undersides) pose in the improvised revetments at Hal Far, mid-1941.

Above right: As a Swordfish wheels overhead, Force 'H' escorts HMS Argus (left, with RAF Hurricanes on its deck) through the Mediterranean towards Malta in late 1940.

Right: With Valletta in the distance, four Hurricane Mk IIs, each with a pair of long-range fuel tanks, await their next sortie. The 'XJ' code on the nearest aircraft is unusual, as it was also used by No. 13 (Bomber) OTU in the UK.

Malta with a dozen Hurricane Mk Is of No. 418 Flight, which were flown off and landed safely at Luqa; these aircraft, together with six Sea Gladiators (recently assembled from storage) and the four Hurricanes already on the island, were formed into No. 261 Squadron under the command of Squadron Leader Duncan Whiteley Balden; ground crews for the new squadron arrived at Malta by submarine.

Thus strengthened, Malta now received three Marylands, which constituted No. 431 Flight under Squadron Leader Eric William Whiteley, their role being photo-reconnaissance throughout the central Mediterranean, with particular emphasis on the Italian fleet. On 10 November, one of these aircraft, flown by Pilot Officer Adrian Warburton, returned to Luqa with complete photographic evidence of the presence of the bulk of that fleet in Taranto harbour (having twice circled the naval anchorage at very low level in the face of heavy anti-aircraft fire to photograph every major warship at close quarters). The following day the carrier HMS *Illustrious*, on patrol nearby, made ready to launch its complement of Swordfish, and that night, led by Lieutenant Commander Kenneth Williamson RN, 21 aircraft attacked with bombs and torpedoes, sinking the battleship

Littorio and severely damaging two others, one of which never sailed again. (Warburton was to gain an outstanding reputation as one of the most courageous of al reconnaissance pilots in the Mediterranean, particularly in Malta, performing countless hazardous sorties over Sicily and Italy during the next two years. He rose to wing commander during that period, was awarded two DSOs, three DFCs and the American DFC – a remarkable testimony to the skill and courage of a pilot who frequently flew unarmed aircraft during his operations.)

A week after the successful attack on Taranto, HMS *Argus* was ready with a new consignment of Hurricane Mk Is for Malta but, owing to confused reports of activity by the Italian fleet, launched the 12 fighters and two 'pathfinding' Skuas at the extreme limit of the Hurricanes' range. Owing to a lack of experience among the pilots, eight of the Hurricanes and a Skua ran out of fuel en route to Malta and were lost.

Notwithstanding this setback, the RAF started flying Wellingtons to Egypt from Britain, staging through Malta, where they paused briefly to carry out a few raids on Italian ports before continuing to the east. Such improvised attacks proved less than satisfactory, and Maynard obtained permission to retain 16 of the

bombers on the island permanently, these being formed into No. 148 Squadron at Luqa on 14 December. Their initial raids were to be flown against Italian forces in Albania in support of the Greeks, but were soon switched to attacks on the main Italian supply ports of Benghazi and Tripoli in Libya in support of General Wavell's bold offensive in the Western Desert.

Italy's recurring setbacks in the Balkans and North Africa, and its inability to close the Mediterranean to British shipping, now prompted Germany to take a hand; before December was out, the crews of Malta's Marylands were bringing back evidence of German bombers in Sicily. Initially they were thought to be equipment for the Regia Aeronautica (and Italian-flown Ju 87Rs had taken part in attacks on Malta), but early in January 1941 their true purpose became all too evident to the garrison and civilian population of Malta.

The '*Illustrious* Blitz'

Thus far Malta had escaped serious attacks by the Regia Aeronautica, the efforts of No. 261 Squadron having first forced the Italians to bomb from greater height (with much reduced accuracy), and then to provide fighter escorts of Fiat CR.42s and Macchi MC.200s. Neither of

Almost certainly seen at Kalafrana, this Sunderland Mk I has seemingly fallen victim to a strafing attack. Its wing spar has fractured close to the starboard inner engine and spilt fuel is well ablaze.

The arrival of the rains reduced Malta's airfields to quagmires. Here a Bren Gun Carrier is seen towing a string of 500-lb bombs to a No. 104 Sqn Wellington Mk II. Note the George Cross displayed on the Carrier.

With a well-known Maltese religious landmark in the background, groundcrew guide a No. 272 Sqn Beaufighter Mk VIF as it taxis from a dispersal at RAF Luqa.

Engaged, for the most part, in maritime operations, the Beaufighter was popular with crews as it was able to provide concentrated firepower and was twin-engined – the latter a comforting feature considering that offensive strikes inevitably involved long periods over the Mediterranean. Beaufighter Mk VIC X8035 'J' (far left) takes to the air from one of Malta's airfields. Another Mk VIC, T5068 'V' of No. 272 Sqn (left), displays the wear and tear brought on by extended operations from Malta.

these aircraft were much of a match for the Hurricanes, few in number though they were.

The deployment of the Luftwaffe's X Fliegerkorps in the Mediterranean was undertaken for three avowed purposes: to secure the Axis supply routes to North Africa, to deny the Royal Navy free rein in the Mediterranean, and to close the Suez Canal. To accomplish these aims it was clearly essential to destroy Malta as a British base. Accordingly, the sighting by an Italian aircraft of a British convoy in the Sicilian narrows signalled the opening of German attacks against Malta and the Royal Navy that were to cost the British dearly in the coming months. The British convoy was in fact part of a complex operation (Operation Excess) that had involved the sailing of a fast convoy

from Gibraltar of three merchantmen for Greece and one for Malta, with an escort (Force H) of a battleship, a battlecruiser, a carrier (HMS *Ark Royal*), two cruisers and 11 destroyers. Another convoy of two merchantmen, escorted by two battleships, a carrier (HMS *Illustrious*), six cruisers and 12 destroyers, had sailed from Alexandria so timed to arrive in the Sicilian narrows as to assume escort for the ships sailing for Greece, allowing Force H to return to Gibraltar. Also at the same time, two cruisers – HMS *Southampton* and *Gloucester* – brought troops to Malta from Alexandria before escorting eight empty merchantmen sailing in the opposite direction.

Shortly after Force H had turned back on the afternoon of 10 January, after a dawn encounter

with a pair of Italian E-boats, Fulmars were launched from *Illustrious* to meet a threat by two SM.79s, just as about 30 Ju 87R-2s of I./StG 1 and II./StG 2, led by Hauptmanns Paul-Werner Hozzel and Walter Enneccerus, arrived over the carrier. For the loss of three aircraft, the German crews scored six direct hits on *Illustrious*, which was probably saved from total loss by its armoured flight deck. As the big ship limped into French Creek at Valletta the following day, Enneccerus was airborne from Trapani and found the cruisers *Southampton* and *Gloucester*, hitting both with 1,100-lb (500-kg) bombs; badly damaged and on fire, the former had to be sunk.

Unfortunately, apart from six Fulmars whose pilots had been unable to land back on

Above: A local lad looks on as an armourer services the twin Vickers 0.303-in 'K' machine-guns from the Albacore in the background. Note the aircraft has been 'tropicalised' with a dust filter fitted to the intake above the engine.

Below: A vic of three torpedo-armed Albacore Mk Is of No. 828 Sqn, Fleet Air Arm (BF710 'S5L' nearest the camera) cruises over Malta for an official photographer. Based at Hal Far (and later Ta Kali), No. 828 Sqn was based on the island for 19 months from mid-October 1941, combining with No. 830 Sqn, for operational purposes, as Naval Air Squadron Malta from March 1942. By mid-1943 the two squadrons had sunk 30 enemy ships and damaged a further 50. As well anti-shipping sorties No. 828 Sqn undertook flare drops for the night bombing of Pantellaria, in the Sicilian Channel, in May 1943.

Above: The arrival of the Beaufort gave Malta the means by which to better confront the considerable amount of enemy shipping in the Mediterranean. This Beaufort Mk II is seen with a torpedo in its semi-recessed bay.

Right: Apparently damaged by flak during a raid on the Italian fleet, this Beaufort Mk II has made a wheels-up landing, probably at Luqa, and is seen as it is towed off the runway by a Valentine tank. Damage seems comparatively light and repairable, limited, it would seem, to its propellers, engine nacelles and lower fuselage.

Illustrious, neither convoy had been able to deliver any fighter reinforcements to Malta. With the badly damaged carrier now attracting Axis bombers like bees to honey, the island's fighter defences faced enormous odds in the coming days.

Further raids by the Luftwaffe

Bad weather and a shortage of armour-piercing bombs delayed the Luftwaffe's return until 16 January, while repairs to the *Illustrious* went ahead with all possible haste. On that day an attack by the Ju 88A-3s of LG 1 on Valletta was followed by the Ju 87Rs of StG 1 and 2; despite a spirited barrage put up by the gun defences (assisted by those of *Illustrious* and the cruiser HMAS *Perth*) which claimed five of the raiders, another direct hit was suffered by the carrier. The cruiser HMS *Essex* was struck by a bomb, which failed to explode, a particularly fortunate circumstance, as the ship was heavily laden with explosives. Eight Hurricanes of No. 261 Squadron and Fulmars of No. 806 Squadron, Fleet Air Arm, joined in and shot down five of the attackers. Two days later more than 60 bombers, with fighter escort, returned to attack Valletta and Luqa airfield. By that evening only

seven RAF fighters and two Fulmars remained serviceable, while Luqa was temporarily out of action. The next day six Hurricanes, a Sea Gladiator and a Fulmar took off to intercept an attack by 50 aircraft, whose crews concentrated on the ships once more; the fighter pilots claimed five victories and the redoubtable gun defences shot down 11 aircraft. British losses amounted to two aircraft in the air and two on the ground, in addition to a Sunderland that was sunk at its moorings in Marsaxlokk Bay. *Illustrious* suffered further minor damage from near misses, but this did not prevent the repairs from going ahead and, on 23 January, the carrier slipped out of Valletta and made all possible speed for Alexandria, where it arrived two days later to start a long period of more lasting repairs. The departure of *Illustrious* gave Malta no respite, however; it simply presented one fewer target.

Among the cargoes recently delivered by sea to the island were two low-looking COL (Chain Overseas Low Type 5) radars, one of which had been set up at Ta Silch, and the other was now being sited at Fort Maddalena on the north coast west of Valletta. As the Ju 87Rs and Ju 88As continued to attack the

airfields of Luqa and Hal Far (from where No. 261's Hurricanes now flew for the most part), new German units joined the assault, and Heinkel He 111s of 4./KG 4 and II./KG 26 systematically sea-mined the approaches to Grand Harbour, Marsamxett harbour and Marsaxlokk Bay. Messerschmitt Bf 109Es of 7./JG 26 (commanded by the much-respected Oberleutnant Joachim Muncheberg) and 1./NJG 3's Bf 110C night-fighters began to appear in Malta's skies, prompting Maynard to emphasise his former orders to the Hurricane pilots to avoid prolonged dogfighting but to worry the bombers. Fortunately, at this moment Air Chief Marshal Sir Arthur Longmore decided that he could spare six more Hurricanes from his reserves in Egypt and, on 30 January 1941, they took off from Gazala in Libya – now in British hands – and landed safely at Ta Kali. They were, however, adequate to do no more than bring one of No. 261's flights up to strength.

The almost total German air superiority now enjoyed in the central Mediterranean discouraged the British Admiralty from attempting any further air reinforcement of Malta by carrier for the time being (preferring to employ the

No. 23 Squadron's Mosquito NF.Mk IIs had their AI.Mk IV radar removed for the night-intruder role in Malta amid concerns that the still-secret equipment may fall into Axis hands. Operating from RAF Luqa over southern Italy in the autumn of 1943 and later detached to Sigonella on Sicily, No. 23 Squadron's were the first Mosquitoes to operate in the Mediterranean theatre.

Almost certainly at Luqa, Baltimores (possibly of No. 223 Sqn) are 'bombed up' and serviced prior to a raid on Axis forces retreating from Sicily. Although a tempting target to Axis bombers, British air superiority over Malta had been established by this time.

carriers HMS *Argus* and *Furious* on the route to Takoradi in West Africa, from where fighters could be flown to the Middle East in greater safety). German and Italian air attacks on the island continued unabated throughout February, and on 26 February a particularly savage raid on Luqa by 30 Ju 87s and 12 Ju 88A-4s (the latter commanded by the legendary Hauptmann Hajo Herrman) destroyed six of No. 148 Squadron's Wellingtons and damaged seven others. Although the defending Hurricanes had succeeded in penetrating the escorting screen of Bf 109Es and MC.200s to shoot down two of the attackers, Maynard now conceded that Malta's own offensive striking force had been virtually eliminated, and reluctantly ordered the surviving bombers to leave the island for Egypt.

Since mid-June 1940, Malta's fighters – never exceeding more than about a score, and usually much fewer – had claimed the destruction of 96 Italian and German aircraft (losses almost precisely confirmed in Axis records) for the loss in air combat of 16 RAF and FAA fighters and 11 pilots. The fighting during the first 10 days of March 1941 claimed three more pilots and seven Hurricanes. By the end of that month only six fighters could be counted as even airworthy.

Salvation came from two sources. Heavy fighting in Cyrenaica and the invasion of the Balkans by German forces resulted in the redeployment of much of X. Fliegerkorps from Sicily to distant bases, and the slackening of Axis pressure in the central Mediterranean encouraged the British Admiralty to sail HMS *Ark Royal* towards Malta on 3 April with 12 Hurricanes, all of which arrived safely. Before the month was out, *Ark Royal* returned once more, this time with 24 Hurricane Mk IIBs which, combining with No. 1430 Flight, now formed No. 185 Squadron at Hal Far. This squadron also absorbed the survivors of No. 261 Squadron, the latter being formally disbanded on 17 May.

More Hurricanes arrive

Believing that, with the departure of the bombers, Malta's teeth had been finally drawn, the Regia Aeronautica and remaining Luftwaffe units in the Mediterranean left the island largely to its own devices, thinking that significant reinforcement would prove impossible. This belief was proved to be mistaken by the arrival of 46 cannon-armed Hurricane Mk IICs in May (from HMS *Ark Royal* and *Furious*) and another 143 Hurricane IIBs and IICs in June, in the course of four operations involving HMS *Ark Royal*, *Furious* and *Victorious*. These aircraft equipped Nos 126, 185 and 249 Squadrons, while six Hurricanes were modified as photo-reconnaissance variants and taken on charge by No. 69 Squadron (which had been formed from a nucleus provided by the Maryland-equipped No. 431 Flight early in 1941).

By the beginning of July, the Hurricane Mk II fighter-bombers had started to regain the initiative with offensive sweeps over Sicily. For example, on 9 July four Hurricane Mk IICs of No. 185 Squadron, led by its CO, Squadron Leader Peter William Olber Mould, attacked the Italian seaplane base at Syracuse, destroying six aircraft and damaging four others with cannon fire. On 26 July six Italian E-boats, escorted by MC.200s, attempted to attack shipping in Valletta's Grand Harbour; the Hurricanes of Nos 126 and 185 Squadrons were scrambled and set about the E-boats, sinking four and causing the other two to surrender. One of the latter was literally 'captured' by No. 185 Squadron, whose Pilot Officer Winton had been forced to bale out of his Hurricane; swimming to the nearest E-boat, he climbed aboard to find the entire crew dead.

Thus emboldened by the strengthened fighter defences, it fell to Malta's newly-appointed Air Officer Commanding, Air Vice-Marshal Hugh Pughe Lloyd, CBE, MC, WC, to make ready for the return of the bomber force. In May a small detachment of Blenheim Mk IVs from No. 139 Squadron flew to Luqa for a fortnight, and in July the whole of No. 195 Squadron arrived on the island, soon to be followed by No. 107, both flying Blenheims at Luqa. By the end of October this airfield hosted the Wellingtons of No. 40 Squadron, together with detachments from Nos 38 and 102, the

Above: Complete with nose art, Baltimore Mk IIIA FA353 of No. 69 (GR) Sqn undergoes maintenance in revetments at RAF Luqa, 1943.

Right: As well as bombing missions, Baltimores undertook reconnaissance tasks. Here a No. 69 Sqn aircraft returns to Luqa, a member of its crew handing over film as the aircraft taxies to a halt.

Spitfire Mk VB BP844 leaves the deck of HMS Eagle on 21 March 1942 during Operation Picket I, the second delivery of Spitfires to Malta. Nine Spitfires were despatched from the carrier, all reaching their destination. Note that the RAF crews followed naval practice and launched with their cockpits open in case a rapid exit was required.

Blenheims of No. 107 Squadron and the PR Hurricanes and Marylands of No. 69 Squadron. At Hal Far were the Hurricane Mk IIs of No. 185, while those of Nos 126 and 249 were based at Ta Kali.

By this time, of course, Rommel's Afrika Korps were fully established in North Africa. The British Commonwealth armies, which had advanced far into Cyrenaica during the previous winter, had been forced back almost to the Egyptian border. Throughout the Axis advance eastwards through Cyrenaica, the Germans and Italians contrived to supply their armies by sea from Europe to the ports of Tripoli and Benghazi. It was such shipping, both in port and on the high seas, that the bombers – as well as the Fleet Air Arm Swordfish based on Malta – constantly attacked, to such effect that roughly three-quarters of all supply shipping available to the Axis in the Mediterranean was sunk or destroyed during the summer and early autumn of 1941 by Allied aircraft and naval forces. Of the 220,000 tons (223520 tonnes) sunk (90 per cent of which was southbound shipping) between 1 June and 31 October, 115,000 tons (116840 tonnes) were accounted for by the RAF and Fleet Air Arm – about 85,000 tons (86360 tonnes) by aircraft based on Malta.

October 1941 found General Sir Claude Auchinleck and the Eighth Army under Cunningham preparing for a new offensive in the Western Desert (Operation Crusader), as Air Marshal Sir Arthur Tedder, now commanding RAF Middle East, mustered 49 squadrons, nine of which were based on Malta. In spite of the losses sustained by the Axis in the previous months, Rommel was also building up his forces in preparation for a new offensive into Egypt. However, his supply situation was so desperate that, at the expense of his forces in Russia, Hitler ordered the Luftwaffe back to Sicily in strength during November.

Although Crusader was launched before Rommel was ready, and did succeed in forcing the Axis armies back through Cyrenaica, once more the newly-established German air strength in the central Mediterranean enabled considerable reinforcements to be sailed to North Africa. The period between December 1941 and June 1942 constituted one of utmost peril for the island of Malta. By mid-December, Lloyd possessed 60 serviceable bombers and 70 fighters; ranged against him in Sicily were about 250 bombers and reconnaissance aircraft and 200 fighters (both German and Italian). During the last week of the year the enemy attacked the island's air bases with 200 aircraft. Moreover, by now the Messerschmitt Bf 109F had replaced the 'Emil', and proved much superior to the Hurricane, while unnaturally heavy raids reduced Hal Far and Ta Kali to quagmires.

Early in January 1942. German air attacks on Malta increased rapidly in ferocity, scarcely a day

Above: With a Vokes filter and long-range belly ferry tank fitted a Spitfire Mk VC is held as its Merlin is run-up before take-off. USS Wasp joined HMS Eagle in ferrying a further 64 Spitfires (of which four were lost) to Malta during May 1942 under Operation Bowery. The successful completion of this duty prompted Winston Churchill to ask the question, "Who says a Wasp cannot sting twice?".

Right: With 14 Grumman F4F-3s of VF-71 visible in the foreground, 12 Spitfire Mk VCs of No. 601 Sqn are seen on the deck of USS Wasp (CV-7) on 19 April 1942, the day the RAF fighters left for Malta during Operation Calendar. A further 35 Spitfires were lashed down below decks, these being brought up to the flight deck with engines running following the launch of those aircraft that had travelled from the UK as deck cargo.

Above: No. 126 Sqn moved from Ta Kali to Luqa and re-equipped with Spitfires in May 1942. Spitfire Mk VB EP257 (top) is believed to have been one of its aircraft and is seen here being guided along an unpaved taxiway, probably at Luqa.

Below: Mk VB ER471 of No. 126 Sqn heads a line up of Spitfires at RAF Luqa in mid-1942, after it had adopted 'MK' codes. No. 126 Sqn later served in Sicily and Italy, but was withdrawn to England to support Operation Overlord in April 1944.

Deliveries of aircraft to Malta by aircraft-carrier

code name	date	carrier(s)	embarked/delivered
HURRY	2 Aug 1940	Argus	12/12 Hurricanes
WHITE	17 Nov 1940	Argus	12/4 Hurricanes, 2/1 Skua
WINCH	3 Apr 1941	Ark Royal	12/12 Hurricanes
DUNLOP	27 Apr 1941	Ark Royal	24/23 Hurricanes
SPLICE	21 May 1941	Ark Royal/Furious	48/46 Hurricanes
ROCKET	6 Jun 1941	Ark Royal/Furious	44/43 Hurricanes
TRACER	14 Jun 1941	Ark Royal/Victorious	48/45 Hurricanes
RAILWAY I	27 Jun 1941	Ark Royal	22/21 Hurricanes
RAILWAY II	30 Jun 1941	Ark Royal/Furious	42/34 Hurricanes
SUBSTANCE	25 Jul 1941	Ark Royal	7/7 Swordfish
STATUS I	9 Sept 1941	Ark Royal	14/14 Hurricanes
STATUS II	13 Sept 1941	Ark Royal/Furious	46/45 Hurricanes
CALLBOY	18 Oct 1941	Ark Royal	11/11 Albacores
PERPETUAL	12 Nov 1941	Ark Royal/Argus	37/34 Hurricanes
SPOTTER	7 Mar 1942	Argus/Eagle	15/15 Spitfires
PICKET I	21 Mar 1942	Eagle	9/9 Spitfires
PICKET II	29 Mar 1942	Eagle	7/7 Spitfires
CALENDER	20 Apr 1942	USS Wasp	47/46 Spitfires
BOWERY	9 May 1942	USS Wasp/Eagle	64/60 Spitfires
LB	19 May 1942	Eagle/Argus	17/17 Spitfires
STYLE	3 Jun 1942	Eagle	31/27 Spitfires
SALIENT	9 Jun 1942	Eagle	32/32 Spitfires
PINPOINT	15 Jul 1942	Eagle	32/31 Spitfires
INSECT	21 Jul 1942	Eagle	30/28 Spitfires
BELLOWS	11 Aug 1942	Furious	38/37 Spitfires
BARITONE	17 Aug 1942	Furious	32/29 Spitfires
TRAIN	29 Oct 1942	Furious	31/29 Spitfires

Summary
361 Hurricanes were despatched over 16 months with the loss of 28 aircraft; 385 Spitfires were despatched over eight months with the loss of 18 aircraft; 20 other aircraft were despatched for the loss of one.

passing on which Valletta's sirens did not sound, often as many as six times. By this time, warning of such raids was provided by two long-range CO and four COL radars, their main site having been established on the high ground at Dingli on the southwest coast of Malta. The raids were being flown by elements of Luftflotte 2 under Generalfeldmarschall Albert Kesselring, and General Bruno Loerzer's II. Fliegerkorps. As the weeks passed, the latter alone increased in strength to more than 400 aircraft, including the Ju 88A-4s of KG 54 and the Bf 109F-4s of II./JG 3 'Udet' and JG 54 'Grünherz'.

Although the Blenheims of Nos 21 and 107 Squadrons managed to make a diminishing number of attacks on enemy bases, even

destroying 11 Axis transport aircraft at Castelvetrano on 4 January, it was obvious that large quantities of supplies and reinforcements were succeeding in reaching North Africa, often undetected and seldom attacked. Once more it was decided to reduce the island's bomber force, and on 22 February the Blenheims were flown to Egypt, leaving only the Wellington ICs of No. 40 Squadron and the anti-shipping Wellington Mk VIIIs of No. 221.

The first Spitfires arrive

All this could not have occurred at a worse time for the Eighth Army, which had advanced deep into Cyrenaica and captured Benghazi. On 21 January Rommel attacked and caught the British ground forces by surprise, and by May they were defending a line south from Gazala. By the end of February, Lloyd could seldom put more than a score of fighters into the air to meet the raids on Malta, and low-level sweeps by German fighters rendered even these efforts extremely hazardous. No convoy, with food, fuel, ammunition or aircraft

reinforcements, had arrived since November. So essential was it that the island's defences be strengthened once more, that on 7 March HMS Eagle launched 15 Spitfire VBs for Malta, led by Squadron Leader Edward John Gracie, RAF – the first such fighters to reach the Mediterranean – covered by four Beaufighters, detached for the purpose. Sixteen more Spitfires followed later in the month.

Although the new fighters gave a welcome boost to the morale of the hard-pressed islanders, they could do little to counter the swarms of enemy raiders which now attacked Malta almost daily. Nevertheless, the US, now at war with Germany, was able to send the carrier USS Wasp to join HMS Eagle and Argus in the Mediterranean with a total of more than 120 Spitfire Mk Vs for Malta during April and May. These reinforcements certainly saved Malta and were, in part, responsible for a reduction in Kesselring's air attacks after mid-May. For their part, the Germans began laying plans to launch an invasion of the island in the autumn, as part of an all-out offensive to drive the Allies out of the Mediterranean. On 1 July, as Axis preparations for this offensive began with increased supplies once more being shipped to Tripoli, Kesselring reopened his

Italian personnel examine Spitfire Mk VC BR112/'X' of 185 Sqn after it crash-landed on the beach at Scoglitti, Sicily on 9 September 1942. Its pilot, Sgt Claude Weaver (an American who had joined the RCAF in 1941), had just shot down an Italian MC.202 but had sustained damage in the process. Weaver was taken prisoner, but was released after the Italian surrender and returned to England, where he joined No. 403 Sqn, RCAF. Sadly he was killed in January 1944, though not before scoring his 12th kill. BR112 was among the aircraft delivered to Malta in April 1942. Its blue paint scheme, hastily applied over the original desert colours on Malta, shows signs of peeling.

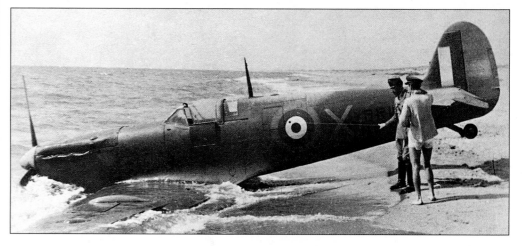

RAF squadrons in Malta, 1940-46

LUQA

unit	dates	aircraft type
No. 21 Sqn	26 Dec 41 – 14 Mar 42	Blenheim Mk IV
No. 23 Sqn	27 Dec 42 – 7 Dec 43	Mosquito Mk II/VI
No. 38 Sqn (det.)	9 Aug 41 – 26 Oct 41	Wellington Mk IC
No. 39 Sqn	20 Aug 42 – 9 Dec 42	Beaufort Mk I
	21 Jan 43 – 27 Jan 43	
No. 40 Sqn	31 Oct 41 – May 42	Wellington Mk IC
	25 Nov 42 – 20 Jan 43	Wellington Mk III
No. 69 Sqn	10 Jan 41 – 7 Feb 44	Maryland/Spitfire/ Hurricane/Mosquito/ Baltimore/Wellington
No. 92 Sqn	14 Jun 43 – 13 Jul 43	Spitfire Mk IX
No. 104 Sqn (det.)	18 Oct 41 – 3 Jan 42	Wellington Mk II
	6 Nov 43 – 21 Jan 43	
No. 105 Sqn	28 Jul 41 – 27 Sep 41	Blenheim Mk IV
No. 107 Sqn	20 Aug 41 – 12 Jan 42	Blenheim Mk IV
No. 108 Sqn	3 Jul 43 – 1 Jul 44	Beaufighter Mk VI
No. 110 Sqn (det.)	1 Jul 41 – 28 Jul 41	Blenheim Mk IV
No. 126 Sqn	1 May 42 – 10 Jun 43	Spitfire Mk VC
No. 139 Sqn (det.)	17 May 41 – 9 Jun 41	Blenheim Mk IV
No. 145 Sqn	14 Jun 43 – 13 Jul 43	Spitfire Mk V
No. 148 Sqn	14 Dec 40 – 9 Mar 41	Wellington Mk IC
	Dec 42	
No. 217 Sqn	10 Jun 42 – 25 Aug 42	Beaufort Mk II
No. 221 Sqn	8 Jan 42 – 26 Aug 42	Wellington Mk VIII
	22 Jan 43 – 31 Mar 43	Wellington Mk XI
No. 223 Sqn (det.)	20 Jul 43 – 10 Aug 43	Baltimore Mk IV
No. 227 Sqn	20 Aug 42 – 25 Nov 42	Beaufighter Mk VI
No. 250 Sqn	Jul 43	Kittyhawk Mk III
No. 252 Sqn (det.)	May 41	Beaufighter Mk I
No. 256 Sqn (det.)	2 Jul 43 – 25 Aug 43	Mosquito Mk XII
	14 Oct 43 – 7 Apr 44	
No. 272 Sqn	Jul 43	Beaufighter Mk VI
No. 417 Sqn, RCAF	Jul 43	Spitfire Mk VB/VC
No. 450 Sqn, RAAF	Jul 43	Kittyhawk Mk III
No. 600 Sqn	25 Jun 43 – 26 Jul 43	Beaufighter Mk VI
No. 601 Sqn	15 Jun 43 – 14 Jul 43	Spitfire Mk V
No. 683 Sqn	8 Feb 43 – 22 Nov 43	Spitfire IV/XI
No. 1435 Sqn	2 Aug 42 – Oct 43	Spitfire Mk VB/VC/IX

HAL FAR

unit	dates	aircraft type
No. 43 Sqn	11 Jun 43 – 14 Jul 43	Spitfire Mk VC
No. 72 Sqn	10 Jun 43 – 17 Jul 43	Spitfire Mk VC
No. 93 Sqn	12 Jun 43 – 14 Jul 43	Spitfire Mk VC
No. 108 Sqn	Jul 44	Beaufighter Mk VI
No. 185 Sqn	27 Apr 41 – 5 Jun 43	Hurricane/Spitfire
	24 Sep 43 – 30 Jan 44	Spitfire Mk VC
No. 229 Sqn	28 Mar 42 – 29 Apr 42	Hurricane Mk IIC
	24 Sep 43 – 30 Jan 44	Spitfire Mk VC
No. 243 Sqn	11 Jun 43 – 14 Jul 43	Spitfire Mk VC
No. 249 Sqn	24 Sep 43 – 27 Oct 43	Spitfire Mk IX
No. 250 Sqn	Jul 43	Kittyhawk Mk III
No. 261 Sqn	1 Aug 40 – 17 May 41	Hurricane Mk I
No. 283 Sqn	6 Apr 44 – 31 Mar 46	Warwick (ASR)
No. 284 Sqn	Jul 43	Walrus (ASR)
No. 605 Sqn	10 Jan 42 – 12 Feb 42	Hurricane Mk IIB

KALAFRANA

unit	dates	aircraft type
No. 228 Sqn (det.)	Jun 40 – Mar 41	Sunderland Mk I
No. 230 Sqn (det.)	Jun 40 – Jul 40	Sunderland Mk I

SAFI

unit	dates	aircraft type
No. 111 Sqn	10 Jun 43 – 15 Jul 43	Spitfire Mk V/IX
No. 112 Sqn	Jul 43	Kittyhawk Mk III
No. 126 Sqn	10 Jun 43 – 23 Sep 43	Spitfire Mk VC/IX

TA KALI

unit	dates	aircraft type
No. 81 Sqn	4 Jun 43 – 20 Jul 43	Spitfire Mk VC/IX
No. 126 Sqn	28 Jan 41 – 1 May 42	Hurricane Mk IIB/IIC
No. 152 Sqn	6 Jun 43 – 27 Jul 43	Spitfire Mk VC
No. 154 Sqn	4 Jun 43 – 20 Jul 43	Spitfire Mk VC
No. 227 Sqn	25 Nov 42 – 1 Mar 43	Beaufighter Mk VI
No. 229 Sqn	3 Aug 42 – 10 Dec 42	Spitfire Mk VC
No. 232 Sqn	5 Jun 43 – 18 Jul 43	Spitfire Mk IV/IX
No. 238 Sqn	Jun 41	Hurricane Mk I
No. 242 Sqn	5 Jun 43 – 22 Jul 43	Spitfire Mk VC/IX
No. 248 Sqn	3 Aug 42 – 13 Sep 42	Spitfire Mk VC
No. 249 Sqn	21 May 41 – 23 Nov 42	Hurricane/Spitfire
No. 272 Sqn	6 Nov 42 – 4 Jun 43	Beaufighter Mk I/VI
No. 603 Sqn	20 Apr 42 – 3 Aug 42	Spitfire Mk VC
No. 605 Sqn	Feb 42	Hurricane Mk IIB

QRENDI

unit	dates	aircraft type
No. 185 Sqn	5 Jun 43 – 10 Oct 43	Spitfire Mk VC
No. 229 Sqn	10 Dec 42 – 24 Sep 43	Spitfire Mk VC
No. 249 Sqn	23 Nov 42 – 24 Sep 43	Spitfire Mk VC

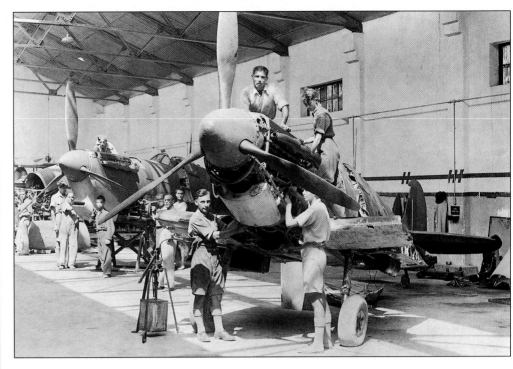

Top: Life for the Malta-based fighters was punishing. Spitfire Mk Vs undergoing repair and maintenance indoors at a Maintenance Unit, location unknown, during 1942.

Right: No. 1435 Squadron operated Spitfire Mk Vs and IXs from Luqa, using a 'V' unit code. This Mk V, seen in 1943, was employed as a 'met' aircraft and occasionally as a target tug. Note the lug fitted below the rudder for the latter role.

attacks on Malta. Two Allied convoys, with a total of 17 merchant ships, had battled their way to the island from east and west during June, but only two merchntmen reached their destination, and those at a cost of one cruiser and four destroyers sunk – despite escorts amounting to two carriers, a battleship, 12 cruisers and no fewer than 43 destroyers.

Keith Park replaces Lloyd

During the first half of July, about 1,000 sorties were flown by German and Italian aircraft against the island, during which 42 were destroyed (or about 10 per cent of the force available) for the loss of 39 Hurricanes and Spitfires, 26 of whose pilots were saved. It was at this time that air command on Malta passed to that supreme fighter exponent, Air Vice-Marshal Keith Park, as Lloyd was given a well-earned rest from his exertions.

If Malta was to survive as an effective offensive base in the run-up to the major Allied operations being planned for the late autumn of 1942, it was imperative that a fresh effort be made to sail another convoy to the island. Operation Pedestal involved the sailing in August of 14 merchant ships through the Gibraltar straits, where their escort was increased to four fleet carriers, two battleships, seven cruisers and 24 destroyers. About 100 aircraft (including four Liberators, a squadron of Beaufighters and an additional squadron of Wellingtons) were flown to Malta to increase Park's strength to some 250 aircraft, in an effort to cover the approach of the convoy, whose presence had become known to

the enemy almost as soon as it entered the Mediterranean. From 11 August, the convoy came under continuous attack from air and sea forces but, at a cost of one carrier (HMS *Eagle*), two cruisers, a destroyer and 18 RAF and Fleet Air Arm aircraft, five merchantmen (including a vital tanker) sailed or were towed into Grand Harbour.

The 55,000 tons (55880 tonnes) of materiel delivered to Malta in Operation Pedestal enabled the defences of the island to be strengthened immeasurably, especially as HMS *Furious* had taken the opportunity to deliver 37 more Spitfires. It was now safe to deploy a squadron of torpedo-carrying Beauforts and one of Beaufighters at Luqa permanently, as Park steadily began to increase his striking power.

By the winter of 1942/43, as fighting on the Russian front claimed the highest priority for aircraft of the Luftwaffe and the great battles of Stalingrad and El Alamein signalled the turn of fortunes for the Axis, Malta's aircraft had seized the initiative, and German plans to invade the island evaporated. Moreover, as Italian aircraft factories came increasingly to feel the punishment of UK-based RAF heavy-bombers, the Regia Aeronautica – always hitherto capable of mounting aggravating and occasionally highly successful attacks in the Mediterranean – entered a sharp decline, from which it was never to recover. At the beginning of 1943 Park possessed four squadrons of Spitfire Mk Vs (Nos 126, 185, 229 and 249), two of Wellington Mk IIs and IIIs (Nos 40 and 104) and two of Beaufighter Mk VIs (Nos 227 and 272), plus No. 23 Squadron with

Three of No. 249 Sqn's battle-scarred Spitfire Mk VCs are seen at RAF Ta Kali during a quiet period in the fighting during 1942.

Right: Four of No. 249 Sqn's Spitfire Mk Vs on patrol off the coast of Malta in 1943. Note that the lead aircraft ('T-A') and nearest ('T-T') have clipped wings while the other two have standard-length wings.

Mosquito night-fighters, No. 39 with Beauforts, and No. 69 with various PR aircraft.

Now that long-range aircraft were based in Egypt, capable of striking enemy ports throughout the central and eastern Mediterranean theatres, the tasks of Malta's aircraft could be confined to searching for, shadowing and attacking enemy shipping at sea, and it was during the crucial period that culminated in the Eighth Army's victorious advance along the length of Libya's coast that Park's aircraft contributed to the eclipse of Axis maritime traffic with North Africa. Moreover, during the vulnerable phase of Allied landings in Algeria (Operation Torch), Malta-based aircraft – particularly the Spitfires – maintained a series of sweeps over airfields in Sicily to prevent any serious attempt by Axis aircraft to interfere with the landings.

During the final stages of the campaign in Tunisia, when enemy shipping sailed in frantic efforts to deliver supplies to the doomed Afrika Korps through ports such as Sfax and Sousse, Allied aircraft, including Malta-based bombers, sank no fewer than 20 supply ships. When the Germans eventually resorted to the use of transport aircraft, such as the painfully vulnerable Ju 52/3m and the ungainly Messerschmitt Me 323, to deliver fuel supplies to the dwindling Axis forces hemmed in on the Cape Bon peninsula, the Malta-based Spitfires were ideally situated to join the massacre.

Invasion of Sicily

Final retribution for the years of trial by fire and explosive was accorded to the people of Malta as preparations were made for the Allied invasion of Sicily. Beginning in June 1943, Air Chief Marshal Sir Arthur Tedder, by then Air Commander-in-Chief, Mediterranean Air Command, started his deployment of an extraordinary concentration of Allied aircraft on the tiny island. By the middle of that month, in addition to two Fleet Air Arm squadrons and two of the South African Air Force, the RAF

Maltese Spitfires

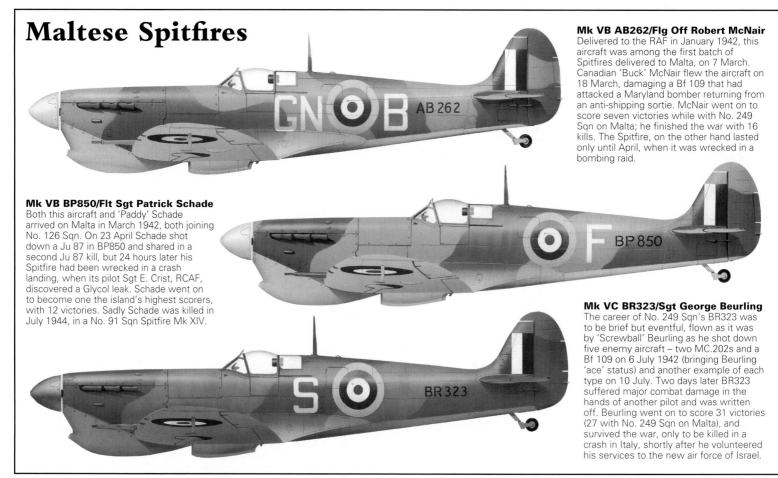

Mk VB AB262/Flg Off Robert McNair
Delivered to the RAF in January 1942, this aircraft was among the first batch of Spitfires delivered to Malta, on 7 March. Canadian 'Buck' McNair flew the aircraft on 18 March, damaging a Bf 109 that had attacked a Maryland bomber returning from an anti-shipping sortie. McNair went on to score seven victories while with No. 249 Sqn on Malta; he finished the war with 16 kills. The Spitfire, on the other hand lasted only until April, when it was wrecked in a bombing raid.

Mk VB BP850/Flt Sgt Patrick Schade
Both this aircraft and 'Paddy' Schade arrived on Malta in March 1942, both joining No. 126 Sqn. On 23 April Schade shot down a Ju 87 in BP850 and shared in a second Ju 87 kill, but 24 hours later his Spitfire had been wrecked in a crash landing, when its pilot Sgt E. Crist, RCAF, discovered a Glycol leak. Schade went on to become one the island's highest scorers, with 12 victories. Sadly Schade was killed in July 1944, in a No. 91 Sqn Spitfire Mk XIV.

Mk VC BR323/Sgt George Beurling
The career of No. 249 Sqn's BR323 was to be brief but eventful, flown as it was by 'Screwball' Beurling as he shot down five enemy aircraft – two MC.202s and a Bf 109 on 6 July 1942 (bringing Beurling 'ace' status) and another example of each type on 10 July. Two days later BR323 suffered major combat damage in the hands of another pilot and was written off. Beurling went on to score 31 victories (27 with No. 249 Sqn on Malta), and survived the war, only to be killed in a crash in Italy, shortly after he volunteered his services to the new air force of Israel.

Left: Wg Cdr Peter Prosser Hanks, CO of the Luqa Spitfire Wing from August 1942 is seen here (centre) chatting to fellow pilots including, to his immediate left, Battle of France ace Sqn Ldr Maurice Stephens, CO of No. 229 Sqn from 13 November.

Right: Canadian Flt Lt George F. Beurling (variously nick-named 'Buzz' and 'Screwball') scored 27 kills while serving with No. 249 Sqn at RAF Ta Kali between June and October 1942.

Below right: P/O Reade Tilley DFC, an American in the RCAF, scored seven victories while with No. 126 Sqn. Here his Spitfire Mk VB is serviced between sorties.

deployed 15 squadrons of Spitfire Mk VCs, one of Spitfire Mk IXs, one of Mosquitoes, a Beaufighter squadron, and two photographic reconnaissance squadrons; to these were added in the next four weeks an RCAF squadron of Spitfire Mk VCs, four Kittyhawk squadrons (including one of the SAAF), one of Baltimores, one of Mosquito Mk XII night-fighters, another Spitfire Mk IX squadron, and the Walrus amphibians of an air-sea rescue squadron – a grand total of 407 aircraft.

Early on 10 July the first Allied forces went ashore on the southern coasts of Sicily. During the preceding hours of darkness, the monotonous drone of scores of glider-towing aircraft had been clearly heard on Malta. As dawn approached, the first Spitfires and Kittyhawks

took off from Luqa, Safi, Qrendi and Hal Far to mount guard over this first great air- and seaborne invasion of Europe.

At the height of Malta's suffering under the assault by enemy bombers, King George VI had approved the award of the George Cross to the island and its courageous people. This was the highest award for gallantry available to civilians, which the King had caused to be instituted in September 1940, at the height of the Battle of Britain. Within its instituting Royal Warrant are the words "the Cross shall be awarded only for acts of the greatest heroism or of the most conspicuous courage in circumstances of extreme danger" Who could deny that the Maltese were well qualified for such an award?

Francis K. Mason

Maltese Spitfire camouflage

As standard Dark Earth/Middle Stone desert camouflage tended to be somewhat conspicuous when viewed over water, the Middle Stone shade was often overpainted with whatever was available locally – often a shade of blue. Spitfires delivered later were finished in 'temperate' Slate Grey/Dark Green camouflage.

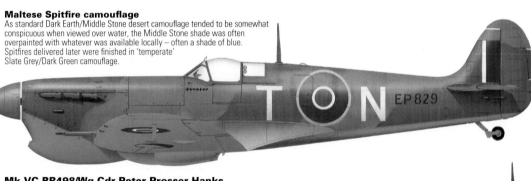

Mk VB EP829/Sqn Ldr John J. Lynch

American John Lynch, a veteran of No. 71 'Eagle' Sqn, scored his fifth victory in this aircraft and went on to command No. 249 Sqn at Krendi. His claim of a Ju 52/3m on 28 April 1943 (one of 3½ he shot down that day) was classed as 'Malta's 1000th victory', Lynch finishing the war with 10 kills, all claimed on Spitfire Mk Vs. Joining the USAF post-war, he was killed in an F-84G in 1956. Ironically, Spitfire EP829 was among the Mk Vs delivered to the Aeronautica Militare Italiana in 1946.

Mk VC BR498/Wg Cdr Peter Prosser Hanks

This Spitfire arrived on Malta during one of the July 1942 reinforcement operations and served with Nos 126, 1435 and 185 Sqns and, finally, the Malta Conversion Flight. In October 1942 the aircraft was the personal mount of Hurricane ace Peter Prosser Hanks, who had been posted to Malta to command the Luqa Wing. During that first month on the island, Hanks added three Bf 109s and a Ju 88 to his score, finishing the war with 13 victories.

Mk VC JK715/Sqn Ldr Evan Mackie

This Mk V is likely to have been the most successful of all the RAF's Mk Vs, having been credited with the destruction of eight enemy aircraft, 1 probable and four shared – all whilst flown by New Zealander Evan Mackie, OC No. 243 Sqn at Hal Far. Of note are its Mk IX-style exhaust stubs fitted at Mackie's request to increase speed. Mackie later flew Spitfire Mk VIIIs in Italy, as CO of No. 92 Sqn, and finished the war with 20 kills, having converted to Tempests, on which he commanded No. 80 Sqn in Germany and, later, No. 122 Wing.

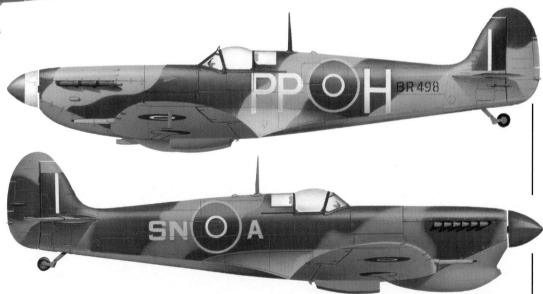

Luftwaffe Markings: Part 3

Tactical Symbols, Markings and Identification Codes of German Military Aircraft 1919-45

'Heinrich-Ulrich', a 10. Staffel Ju 88 of an unidentified bomber unit, clearly has a training role. This is indicated by the large white numeral '17' carried on its vertical tail surface. The aircraft of many IV. Gruppen of frontline Kampfgeschwader were used to train replacement crews.

As the war progressed, changing circumstances and operational requirements not only led to some revisions of, and additions to, the two basic systems of markings already described, they also resulted in certain branches of the flying arm – the ground-assault and transport units, for example – introducing their own marking schemes for tactical formation and recognition purposes. Without venturing too deeply into the quagmire of wartime marking minutiae, some of the more important developments may be summarised in this concluding article.

Fighters

Most new Jagdgruppen which were added to existing Geschwadern after the outbreak of war, and most new Jagdgeschwader which were themselves activated during the course of hostilities (JGs 4,5 and 11, for example), fell into line with the basic system. Some units, however, adopted additional coloured markings to meet special situations. As the only large fighter formation stationed in north-west Germany at the beginning of 1943, JG 1 added black and white horizontal stripes and checkerboards to the cowlings of its Fw 190s as an aid to instant air-to-air recognition during the opening rounds of its long-fought campaign against the United States 8th Air Force's daylight incursions into Reich airspace. Towards the end of that same year, at the opposite extremity of Hitler's innermost 'Festung Europa' – in Austria and along the south-eastern approaches – the Bf 109s of JG 27 carried all-white rudder and vertical tail surfaces (similar to those first used by JG 26 in immediate pre-war manoeuvres) to indicate Staffel and Schwarm leaders engaged against the US 15th Air Force striking northwards from Italy.

Several other autonomous Jagdgruppen and Staffeln which played brief, or minor, roles in the defence of the Reich during these early months also displayed certain variations. The short-lived Jagdgruppen 25 and 50, established during the latter half of 1943 to combat not only the American heavies, but also high-flying reconnaissance Mosquitos of the RAF, elected to carry their individual aircraft numbers

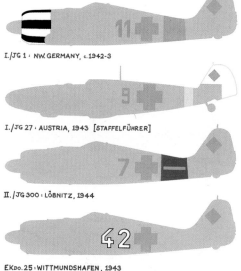

I./JG 1 : N.W. GERMANY, c.1942-3

I./JG 27 : AUSTRIA, 1943 [STAFFELFÜHRER]

II./JG 300 : LÖBNITZ, 1944

EKDo. 25 : WITTMUNDSHAFEN, 1943

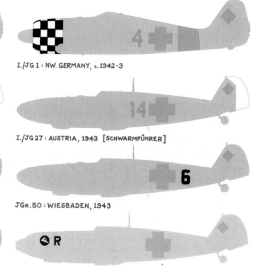

I./JG 1 : N.W. GERMANY, c.1942-3

I./JG 27 : AUSTRIA, 1943 [SCHWARMFÜHRER]

JGR.50 : WIESBADEN, 1943

WERKSCHUTZSTAFFEL FIESELER, 1940 [PILOT: ANTON RIEDIGER]

– in the appropriate Staffel colour – aft of the cross. In addition, a number of aircraft plants, particularly those manufacturing the Bf 109, set up their own factory defence squadrons (Werkschutzstaffeln)

during the course of the war. Although perhaps not part of the Luftwaffe proper, they too bore their own distinguishing markings. One of the first such squadrons was that established by the Fieseler factories (Fieseler had been part of the Bf 109 production programme since 1938). In 1939-40 its Bf 109Es displayed the Fieseler company emblem, together with the initial of the works test pilot who flew the fighter – both in blue – on their engine cowlings.

This Bf 109G-6, flown by Leutnant Emil Clade of 7./JG 27 in December 1943, displays the white rudder denoting a Schwarmführer (i.e. a leader of a formation of four aircraft) and has a white Mediterranean fuselage band.

Bombers

As with the fighters, most subsequent wartime additions to the ranks of the bomber arm adopted the basic system which had been laid down for them. One minor refinement was the decision by some units to repeat the aicraft's 'last two' (or sometimes just the individual letter) on the leading edge of the wing; presumably for purposes of ground-marshalling. A number of aircraft types, among them the Fw 200 and He 177, likewise carried their individual letter repeated on the front of the nose.

The application of temporary night finish to bombers participating in the Blitz of 1940-41 often resulted in part of the fuselage code's becoming obscured. The individual aircraft letter, however, was normally either carefully retained, or re-applied over the matt black camouflage; sometimes simply in chalk. Other units took to repeating the 'last two' in small letters on the tailfin. This latter became common procedure on the Do 17s, and later Do 217s, of KG 2 operating by night over the United Kingdom and was, at times, extended to include the entire four-part code (a practice also encountered on some Ju 188s towards the end of the war when some bomber units displayed a small four-part code on the tailfin, either in conjunction with a single individual aircraft letter behind the fuselage Balkenkreuz, or in lieu of fuselage coding altogether).

But the most noticeable and commonplace wartime development of the four-part system was the reduction of the first half of it – the parent unit letter/number code combination (carried to the left of the Balkenkreuz) – to about a fifth of its former size. This occurred throughout all units of all branches using the system. But only one Gruppe, IV./KG 51, is so far known to have reduced the size of the final (Staffel code) letter as well; its Me 410s for a while displaying only the individual aircraft letter at the normal size. Tactical markings were also revived during the latter stages of the war. In the west, the coloured tailfin tips (top or bottom) applied to some Do 217s of the 'pathfinding' KGs 6 and 66 are believed to have been

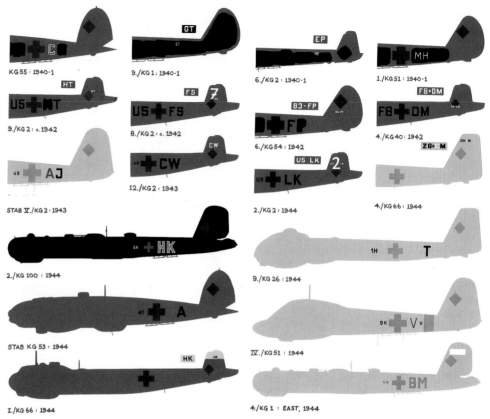

used to indicate machines carrying special radio-guidance equipment. On the Eastern Front, the Luftwaffe's last 'mass' bombing raids – by up to 50 or more He 177s of KG 1 at a time – resulted in the reintroduction of white bars on the vertical tail surfaces somewhat reminiscent of the heady days of the Battle of Britain. Presumably intended for tactical formation rather than recognition purposes, KG 1 added to the earlier system by also utilising a white triangle to identify the Staffel leaders' aircraft.

Right: Although most temporary black night finishes left some indication of aircraft identity, this He 111 – equipped with the unsuccessful balloon fender device – appears to have taken matters to the extreme. In fact, the aircraft was from 4./KG 27 (coded 1G+ZM) and hit a hill near Lulworth Cove, Dorset on 22 May 1941. The retention of the glaring white fuselage cross seems to defeat the object of night camouflage – unless, of course, the camouflage was rubbed off after capture specifically for this photograph.

Below: He 177 (6N+HK) of 2./KG 100 is seen being prepared for a night raid during Operation Steinbock, the 'mini Blitz' on the UK in early 1944. Note the individual aircraft letter 'H' repeated on the nose. Although the phonetic alphabet listed 'H' as 'Heinrich', this Staffel's aircraft were all given female names appropriate to their individual letter. This machine carried Helga on the port side of the nose.

Right: Here we see a good example of the reduction in size of fuselage codes on this Ju 188 of III./KG 26 after capture by the Allies in Norway at the end of the war. '1H' – the code for KG 26 – is barely visible between the fuselage roundel of its new owners and the Air Ministry AM113 identity number forward of the tailplane.

Zerstörer

Having been formed out of the pre-war Jagdgeschwadern, some Zerstörer units had commenced hostilities wearing a combination of official four-part code, plus fighter-type Stab chevrons. These latter embellishments gradually became less common, however, and the overriding feature of wartime Zerstörer markings – due firstly to the number of early unit redesignations, followed by their wholesale disappearance into the ranks of the night-fighter arm, and then the subsequent reactivation of some – is the confusing plethora of Geschwader codes that were used. The Zerstörer arm does, however, provide another of the few direct anomalies (rather than mere variations) associated with the four-part code system. The semi-autonomous Zerstörerstaffel of Bf 110s which operated on the Arctic front – attached first to JG 77 and then to JG 5 – initially took a two-letter code sequence ('LN'), rather than a standard letter-number combination, as its unit identification. It also used 'R' as its fourth (Staffel code) letter. This would normally indicate a 7. Staffel machine; although, in this instance, the unit operated as the first Zerstörerstaffel of JG 77; i.e. 'LN+KR' was 'K-Kurfürst' of 1.(Z)/JG 77. When it later became part of JG 5, as that Geschwader's 13. Staffel, a new unit code combination was issued, after which any subsequent 'K-Kurfürst' would have been correctly marked '1B+KX'. (There were a few more examples of two-letter unit codes, e.g. the 'SB' of Sonderstaffel Buschmann (the Buschmann Special Squadron; composed of Estonian volunteers). But, as its name suggests, this – and others of its kind – were special cases.

By the mid-war years, most of those Zerstörer units which had survived the depredations of front-line service (the Bf 110 had not fulfilled the expectations of its principal champion, Hermann Göring), and which had escaped the clutches of night-fighter C-in-C General Josef Kammhuber, found themselves deployed in the defence of the Reich; in which capaci-

Looking, at first glance, like a standard four-letter Stammkennzeichen (factory-applied code), the 'first two' of this aircraft's markings in fact identify its parent unit: SB = Sonderstaffel Buschmann (the Buschmann Special Squadron). This coastal patrol unit of Estonian volunteers flew a hotch potch of aircraft, including this indigenous PTO-4.

Left: Well wrapped up against the Arctic cold, Bf 110G '1B+AX' of 13.(Z)/JG 5 has another example of a small unit code applied.

ty they were usually identified by either white, or yellow, rear fuselage bands. One of the last such units of all, II./ZG 76, reverted to its roots late in 1944 by adopting standard Jagdgeschwader-style Stab chevron and numeral markings ... albeit, perversely, with a small 1940-era "M8" unit identity code sometimes tucked alongside!

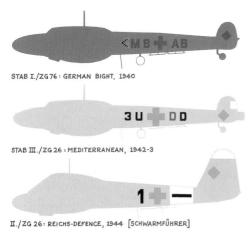

STAB I./ZG 76 : GERMAN BIGHT, 1940

1.(Z)/JG 77 : ARCTIC, 1941

13.(Z)/JG 5 : ARCTIC, 1943-4

STAB III./ZG 26 : MEDITERRANEAN, 1942-3

6./ZG 76 : REICHS-DEFENCE, 1944

6./ZG 26 : REICHS-DEFENCE, 1944

II./ZG 26 : REICHS-DEFENCE, 1944 [SCHWARMFÜHRER]

STAB II./ZG 76 : REICHS-DEFENCE, 1944

II./ZG 76 : REICHS-DEFENCE, 1945

Night-fighters

The Luftwaffe's first operational night-fighters comprised some individual Staffeln of Ar 68 biplanes, plus a single Gruppe of early Bf 109s. But whereas the former carried standard fighter markings of the time (i.e. the white numerals of a 10. Staffel), the Bf 109s of IV.(N)/JG 2 did not display any fourth Gruppe symbol. Instead, each machine bore its individual number aft of the fuselage cross, and a letter 'N' (for Nacht = night) of equal size in front of it. Both number and letter were in the appropriate Staffel colour. The initial 'N' – albeit now smaller than the individual aircraft number – was later reintroduced on some single-seaters (Bf 109s and Fw 190s) during the 'Wilde Sau' period of the night-fighting campaign. But when the first Bf 110 Nachtjagdgruppe proper was established in mid-1940 – by redesignating I./ZG 1 – both it, and almost all its twin-engined successors, used the standard four-part code system. There were, of course, the inevitable

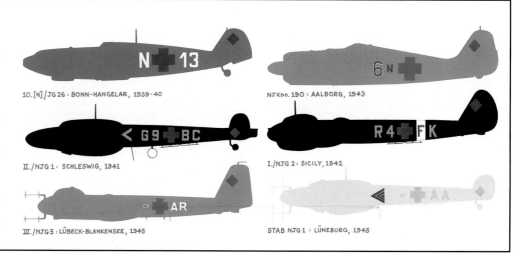

10.[N]/JG 26 : BONN-HANGELAR, 1939-40

NJKdo. 190 : AALBORG, 1943

II./NJG 1 : SCHLESWIG, 1941

I./NJG 2 : SICILY, 1942

III./NJG 5 : LÜBECK-BLANKENSEE, 1945

STAB NJG 1 : LÜNEBURG, 1945

variations. Some early night-fighters, finished in all-black camnouflage, carried the entire code in either dull-red or grey. Certain units, e.g. NJG 1, not only repeated the individual aircraft letter on the front of the nose, they also displayed a small Roman numeral (indicating the Gruppe) next to the night-fighter badge below the cockpit. NJG 1 also used day-fighter style chevrons to indicate their Stab machines. This was a practice they continued, at least in part, right up until the end of the war; as witness the triple chevrons carried by Bf 110G 'G9+AA', the aircraft of the unit's last Geschwaderkommodore, which was 'borrowed' by two eastern European NCOs to escape to neutral Sweden in May 1945.

Above: These Bf 109D night-fighters of 11.(N)/JG 2 are seen at Trondheim/Vaernes in May 1940. The unit scored no known night kills during the Norwegian campaign, the deployment having reportedly been made for largely propagandist purposes.

Below: Leutnant Uellenbeck of II./NJG 1 crash landed BF 110C 'G9+BC' at Schleswig at 02.30 hours, 9 May 1941 after being hit by 'friendly' flak. The chevron forward of the fuselage code seems to indicate that Uellenbeck was currently Gruppen-Adjutant, or at least flying the latter's machine!

Stukas

The Ju 87s of the Stuka arm remained remarkably faithful in their interpretation of the four-part code system throughout their increasingly fraught wartime career. But here, too, some discrepancies did occur. Perhaps the most noticeable of these was the Stukas' tendency, more than any other type of unit, to retain their original Stammkennzeichen (see 'Trainers', below) on the undersides of the wing. And at least one early Gruppe, III./StG 51, is also known to have used a very light shade (possibly grey), rather than the standard black, for its fuselage codes. More commonly, many units made a practice of repeating the individual aircraft letter on the front of the wheel spat. Additional tactical markings, however, were few; although some Gruppen – including those of St.G 2 – did at times sport diagonal rudder stripes; these, like the fuselage bands of the Polish campaign, are believed to have been used primarily to indicate Stab machines and other formation leaders, and were presumably intended to facilitate regrouping after the dive.

Some Stuka commanders also chose to carry fighter-style chevrons in conjunction with the standard code system. The most famous and successful of them all, Oberst Hans-Ulrich Rudel, went one better. He continued to fly a tank-busting Ju 87G long after the remainder of his Geschwader had converted to the Fw 190. No longer a dive-bomber, the cannon-armed 'G' variant was officially

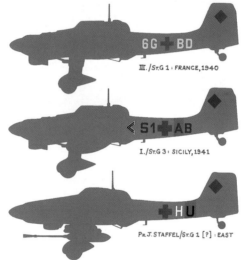

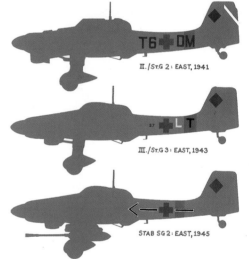

6G+BD — III./STG 1 : FRANCE, 1940	T6+DM — II./STG 2 : EAST, 1941
S1+AB — I./STG 3 : SICILY, 1941	LT — III./STG 3 : EAST, 1943
HU — Pz.J.STAFFEL/ST.G 1 [?] : EAST	STAB SG 2 : EAST, 1945

classified as a Panzerjäger (literally a 'tank-hunter' or, in Luftwaffe parlance, a 'tank-fighter'). Taking the 'Jäger' connotation to its natural conclusion, Rudel elected to have his machine finished in full fighter fig; complete with 1937-pattern Geschwaderkommodore fuselage markings and wartime spiral spinner! (The same combination looked less out of place on the Fw 190D-9 he sometimes consented to fly during the very closing weeks of the war.)

Above left: Another fighter-pattern Gruppen-Adjutant chevron is shown here, this time on a Ju 87B of a Stukagruppe – I./StG 76. This code is a good example of the multi-use of some codes. 'F1' was used throughout the war by KG 76 and was retained by I./StG 76 when it was redesignated III./StG 77.

Left: In this well-known shot, the Ju 87G of Oberst Hans-Ulrich Rudel (the Kommodore of SG 2) carries a fighter-style spiralled spinner, textbook pre-war Geschwaderkommodore markings (chevron and bars) and, just visible on the port wing leading edge, the yellow wraparound chevron to aid recognition from the ground.

Above: This heavily dappled Ju 87D of Stukageschwader 2 Immelmann is seen over the Eastern front. Of note are its yellow theatre markings (fuselage band and wing tip underside), the first two of its Stammkennzeichen still visible under its wing ('BH-??'), its small unit code 'T6' on the fuselage band and the aircraft letter carried on both wheel spats.

Fighter-bombers and ground-assault

If the history of Stuka markings is one of relative consistency, that of the Luftwaffe's various ground-assault units reflects the complexity of their origins and wartime career.

The first fighter-bomber, or Jabo, sorties – those mounted during the Battle of Britain by the Channel-based Jagdgeschwadern – were carried out by Bf 109s with nothing to indicate their special role other than the physical presence of the hastily-attached bomb racks themselves. It was not until the first dedicated Jabostaffeln were activated the following year that specialised markings really began to be introduced; 10.(Jabo)/JG 2 displaying a Stab-type chevron and bar behind the fuselage cross, both these – and the aircraft's individual number – being in blue, and 10.(Jabo)/JG 26 opting for a white bomb motif on the rear fuselage. A number of Jabostaffeln, together with a redundant Zerstörergruppe, were subsequently amalgamated into a so-called Schnellkampfgeschwader (fast bomber group). This unit, SKG 10, appears then to have used individual coloured letters aft of the fuselage Balkenkreuz as a means of identification for its front-line Staffeln operating against the UK out of northern France; Stammkennzeichen for its Mediterranean-based component; and a standard fighter-style system (complete with numerals and rear fuselage disc) for its IV. (Replacement) Gruppe! In contrast, the Luftwaffe's only other Schnellkampfgeschwader – SKG 210, created around a test unit bearing the same numerical designation which had flown a mix of Bf 109s and Bf 110s during the Battle of Britain – used a standard four-part code throughout its existence.

But it was the Schlacht, or ground-assault, units which were to display the widest variety of markings. There was only one Schlachtgruppe upon the outbreak of the Second World War. Equipped with the obsolescent Henschel Hs 123, this unit, II.(Schl)/LG 2, used the standard four-part code of the period; the Kommandeur's machine, 'L2+AC', carrying, in addition, a variation of the old biplane-pattern double chevron on the upper wing and a white stripe along the dorsal spine. By the end of the French campaign, however, the four-part code had given way to contemporary fighter-type markings: an individual number forward of the fuselage Balkenkreuz, and a horizontal bar aft of it. Shortly thereafter the Hs 123s themselves disappeared, and the Gruppe took part in the Battle of Britain flying the Bf 109E in completely new markings.

These heralded the reappearance of the black triangle symbol of the ground-assault forces, which had first been seen on the Hs 123-equipped Fliegergruppen activated as an emergency measure at the time of the Sudeten crisis in September 1938. In addition to the triangle, which was located ahead of the Balkenkreuz, each Bf 109 also carried an individual aircraft letter, in its appropriate Staffel colour, on the rear fuselage. The self-same markings adorned the refurbished Hs 123s when they were returned to front-line service for the campaign in the Balkans, and the subsequent invasion of the Soviet

Right: Bf 109F-4/B 'Blue 1' was flown by Oberleutnant Frank Liesendahl, Staffelkapitän of 10.(Jabo)/JG 2 'Richthofen' in April 1942. The chevron and bar, also in blue, is the Jabostaffel emblem, the aircraft being used largely for anti-shipping strikes in the English Channel; note the scoreboard on the fin.

Left: Hs 123 biplanes of II./SchlG 1 are seen on the Eastern Front in 1942. Note the combination of an individual letter plus the II. Gruppe horizontal bar part-superimposed over the yellow theatre band. Aircraft 'L', in the foreground, also displays an Adjutant's chevron (in black) ahead of the letter.

Lower left: This Bf 109F-4/B of 10.(Jabo)/JG 26 carries the unit's 'falling bomb' emblem on the rear fuselage. Note also the Channel front markings (yellow cowling and rudder).

Below: Black Schlacht triangles aft of the cross and yellow theatre bands identify these Fw 190F-2s of II./SchlG 1. Note also the Gruppe's stylised 'Mickey Mouse' badge on the cowling of the third aircraft.

Union. The sturdy biplanes even survived alongside Bf 109Es when II.(Schl)./LG 2 was redesignated as I./Sch.G 1. And when a II./Sch.G 1 was activated, its Bf 109Es also used the triangle/letter combination, albeit reportedly in the reverse order: the triangle now appearing behind the Balkenkreuz. The two specialised anti-tank Staffeln of Sch.G 1, equipped with Hs 129s, also sometimes carried the ground-assault triangle; 4. and 8. Staffeln likewise displaying it fore and aft of the fuselage Balkenkreuz respectively. When the triangle was not used, Staffel identity was apparently indicated either by the position of the individual aircraft letter alone, or by the use of a II. Gruppe horizontal bar. Staffelkapitäne added a single chevron ahead of their individual letter. The second of the two original Schlachtgeschwader – Sch.G 2, also comprising two Gruppen, plus two Hs 129 anti-tank Staffeln – is believed to have employed the same system for a time. But when the four above anti-tank Staffeln later merged to become IV.(Pz)/SG 9, they adopted standard fighter-style markings with Stab chevrons, individual numbers and IV. Gruppe disc.

In autumn 1943 the four component Gruppen of Sch.Gs 1 and 2 were split up among the new,

Jabos

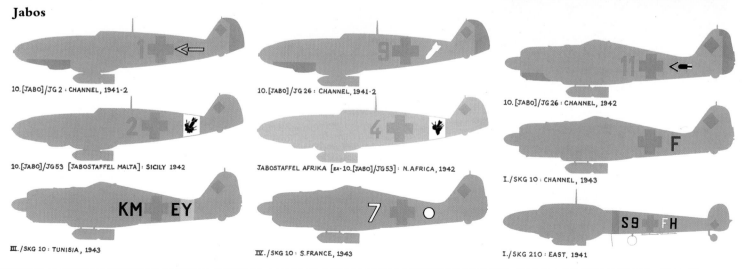

10.[JABO]/JG 2 : CHANNEL, 1941-2

10.[JABO]/JG 53 [JABOSTAFFEL MALTA] : SICILY 1942

III./SKG 10 : TUNISIA, 1943

10.[JABO]/JG 26 : CHANNEL, 1941-2

JABOSTAFFEL AFRIKA [ex-10.[JABO]/JG 53] : N. AFRICA, 1942

IV./SKG 10 : S.FRANCE, 1943

10.[JABO]/JG 26 : CHANNEL, 1942

I./SKG 10 : CHANNEL, 1943

I./SKG 210 : EAST, 1941

First generation Schlacht (Sch.G)

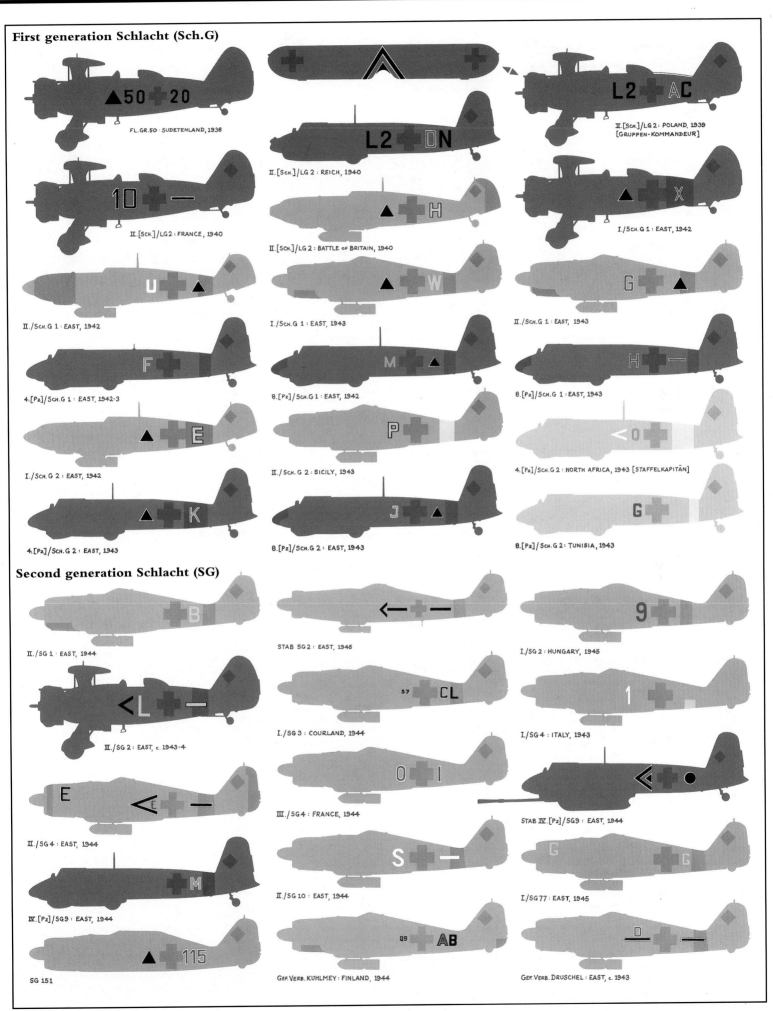

FL.GR.50 : SUDETENLAND, 1938

II.[Sch.]/LG 2 : REICH, 1940

II.[Sch.]/LG 2 : POLAND, 1939 [GRUPPEN-KOMMANDEUR]

II.[Sch.]/LG2 : FRANCE, 1940

II.[Sch.]/LG 2 : BATTLE of BRITAIN, 1940

I./Sch.G 1 : EAST, 1942

II./Sch.G 1 : EAST, 1942

I./Sch.G 1 : EAST, 1943

II./Sch.G 1 : EAST, 1943

4.[Pz]/Sch.G 1 : EAST, 1942-3

8.[Pz]/Sch.G 1 : EAST, 1942

8.[Pz]/Sch.G 1 : EAST, 1943

I./Sch.G 2 : EAST, 1942

II./Sch.G 2 : SICILY, 1943

4.[Pz]/Sch.G 2 : NORTH AFRICA, 1943 [STAFFELKAPITÄN]

4.[Pz]/Sch.G 2 : EAST, 1943

8.[Pz]/Sch.G 2 : EAST, 1943

8.[Pz]/Sch.G 2 : TUNISIA, 1943

Second generation Schlacht (SG)

II./SG 1 : EAST, 1944

STAB SG 2 : EAST, 1945

I./SG 2 : HUNGARY, 1945

II./SG 2 : EAST, c. 1943-4

I./SG 3 : COURLAND, 1944

I./SG 4 : ITALY, 1943

II./SG 4 : EAST, 1944

III./SG 4 : FRANCE, 1944

STAB IV.[Pz]/SG 9 : EAST, 1944

IV.[Pz]/SG 9 : EAST, 1944

II./SG 10 : EAST, 1944

I./SG 77 : EAST, 1945

SG 151

GEF.VERB. KUHLMEY : FINLAND, 1944

GEF.VERB. DRUSCHEL : EAST, c. 1943

Nachtschlachtgruppen

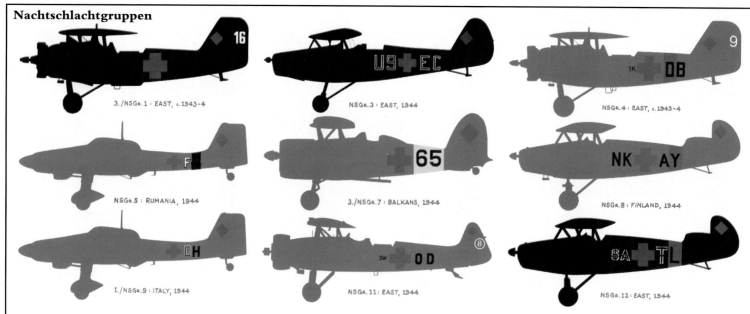

3./NSGr.1 : EAST, c.1943-4

NSGr.3 : EAST, 1944

NSGr.4 : EAST, c.1943-4

NSGr.5 : RUMANIA, 1944

3./NSGr.7 : BALKANS, 1944

NSGr.8 : FINLAND, 1944

1./NSGr.9 : ITALY, 1944

NSGr.11 : EAST, 1944

NSGr.12 : EAST, 1944

second-generation Schlachtgeschwadern (now abbreviated as SGs) which were formed out of the collective redesignation of what had previously been the Stuka arm (plus the Gruppen of SKG 10). The black triangle disappeared (apart from its retention on some training Fw 190s) amid the general upheaval. And from now until the end of the war not just every Geschwader – but very nearly every Gruppe of every Geschwader – seems to have gone its own way in its choice of markings: some opted

to retain their ex-Stuka four-part code system, others chose fighter-style numerals and symbols, and yet others individual identity letters; the latter on either fuselage or engine cowling. And while it has not yet proved possible to isolate and identify the twenty-plus Gruppen involved, the accompanying diagrams/illustrations offer some indication of the wide range of markings carried by the Schlachtgeschwadern of the later war years.

Similarly, those 'poor relations' of the ground-

assault arm, the fourteen nocturnal Nachtschlachtgruppen – the majority flying a motley collection of antiquated trainers, second-line, or foreign machines – appear to have been given an equally free hand in the selection of their markings. Several were obviously allotted unit identity code combinations, allowing them to apply standard four-part fuselage markings. But many others simply sported an individual number or letter on fuselage or rudder. Again, not all have yet been identified.

Above: An unusual four-figure code was used on the Ar 66Cs of the Latvian-manned Nachtschlachtgruppe 12 in 1943. '6A' was the NSGr 12 code, but the 'last two' ('TN' and 'RU' on these aircraft) do not fit in with a single (I.) Gruppe system in which the last letter should be 'H', 'K' or 'L'. It is possible that the aircraft carried their Stammkennzeichen and that the 'first two' were simply overpainted and replaced by '6A'.

Above: As protection against ground strafing, the upper part of the white theatre band, the tail swastika and upper surface wing crosses on this I./SG 4 Fw 190F-8 have been overpainted. An individual number is used for aircraft identification.

In contrast, this unidentified III./Gruppe (note vertical bar behind fuselage the cross) Fw 190 of an Eastern Front Schlachtgeschwader uses a single letter to identify its aircraft.

Transports and gliders

The Luftwaffe's wartime transport fleet grew out of two Gruppen activated in the late 1930s. Initially known as Kampfgruppen zur besonderen Verwendung (special-purpose bomber wings), these early units were intended specifically for paratroop-training rather than for general transport duties. And in order to correspond to the contemporary paratroop battalion of HQ staff and four companies, each KGr.z.b.V. was likewise organised, from the outset, into a Stab and four Staffeln. This basic formation was to be retained throughout the war.

At first, the two Gruppen carried their own form of four-digit code: 01 or 02 in front of the fuselage cross to indicate the Gruppe itself, and a two-number sequence from 01 to 53 to identify the individual aircraft (a Gruppe's comprising, on paper, five Stab machines plus four Staffeln each of 12).

When the standard four-part code was introduced immediately prior to the war, the two Gruppen (since joined by a third and fourth) were given a common Geschwader identity code-combination. This was carried, as normal, to the left of the fuselage cross. To the right of the Balkenkreuz, however – while the fourth-place (Staffel code) letter remained basically the same as before – the colour of the third (individual identity) letter began to differ after the third Staffel; for instead of their being recurring cycles of three (white, red, yellow), there were now cycles of four Staffeln per Gruppe (white, red, yellow, blue):

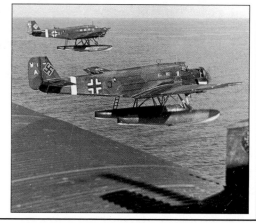

'Somewhere over the Mediterranean' these Ju 52 floatplanes of Lufttransportstaffel (See) 1 carry standard tactical tail markings. Their unit code was '8A', with the unusual fourth letter 'J'.

Transports

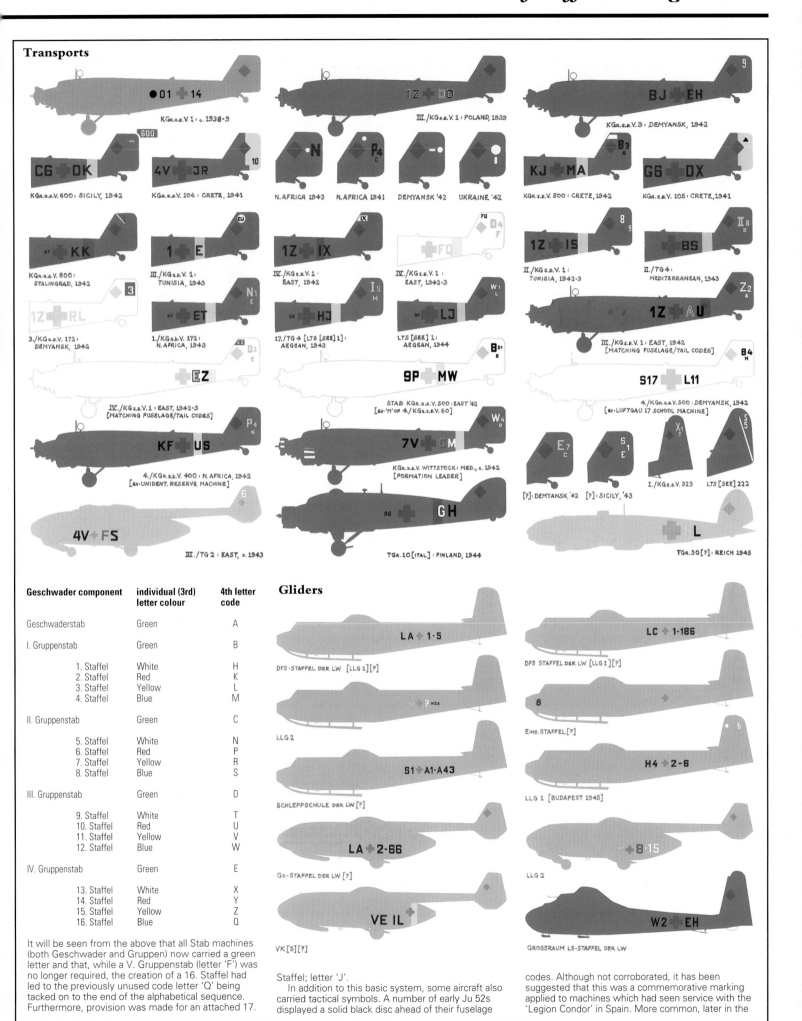

Geschwader component	individual (3rd) letter colour	4th letter code
Geschwaderstab	Green	A
I. Gruppenstab	Green	B
1. Staffel	White	H
2. Staffel	Red	K
3. Staffel	Yellow	L
4. Staffel	Blue	M
II. Gruppenstab	Green	C
5. Staffel	White	N
6. Staffel	Red	P
7. Staffel	Yellow	R
8. Staffel	Blue	S
III. Gruppenstab	Green	D
9. Staffel	White	T
10. Staffel	Red	U
11. Staffel	Yellow	V
12. Staffel	Blue	W
IV. Gruppenstab	Green	E
13. Staffel	White	X
14. Staffel	Red	Y
15. Staffel	Yellow	Z
16. Staffel	Blue	Q

Gliders

It will be seen from the above that all Stab machines (both Geschwader and Gruppen) now carried a green letter and that, while a V. Gruppenstab (letter 'F') was no longer required, the creation of a 16. Staffel had led to the previously unused code letter 'Q' being tacked on to the end of the alphabetical sequence. Furthermore, provision was made for an attached 17. Staffel; letter 'J'.

In addition to this basic system, some aircraft also carried tactical symbols. A number of early Ju 52s displayed a solid black disc ahead of their fuselage

codes. Although not corroborated, it has been suggested that this was a commemorative marking applied to machines which had seen service with the 'Legion Condor' in Spain. More common, later in the

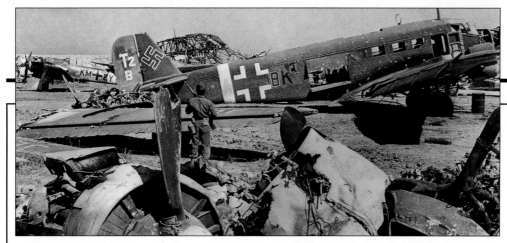

Left: This wrecked Ju 52, captured in Tunisia, is a prime example of an aircraft with fuselage and tail codes that match. The fuselage code reads '8T+BK', whereby '8T' (small, behind the fuselage band) is the unit designator for KGrzbV 800, 'B' is the individual aircraft letter and 'K' denotes 2. Staffel of the Gruppe. This is corroborated by the tactical code on the tail. Here the 'T' signifies KGrzbV 800, '2' is for 2. Staffel and 'B' is the aircraft letter. KGrzbV 800 was later redesignated III./TG 2.

war, were the white bands seen on engine cowlings (and sometimes tailfins) indicating Stab machines and formation leaders.

But it was mainly on the rudder that the widest variety of markings were to occur. Some Gruppen divulged their actual identity; KGr.z.b.Vs 9 and 600, for example, both displayed their unit number on the rudder for all to see. Other Gruppen indicated just the aircraft's 'last two'; either by repeating the letters themselves, e.g. 'FS', (normally on some sort of light background added to fin or rudder), or by a simple numerical code, whereby the same 'FS' would be translated into an '8' with with a smaller '6' diagonally below it; i.e. the sixth aircraft ('F'-Friedrich) of the 8. Staffel. Later still, when a number of Gruppen were collected into Transportgeschwadern, some used a three-part rudder marking comprising a Roman numeral (Gruppe) and an Arabic numeral (Staffel), with a letter (individual aircraft identity) below the two.

Despite the talk of Geschwader, for practical purposes the transport arm was – and remained – organised upon a Gruppe basis. As the war progressed, however, specific operational needs and, later, emergencies (from early airborne assaults, through supply airlifts, to the final evacuations) gave rise to a whole series of urgent demands for yet 'one more all-out effort' on the part of the hard-pressed transport units. These, in turn, resulted in the setting up of a succession of *ad hoc* formations composed of whatever strength was available at the time. Thus existing Gruppen would find themselves operating alongside others hastily put together from individual aircraft drawn from as many as 20 or more different sources: from other transport units, schools, specialist training establishments, rear-area pools and even the civil fleet. These latter Gruppen could thus comprise a collection of 50 or more machines bearing a wide range of confusing and conflicting fuselage markings.

To identify these various Gruppen, a three-part tactical rudder code system gradually evolved. This consisted of a large letter to indicate the Gruppe, followed by a number – invariably smaller – specifying the Staffel. Below these two, and smaller, came the individual aircraft letter. While seemingly chosen at random, the Gruppe code letter was, in fact, often

Glider codes are still something of a mystery, but one source suggests that the 'LB' ahead of the fuselage cross on this DFS 230 indicates its being part of II./LLG 1 (Luftlandgeschwader, or air landing group). The numerals aft of the cross, '1-91', may refer to a platoon or troop or perhaps the numbers of the airborne forces assigned to each glider.

provided by the initial of the unit's first Kommandeur, or sometimes of the location where it was activated. Some of the letters identified to date (several having been used at different periods by different units) are listed below (with the Gruppen's later identities given in brackets):

B	KGr.z.b.V. 500 (II./TG 4)
D	IV./KG.z.b.V. 1
H	KGr.z.b.V. 106 (III./TG 2), KGr.z.b.V. 400 (III./TG 4)
K	Einsatzgruppe Kupschus KGr.z.b.V. Frankfurt
N	I./KG z.b.V. 172 (IV./TG 3)
P	KGr.z.b.V. 400 (III./TG 4), II./TG 1
T	KGr.z.b.V. 800 (III./TG 2)
W	KGr.z.b.V. Wittstock (Stab TG 5)
X	I./KG z.b.V. 323 (I./TG 5)
Y	II./KG z.b.V. 323 (II./TG 5)
Z	III./KG z.b.V. 1.

(Two autonomous maritime Staffeln also used rudder code markings. But whereas the Blohm und Voss flying boats of Lufttransportstaffel (See) 222 simply carried an 'S', together with an individual aircraft number (the two sometimes accompanied by a diagonal white stripe); the Ju 52 floatplanes of

Lufttransportstaffel (See) 1 used the full three-part system: the initial 'W' as the unit code, plus a somewhat superfluous '1' to identify the (sole) Staffel, and then the individual aircraft letter.)

In long-established Gruppen, the information imparted by the three-part rudder code usually tallied with that contained within the fuselage unit markings. In the majority of those wartime Gruppen put together from a variety of sources, however, the two systems were – more often than not – completely at variance. In these cases, it is always the rudder code which takes precedence and establishes current unit ownership; the contradictory fuselage markings serving no purpose other than to indicate the aircraft's previous identity.

In discussing the Luftwaffe's transport arm, mention should obviously be made of the assault- and supply-glider units. But here, in the continuing absence of official documentation, the researcher draws an almost complete blank. Not even the ex-glider pilots themselves, when asked, are able to supply the reasons for, or the meaning of, the strings of hyphenated numbers applied to some gliders. Those simply bearing individual numbers, or four-letter groups, remain equally anonymous; and it is only in the few cases where a known unit code has been allocated that positive identification may be made.

Schools and the training organisations

To obtain a brief, but comprehensive, overview of the Luftwaffe's trainer markings, it is necessary to go back to 1936 and the introduction of the first purely military alphanumeric code system. While the operational units (and some advanced weapons training establishments) adopted this later, the bulk of the Luftwaffe's training aircraft retained civilian-style codes consisting of the familiar initial 'D' and four-letter block separated by a hyphen. To indicate their military status, however, Balkenkreuze were added to the wing extremities and positioned in the very centre of the fuselage code, dividing the 'D', hyphen and classification letter from the aircraft's 'last three'.

At the beginning of 1939 the initial 'D' was then replaced by the letters 'WL' (indicating 'Wehrmacht-Luft', or 'Armed forces-Air'; the same prefix as seen on all Luftwaffe vehicle registrations). At the same time, a distinction was drawn between unarmed basic trainers, and those carrying military equipment – by the inclusion – or otherwise – of wing and fuselage Balkenkreuze.

Finally, from the late summer of 1939, all Luftwaffe aircraft were allotted a standard four-letter identity code. This Stammkennzeichen, as it was called, was applied in the factory (from blocks allocated by the Luftwaffe) and – like the RAF's and USAF's serial numbers –

Advanced fighter trainers displayed their school numbers on wide, coloured fuselage bands. Messerschmitt Bf 109E '23' (left) and Arado Ar 96B '3' (below) were typical of the machines equipping the 13 Jagdschulgeschwader (fighter training groups).

constituted the aircraft's basic service identity (as opposed to the Werk-Nummer, which was simply the constructor's number). All machines normally carried their Stammkennzeichen during their acceptance trials up to, and including, delivery to an operational unit, whereupon the Stammkennzeichen was usually overpainted by the appropriate unit code markings (the Verbandskennzeichen).

All second-line and training aircraft retained their Stammkennzeichen markings, however; displaying the four-letter code on the fuselage sides (divided by the Balkenkreuz), and across the wing lower surfaces. The

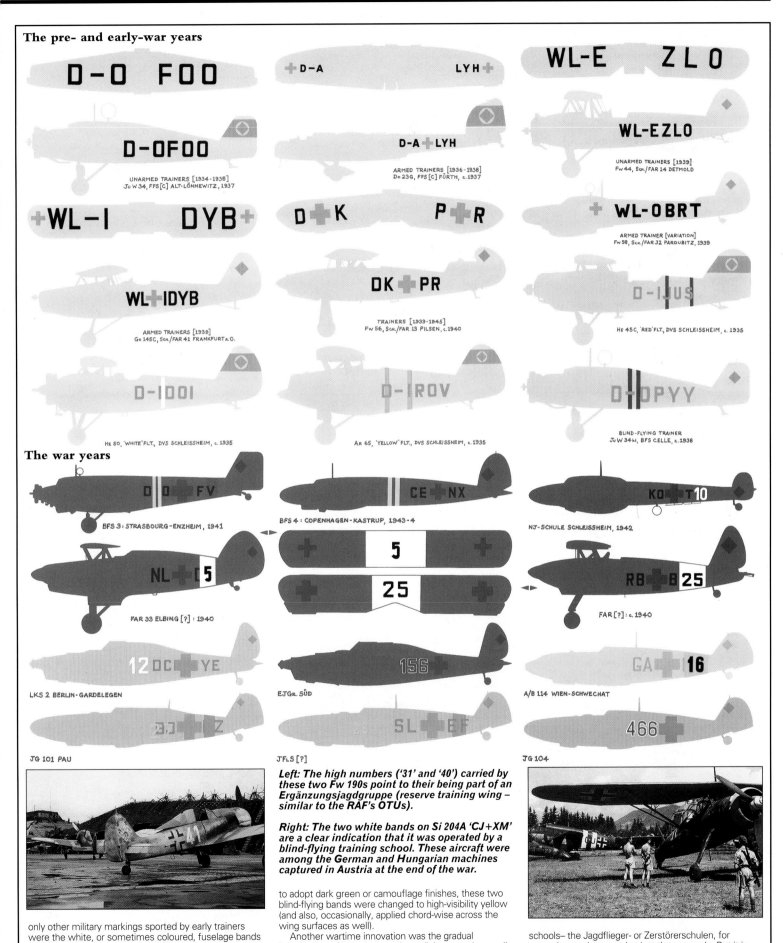

The pre- and early-war years

UNARMED TRAINERS [1934-1938]
Ju W 34, FFS [C] ALT-LÖNNEWITZ, 1937

ARMED TRAINERS [1936-1938]
Do 23G, FFS [C] FÜRTH, c.1937

UNARMED TRAINERS [1939]
Fw 44, SCH./FAR 14 DETMOLD

ARMED TRAINERS [1938]
Go 145C, SCH./FAR 41 FRANKFURT a.O.

TRAINERS [1939-1945]
Fw 56, SCH./FAR 13 PILSEN, c.1940

ARMED TRAINER [VARIATION]
Fw 56, SCH./FAR 32 PARDUBITZ, 1939

He 45C, 'RED' FLT, DVS SCHLEISSHEIM, c.1935

He 50, 'WHITE' FLT, DVS SCHLEISSHEIM, c.1935

Ar 65, 'YELLOW' FLT, DVS SCHLEISSHEIM, c.1935

BLIND-FLYING TRAINER
Ju W 34 hi, BFS CELLE, c.1938

The war years

BFS 3: STRASBOURG-ENZHEIM, 1941

BFS 4: COPENHAGEN-KASTRUP, 1943-4

NJ-SCHULE SCHLEISSHEIM, 1942

FAR 33 ELBING [?]: 1940

FAR [?]: c.1940

LKS 2 BERLIN-GARDELEGEN

EJGr. SÜD

A/B 114 WIEN-SCHWECHAT

JG 101 PAU

JFLS [?]

JG 104

Left: The high numbers ('31' and '40') carried by these two Fw 190s point to their being part of an Ergänzungsjagdgruppe (reserve training wing – similar to the RAF's OTUs).

Right: The two white bands on Si 204A 'CJ+XM' are a clear indication that it was operated by a blind-flying training school. These aircraft were among the German and Hungarian machines captured in Austria at the end of the war.

only other military markings sported by early trainers were the white, or sometimes coloured, fuselage bands introduced by some schools to differentiate between the machines of different flights; and the standard two narrow brick-red bands – usually carried around the mid-fuselage – which denoted blind-flying trainers. As the war progressed, and training aircraft of all types started to adopt dark green or camouflage finishes, these two blind-flying bands were changed to high-visibility yellow (and also, occasionally, applied chord-wise across the wing surfaces as well).

Another wartime innovation was the gradual introduction of large two- or three-digit numerals, usually in conspicuous white or yellow. These were often carried in conjunction with the four-letter Stammkennzeichen; either alongside, or sometimes partially obscuring it. In later years some advanced

schools– the Jagdflieger- or Zerstörerschulen, for example – took to wearing just the numerals. But it is normally not too difficult to distinguish between an advanced trainer and an operational fighter. The former rarely carried any other tactical markings, and the numbers tended to be much higher; anything above the mid-1920s (unless, perhaps, belonging to one of the experimental Erprobungskommandos, which numbered their machines consecutively) was probably a trainer – anything displaying three figures certainly was. The final training stage which most Luftwaffe pilots went through was the Ergänzungsgruppe, or replacement wing. This was roughly on a par with the RAF's OTU. But the German system was organised somewhat differently; many front-line units, particularly the Kampfgeschwader, having their own such replacement wing (usually as the IV. Gruppe) attached directly to them. The aircraft operated by these units also normally displayed unmistakably large white, or yellow, numerals (on tails, noses, engine nacelles and/or wings according to preference); but in their case in conjunction with otherwise standard unit codes and operational markings.

ZERSTÖRER-SCHULE NANCY — 4

FFS [C] : c. 1941 [UNIDENT.] — S A + 26HN

ZERSTÖRER-SCHULE [?] — 1 — DE + MP

SG 101 : PARIS-ORLY — 10 — GM + OG — 19 — 19

II./ZG 101 — — 62

FFS [C] 4 : SPROTTAU, 1941 — RN + NF

STUKA-SCHULE FOGGIA — SH + SV — 22

17 — 17 — 34

STUKA-SCHULE TOURS — 19 — TE + F

IV./KG 1 — V4 + HU — 17

IV./KG 54 — B3 + LX — 34

The closing stages of the Second World War witnessed some of the most colourful markings ever carried by the Luftwaffe. Since the days of JG 1's checkerboard Fw 190s' sole guardianship of north-west Germany, the defence of the Reich both by day and by night had become the Luftwaffe's one major 'growth industry'. By late 1944 a total of some 17 Jagdgeschwader were either wholly, or partly, engaged in the business of defending metropolitan Germany. And each of these units was allocated a distinctive coloured rear fuselage band, or bands, as a means of instant identification.

These final months also saw the dawn of the jet age. But if the Luftwaffe's jet- and rocket-powered aircraft did not introduce any innovative marking systems, and were not themselves intrinsically colourful, they did give rise to some other very flamboyant markings on the piston-engined fighters charged with their protection.

The defence of the Reich

By the end of 1944 the bulk of the Luftwaffe's fighter forces – some 17 Jagdgeschwader (or parts thereof) – were actively engaged in the daylight defence of the Reich. As a means of rapid air-to-air identification during their battles with the American heavy bombers, and – more importantly – with the overwhelming numbers of fighters which protected them, each of the 17 was allocated its own distinctive coloured rear fuselage band, or bands. At least one Industrieschutz-Schwarm (industrial defence flight; service successors to the works' own earlier factory defence squadrons) is also known to have used such a band. But, as mentioned earlier, those few surviving Zerstörergruppen which had soldiered on into the defence of the Reich do not appear to have been included in this system; although some did carry

white or yellow theatre-style rear fuselage bands at certain stages of the campaign. Only the Me 410s of II./ZG 76 displayed different coloured bands. These, however, are believed to have been used simply to identify the individual Staffeln within the Gruppe.

Depending upon one's interpretation of the colour rendition in this photograph, this Fw 190D could have belonged to JG 2, JG 4 or JG 6.

The white 'defence of the Reich' band was allocated to JG 3 and is seen here on an Fw 190A-8 Sturmjäger of IV.(Sturm)/JG 3 'Udet', mid-1944. The abbreviated 'wavy line' marking was used by a number of IV.Gruppe fighter units late in the war.

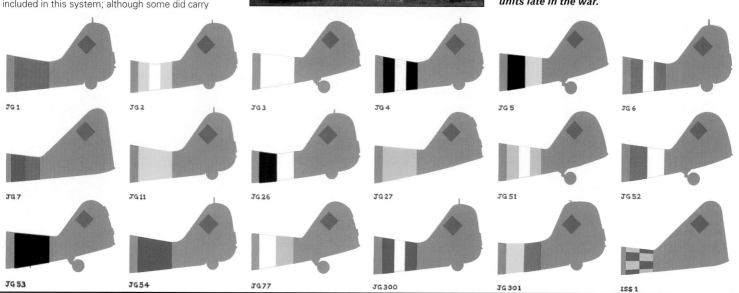

JG 1   JG 2   JG 3   JG 4   JG 5   JG 6

JG 7   JG 11   JG 26   JG 27   JG 51   JG 52

JG 53   JG 54   JG 77   JG 300   JG 301   ISS 1

The jet age

Although undoubtedly revolutionary in design, the Luftwaffe's jet- and rocket-powered aircraft did not, in themselves, give rise to any new markings systems. Generally, those machines operated by bomber units (e.g. the Ar 234s of KG 76 and the Me 262s of KG 51) retained contemporary bomber-style markings (as, paradoxically, did the Me 262s of KG(J) 54); while the fighters (e.g. the Me 262s of JG 7 and the Me 163s of JG 400) carried standard coloured numerals either on the nose, or alongside the fuselage cross. (But at least one Me 262 Stab machine exhibited some of the fighter arm's old individuality by reviving the pre-1937 biplane practice of displaying horizontal bars either side of the Balkenkreuz!). Me 262 night-fighters and reconnaissance aircraft also used numerals for individual identification (as, in fact, did the majority of all late-war single-seat reconnaissance machines). Other than the yellow mid-fuselage band seen on most Me 262s of III./EJG 2, the only coloured trim seems to have been that applied to the nose cone and jet intakes of some machines. Although this was used mainly for purposes of Staffel identification,

These Me 262s, reportedly of Kommando Nowotny, carry the yellow mid-fuselage band later associated with III./EJG 2.

some multi-coloured nose bands may have been purely decorative. The one striking exception was the distinctive red arrow which adorned the nose of nearly every one of the 40-odd He 162 Volksjäger of the Einsatzgruppe/JG 1 which were lined up either side of the runway at Leck in May 1945 awaiting surrender to the British.

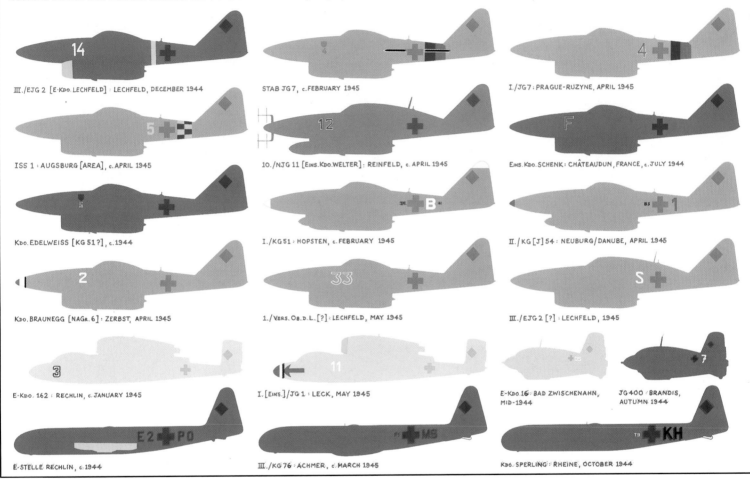

III./EJG 2 [E-Kdo. LECHFELD] : LECHFELD, DECEMBER 1944

STAB JG 7, c. FEBRUARY 1945

I./JG 7 : PRAGUE-RUZYNE, APRIL 1945

ISS 1 : AUGSBURG [AREA], c. APRIL 1945

10./NJG 11 [EINS. KDO. WELTER] : REINFELD, c. APRIL 1945

EINS. KDO. SCHENK : CHÂTEAUDUN, FRANCE, c. JULY 1944

KDO. EDELWEISS [KG 51?], c. 1944

I./KG 51 : HOPSTEN, c. FEBRUARY 1945

II./KG [J] 54 : NEUBURG/DANUBE, APRIL 1945

KDO. BRAUNEGG [NAGR. 6] : ZERBST, APRIL 1945

1./VERS. OB. D. L. [?] : LECHFELD, MAY 1945

III./EJG 2 [?] : LECHFELD, 1945

E-KDO. 162 : RECHLIN, c. JANUARY 1945

I. [EINS.]/JG 1 : LECK, MAY 1945

E-KDO. 16 : BAD ZWISCHENAHN, MID-1944

JG 400 : BRANDIS, AUTUMN 1944

E-STELLE RECHLIN, c. 1944

III./KG 76 : ACHMER, c. MARCH 1945

KDO. SPERLING : RHEINE, OCTOBER 1944

Recognition from the ground up

Many jet bases had one or more flights of piston-engined fighters tasked with protecting the 'Turbos' when these were at their most vulnerable; at take-off and landing. Marauding Allied fighters were a constant menace, and such airfields were also ringed with Flak defences. And in order to stand the slightest chance of survival in the hail of fire which invariably greeted the approach of any non-jet (and that of many Me 262s as well!), the Bf 109s and Fw 190s of these airfield protection Schwärme had to be instantly recognisable from the ground. To this end, their entire undersurfaces were striped; either simply in black on the normal light undersides, in black and white, or even – according to some sources – in red and white.

Meanwhile, not many miles to the east, the few remaining ground-assault Gruppen attempting to stem the tide of Soviet armour pouring across the plains of Hungary were likewise suffering attrition from 'friendly' fire thrown up by army and Waffen-SS units alike who, from bitter experience, had long ago learned to regard anything with wings as hostile until definitely proven otherwise. So here, too, an instant aid to recognition from the ground became paramount. SG 2's answer

was to apply a large yellow chevron inboard of the port wingtip, across the undersides and wrapped around the leading-edge, of all its Fw 190s. Kommodore

Oberst Rudel's 'Stuka in fighter's clothing' received the same treatment.

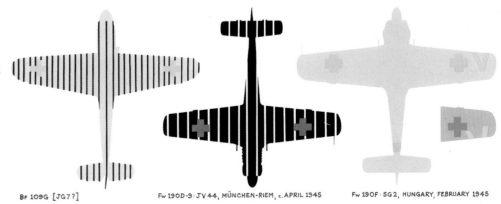

BF 109G [JG 7?]

FW 190D-9 : JV 44, MÜNCHEN-RIEM, c. APRIL 1945

FW 190F : SG 2, HUNGARY, FEBRUARY 1945

It is, perhaps, ironic that a survey of the tactical markings of an air arm, whose wings had once overshadowed the continent of Europe from the Biscay to the Black Sea, from the Arctic to the Aegean, should close on such a note: with some of the survivors of that arm including the most highly-decorated officer of them all being forced to seek means of marking their machines in order to protect themselves from their own! **John Weal**

INDEX

Page numbers in **bold** refer to an illustration

INDEX

Picture acknowledgments

Front cover: via Robert F. Dorr. **4:** Convair. **5:** Aerospace, via Robert F. Dorr. **6:** Convair (three), US Navy. **7:** Convair (two). **8:** Convair via San Diego Aerospace Museum (four). **9:** Convair via San Diego Aerospace Museum (two), Convair. **10:** Convair via San Diego Aerospace Museum (seven). **11:** Aerospace, Convair via San Diego Aerospace Museum (two), Convair. **12:** US National Archives, Convair (two). **13:** via National Museum of Naval Aviation, Convair via San Diego Aerospace Museum (two). **14:** Aerospace, via National Museum of Naval Aviation, Convair. **15:** via Harry Gann, US Navy. **16:** Aerospace, Chuck de Vlaming via Larry Davis (LD), via Robert F. Dorr. **19:** USAF Museum via LD, Dave Graben via LD. **19:** via Terry Panopalis, Chuck de Vlaming via LD. **20:** via Terry Panopalis (two), USAF via LD, Aerospace. **21:** USAF, Fairchild-Hiller, Aerospace. **22:** James E. Rotramel, USAF via LD (two). **23:** Aerospace, via Philip Birtles, via Ian Thirsk, BAe via Philip Birtles, via Philip Birtles. **24:** USAF via LD, USAF. **24:** USAF via Robert F. Dorr (two), Paul Chesley via LD, USAF. **26:** Joe Michaels, US National Archive, USAF via LD. **27:** Paul Chesley via LD, John Julian via LD. **28:** Barry Miller via LD, Tom Cope via LD, Aircraft Publicity Bureau via LD. **29:** USAF via LD, Terry Panopalis, Dennis Hayes via LD. **30:** via LD (two). **31:** Robert Amos via LD, via LD. **32:** via LD, Ralph Kuster via LD, LD (two), Aircraft Publicity Bureau via LD. **33:** Doug Remington via LD, Brent Danner via LD, Tom Waller via LD, LD. **34:** Robert Amos via LD, Dave Graben via LD (two). **35:** via LD, Aerospace, Joe Bruch via LD, Art Krieger via LD. **36:** via LD, John Julian via LD, Marty Isham via LD. **37:** USAF via LD, James Rotramel, USAF via LD. **38:** Charles E. Brown/RAF Museum, **40:** de Havilland (three). **41:** BAe, via Martin Bowman (MB), de Havilland, Aerospace. **42:** via MB, BAe via Philip Birtles, Hawker Siddeley via Philip Birtles, via Philip Birtles. **43:** Aerospace, via Philip Birtles, via Ian Thirsk, BAe via Philip Birtles. **44:** BAe via MB, Imperial War Museum (IWM), de Havilland. **45:** via MB (two), BAe via MB. **46:** IWM, Aerospace. **47:** via MB, IWM. **48:** de Havilland, Aerospace. **49:** Aerospace, via MB, Charles E. Brown. **50:** Aerospace, via MB. **51:** Charles E. Brown/RAF Museum, via MB (two). **52:** via MB, Charles E. Brown. **57:** IWM (two), via Ian Thirsk. **58:** Aerospace, **59:** de Havilland (two), Aerospace (two). **60:** Charles E. Brown (two), via John Fricker, BAe via Philip Birtles. **61:** via MB, Aerospace (two), via Philip Birtles, de Havilland via MB. **63:** US Navy, de Havilland, Aerospace. **64:** IWM, via MB (four). **65:** IWM (two). **66:** via MB, Aerospace. **67:** Aerospace (two), via MB. **76:** via MB. **77:** de Havilland, RAF via MB, Aerospace (two), Charles E. Brown via MB, Dave Willis, MoD via MB, via MB. **78:** USAF (two), via MB (two). **79:** via MB (two). **80:** via MB (five). **82:** via MB (two). **83:** Aerospace, via MB, RAF. **84:** via Philip Birtles, via Ian Thirsk, Aerospace (two), RAF. **85:** via MB (three). **86:** Aerospace (five). **87:** John Fricker, Aerospace, Harry Gann (two). **88:** Harry Gann, Aerospace, via MB. **89:** Spartan Air Services, Aerospace, Philip Birtles, BAe via MB. **90:** via MB, IWM, Aerospace, John Fricker (two). **91:** RAAF via Ian Thirsk, via Ian Thirsk, via Shlomo Aloni, BAe via MB, via MB (two). **92:** BAe via Tony Buttler, de Havilland via Tony Buttler, Tony Buttler. **93:** BAe via Tony Buttler, BAC via Terry Panopalis, de Havilland. **94:** Bristol. **95:** Bristol via Mike Stroud, Bristol (two), DERA via Tery Panopalis. **96:** Bristol Siddeley, BAe via Tony Buttler, Bristol via Mike Stroud, Aerospace. **97:** Bristol, DERA via Terry Panopalis. **98:** via Tony Buttler (two). **99:** C. D. Hollis via Tony Buttler, Tony Buttler (two). **100:** BAe via Tony Buttler (two), Bristol. **101:** BAC via Terry Panopalis, DERA via Terry Panopalis, via Tony Buttler. **102:** Aerospace. **103:** Hawker Siddeley via Bill Upton, Dave Menard, Canadian Armed Forces (CAF). **104:** Avro Canada via Bill Upton, Aerospace. **105:** W. J. Balogh, Aerospace, Avro Canada. **106:** Avro Canada, Avro Canada via Terry Panopalis, Aerospace. **107:** Aerospace (two), Marty Isham via Jeff Rankin-Lowe. **108:** Aerospace, via Bill Upton, Gloster Aircraft. **109:** Aerospace, Dave Menard, Gloster Aircraft. **110:** Avro Canada via Terry Panopalis, Aerospace, W. J. Balogh. **111:** Avro Canada via Bill Upton (four). **112:** Avro Canada via Bill Upton (four). **113:** Avro Canada via Bill Upton (two), via Bruce Robertson. **114:** via Peter R. Foster, Ray Moneta via Andrew Cline. **115:** Andrew H. Cline (nine), Regent Dansereau, Peter Handley via Andrew H. Cline. **116:** Avro Canada via Bill Upton, Hawker Siddeley via Bill Upton (two), Aerospace. **117:** Avro Canada via Bruce Robertson, Avro Canada, CEPE. **118:** Avro Canada (two), National Defence (two). **119:** Avro Canada via Bill Upton, Avro Canada. **120:** National Defence, Avro Canada, Orenda via Bruce Robertson, NRC via Bill Upton. **121:** Aerospace, via Terry Panopalis, Avro Canada, Fairey Engineering Limited. **122:** Larry J. MacDougal, D. MacIntosh, DND via Bill Upton, Avro Canada via Bill Upton. **123:** Avro Aircraft. **124:** Aerospace, Avro Canada. **125:** Aerospace (two), Dave Menard. **126:** Avro Canada, Larry J. MacDougal, DND via Andrew Cline. **127:** W. J. Balogh, Canadian Armed Forces, Andrew Thomas, R. E. Kling. **128:** Aerospace (two), via Terry Panopalis, Duncan MacIntosh. **129:** Aerospace, Aerospace (two), W. J. Balogh. **130:** Aerospace, D. N. Drew, CAF. **131:** via Terry Panopalis, Avro Canada via Bill Upton, Aerospace, Terry Panopalis. **132:** Aerospace (three). **133:** Aerospace, Duncan MacIntosh. **134:** IWM (four). **135:** Aerospace (two). **136:** Aerospace (two), IWM (three). **137:** via Dr A. Price, IWM (three), RAF Museum. **138:** Aerospace, IWM (four). **139:** Aerospace (two), IWM (three). **140:** IWM (three). **141:** IWM via Dr A. Price (two), US National Archives via Dr A. Price (two). **142:** IWM via Dr A. Price (three). **143:** IWM via Dr A. Price. **144:** IWM, via Dr A. Price. **145:** IWM, Aerospace, IWM via Dr A. Price. **146:** Bundesarchiv (two). **147:** via John Weal (two), MoD. **148:** via John Weal, Bundesarchiv via John Weal. **149:** via John Weal (three), Aerospace (two). **150:** via John Weal (two), Aerospace (two). **152:** via John Weal, Bundesarchiv (three). **154:** IWM via John Weal, via John Weal, Aerospace (two). **155:** IWM via John Weal (two). **156:** via John Weal (two). **157:** via John Weal.